VISITING GRANDCHILDRE
ECONOMIC DEVELOPMENT in the MARITIMES

MW00743937

During his successful campaign to become Conservative Party leader in the spring of 2004, Stephen Harper said of the Maritime provinces, 'We will see the day when the region is not the place where you visit your grandparents, but instead more often than not the place where you visit your grandchildren.' In *Visiting Grandchildren*, policy analyst and scholar Donald J. Savoie explores how Canadian economic policies have served to exclude the Maritime provinces from the wealth enjoyed in many other parts of the country, especially southern Ontario, and calls for a radical new approach to government policy that affects regional development.

Savoie reviews the long history of largely ineffectual federal programs directed particularly at the Maritime provinces. In the process, he debunks the myth that this region has received more than its fair share of federal funds. He advocates reform of national policies, focusing on proven ways to enhance growth in underdeveloped areas and thus reduce regional economic disparities.

Visiting Grandchildren looks to history, geography, and to the workings of national political and administrative institutions to explain the relative underdevelopment of the Maritime provinces. Savoie argues that the region must strive to redefine its relationship with the national government and with other regions, and that it must ask fundamental questions of itself about its own responsibility for its present underdevelopment, if it is to prosper in the twenty-first century. Savoie's work serves as a blueprint for a new way of envisioning the Maritime region.

DONALD J. SAVOIE holds the Canada Research Chair in Public Administration and Governance at l'Université de Moncton.

DONALD J. SAVOIE

Visiting Grandchildren: Economic Development in the Maritimes

UNIVERSITY OF TORONTO PRESS
Toronto Buffalo London

© University of Toronto Press Incorporated 2006
Toronto Buffalo London
Printed in Canada

ISBN-13: 978-0-8020-9054-6 (cloth)
ISBN-10: 0-8020-9054-0 (cloth)

ISBN-13: 978-0-8020-9382-0 (paper)
ISBN-10: 0-8020-9382-5 (paper)

Printed on acid-free paper

Library and Archives Canada Cataloguing in Publication

Savoie, Donald J., 1947–
    Visiting grandchildren : economic development in the Maritimes / Donald
J. Savoie.

    Includes bibliographical references and index.
    ISBN-13: 978-0-8020-9054-6 (bound)
    ISBN-10: 0-8020-9054-0 (bound)
    ISBN-13: 978-0-8020-9382-0 (pbk.)
    ISBN-10: 0-8020-9382-5 (pbk.)

    1. Maritime Provinces – Economic conditions.   2. Regional
planning – Maritime Provinces.   3. Canada – Economic conditions –
Regional disparities.   4. Canada – Economic policy.   I. Title.

HC117.M35S39 2006   338.9715   C2005-905770-X

University of Toronto Press acknowledges the financial assistance to
its publishing program of the Canada Council for the Arts and the
Ontario Arts Council.

University of Toronto Press acknowledges the financial support for
its publishing activities of the Government of Canada through the
Book Publishing Industry Development Program (BPIDP).

To Jean and Benjamin Higgins

Contents

Preface

In the summer of 2002 Paul Martin, then Canada's finance minister, called me without any forewarning. He opened the conversation with a question – 'What is the problem in Atlantic Canada and what is the solution?' It is a question that many other Canadians have been asking in recent years. The question led to a lively and, for me at least, fascinating discussion. I responded to his initial question by observing that it was a great deal easier to talk about the problem than about solutions, adding that I would much prefer to focus our discussion on the Maritime region rather than on Atlantic Canada. The concept of Atlantic Canada is mostly a myth created by policy makers from away. The three Maritime provinces have long-standing historical ties, share many common political and economic concerns, and have strong trade ties. Newfoundland and Labrador has a different history, a different culture, different trade patterns, and different economic challenges. Put another way, although I am from Moncton, New Brunswick, I consider Cape Breton, Prince Edward Island, and Nova Scotia to be part of my region. I have long argued for Maritime union, though I have come to accept that full political union will not become a reality, at least not in my lifetime. I do not, however, consider Newfoundland and Labrador to be part of my region any more than I do, say, Manitoba. There is a unique business culture in the Maritimes, and a thriving business network. The Toronto *Globe and Mail* ran an article on the region's business connections and reported that business leaders from 'the three Maritime provinces ... say that Newfoundlanders have their own close network that can be equally effective.'[1] I am sure that many Newfoundlanders and Labradorians feel the same way about the Maritimes. The only thing that the Maritimes and Newfoundland and Labrador have in common is that we share part of the Atlantic Ocean and we are classified as have-less regions.

No doubt my views left Mr Martin *sur sa faim*. It certainly left me with the desire to answer his question more fully – hence this book. But the prime minister is hardly alone in searching for economic solutions for the region. In the heat of the 2004 general election campaign, Stephen Harper had this to say on a visit to the Maritime provinces: 'Some day, when this province gets its fair share from Confederation ... New Brunswick will be less a place where you visit your grandparents, and more a place where you visit your grandchildren.'[2] For Harper, the region's economic problems stemmed from Confederation. But this begs the question — what is the solution or, to put it another way, how can the region secure its fair share from Confederation?

The question and answer explain the book's rather ambitious, if not pretentious, title. But Martin's question and Harper's answer speak to the impatience many policy makers in Ottawa, public policy analysts, and Canadians generally have with the pace of economic development in the Maritime provinces. There is a strong appetite for solutions, for reducing federal transfer payments to the region, and for seeing more self-sustaining economic activities take root. In brief, if there is a thirst for a solution in the rest of Canada, imagine what it is like in the Maritime region. That said, I warn the reader at the outset that this book does not offer a 'definitive' solution to the Maritimes' economic woes. My goal is to initiate a comprehensive debate on the economic problems confronting my region and to canvas possible solutions. This explains why I have chosen to look at the problem both from a regional and a national perspective and to spend a great deal of time reviewing Ottawa's policies for economic and regional development over the years.

I love everything about Canada, except its constitutional marital arrangement. I believe firmly that something is not right with the way our national political institutions operate. This has something to do with what has been labelled Canada's democratic deficit. But, to my mind, the issue is broader still, though it may well be directly related to the democratic deficit. I have come to the conclusion that Canada will never be completely at peace with itself until we sort out better how all regions relate to the national government. I am firmly of the view that my region needs to find the answer and its economic future within Canada's framework.

I have, for example, long supported the reform of Canada's Senate, and I could never understand why Maritimers or, for that matter, all of Atlantic Canada would not join forces with western Canada to push for Senate reform. With few exceptions, political or business leaders in the Maritime provinces have not taken much interest in the question. I have written about its importance and in numerous media interviews have put the case for joining forces with western Canada to advocate Senate reform, but my plea, it seems, has fallen mostly on deaf ears, at least in my own region. I even had a disagreement on this issue with Prime Minister Martin, refusing to endorse publicly his Osgoode Hall speech on democratic deficit because it did not deal with Senate reform. How, I asked, could we possibly address Canada's democratic deficit without making any reference to the one political institution that is fundamentally undemocratic and has never fully assumed its responsibility of speaking on behalf of the regions?

I write all of the above so that the reader will know why I set out to write this book. I have a responsibility to my peers in the academic community and to the reader to present an objective perspective. I try to do this as best as I can, but only my peers and the reader will be able to determine if I were successful. My fondest hope is that this book will contribute, in some modest way, to better public policy for Canada and a stronger economic future for the three Maritime provinces.

I have many people to thank. I owe Professor Benjamin Higgins a great deal. We became close friends in the mid-1980s and remained so until his death in May 2001. He visited the Université de Moncton every year from 1985 to 1995. We worked together on a number of projects and co-authored several articles and two books. I also co-edited a book in his honour and co-edited with him a book in honour of François Perroux. Benjamin Higgins fell in love with the Université de Moncton and the Maritime provinces and in turn both fell in love with him and his wife Jean. I have fond memories of both, their remarkable zest for life, their complete lack of pretension, and their thirst for knowledge. I had the good fortune of visiting them in 1993 on their ranch in Australia to work with Ben on our book *Regional Development Theories and Their Application*. I borrow from that book, and it is fitting that I dedicate this book to Ben and Jean.

I also borrow from my earlier books on regional development – in particular, *Regional Economic Development: Canada's Search for Solutions*. The reader will note that I reproduced in large measure four chapters from an earlier book. Chapters 4, 5, 6, and 7 provide an account of federal regional development programs from their beginning to the early 1990s. I saw no need to rewrite history, but I felt that the chapters were extremely important to the central purpose of this book.

My earlier work on regional development has brought me in direct contact with scholars and practitioners who have made important contributions to the field, including François Perroux, Tom Courchene, John Friedmann, William Alonso, Niles Hansen, and Lloyd Rodwin. I collaborated closely with Tom Courchene and we became friends. I organized a conference in honour of François Perroux. He participated at the conference and tabled a paper – what would be his last contribution to the literature. I have his original paper in my office with handwritten notes in the margin. I am in debt to these and many other authors, as the endnotes to this book reveal.

I also had the good fortune to work closely on economic development with many practitioners, notably Roméo LeBlanc, Pierre De Bané, Elmer MacKay, Gérard Veilleux, Richard Hatfield, Senator Lowell Murray, and Frank McKenna. In 1986, I was asked by former prime minister Brian Mulroney to prepare a report on the establishment of the Atlantic Canada Opportunities Agency. Some three years later, I was asked by Jean Chrétien to prepare a policy paper on regional development, one of six he tabled during his successful bid in 1990 to lead his political party. I also interviewed both Jean Marchand and Tom Kent, key architects of Canada's regional development policy in the 1960s, for an earlier book on regional development. All these people were generous with me, provided important insights into public policy and how government decides, and I would like to thank all of them for their assistance and support.

I owe a special thank you to Alex Colville for agreeing to allow one of his paintings to be reproduced for the cover. I am told that it is not something that he does lightly, and for this reason alone the gesture is greatly appreciated. In explaining his decision, he wrote that he admired my work on behalf of my region, but sometimes felt that I was 'a voice crying in the wilderness.' He added: 'of course, that are also good things in the wilderness and perhaps you and I speak of them in similar voices.' It is difficult to imagine a greater compliment from a most distinguished Maritimer.

I am also in debt to the regional economic development field itself, a field that provided my first academic appointment, generated material for a number of my publications, and gave rise to fascinating discussions and experiences. I have, however, decided to exit the field with this book. In future I intend to write about public administration and governance, given my current appointment with the Canada Research Chair in Public Administration and Governance. I will never, however, lose interest in regional issues, and I will keep a close watch on new developments. I will also make it a point to strongly encourage students of public policy to undertake research in economic development and regional studies.

I owe a special thank you to Ginette Benoit. We have worked together for nearly twenty-five years, and I cannot imagine a scholar being better served. I will simply say that I could not have accomplished what I have done without her assistance and her ability to organize my work and my agenda. I also would like to thank Joan Harcourt, who, as she always does with my work, read the study when it was in manuscript form and made numerous improvements.

Abbreviations

ACOA	Atlantic Canada Opportunities Agency
ACTP	Atlantic Canada Tourism Partnership
ADA	Area Development Agency
ADB	Atlantic Development Board
ADIA	Area Development Incentives Act
AECL	Atomic Energy of Canada Ltd
AEP	Atlantic Enterprise Program
AIF	Atlantic Innovation Fund
AIMS	Atlantic Institute for Market Studies
AOP	Atlantic Opportunities Program
APEC	Atlantic Provinces Economic Council
ARDA	Agricultural Rehabilitation and Development Act (later, Agricultural and Rural Development Act)
BNA Act	British North America Act
CAP	Canada Assistance Plan
CFI	Canada Foundation for Innovation
CHST	Canadian Health and Social Transfer
CIDA	Canadian International Development Agency
DEVCO	Cape Breton Development Corporation
DFO	Department of Fisheries and Oceans
DIPP	Defence Industry Productivity Program
DIST	Department of Industry, Science, and Technology
DREE	Department of Regional Economic Expansion
DRIE	Department of Regional Industrial Expansion
ECB	Enterprise Cape Breton
ECBC	Enterprise Cape Breton Corporation
EDC	Export Development Canada

EPF	Established Program Financing
ERC	Expenditure Review Committee
ERDA	Economic and Regional Development Agreements
FEDC	federal economic development coordinator
FedNor	Federal Economic Development Initiative for Northern Ontario
FRED	Fund for Rural Economic Development
FTA	Canada-U.S. Free Trade Agreement
GDA	General Development Agreements
GDP	gross domestic product
IRAP	Industrial Research Assistance Program
IRDP	industrial and regional development program
IT&C	Department of Industry, Trade, and Commerce
MSERD	Ministry of State for Economic and Regional Development
NAFTA	North American Free Trade Agreement
NDP	New Democratic Party
PCO	Privy Council Office
PMO	Prime Minister's Office
P&P	Priorities and Planning
PWGS	Department of Public Works and Government Services
R&D	research and development
RDIA	Regional Development Incentives Act
SMEs	small and medium-sized enterprises
TPC	Technology Partnerships Canada
WD	Western Economic Diversification Canada
WTID	Western Transportation Industrial Development

VISITING GRANDCHILDREN:
ECONOMIC DEVELOPMENT IN THE MARITIMES

1 Introduction

This book has two objectives: to examine past government efforts to promote economic development in the Maritime provinces and to lay the foundation for improved public policy. It is, of course, possible to look at Canada in several ways, according to ecological, physiographic, economic, or political criteria. The most common approach, however, has been to regard provinces and regions as synonymous.[1]

In this book, I have chosen to view the three small Maritime provinces as a single region. I do this for several reasons. For one thing, I am a Maritimer both by birth and by choice, and I have a deep attachment to the region and its people. For another, the Maritimes as a 'region' has deep historical roots in Canada. For example, it should be remembered that the 1864 Charlottetown Conference was originally called to discuss Maritime union. Then, representatives from the Canadas came to persuade Maritimers to join a larger union. More recently, in 1965 the legislatures of Nova Scotia and New Brunswick passed resolutions calling for a Maritime Union study. Yet another reason for viewing the Maritime provinces as a region is that there is a widely held perception that the Canadian government has spent more funds pursuing economic development in these provinces than anywhere else in the country, and, further, that these efforts have not been a resounding success. The region is also an ideal setting to review public policy in the field – it is relatively small, thus making it a good laboratory in which to test past endeavours, to find out what works, what does not, and why. The economic underdevelopment of the three Maritime provinces has puzzled policy makers for over a century. It has been the subject of royal commissions and has given rise to a plethora of government programs designed to alleviate the situation.[2] The hope is that this book will foster a greater understanding of the economic challenges confronting all peripheral regions, promote a public debate, provide public-policy prescriptions, and encourage new research in the area.

The espousal of Keynesian economics following the Second World War led to the attempt by governments to deal with economic disparity by promoting new economic opportunities in disadvantaged regions. These efforts have in turn given rise to a catalogue of lessons learned and to a body of literature on the subject.[3] We draw on both. Yet, regional economic development has, at least in Ottawa, had an uneasy existence from the very beginning. Tom Kent puts it succinctly: 'From the point of view of almost all conventional wisdom in Ottawa, the idea of regional development was a rather improper one that some otherwise quite reasonable politician brought in like a baby on a doorstep from an election campaign.'[4]

Many economists have a 'prejudice against' regional economic development on the grounds that such policies compromise efficiency in resource allocations.[5] They see little merit in encouraging the regional distribution of economic activities, believing that capital and labour will inevitably migrate to regions and communities that generate the highest level of profit or wage. Meanwhile, most public policy analysts prefer looking to the national (macro) level and to the (micro) level of the industry, enterprise, and the household in their work. National bureaucracies, as Tom Kent discovered, have a similar bias. The Canadian civil service, as is the case elsewhere, is organized along sectoral lines. Civil servants are not known to draw battle lines often, but when they do, they are likely to do so on sectoral matters and on the program interests of their own departments, as opposed to those of other departments. Civil servants often equate any regional venture with politics rather than with sound public policy. An economist in the Department of Finance in Ottawa would insist that 'regional development measures' is a phrase that may have succeeded politically, but that there is precious little evidence that it has done so from the standpoint of public policy. Accordingly, he or she would argue that such measures should be evaluated from a political perspective and that the less public funding committed to them, the better. In any case, as is well known, Keynesian economics has fallen out of favour in recent decades. It has been blamed for inhibiting private initiative, efficiency, and economic growth while creating a bloated bureaucracy and a large government debt. When people want to prove this, they point to the results of the various regional economic development policies – policies that have been on the defensive for the last twenty-five years.

There is no doubt that regionalism and regional economic development are sustained by a political constituency. The boundaries of politics are defined by geography, by an electorate with community and regional interests to advance. Politicians represent their constituents – and the constituents' idea of an effective member of Parliament in Ottawa is someone who is able to bring the bacon home to the riding. This is not, by any stretch of the imagination, a view restricted to the outlying provinces. John Bryden, an Ontario MP, commenting on the 2004 Liberal nomination fracas in Hamilton observed that 'the battle is largely about who will be Hamilton's political boss. Liberal politicians have long been judged on the spoils they bring back to Hamilton.' He added, 'The role of the politicians is to get money from Ottawa for Hamilton.'[6] The incumbent MP for Ottawa-Orleans, Eugène Bellemare, lost his party's nomination in 2004 because he could not bring home the bacon. The winning candidate, Marc Godbout, explained: 'Mr. Bellemare lacked a strategy to get the east end [Ottawa] out of the rot it found itself in ... Of the 450 buildings owned or leased by the federal government in Ottawa, only two were in the riding.'[7] If politicians in Hamilton, an important urban centre not far from Toronto, one of the world's economic hot spots, and Ottawa, benefiting as it does from the large federal government presence in the city, are judged on their ability to 'deliver the goods,' then one can only imagine what it must be like for an MP representing a disadvantaged riding in a peripheral region of the country.

There is also a disconnect between political and economic development time. Politicians must have an immediate impact in promoting the interests of their constituencies, given that they enjoy only a four- to five-year mandate, and even less if they are members of a minority government. On the other hand, economic development isn't achieved overnight. This is particularly so in a region, like the Maritime provinces, that requires a comprehensive strategy designed to address, among other things, human resources development, infrastructure, and innovation.

Federal politicians, like their provincial counterparts, represent constituencies or geographic spaces that vary greatly in size and population. Their continuing success is directly tied to how well they are perceived by their constituents as advocating their interests. Once elected, under our Westminster model of parliamentary government, a small minority of them, drawn from the same political party, will come together to form the government. The prime minister and provincial premiers will draw on their respective cabinets and civil service for advice. Prime ministers and their governments are expected to promote the interests of the nation, while provincial premiers and their governments are expected to promote the interests of their provinces. The administrative side of government is organized to support first ministers and their cabinets in defining and pursuing sectoral opportunities, again from either a national or a provincial perspective. Thus, from the public service standpoint, the geographical perspective is national or provincial, not regional or community-based. The latter responsibility is left to regional, municipal, or local politicians. But this is not the way the local MP, MPP, or MLA will see things. They expect the machinery of government as a whole to support their efforts to promote the economic interests of their constituencies.

This book takes the view that nations, in our case Canada, are in fact collections of regions (geographical spaces). Each region, in turn, has its own society and its own economic, political, and power structure. The degree to which these spaces are integrated into a unified national economic, social, political, and administrative system, and into regional and global economies, varies a great deal from region to region, and these variations go a long way to explaining differences in performance (economic, social, and political) from country to country.[8]

When performance is unsatisfactory, one can make the case that government intervention is required at the regional and community level, not just at the macro or micro levels. But what action should be taken? Different regions, different spaces, and different communities have different resource endowments, physical and human. Since neither people nor resources are spread evenly through space, there are necessary choices and decisions to be made as to what economic activities should be carried out and where. Proximity to markets (people) and to resources as well as calculations as to production costs and transport costs will, among others, be considerations in these decisions. More recently, access to information, to innovations, and to new knowledge has been added to the list of important considerations. The aggregation of these decisions will determine the location of industry and other economic activities, and thus the location of population, the location and size of cities, and the urban hierarchy. But no government, however laissez-faire it may claim to be, will stand idly by when a region is suffering economically. Governments do intervene, though political ideology and fiscal restraints will often shape the nature and degree of intervention.

Therein lies the rub. Economic theory, economic development planning, the workings and the planning capacities of government bureaucracies are one thing. Political circumstances and requirements are quite another. Complicating the dilemma is how government is structured. The machinery of government is not policy neutral, and how a government is organized will shape its policy response to various challenges. Thus, this book is about politics, public policy, history, economics, and public administration – admittedly an ambitious agenda that may not appeal to the specialist with an intimate knowledge of specific issues, the current fashion in the public policy literature being to focus on a relatively narrow field. There is, of course, a great deal to commend this approach, nor would I wish to challenge it. However, I have become convinced that the economic problems intrinsic to the Maritime provinces require a broader palette, a willingness to take a more comprehensive look at various forces confronting the region. Ben Higgins, a leading student of economic development in the last century, long insisted that to define economic prescriptions for a region one must be prepared to do so from a multidisciplinary perspective.[9] I take his advice to heart in this book. That said, I fully recognize that there is a risk that I may not meet expectations. But the risk is well worth taking if it encourages others to undertake new research in Canadian regionalism and economic development.

This book turns to history, to economic data, and to Ottawa's regional economic development policy and efforts over the years to look for a new approach to an old problem. We examine the federal regional policy from a Canada-wide perspective, as well as from a strictly Maritime one, because of the light it sheds on Ottawa's commitment to the various regions, and on what may work and what does not.

The reader will note that I spend a great deal of time on history and on outlining, in some detail, past federal attempts to promote economic development in Canada generally and in the Maritime provinces in particular. There are several reasons for this. For one thing, together they help to explain the problem, and it would be foolish to search for a new approach without drawing on the past. For another, I have become deeply concerned with the historical amnesia of both students and practitioners of economic development. This in turn has led to embedded ideas among many national policy makers and their advisers that have inhibited development of effective policies to promote economic development in the three Maritime provinces.

Students in the economic development field increasingly use highly

mathematical and technical models to determine the location of economic activities. These models have their merit, of course, but they
cannot provide a complete explanation. To be sure, neither can history
or a detailed account of past ventures do so, but they can make a
contribution to the task, if only to point out the pitfalls.

Practitioners have also lost sight of the history to their own work. In
the fall of 2003 I gave a presentation on regional development policy to
senior officials at Industry Canada. I spoke about Trudeau's reasons for
establishing the Department of Regional Economic Expansion (DREE),
why he later abolished it, and why Mulroney established the Atlantic
Canada Opportunities Agency (ACOA) and other regional development agencies in 1988. To a person, they thanked me for giving them
the history of Ottawa's regional development policy. The great majority
of the participants were unfamiliar with seminal policy moments.
Though I was speaking about relatively recent events, and to individuals with a direct interest in the field, it was as if I were talking about
ancient history.

Later, when I was the Simon Reisman Visiting Fellow at the Treasury
Board (2004), I came to understand this historical vacuum better. Governments now all too often make policy by announcement. Power Point
presentations have replaced the discussion papers that were once attached to Memoranda to Cabinet and that were an important part of the
cabinet decision-making process. Perhaps because of the perverse
aspects of Access to Information legislation, perhaps because policy
making now has to be generated quickly to respond to a new, more
demanding political environment, or perhaps because far too many
cabinet documents are now prepared by outside consultants rather
than by career officials, government departments today rarely produce
discussion papers. The policy-making process has become ahistorical,
and both sound public policy and the lessons that might be learned
from history are the worse for it. As one knowledgeable official co-
gently observed, 'Power Point presentations are easier to produce than
discussion papers because often one only has to state a point, not
defend it, or support it by building a carefully crafted and well-
reasoned paper.'[10]

And there is more. Senior government officials no longer serve in the
same department for very long, nor do they now come up through the
ranks of a line department, as in the past. The longest-serving deputy
minister in a federal department in 2004 had been in the position for
only five years. Between 1984 and 2004, we have had six clerks of the

Privy Council Office, seven secretaries of the Treasury Board, twelve deputy ministers of Industry, and seven deputy ministers of Finance.[11] Institutional memory, thus, has become a rare commodity in government. It is my hope that this book will provide students and practitioners with knowledge of what has been attempted in the field and why. It sets economic development in the Maritime provinces in a broader context precisely for this purpose.

The book's central thesis is that, to prosper, each Canadian region requires a different relationship with the federal government and with national policies. Only Ontario has been able to develop this relationship, benefiting as it does from national policies. Canada's regional structure, its diversity, and its economic circumstances are such that national economic development policies can never apply equally well in all regions. Some will invariably gain from such policies while others will not or will benefit substantially less.

Our national political and administrative institutions have a national policy mindset. No national government – and, for that matter, no neoconservative economist – will allow market forces complete freedom to dictate the pace of development in the national economy. They have always favoured policies that strengthen the national economy vis-à-vis the United States and, more recently, the global economy. Laissez-faire economics has its place, but not in every sector, not in every region, and not for all time.

Canadian policy makers have since the late 1870s sought to grow a national economy through national policies. These national policies are not without significant implications for Canada's regions. But this begs the question: What is national and what is regional? When I put this question to a senior Finance official in Ottawa, he answered, 'It is important to understand that 64 per cent of Canada's gross domestic product is located in central Canada. There is no getting around this. And so when you design national economic policies and programs, you will invariably be drawn to that reality.'[12] Tom Courchene is one of Canada's leading and most prolific neoconservative writers. However, his confidence in market forces has its limits, and in recent years, for example, he has written about the need to have a new national government department to deal with globalization and the knowledge information revolution.[13] Government intervention may not be appropriate at the regional level, but it seems that it is at the national level to pursue national objectives.

It is not too much of an exaggeration to write that national economic policies and programs have been designed to make the national (for the most part here, read southern Ontario) economy compete better with the American or with other national economies. From time to time, they have also been adjusted to promote national unity (here, one should read making Canadian federalism viable in Quebec). Our national political institutions also have a built-in bias that favours some regions (those with the most seats) over others. Our parliamentary system is based on the Westminster model, and our government organization and public service took guidance from British experience. The British institutions took shape in a unitary state where power was concentrated in the hands of the monarch and where a large population was concentrated over a relatively small territory. In Canada, political power is concentrated in the hands of the prime minister and a few key advisers. Unlike Australia, for example, our Senate is not elected and likely for this reason it has not been very effective in representing regional interests within national political institutions. Unlike Britain, Canada's population is relatively small and spread out over a vast territory. Canada's population density is 1 per cent that of Great Britain.[14]

The fact that Canada's political institutions were born and given shape in Britain, a unitary state, is vitally important. Sir John A. Macdonald and a number of Fathers of Confederation wanted one national government and saw little need for another order of government. The hope was to bring the Maritime provinces into a legislative union with the Canadas. Failing that, their goal, as our constitution makes clear, was to create a constitution similar in principle to that of the United Kingdom. As James Mallory explains, however, 'the British constitution has grown up within the framework of a homogeneous community and a unitary state.'[15] Not so Canada. One hundred years after Confederation, the Canadian provinces were becoming assertive in their relations with the national government, an assertiveness that could, in good part, be traced back to economic sources.[16] The outer provinces came to see that, all too often, things 'national' equalled the economic interests only of Ontario and Quebec.

The 'national' media also defines what is national to be bounded by Ontario and Quebec. Journalists have never described Lester Pearson, Pierre Trudeau, Brian Mulroney, Jean Chrétien, or Paul Martin as being regional politicians. However, Lawrence Martin writes that 'Like Preston Manning, Stephen Harper bears a regional stamp.'[17] The same was said about John Diefenbaker.[18] It seems that Ontario and Quebec politicians become national politicians simply by being from one of those provinces, while politicians from the West, the Maritimes, and Newfoundland and Labrador can wear a national stamp only through considerable effort, if at all. I was struck, as probably many Maritimers were, by the reactions in the media to John Manley's being moved out of the industry portfolio in 2004. Edward Greenspon praised Manley in the *Globe and Mail* for his ability to think 'national' and pointedly asked whether his replacement, Brian Tobin, will 'be an Atlantic minister or a national minister.'[19] A few days later Campbell Morrison, a columnist, wrote in the *Moncton Times and Transcript* that 'If Brian Tobin succeeds at nothing else, at least he has dislodged John Manley from the key Industry portfolio ... [Manley's] primary concern has been the high-tech sector, which by happy coincidence is based largely in Ottawa, and the aerospace sector in Montreal and Toronto.'[20] For Maritimers, however, Ontario's Manley was as much a regional minister as was Newfoundland's Tobin. Manley also practised the art of *deux poids, deux mesures*. He consistently refused to assist the New Brunswick shipbuilding industry, on the grounds that it was not part of the new economy. However, witness his attempt to come to the rescue of the Ottawa Senators with federal funding. Surely one would be hard pressed to make the case that a hockey team is part of the new economy while the shipbuilding industry is not.

But what about the Maritime provinces? Where *do* they fit in relation to the national policy and to political requirements (here, read winning seats)? When the national economy is considered to be sufficiently strong to compete in the global economy (here, read not very often), federal government policy makers will design special programs and increase federal transfers for the region. Brian Crowley has described these efforts as 'guilt money' coming from central Canada.[21] National policy makers will not, however, examine national policies and programs in order to assess their impact on the Maritime provinces and make any remedial adjustments to them.

Guilt money has taken various forms. Indeed, the programs it has sponsored have not lacked for flexibility. The program goals, however, with some significant exceptions, have been unclear. This, in turn, explains why we have not been able to assess their success with any degree of certainty. In recent years, guilt money programs have been considerably more discriminating and focused. But the perception lingers that they have been and continue to be bad investments. More, they have never been able to compensate for the fact that national policies do not apply equally in all regions. To be sure, not all transfers to provincial governments and individuals were designed to promote economic development.

But that is not all. The flow of these programs has been carefully monitored so that the tap opens when the national economy can afford it and Maritime seats may be needed to secure a majority government mandate. However, as this book suggests, the tap is quickly adjusted and the flow directed to other purposes when there is a need to strengthen the 'national' (that is, Ontario) economy or national unity (with the diversion of funds to Quebec). The economic interests of the Maritime provinces can never be part of the national interest or even accommodated in national policies. Since the 1880s, the economic interests of the Maritime provinces have been treated as one-off, somehow disconnected from national policies. That said, national policy and national political and administrative institutions are not the only reason for Maritime decline and its relative underdevelopment, and we will explore other causes.

As local economic development officials know all too well, there are a number of accepted truths that, to a certain extent, apply in this matter: success breeds success, failure breeds failure, new Canadians go where their compatriots have settled, proximity to markets still matters a great deal, economic development does not take place in a vacuum, and there has to be a valid reason for new economic activities to take root.

At the risk of sounding repetitive, national politics is dominated by Ontario and Quebec because both provinces hold the key to a majority government and because Canada does not have an effective second chamber in Parliament to speak on behalf of the smaller provinces. National policy making is fed by an Ontario-Quebec focus dominated by a senior public service concentrated in Ottawa and by policy groups, networks, think-tanks, and consultants, also largely in Ottawa. Their overriding preoccupation is to build a national economy that can compete with the Americans under NAFTA and in the global economy. Viewed from this perspective, Canada's national economy is small, and every effort must be made to concentrate its strengths. The omnipresence of the U.S. economy, the desire to be economically competitive, and the never ending desire to promote national unity and to demonstrate that Canadian federalism is viable for Quebec explain the behaviour of national policy makers and their advisers. Indeed, these forces are behind every seminal moment in national policies, from the establishment of Crown corporations to the design of national economic development strategies. Meanwhile, the economy of the Maritime provinces has been viewed, at best, as a puzzle for national policy makers and, at worst, as a burden on the national economy. Provincial politicians have been left on their own to try to come up with solutions, solutions that by definition can never measure up to those charged with promoting the national economy on the world stage. The result is that the Maritime economy has been sidelined in terms of national economic development policies and programs. Call it guilt money or what you will, it remains that the Maritime economy has always been viewed as an add-on, a special case, a lagging region, a problem to be addressed by special measures.

Policy makers have occasionally acknowledged that national policies have long favoured central Canada. The 1940 Report of the Rowell-Sirois commission is one such example, and the government's eventual response to its findings speaks directly to this admission. The proposed solution was to design redistributive policies and special regional measures to compensate the Maritime provinces for national policies geared towards the generation of wealth in central Canada – in other words, guilt money. The development measures were tolerated only so long as they did not threaten the national economy. In time, however, they came to be considered an important instrument of national unity and thus were expanded to cover other regions. But again they were always thought to be 'one-off' measures, never an integrated part of national policies and programs.

This study points the way to a workable solution to the search for a viable Maritime economy. The first step involves the Maritime provinces themselves resolutely breaking away from guilt money, once and for all. This suggestion is hardly new. Indeed, it has been made time and again by a variety of economists, observers, and think-tanks. But what should the next step be?

If one accepts that the Maritime economy has been peripheral to national policies and programs and that this situation is, at least in part, responsible for the region's relative underdevelopment, then ways must be found to have the region's economic circumstances brought right into the centre of government, where policies and programs are defined. The goal should be to integrate the Maritime economy better into already thriving economies, whether in Canada's national economy or in the regional economies of New England and the eastern seaboard of the United States.

This book calls for a radically new approach, one that recognizes that what is good for the Maritime provinces is good for Canada no less than what is good for Ontario is good for Canada. Long-run growth rates tend to be highest in countries undergoing long-run regional convergence, as a result of the operation of a 'ratchet effect'; that is, regions take turns at high growth, the slow-growth region of one period becoming the high-growth one of the next, with none moving from slow-growth to decline.[22] This cannot be accomplished by ad hoc regional economic development programs, or guilt money, or both.

The Approach

This study seeks to test several hypotheses:

- Canada's national political institutions are designed for a unitary state, not for a federation. These institutions have shaped national policies and programs at an important cost to the Maritime economy.
- The government of Canada has consistently misdiagnosed the patient in developing economic prescriptions for the Maritime provinces.
- The regional perspective – critical to smaller regions such as the Maritime provinces – has never been properly defined or pursued in the national public policy.
- The federal government's national policy perspective and objectives and national unity efforts have been code words to pursue the regional political and economic interests of Ontario and Quebec.
- Historical accidents and historical events, with the latter shaped by the workings of our national political and administrative institutions, go a long way to explaining the region's underdevelopment.
- Ideas that have no historical basis have become embedded in our national political administrative institutions. These, in turn, have made evidence-based policy advice at the national level difficult to produce.

Organization of the Study

The study has eleven chapters. In chapter 2, we look to history to see how the Maritime provinces have defined their place in Confederation. Canada's birth was motivated by regional self-interest rather than by patriotism. Ontario wanted to counterbalance Quebec and co-opted the

Maritime provinces for help to achieve this goal. The country's political institutions were designed with this goal in mind, and the Maritime provinces have paid a steep political and economic price ever since. Not present in 1867, but very much so today, are the Western provinces. They share with the Maritimes a strong sense that the national political and administrative institutions have never accommodated their economic circumstances and interests to anything like the same extent that they have those of Ontario and Quebec.

Chapter 2 also discusses the region's economic strengths and trade patterns before Confederation. It reports on why and how New Brunswick and Nova Scotia joined with the Canadian colonies to create Confederation. It reviews the creation of the National Policy and its impact on the region. The chapter examines the economic forces that shaped Canada's economic development in the early part of the last century and also the influence of Keynesian economics after the 1930s. It reports on the Maritime Rights Movement and on early federal efforts to promote economic development in the Maritime provinces.

In chapter 3 we review the most important economic development theories and prescriptions advanced to promote economic development, particularly in slow-growth regions. The purpose is to draw from the literature lessons that may apply to the Maritime region. My own experience in government and in advising government reveals that many practitioners are often unaware of what the seminal essays on economic development have to say about their work. I do not in this study seek to put forward another general analytical framework or a new all-encompassing theory. My goal is much more modest. I am convinced, however, that it is not possible to examine federal efforts in the field without first reviewing the literature. Accordingly, we focus on those theories and approaches that are relevant to the Canadian context.

In chapter 4 we review the government of Canada's first regional economic development programs. These began in the early 1960s and continue to this day. The early ventures were modest, but they laid the groundwork for subsequent programs. The chapter discusses Trudeau's initial contribution to regional development, in particular the establishment of the Department of Regional Economic Expansion.

In chapter 5 we look at the first of many revisions made to Canada's regional economic development policy. Concerns about national unity, dissatisfaction with the visibility of federal funding, and the perceived weakening in Ontario's economy in the early 1980s were critical to the revisions. A new approach to federal-provincial relations was introduced, one that involved generous federal-provincial agreements to deliver the bulk of federal efforts in the field.

Chapter 6 turns to Mulroney's changes to his predecessor's approach. We discuss the establishment of ACOA and its emphasis on entrepreneurship. Mulroney decided to locate the head office outside of Ottawa and to decentralize operations to provincial offices. ACOA led to a new approach, not only in the type of efforts sponsored but also in federal-provincial relations. In the early days of federal regional development efforts, the focus was on eastern Quebec, the three Maritime provinces, and Newfoundland and Labrador. In time, they were extended to cover other regions. New agencies were established for western Canada, for Quebec, and for Northern Ontario.

Canadian prime ministers, as far back as Diefenbaker, have sought to leave a legacy in the field of regional economic development (Diefenbaker with the Agricultural Rehabilitation and Development Act, Pearson with the Fund for Rural Economic Development, Trudeau with DREE, and Mulroney with ACOA and Western Economic Diversification Canada). In chapter 7 we look at Chrétien's decade in power. Chrétien left the machinery of government intact, but he also introduced important changes, including the promotion of research and development and the elimination of cash grants to private firms.

In chapter 8 we consider the various suggestions that the region heal itself or pick itself up by its own bootstraps, including a movement to promote political union of the three Maritime provinces to strengthen the region's economy. We also examine the concept of entrepreneurship that took root in the late 1980s and its application to the Maritime provinces.

Using census and other data from Statistics Canada, from research institutes, and from various government departments, in chapter 9 we compare the economy of the Maritime provinces in 2001 to that in 1961. We chose these two dates because the period covers Canada's most ambitious years in the regional economic development field. We look at various indicators to document the region's economic progress and to assess Ottawa's efforts in the region. The purpose is to determine whether the Maritime region made economic progress over the forty-year period.

In chapter 10 we look at the place of the Maritime provinces in Confederation. Some believe that the region benefits from federal policies and programs and that these have not inhibited economic development. Others take the opposite view. In this chapter we look at the economic policies of the federal government, the role of the federal public service, and the relationship between the region and the national government to assess their impact on the Maritime provinces and their development.

In chapter 11 we seek to enumerate the different reasons for the region's relative underdevelopment and offer suggestions as to how the Maritime provinces might prosper again. In this vein, we look to history, accidents of geography and history, historical events, and the workings of national political and administrative institutions. We argue that the region must strive to redefine its relations with the national government and with other regions, that it must ask fundamental questions of itself about its own responsibility for its present underdevelopment. This study argues that the region needs to develop a cooperative mindset, be proactive, create new historical events, and embrace the market, if it is to prosper in the twenty-first century.

Information for this study comes from a number of sources, including published and unpublished government documents. Several senior government officials made available information and material that proved extremely valuable in completing the research. I also draw on some of my earlier work on regional economic development.[23] I consulted a number of current and former government officials (twenty-five interviews) between October 2003 and September 2004. Off-the-record interviews were done to elicit the most candid comments. A list of potential respondents was developed on the basis of what information and answers were required to complete the research. The interviews were largely unstructured and each was tailored to the position of the respective respondent. Accordingly, a series of common questions were not put to all.

2 History Matters

In economic development, as in other things, history matters, and success breeds success much as failure breeds failure. The Maritime provinces have long been classified as a have-not region. Their economic progress in the last century was very tentative and, even then, only in a few areas. Significantly, many of the gains in per capita income and in high-quality public services that have been achieved over the last forty years or so can be directly attributed to federal transfer payments, which can also create an economic dependency. Moreover, the region actually lost ground in many sectors in the last century. All in all, for much of the twentieth century, economic development in Canada was concentrated in the Quebec City–Windsor corridor, in the oil- and gas-producing provinces of western Canada, and in resource-rich British Columbia. Anyone calling for economic development elsewhere in the country was shouting into the wind. With the exception of Newfoundland and Labrador, nowhere was this more apparent than in the Maritime provinces.

In this chapter we provide a brief historical journey through the Maritime provinces. Many Maritimers are convinced that most of their economic woes stem from Canada's constitutional arrangements and its political institutions. We need to explore this issue, while acknowledging that it is not possible to determine exactly to what extent this may be so. It would be like trying to ascertain how many children would not have been born in Canada in the absence of Ottawa's former family allowance program.[1] But we need to examine how the Maritime provinces have come to define their place in Confederation: it is simply not possible to engage Maritimers in a debate about economic development without first dealing with the role of the federal government and national policies. Thus, history matters.

In the Beginning

The three Maritime provinces did witness a golden era (c. 1800–66). As many historians have pointed out, they experienced substantial growth from 1800 to Confederation, based on a trading system that linked the region with the West Indies, New England, and Britain. Entrepreneurs from the three Maritime provinces were able to exploit the 'most important staples of fish and timber' throughout the era of 'wood, wind and sail.'[2] They were also able to compete with New England to the point that the region's 'shipping industry grew rapidly [and] at its height in the 1860s it ranked fourth among merchant marines of the world. The colonial financial system ... included nine dozen banks, among which were the two most stable financial institutions in British North America [and] numerous marine and other insurance companies which played leading roles in the economy of the region.'[3] Some of these would later rank among Canada's most important financial institutions, notably the Royal Bank of Canada and the Bank of Nova Scotia. A leading Canadian historian of the last century, J.M.S. Careless, described Halifax of the 1850s as 'the wealthiest, most advanced metropolitan city in the British North American Provinces.'[4] Nova Scotia was also a leader on the political front, and it was the first jurisdiction in the British North American colonies to introduce responsible government.

Halifax was not the only bright spot in the region. Saint John also had a thriving economy for much of the nineteenth century. The first incorporated city in Canada (1783), it was home to Canada's first chartered bank, the Bank of New Brunswick, established in 1820. The city's shipbuilding capacity had an international reputation. The *Marco Polo*, built in 1851, sailed from Britain to Australia and returned in about five months. It was the first ship to circumnavigate the globe in less than six months. It became known as the fastest ship in the world, and to this day Saint John takes great pride in this accomplishment.

Prince Edward Island also had a vibrant economy and a strong shipbuilding industry. It is important to stress that from 1815 to the 1860s, the entire region enjoyed a period of spectacular growth in shipbuilding. In those days of wooden ships, even small communities had their own shipyards because both good timber and the necessary skills were readily available. In addition, agriculture in Prince Edward Island flourished with the introduction of reciprocity with the United States in 1854, which led to a strong demand for agricultural products from Prince Edward Island, especially during the Civil War.

The 1854 reciprocity agreement with the Americans also cleared the way for the export of fish, lumber of all kinds, coal, gypsum, stone, lard, and other products to a growing market to the south.[5] The twelve years during which the trade agreement was in place were prosperous ones for the Maritime provinces. As two economic historians have noted, 'If we take the value of the exports of each province separately to the United States in 1854 as 100, by 1866 New Brunswick exports had risen by 400, Nova Scotia's to 208 and Prince Edward Island to 131.'[6] But that is not all. As world trade expanded during this period, demand for wooden sailing ships was strong, as for long trips, 'particularly to parts of the world with few coaling stations, these vessels [i.e., those built in the Maritimes] were still unrivalled.'[7] The steamship had limited impact on sailing ships until the 1870s. Historian D.A. Muise sums up this period well when he writes that the 'emergence of a powerful locally-based merchant marine that carried regional products also made regionally-based shippers a force to be reckoned with ... Later generations would look upon this era as the region's golden age.'[8]

Historians also note that the Maritime provinces had less in common with the United Province of Canada than they did with New England. Communications and trade with New England were stronger than with the Canadas. In brief, the region was oriented towards the Atlantic and New England, not to the St Lawrence. Leaving aside Halifax and Saint John, most communities were relatively isolated from one another. Given the region's economic structure and its main exports, the Maritime population resided in small rural villages and hamlets. The smaller communities were for the most part self-contained, prospering or surviving on fish, timber, and shipbuilding. They looked to Saint John and Halifax, to the New England states, to the West Indies, and to Britain to sell their products. As George Rawlyk and Doug Brown wrote, 'at the time of Confederation, Nova Scotia, New Brunswick and Prince Edward Island had relatively little in common with the Canadas.'[9] There were no roads or rail connections between the Maritimes and the Canadas. All this is to say once again that the Maritimes looked to the sea, to the fishery, to timber, agriculture, and shipbuilding for economic development, and this strategy worked.[10]

Aboriginals and immigrants, mostly from western Europe, developed the region. The Mi'kmaq and Maliseet had long survived as hunters, fishers, and gatherers well before the Acadians and, later, the Highland Scots and southern Irish arrived. The arrival of thousands of American Loyalists in 1783–4 (including approximately 14,000 in Saint John alone) forced a political restructuring of the region. The population suddenly doubled, and the British government divided the colony into a number of new provinces – Nova Scotia, Cape Breton (which rejoined Nova Scotia in 1820), and New Brunswick.

The Maritime provinces continued to have strong population growth between 1800 and Confederation. New Brunswick's population grew from 20,000 in 1803 to 252,000 in 1861, Nova Scotia's population grew from 82,000 in 1817 to 330,000 in 1861, and Prince Edward Island's from 25,000 in 1822 to 80,000 in 1861.[11] This growth almost kept pace with the Canadas. The region's population grew by 24.6 per cent from 1851 to 1861, compared with 34.7 per cent for the United Province of Canada and by 15.5 per cent between 1861 and 1871, compared with 13.8 per cent for the Canadas/Ontario and Quebec.[12] As George Rawlyk wrote, 'the Yankees migrated to the southern end of Nova Scotia and to fishing townships on the south shore, the "Foreign Protestants" to Lunenburg County, south of Halifax, the Highland Scots to Cape Breton Island, a mixture of Scots, Irish, Americans and English to Prince Edward Island, the Irish along the Miramichi River Valley in New Brunswick and the Loyalists to the Saint John River basin.'[13] The Loyalists in southern New Brunswick had little in common with the Acadians who returned to the region within twenty years of their expulsion (1755–61) to settle along the New Brunswick coast, in southwestern and northern Nova Scotia, and in the northeast end of Prince Edward Island. There were few reasons for Loyalists and Acadians to be in contact, given their different culture and language, the limited role of government, and the nature of the local economy.

All these communities were relatively self-contained. We are told, for example, that 'a man could build his own ship, grow his own cargo, sail it to the West Indies himself, sell both ship and cargo, and return with a handsome profit to show for his enterprise.'[14] Trade was both far flung and important to Maritime communities, and the region was much more dependent on trade than was the colony of the Canadas (see table 2.1).

The Maritimes and Confederation

Historians have documented how and why New Brunswick and Nova Scotia (and later Prince Edward Island) joined forces with the Canadian colonies to create Confederation. There is no need to review this in any detail: it will suffice to highlight some developments.

In the early 1860s high-profile political leaders (for example, Leonard Tilley in New Brunswick and Charles Tupper in Nova Scotia) began to

TABLE 2.1
Trade per capita – 1860

	Exports ($)	Imports ($)	Total ($)
United Province of Canada	12.57	13.72	26.29
Nova Scotia	19.45	26.40	45.85
New Brunswick	17.63	27.83	45.46
Prince Edward Island	12.35	13.83	26.18
Maritime colonies	17.89	25.41	43.30

Source: S.A. Saunders, *The Economic History of the Maritime Provinces* (Fredericton: Acadiensis, 1984).

advocate a political union of the three Maritime provinces as a means to ensure greater economic stability for the region. Tupper and Tilley arranged a meeting in 1864 in Charlottetown to discuss the idea. They believe that political union held a number of advantages, including a solid foundation on which to construct the Intercolonial Railway. At the time, they had a good deal of public support. Donald Creighton wrote that union 'had become a public issue, openly discussed and strongly supported. It even showed some ... signs of becoming a popular movement.'[15] There were several reasons for this, including a 'negative one of antagonism toward Canada ... swept along ... on a wave of hatred of Canadian duplicity and domination.'[16] In any event, by the mid-1860s, one by one the legislative assemblies of the three provinces agreed to participate in a conference to devise a blueprint for Maritime union. Unexpectedly, however, the governor of British North America asked if the Canadian government could send delegates to the conference to make a case for a larger political union. The rest of the story is, of course, well known.

Other forces at play also favoured integration into a larger union rather than a regional one. At the political level, Britain – the mother country to many Maritimers – was sending out messages strongly supporting Confederation. Fenian raids, including one in 1866 along the Maine–New Brunswick border, also pointed to the benefits of colonial union. In addition, the failure of the reciprocity trade negotiations with the Americans in 1866 provided yet another strong influence in favour of Confederation.

The failed reciprocity negotiations in particular posed a daunting challenge to the colony of the Canadas, which was much more dependent on the American market than were the Maritime provinces, as

TABLE 2.2
Exports to the United States as percentage of total exports

Year	Canada	Nova Scotia	New Brunswick	Prince Edward Island
1853	45.7	25.8	11.4	21.1
1855	70.6	32.7	14.9	21.9
1856	62.9	30.1	16.2	16.8
1859	61.4	33.2	22.0	49.2
1860	58.4	33.7	27.1	38.7
1862	49.3	32.1	23.1	29.7
1863	52.1	28.5	24.2	50.4
1864	62.5	34.1	25.0	38.2
1866	70.4	40.1	29.1	8.8

Source: S.A. Saunders, *The Economy History of the Maritime Provinces* (Fredericton: Acadiensis, 1985), 53.

table 2.2 reveals. This is all the more remarkable because, as we saw in table 2.1, total exports per head were much higher for the Maritime colonies than for the Canadas.

The Canadas had an acute need for new markets. The Maritime provinces held promise not only because they constituted a significant market, but also because they shared something in common – they were British colonies. As S.A. Saunders writes, 'The colonies had to carry on ... diplomacy with the rest of the world through the Colonial Office in London, and, in doing so, often found that they held many interests in common.'[17]

The loss of reciprocity was bound to affect the Maritime local economy. The region was isolated from the Canadas, and it had to follow old routes in order to trade with them. There were also increasing signs that the age of sail was coming to an end. The railway was the future, and many Maritimers felt that they could strengthen their economy by establishing a direct rail connection with the Canadas. In this way they could access new markets while the Canadas could lessen their dependence on American seaports, given that their own ports were ice-bound during winter. The Canadians assured Maritimers that under a new union they would use Maritime ports in the winter, and this would mean new trade traffic and commercial prosperity in the Maritimes.

The British North American colonies also shared a common problem – a weak fiscal position precisely at a time when money was needed to finance railway construction. The Canadian Fathers of Confederation pledged to build an intercolonial railway linking central Canada to Nova Scotia and included this commitment in the British North America (BNA) Act. Many of the region's economic elites became railway promoters, though some did favour a western extension railway to Maine to link with American lines rather than to Montreal and Toronto.[18]

Despite assurances by the Canadas on the benefits of Confederation, debate on the issue in the Maritimes was heated, and there were many voices opposing union with Canada. In fact, there was no enthusiasm for Confederation in the region at all. Prince Edward Island opposed union, and the 72 Resolutions were never submitted to the legislatures of Nova Scotia and New Brunswick. The pro-Confederation party was defeated soundly in New Brunswick in 1865. The only support Tilley in New Brunswick and Tupper in Nova Scotia could secure from their legislatures was in the form of resolutions to continue negotiations in London in 1866. As is well known, Tupper was able to bring Nova Scotia into Confederation without an election, but his party suffered resounding defeats in both the provincial and federal elections held in the fall of 1867 (36 out of 38 anti-Confederationists were elected to the provincial legislature and 18 out of 19 in Ottawa).[19]

There is plenty of evidence to suggest that 'collusion' between the Colonial Office, New Brunswick's lieutenant-governor, Arthur Hamilton Gordon, and the pro-Confederation forces operating outside the province was the key factor in New Brunswick's joining the Canadian federation.[20] It is worth quoting historian W.S. MacNutt on this point:

> Compared with the plight of the defeated states of the Southern Confederacy, of the German principalities taken captive by Bismarck in 1866, New Brunswick stood in a position that was proud and free. But like these she bowed to the will of those from without. Tilley, Mitchell, Fisher, were servants of the Canadian initiative. Behind the adroit persuasions of Macdonald and his colleagues in Canada lay the authority of the British government, not forced but nevertheless strongly asserted, working for the composite solution British world interests required. The problem had not been of New Brunswick's making, but she was compelled to recognize its existence. Her elemental loyalties powerfully invoked, exposed to the appeal of building a new and great nation whose promise hung upon imponderables, pressed by the impact of immediate events, cajoled by rather flimsy assurances of commercial prosperity, and somewhat bribed, the province entered Confederation with very little grace and no gratitude.[21]

Many Maritimers feared that Ontario and Quebec would dominate the new central government (the Maritime region's population would be less than 25 per cent of that of the new union). Ontario insisted that 'representation by population' be granted to the House of Commons, but Maritimers strongly objected. A leading political figure in New Brunswick, Albert Smith, urged the Fathers of Confederation to borrow a page from the Americans and provide for equal representation in the Upper House for each province, a limitation on the number of representatives in the Lower House from the larger provinces, and a court to decide upon cases of disputed jurisdictions. Without a capacity to check the power of representation by population in the House of Commons, many Maritimers feared that their voice would be drowned out, leaving them unable to protect the region's interests. There was, for example, widespread fear that Maritime resources would be used by the new government to develop Canadian canals and to open up the West. There were also concerns early on that the region would not benefit a great deal from being linked to central Canadian market.[22] It became evident that 'true power' would reside with the House of Commons, that its members would be elected 'through rep by pop' and that the Fathers of Confederation had 'realized that the many compromises involved in creating the Senate had rendered it useless.'[23]

Ontario representatives argued persuasively that the Maritime provinces could always count on Quebec if their province ever attempted to dominate Confederation. It would have been difficult to assume in 1867 that Quebec would ever agree to support Ontario's economic interests, and vice versa. In addition, in the pre-Confederation discussions, it was agreed that the Maritimes would have one-third of cabinet posts to compensate for the representation by population in the Commons. This, however, was not enshrined in the constitution. In addition, Ontario explained that the new central government would assume responsibility for all existing provincial debts and take charge of building the railway. This was important for New Brunswick and Nova Scotia. The region had not been able to agree on a comprehensive approach, so that railway construction proceeded on a piecemeal basis. For example, Halifax was linked to Truro and Windsor, and Saint John with Moncton but not with the Nova Scotian capital. In addition, the region had a difficult time trying to raise capital for railway construction.

What was important for Sir John A. Macdonald and his colleagues from Ontario was the establishment of a strong central government. As

Roger Gibbins writes, 'a strong central government was seen as a necessary condition for economic and political survival.'[24]

Second Thoughts

Even in the era of limited government at the time Canada was born, there were soon grave concerns about how the smaller provinces were being treated in the new federation. It quickly became apparent to Nova Scotia and New Brunswick that Ottawa would, in the words of W.T. Easterbrook and Hugh Aitken, look to 'the central place of the St. Lawrence area as the basis for continental expansion.'[25] The new country's economic strengths would be located between Windsor and Quebec City, and Ottawa would take the lead in promoting development in that region.

Not long after New Brunswick and Nova Scotia signed on as partners in Confederation, a number of Maritimers began to have second thoughts about the wisdom of doing so. Indeed, from the 1870s to the late 1920s, there was deep resentment in some quarters towards Confederation and its growing negative impact on the Maritime economy. More than a few Maritime politicians argued publicly that they felt betrayed by the terms of the union, and some even recommended that the region should leave the Canadian federation before it was too late. Feelings ran high. One politician argued that a 'loyal and contented people had been converted by an act of parliament into a state of serfdom to Canadian greed and spoliation.'[26] Another suggested that 'the iron-gloved hand of Canadian greed will still be clutching at the tax strings of the Maritime provinces and meanwhile the stream of emigration will be like the brooks as described by Tennyson as running on forever and the cities will be drying up.'[27]

The concerns of Maritimers were many, including the apparent inability 'to protect the interest of a smaller province in a federal rather than a legislative union where the Canadians would inevitably dominate any House of Commons selected on the basis of representation by population.'[28] Quite apart from the terms drawn up in Quebec, New Brunswick and Nova Scotia resented the fact that they were greatly underrepresented in the federal public service. The new service consisted of 'little more than' the old bureaucracy of the old United Province of Canada.[29] But there were also other, perhaps related, concerns. For instance, Maritimers became convinced that Ottawa could never appreciate that harbours were as critical to many Maritime communities as roads and canals were to central Canada. Nor would Ottawa give proper attention to trade issues affecting the region.

For many, more critical still was the question of where industry would be concentrated in the country, since the Maritimes simply could not compete with the vote-rich provinces of Ontario and Quebec. Ernest Forbes explains that it soon became clear that whenever there was regional competition, Ottawa invariably opted for Ontario and perhaps also Quebec. He points out, for example, that Ottawa simply said, 'We can't have a tariff on coal because Ontario needs to import if from the United States. They took the tariff off and were able to create an iron and steel industry in Ontario.'[30] That decision alone shifted important economic power to central Canada and served to eliminate the advantages previously enjoyed by Cape Breton coal producers.

Historians have produced a veritable catalogue of misguided federal policies, at least from the perspective of the Maritimes. Hugh Thorburn sums it up well when he observes that 'In the long run the federal government's tariff, transportation, and monetary policies have worked to the general disadvantage of New Brunswick.'[31] Policies were struck in Ottawa to meet national objectives, which, to a Maritimer, became a code phrase meaning the economic interests of Ontario and Quebec only. What was good for central Canada was invariably perceived in Ottawa to be good for Canada as a whole, but the same reasoning would never apply in the Maritimes. Ottawa's monetary policy during the 1930s – and for that matter ever since – reflected economic circumstances in Ontario and Quebec, often at the expense of the Maritimes. Canada, it will be recalled, refused to devalue its currency during the depression of the 1930s, while many other countries did. New Brunswick, like the other two Maritime provinces, 'was exposed to a two-way squeeze: from high and rigid prices for the manufactured goods she had to buy (from central Canada), and from difficult selling conditions in the export markets upon which she depended.'[32]

National Policy

Much has been made of Canada's 'National Policy' and its impact at the regional level. Historians tell us that the term applies 'both to the programme of creating a Canadian nation' and to a 'system of protective tariffs which was adopted in 1878.'[33] The protective tariffs have been largely attenuated, but the National Policy, in its essential elements, has endured. For example, the canals of the St Lawrence were deepened as Canada took form. In 1951, legislation was enacted to create the St Lawrence Seaway Authority, a Crown corporation with a mandate to build a deep waterway between Montreal and Lake Erie, either in cooperation with the United States or on its own.

The National Policy would also serve to promote Canada's manufacturing sector and, in doing so, to favour the Windsor–Quebec City corridor. Tariffs were both a matter of government revenues and protection. Canadian manufacturers looked to domestic markets for growth because there were few alternatives available. Manufacturers argued that the domestic market should be reserved for them, given the failure to achieve lasting reciprocal trade relations with the United States. Ottawa agreed, since it had 'become apparent that a more rapid rate of industrialization was essential if progress was to be made with plans for a better balanced, more diversified and more tightly integrated economic development. Without a strong industrial base, there could be little hope of lessening Canada's dependence on external conditions for prosperity.'[34] The National Policy offered precious little to the Maritime provinces – it emphasized an east-west continental economy and, by ricochet, it protected emerging central Canadian producers. It meant that Maritimers would have to import their manufactured goods from Montreal and southern Ontario or pay duties of 50 per cent in some instances to import goods from traditional sources such as England. In brief, Maritimers concluded that under the National Policy they were compelled to buy what they consumed in a substantially protected home market but had to sell their products in a virtually unprotected one.

Over time, economic protectionism and the National Policy forced producers in the Maritimes to ship their goods on expensive rail routes to central Canada rather than on ships to their traditional export markets in the New England states and elsewhere. Canada's east-west trade patterns, which were artificially created through the National Policy, promoted a shift to overland trade, for which the three Maritime provinces were geographically ill-suited and, in time, served to make the region an 'isolated extremity of Canada.'[35] The emerging trade patterns were artificial in the sense that they were created by political decisions, not by market forces.

Some observers argued that the National Policy and protectionism served to undercut the region's trading advantages in water-borne shipping. David Alexander summed up the impact of the National Policy on the region in this way: 'In the Maritimes, underdevelopment seems a sorry descent from those heady days when the region possessed one of the world's foremost shipbuilding industries, the third or fourth largest merchant marine, financial institutions which were the core of many of the present Canadian giants, and an industrial structure growing as fast as that of central Canada.'[36] The National Policy also encouraged American firms to establish branch plants in Canada. However, because of the imposed east-west trade patterns, precious few of these firms picked a Maritime location to serve the 'national' domestic market. Thus, Maritimers could legitimately claim that there was no place for them in the National Policy. From time to time, the federal government has come to terms with the fact that Confederation dealt the Maritimes a bad hand. One keen observer of New Brunswick politics, for example, wrote in 1961 about the 'enormous economic disabilities under which [the] region has been labouring since the inauguration of the National Policy,' with the result that New Brunswick and, more generally, Maritime politicians have been 'cast in the role of supplicants pressing on whatever pretext that can be devised for better terms from Ottawa.'[37]

A number of Maritime politicians even sought to take the region out of Confederation. As late as May 1886, the Fielding government in Nova Scotia proposed that 'the financial and commercial interests of the people of Nova Scotia, New Brunswick and Prince Edward Island would be advanced by these provinces withdrawing from the Canadian federation and uniting under one government.'[38] But in reality few in the legislature actually believed this would happen. For one thing, there was no indication, let alone assurance, that the British government would agree to let Nova Scotia, or any other Maritime province, leave Confederation. For another, the purpose may well have been to demonstrate to Ottawa that the region was paying too high a price by being in the Confederation. It was more of a *cri du coeur* than the basis for a true secessionist movement. Indeed, the region's anti-Confederation movement, never large to begin with, would eventually disappear without leaving much of a trace. But the region's deep sense of betrayal and grievance would not.

As time passed, Maritimers saw their economy whittled away and their political influence wane. The number of Maritime seats in the House of Commons declined from 43 seats in the 1870s to 31 in 1921. New Brunswick's fell from 16 to 11. Yet, the size of the House of Commons increased from 206 seats in 1874 to 235 in 1921. Worse still, it was clear even then that the Senate, the upper house, did not have the political clout or legitimacy to safeguard regional interests in national policy making as the United States Senate had. The result is that political leaders from the two largest provinces of the country could put in place a 'national' policy that favoured their own provinces over the others, establish Crown corporations in their own regions, and establish tariffs that benefited largely their own regions, all the time knowing that they would never be called to account by an upper house speaking on behalf of regional interests.

For their part, Maritime MPs became well versed in the rhetoric of regional protest and in calling for 'better terms' from Confederation. But things began to change as far back as the early 1890s, as party loyalty started to take precedence over regional loyalty in Ottawa. Apart from a brief period in the 1920s, Maritime interests took a back seat to partisan politics at election time and in the House of Commons.[39]

This view that nation building was essential for Canada to lessen its dependence on external conditions and that special measures were required given both its small population and its small manufacturing sector became conventional wisdom. C.D. Howe, for example, favoured either private monopoly regulated by government controls or Crown corporations to create a strong manufacturing sector. Howe's decision during the Second World War to locate the bulk of wartime production in central Canada speaks to the underlying goal of the country's economic development policy. It also had serious implications for the Maritime provinces. Howe, it will be recalled, was an extremely powerful minister in the governments of Mackenzie King and Louis St Laurent. He served as minister in various departments between 1936 and 1957, including transport, munitions, reconstruction, and industry. At the start of the Second World War, Canada had fifteen Crown corporations. Thirty-two were added during the war years, as Ottawa believed they were better suited to lure business people to manage war programs than a typical government department would be. In addition, Howe felt that a successful war effort required a highly decentralized form of administration, such as that provided by the Crown corporation model. Sir Robert Borden, who established Canadian National Railways as a Crown corporation in 1919, explained the advantages of such corporations: they were designed to promote business-like management, financial autonomy, and a degree of freedom from direct political interference.[40] Howe saw these attributes as being tailor-made for a successful war industry. At the same time, Crown corporations represented a significant new source of investments, with the potential to generate a great deal of new economic activity. Indeed, they would provide the basis for future development in the manufacturing sector in the postwar years.[41] For example, wartime Crown corporations gave rise to, among others, aircraft manufacturers, synthetic rubber producers, an advanced technology company called Research Enterprises. Virtually all of the new corporations, however, were established in the Montreal-Windsor corridor; not a single one was located in the Maritime region.[42]

Although many of the Crown corporations established during the war were later disbanded, some continued, including Polysar and Canadian Arsenals Limited. Crown corporations served the war effort very well, but they also served in the long run to considerably strengthen central Canada's manufacturing sector. And that was not all. The Department of Munitions and Supply made extensive new investments in Canadian industries, but by 1944 only about 3.7 per cent of these had been made in the Maritimes, mainly for aircraft and naval repair. In fact, even the bulk of the shipbuilding for the war was carried out elsewhere. Historians are now agreed that 'C.D. Howe and his bureaucrats favoured the concentration of manufacturing in central Canada.'[43]

Thus, the Maritimes essentially were left on the outside looking in as the country's wartime manufacturing sector started to take shape. To make matters worse, the migration or the 'assignment' of skilled labour to war industries in central Canada made it very difficult for the region to promote its own manufacturing sector in the postwar years. Here again, political decisions rather than market forces strengthened central Canada's position in the manufacturing sector. It is important to stress that C.D. Howe and others of like mind set out to build a nation, not regions, and concentrating industrial development made sense from this perspective. That practice had an added bonus – it made sense from a political perspective, given that the concentration of industry would be in vote-rich Ontario and Quebec.

It is now well established that the manufacturing sector in the Maritimes stagnated during much of the twentieth century. In addition, though the region was fairly strong economically, relative to both national and international standards at the moment of Confederation, its position deteriorated during the first half of the twentieth century. We now know, for example, that relative to Canada, the Maritimes accounted for 14 per cent of goods produced in 1880, only 9 per cent in 1911, and 5 per cent in 1939.[44]

We noted earlier that population growth in the Maritimes, by and

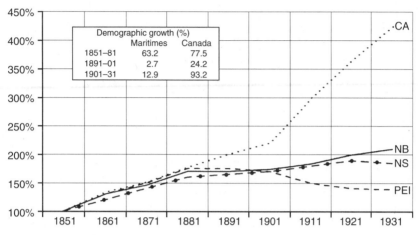

Source: Statistics Canada, *Historical Statistics of Canada*, cat. 11-516-XIE.

Figure 2.1
Population growth rates in the Maritimes and Canada, 1851–1931

large, followed the Canadian average from 1800 to Confederation. However, from 1891 on, the region's population growth rate has stagnated, as figure 2.1 clearly indicates.

Missing Urbanization

A good number of economists maintain that the economic vitality of a region is tied directly to the development of an urban structure.[45] Urban areas, notably in the twentieth century, became in no small measure the shapers of economic development. Larry McCann explores what he labels the Great Transformation in Canadian society that lasted from Confederation to 1929.[46] At the turn of the twentieth century, the Maritime economy shared an overall urban-rural structure similar to Canada's. Twenty-nine years later, however, central Canada was making great strides towards industrial and urban maturity, but not the Maritimes. There are many indicators confirming this development. For example, at the end of the First World War, Ontario and Quebec were passing the halfway point in climbing the urbanization ladder, while the Maritimes were barely a quarter of the way up the same ladder. New Brunswick today is only where Ontario and Quebec were at the end of the First World War.

TABLE 2.3
The industrialization and urbanization of the Maritimes and Canada during the great
transformation, 1890–1929*

	Maritimes		Canada	
	1890–1	1929–31	1890–1	1929–31
Total population	880,737	1,009,103	4,883,239	10,376,786
Percentage of population, urban	16.5	36.3	29.8	52.5
Number of urban places				
(1,000+ population)	41	53	274	503
Gross value of production				
Primary Industries ($000s)	77,993	150,163	585,625	2,061,585
Manufacturing ($000s)	56,514	108,354	623,205	1,802,960
Labour force distribution (%)				
Primary	54.8	47.9	50.0	34.0
Secondary	21.4	17.0	25.3	25.3
Tertiary	23.8	35.1	24.7	40.7

*Population and labour force data are for 1891 and 1931.
Sources: Canada, Census of Canada, 1891 and 1931 (Ottawa); D. Alexander, 'Economic Growth in the Atlantic Region,' Acadiensis 8 (1978): 60; Alan G. Green, Regional Aspects of Canadian Economic Growth (Toronto: University of Toronto Press, 1971), Appendix C.

Table 2.3 compares developments in the Maritimes and Canada during the Great Transformation. The findings are revealing. The gross value of production in the manufacturing sector tripled in Canada between 1850 and 1931 while it doubled in the Maritimes. Between 1920 and 1926 alone, the number of manufacturing jobs in Amherst, Dartmouth, Halifax, New Glasgow, Sydney, Truro, Moncton, and Saint John fell to 14,000 from 25,000 (or by 44 per cent) and about 150,000 Maritimers left the region. Between 1890 and 1937 the Maritimes' position relative to Canada in manufacturing gross value per capita shrank to 42 from 68 per cent. An important reason for this drop is that the Maritimes did not benefit from federal government decisions as to where to establish defence-related industries during the First World War.

If one isolates Ontario from the national average, we see that the province's urbanization level increased the most of any province, from 35.0 per cent in 1891 to 63.1 per cent in 1931.[47] The Maritimes, meanwhile, increased to only 36.0 per cent from 16.5 per cent. The impact of the National Policy may not in itself entirely explain this development, but it does explain some of it.

We introduced this chapter by observing that in economic development, success breeds success. Given the findings in figure 2.1, it should come as no surprise that the last influx of immigrants from southern and eastern Europe would pick Ontario and the western provinces over the Maritimes to find a job and seek a new life.[48] It is no exaggeration to say that the big Canadian immigration waves left the Maritimes virtually untouched. Indeed, many Maritimers joined new Canadians in choosing to leave their homes and move to central and, later, western Canada.

Canada witnessed strong economic growth starting in 1940, which extended well beyond the immediate postwar period. As already noted, the war industries created new economic activities and generated employment. But there were two other important forces at play – Keynesian economics, which came in fashion in the postwar period, and a high level of foreign investment.

The Keynesian revolution captured the Department of Finance and the federal treasury of Canada, as it did elsewhere. Towards the end of the Second World War, the Canadian government presented Parliament with a major policy paper, which was clearly Keynesian in outlook. It said, 'The Government will be prepared, in periods where unemployment threatens, to incur deficits and increases in the national debt resulting from its employment and income policy ... In periods of buoyant employment and income, budget plans will call for surpluses.'[49] Not only the government but also Canadians in general willingly accepted the new direction. They had emerged from the war determined never to permit another depression of the kind witnessed in the 1930s. By war's end, the public's confidence in the ability of government to intervene and to manage the economy was high. Large latent demand and rapid population increase, combined with the realization that the government management of the war effort had been successful, gave governments carte blanche to expand. Canadians had learned during the war 'that governments were able, in moments of crisis, and when moved by an all-consuming goal, to lead the country to high levels of economic activity and employment.'[50] Not only did the allies win the war but the government had also run the war economy well. Unemployment had fallen virtually to zero, yet prices had been held down. Growth of productivity and real GNP was accelerated, inequalities among social groups diminished, civilian consumption actually increased, there were no balance of payment crises, and foreign exchange rates remained stable. When the war ended, everyone was prepared for measures to counter a return of the depression years. But the expected severe economic downturn did not materialize, and the Keynesian-inspired measures proved unnecessary. Still, governments (in particular, the federal government) were convinced that they possessed 'a new arsenal of economic policy' to achieve high employment and generally manage the economy.

Harold Innis, arguably Canada's leading economist of the twentieth century, saw a basic flaw in Keynesian demand and management techniques, which he felt would serve to aggravate rather than attenuate existing regional differences in economic well-being. He bluntly stated that full employment policies would 'become a racket on the part of the central provinces for getting and keeping what they can.'[51]

Keynesian economics did enable Ottawa to fine-tune the national economy, but the economic slide that started in the Maritimes a few years after the implementation of the National Policy simply continued. This slide was reflected in population figures. Canada's overall population grew from 12 to 18 million between 1946 and 1961, thanks to a strong birth rate and 2 million new immigrants. Meanwhile, the Maritimes experienced a net out-migration of 90,000, or 8 per cent of the population, in the 1940s; 85,000, or 7 per cent, in the 1950s; and 95,000, or 6.6 per cent, in the 1960s. Maritimers were continuing to go down the road to central Canada to secure a job, often in the growing manufacturing sector. And this trend was not without political implications, given that the Senate has not been able to perform its role on behalf of the regions. The population of the Maritimes dropped to 9 per cent of the nation in 1961 from 20 per cent in 1871.[52]

The Maritime Rights Movement

By the 1920s regional grievances in the Maritimes reached the boiling point. One of the reasons that led the Maritimes to sign on to a larger political union – railway construction – had been turned on its head, at least from the region's perspective. The Canadian National Railway was mandated to play a key role in managing Canada's railway system, and the integration of the Intercolonial into the national railway system spelled bad news for the Maritimes. Freight rates for Maritime producers to ship to central Canada skyrocketed, and it became all too clear that they could no longer compete in that market. The railway became a *bête noire* for the Maritimes and 'probably the single most important source of anti-Ottawa animus.'[53] Western farmers were able to obtain a renewal of the Crow's Nest Pass Agreement on freight rates in 1927, but Maritimers were unable to secure assistance to deal with a '40 percent increase in freight rates.'[54] Maritimers also blamed Ottawa for the underutilization of their ports.

As is well known, a Maritime Rights Movement came into being in the 1920s. There is now a whole body of literature on the movement, its supporters, its demands, its successes, and its failures.[55] One point is worth stressing – it was non-partisan. As Ernest Forbes explains, the movement had no specific founder or leader, and all the political parties tried to use the protest movement. But, he adds, the movement was essentially a spontaneous expression of the economic and social frustrations of Maritimers. In the process, however, it brought home the point that the region had been turned into a supplicant. There was less talk of secession from Canada (in fact, key members of the movement declared their full support for the nation) and more about the region's becoming an equal participant in the country's economic development. The agenda was one of redress, of bringing pressure to bear on Ottawa to see the light and to deal with real regional grievances. The movement gained credibility to the point that in the 1921 general election 'regional anger had created a force stronger than party loyalty.'[56]

The movement met with some success. First, the Conservatives under Arthur Meighen responded to some of its demands, as then did the Liberals, under Mackenzie King. The region used its political clout to punish Meighen in 1921 (the Liberals won twenty-five of the region's thirty-one seats) and then King in 1925 (the Conservatives won twenty-three of twenty-nine seats). The results of the 1925 election, as is well known, led to a period of political and even constitutional instability in Ottawa. Through the efforts of the movement and its political impact, the supplicant was able to secure *some* concessions. For example, in 1922 it saw a 7.5 per cent decrease in freight rates and the 're-establishment' of Atlantic regional headquarters of the Canadian National Railways in Moncton (the Canadian government established Canadian National Railways in 1917–19, and in doing so had closed the head office of the Intercolonial Railroad located in Moncton and moved the staff to Toronto).

The Duncan Commission

These measures were not enough to satisfy the region, and so King finally decided in 1926 to appoint a royal commission – the Duncan

Commission – to 'focus the discussion into a practicable program.'[57] The chair of the commission, Sir Andrew Duncan, deliberately set out to concentrate on finding 'practical solutions' to economic problems, and, as he wrote in the conclusion of his report, he avoided trying to find 'palliatives for the dissatisfaction and political unrest which have been prevailing in that part of the Dominion.'[58] Still, Duncan, a British coal-mining authority, did challenge the view that Confederation was the sole reason for the Maritime's economic difficulties. The Nova Scotia government in its presentation to the commission argued that national policies had forced the region into a condition of 'dilapidation and decay.'[59] The Duncan Commission did acknowledge the region's economic difficulties and decline since joining Confederation, but it insisted that factors other than Confederation had been at play, buying into the argument that the decline of the maritime economy was a result of the obsolescence of 'wind, wood and sail.'[60] Still, when it came to explaining the region's underdevelopment, it often pointed to decisions taken in Ottawa.

The contribution of the Duncan Commission was limited by several restrictions placed on its mandate. It was told, for example, not to deal with tariff and trade issues because they were 'a matter properly to be considered by the Tariff Advisory Board.'[61] It did, however, urge the board to move on several issues of direct interest to the Maritimes.

On the question of freight rates and transportation, the commission reported that it had 'definitely [come] to the conclusion that the rate structure as it has been altered since 1912 has placed upon the trade and commerce of the Maritime Provinces a) a burden which, as we have read the pronouncements and obligations undertaken at Confederation, it was never intended it should bear and b) a burden which is, in fact, responsible in very considerable measure for depressing abnormally in the Maritimes today business and enterprise which had originated and developed before 1912 on the basis and faith of the rate structure as it then stood.'[62]

The commission also looked at the steel industry in the region. Again, it noted that it was beyond its mandate to deal with tariff and trade issues. But, it observed, 'Independent evidence of an expert character was given to us, that if due regard were paid to the economic unit of production in steel, there was no reason why it should not be produced as efficiently and cheaply in Nova Scotia as anywhere else in Canada.' It added: 'A calculation was given to us which shows that as a result of the operations of the Customs Tariff, if labour employed in the production of iron and steel and its raw products is taken as the unit for measuring protective value, the protection afforded to Nova Scotia is only 28 per cent, whereas in Canada the protection to labour is between 85 per cent and 100 per cent.'[63]

There is no denying that the fact that the commission was not allowed to deal properly with tariff and trade issues – which in many ways went to the heart of the problem, given that it was increasingly clear that many of its producers could not compete in the national market – inhibited its ability to come up with a complete set of practical solutions. In addition, as it became all too clear later, King's objective in establishing the commission was to defuse Maritime agitation and to engage in a policy of delay. He succeeded.

The region would never again embrace the kind of non-partisan approach to applying pressure on the federal government as it did under the Maritime Rights Movement. Never again would the region vote strategically as it did in the 1921 and 1925 general elections. Maritimers, even more than the other regions, came to embrace established national political parties and remain loyal to them. Regional grievances would eventually give rise to new political parties in the west (Reform) and Quebec (Bloc Québécois), but not in the Maritime provinces.

The federal government began to sponsor a series of special studies, inquiries, and royal commissions to deal with specific issues confronting the region. The Duncan Commission was the most important of these. The commission was allowed to find practical solutions to the Maritimes' difficulties, but not at the expense of Ontario's economic interests. The fact that Duncan was instructed not to deal in any concrete terms with tariffs and trade issues is ample evidence of this. Duncan also completely ignored the impact of the region's declining representation in the House of Commons and its implications for the three Maritime provinces.

Clearly, the commission was also established to deal with a problem not on the official agenda. When things appeared to get out of hand in political terms, as they did in 1921 and 1925, commissions and special inquiries could serve a useful purpose: They could be used as diversionary tactics. Mackenzie King (of the famed comment, 'conscription if necessary but not necessarily conscription') was, as history now makes clear, a master in the art of delay to avoid dealing with pressing public policy issues. King successfully employed his considerable skills in the case of the Maritime Rights Movement.

That said, the Duncan Commission's findings did have some impact. Though the King government was able to sidestep much of what the commission had to say, it did not ignore the recommendation to reduce Canadian National Railway rates, with the carrier to be compensated by federal subsidy. A special assistance program was introduced in 1927, establishing Maritime rates 20 per cent lower than rates elsewhere. It was revised in 1957 to 30 per cent and in 1969 was extended to highway carriers. A further revision in 1974 provided an additional 20 per cent reduction for selected commodities moving to markets outside the Atlantic region. A federal-provincial committee determined which products were eligible for the rate subsidy. New products manufactured in the region could be added to the list. For example, wheel weights for automobiles were declared eligible when a firm in Nova Scotia began manufacturing them. Total payments under the freight-assistance programs amounted to $60 million in 1980 and $63 million in 1981. By 1990–1, payments under the Maritime Freight Rates Act (railway) and under the Atlantic Region Freight Assistance Act (railway, marine, and trucking) amounted to nearly $100 million.[64] This program remained in place until 1994, when the Chrétien government launched a major program review to repair Ottawa's balance sheet. All departments were asked to make significant spending cuts. Doug Young, then transport minister and New Brunswick's representative in the federal cabinet, volunteered to sacrifice the subsidies as part of his department's contributions to the program review, and the freight rates assistance for the region is now history.

New measures resulted from the Duncan report's findings but they were hardly as ambitious or (in the end) as effective as the Maritime Rights Movement had initially hoped. Follow-up measures from the Duncan Commission included modest adjustments to federal subsidies to the three Maritime provinces, but slowly and surely the findings of the commission disappeared from the public policy agenda. Historian David Frank sums up the legacy of the report in this fashion: 'The failure of the report and the weakness of subsequent action may simply have increased Maritime cynicism about the prospects for achieving significant changes through the political process ... For many Maritimers it simply confirmed their sceptical appreciation of the weakness of the hinterland within the Canadian state.'[65] Regional ministers from the Maritime provinces would still do their best to secure the odd project for their province, but there was little appetite left in Ottawa to take a broad, comprehensive approach to economic development in the Maritimes. The Great Depression was soon on Canada's doorstep, and the prime minister was in no mood to make concessions to the Maritimes.

The above combined with the fact that the Maritimes' political influence in the House of Commons continued to decline as western Canada kept adding new seats, pushed Maritime concerns to the background. If Maritimers look back to the period just before Confederation as the region's golden age in economic terms, they can look to the 1920s, when they were able to put aside partisan considerations at election time, as its golden age in political terms.

This is not to suggest that Maritime provincial governments gave up on pressing their claims on Ottawa. In 1944 the Nova Scotia government, for example, appointed a royal commission containing high profile and credible members from outside the province to review the 'province's disabilities in Confederation.' The commission decided to focus on tariff issues. Commission staff sought to provide a cost-benefit estimate of tariffs by calculating the amount by which the tariffs raised prices in each province and subtracting any increases deemed beneficial. To the surprise of no one, the three Maritime provinces came out the heavy losers.[66]

But there has never been any market in Ottawa for this line of thinking, and the Nova Scotia royal commission had precious little impact. Federal government payments to the three provinces could be adjusted, but tariffs went to the heart of the Ontario and Quebec economy. The nation's political power, concentrated in these two provinces, would decide on its own terms if tariffs could be changed and by how much. Tariffs were central to the health of the 'national' economy, and the 'national' interest was not about to be sidetracked by regional concerns.

Defining the Nation through Government Initiatives

From the mid-1930s onward, Maritime concerns became subsumed into the nation's broader socioeconomic problems. By then, many in Ottawa probably started to accept as inevitable the decline of the Maritime economy, given its location on the periphery of a tariff-protected Canadian market. In any event, the nation had bigger issues to address. The Great Depression was one, but so was the federal government's apparent inability to respond to the challenges it presented. If the National Policy constituted the first phase in Canadian nation building, the federal government's spending power would constitute the second.

The Great Depression had, in a very harsh manner, revealed Ottawa's inability to use public policy to deal with a disastrous economic downturn. In addition, many leading intellectuals and Canadian nationalists in Ontario became disturbed over the resurgence of assertions of provincial rights. The establishment of the Bank of Canada in the late 1930s brought a new policy capacity to Ottawa, and the Department of Finance, during this same period, started to hire bright young economists, one of whom, Bob Bryce, had studied at the feet of Lord Keynes at Cambridge. Keynesian economics, which advocated a government's spending its way out of economic depressions had, as already noted, come into fashion in Ottawa. But Ottawa could not do this, if only because provincial governments were, on the whole, more concerned with trying to balance their budgets by cutting spending and raising taxes than with introducing new spending measures to stimulate economic activities. Such practices were precisely what Lord Keynes argued would serve only to make things worse.

Mackenzie King decided in 1937 to establish a royal commission (the Rowell-Sirois Commission) to carry out 'a re-examination of the economic and financial basis of Confederation and of the distribution of legislative powers in light of the economic and social developments of the last seventy years.'[67] The problem, as seen from Ottawa, was straightforward. Canada's constitution, the British North America Act, has granted the federal government all the necessary power to implement the National Policy, but times had changed, and the act was ill suited to respond to current realities. In light of the Depression years and the development of the modern state, Canada required access to public policy levers that the act had given to the provinces. The key ones were in the areas of social welfare and the implementation of macroeconomics policies such as those inspired by Keynesian economics,[68] and no longer in managing tariffs and trade issues.

It came as no surprise, then, that the 1940 Rowell-Sirois Report stressed the need for integrating federal-provincial fiscal policies more effectively and, at the same time, sought to give Ottawa a much stronger hand in managing them. By the time the report was tabled, Ottawa had already moved to carve a role for itself in the social policy field. It had, for example, secured a constitutional amendment to allow the federal government to assume full responsibility for unemployment relief, which enabled it to establish an Unemployment Insurance Fund. In addition, as part of managing the wartime economy, the federal government was able to convince the provinces to leave the income tax field for the duration of the war in return for grants calculated on estimates of what the provinces would have collected. When the war ended, Ottawa tried to retain its monopoly of income tax, but the provinces were in no mood to agree. It had been only thirty years since the provincial governments had granted 'consent' for the federal government to enter the income tax field. They were not about to vacate the field completely to let Ottawa have a free hand in imposing new taxes. The result was the development of an elaborate system of sharing of both revenues and responsibilities, the remnants of which can still be found today in health, education, and social services spending. It was not Ottawa's preferred option, but it would have to do. It did, however, hand the federal government a great deal of power over the country's fiscal policies. Historian W.L. Morton has labelled the 1936–49 period 'the Revival of National Power.'[69] The Revival of National Power served Ontario well. As John Ibbitson writes, 'after the Second World War, Queen's Park and Ottawa collaborated to ensure that the rest of the federation served the interests of the economic heartland.'[70]

Why, one may ask, would Maritime premiers agree to an expanding role for the federal government? Certainly, they would know from memory the havoc the National Policy had wreaked on the region and the reasons for the rise of the Maritime Rights Movement. They would also have had a first-hand appreciation of the bias C.D. Howe and his bureaucrats had for central Canada. In addition, Oxford-educated New Brunswick premier J.B. McNair understood the finer points of the Canadian constitution probably better than many of the other provincial premiers, and one can only assume he was well aware New Brunswick no longer had the political clout to influence Ottawa in the event the federal government was able to carve out a greater role for itself. Furthermore, McNair had repeatedly stressed the importance of provincial autonomy.

There were, it appears, two reasons for New Brunswick's support for an expanded role for the federal government. First, when McNair replaced Dysart as premier in 1940, New Brunswick was literally on the edge of bankruptcy and the 'province's Montreal bankers were threatening to foreclose.'[71] With the bankers at its throat, the province was hardly in a position to bargain with Ottawa from a position of strength. Indeed, it needed Ottawa's financial help simply to continue to operate. Added to all of this was the fact that McNair was both a partisan Liberal and a strongly committed supporter of Ottawa's war effort. Partisan politics had come to matter a great deal more in New Brunswick in the

1940s than it had in the 1920s, and McNair took a back seat to no one when it came to partisan politics.

Second, Maritime premiers would have had reason for some optimism in supporting the findings of the Rowell-Sirois Report. While it is true the report did not look directly at tariff issues, trade patterns, or, for that matter, economic development, it did the next-best thing, at least from a Maritime perspective. It recommended 'that the wealth produced nationally should be taxed nationally and redistributed on a national basis, instead of being taxed in the main by the central provinces for the benefit of the central provinces.'[72] In other words, while the commission did not want to change where wealth was being produced in the country, it argued that the benefits from it should be shared nationally. The national economy should be promoted, but dividends flowing from it should be shared with all regions.

The commission heard briefs from both the Maritimes and the Prairie provinces that their economic woes were largely the result of the National Policy. It agreed with this assessment and concluded that those provinces that were impoverished by the National Policy, which was implemented in the 'general interest,' should be compensated with 'public expenditures.' Though the commission had precious little to say about how to go about this, it had plenty to say about the fiscal capacity of the provinces. It recommended the introduction of national adjustment grants that would favour the poorer provinces. Janine Brodie sums up the findings of the Rowell-Sirois Commission well when she writes that 'the grants would simply help to underwrite some of the social costs of uneven development within certain political jurisdictions [for example, New Brunswick] while the economic relationships that promoted uneven development remained unchallenged.'[73] Thus, the idea of some form of fiscal equity in Canada was born.

When Prime Minister Mackenzie King sought to overhaul Canada's taxation and social policy infrastructure and implement the findings of the Rowell-Sirois Report at a federal-provincial conference, he met with firm and highly vocal opposition from both Ontario and Quebec. The notion that Quebec would never side with Ontario – a point made by Canadians to convince Maritimers to join Confederation – no longer held. Indeed, King was told in no uncertain terms by the premiers of Ontario and Quebec that the initiative was a non-starter, so much so that Ontario premier George Drew 'hysterically characterized [the reform package] as Hitlerism.'[74] But Quebec and Ontario's opposition served another purpose: 'The central Canadian premiers' opposition confirmed the Maritime premiers' good opinion of King's plans.'[75] Given Ontario and Quebec's opposition and the preoccupation with the war effort, Ottawa was not able to proceed with a massive overhaul of the country's social policy infrastructure, secure control of an important source of provincial revenues – income tax – or introduce a national adjustment grant initiative. Still, Ottawa would continue to expand its role in many policy areas through its spending power, and the idea of introducing unconditional grants to the provinces with a bias to poorer provinces would re-emerge later.

The Gordon Commission

Some fifteen years after the Rowell-Sirois Commission tabled its findings, the St Laurent government asked Walter Gordon to chair yet another royal commission, this one on Canada's economic prospects. The Maritime region decided to play an active role in the work of the Gordon Commission, and the region prepared twenty-three submissions. Virtually all of them 'were couched in the now familiar language of regional grievance.'[76]

The Gordon Commission is probably best known for expressing deep concerns over the impact of foreign ownership in the Canadian economy. But it also had important things to say about the deepening patterns of uneven development. It went beyond the issue of fiscal need to suggest ways to improve the performance of regional economies. Still, the commission decided not to address 'the causes of uneven development' between the regions.[77] Such inequity was taken as a given that needed not to be revisited. Instead, the challenge, as the commission saw it, was to find ways to promote economic development in slow-growth regions without hurting the stronger provinces, in particular Ontario.

Hugh John Flemming, then New Brunswick premier, played a lead role on behalf of the Maritime provinces in the work of the Gordon Commission and in making representations to Ottawa in support of the region. He decided to organize a major conference in New Brunswick on the region's economic prospects and invited the other three Atlantic premiers to participate. He felt that having four provinces speaking for a new economic agenda would force Ottawa to take the proposed agenda seriously. The other three premiers agreed, and the first ever conference of Atlantic premiers was held in Fredericton on 9 July 1956.

Flemming led the charge, arguing the region should press Ottawa for subsidies based on fiscal need, assistance for resource development, a new regional transportation policy, different monetary and fiscal policies to stimulate economic development, and a new tariff policy geared to the region's economic interests. Nova Scotia premier Henry Hicks recommended they ask Ottawa to place more defence industries and contracts in the region.[78] The region had become more demanding. The focus was no longer restricted to fiscal needs for provincial governments but on a helping hand to promote economic development.

At the same time, however, there were concerns increasingly being heard in Ottawa that the federal government ought not to play regional favourites; that is, Ottawa should not agree to any special concessions for the Maritime provinces unless it was prepared to make them available to the other regions. Equalization in the mid-1950s meant something very different than it does today, and the prevailing view was that all federal payments to the provinces should be made on an 'equal' basis. New Brunswick historian W.S. MacNutt rebutted this view by writing, 'Where is the equalization in the operation of tariff policy, ... in the St. Lawrence Seaway, in the pipeline contract? We can say that, since we started on fairly even terms in 1867, equalization as seen from Ottawa has had some curious results.'[79] In its last budget, the St Laurent government announced plans to introduce annual equalization payments to the have-less provinces. By that time, the Gordon Commission had also submitted an interim report and recommended that 'a bold, comprehensive and coordinated approach' be implemented to resolve the underlying problems of the Atlantic region, which, in the commission's opinion, required special measures to improve its economic framework. These recommendations included a federally sponsored capital-projects commission to provide needed infrastructure facilities to encourage economic growth and measures to increase the rate of capital investment in the region.

In many ways the commission was breaking new ground in advocating the involvement of the private sector in promoting development in slow-growth regions. Perhaps for this reason the commission expressed concerns about any negative impact on other regions. It argued that 'special assistance put into effect to assist these areas might well adversely affect the welfare of industries already functioning in more established areas of Canada.'[80] The point was clear enough: the government could assist the Maritime provinces, but not at the expense of other regions, notably Ontario. However, the fact that Ontario benefited from national policy and the war efforts at the expense of the Maritimes did not seem to figure in the equation.

Discovering Regional Development

Looking back, it is now clear that the election of John Diefenbaker as prime minister constituted a watershed for the Maritime provinces. Unlike the long-serving prime ministers, Sir John A. Macdonald, Sir Wilfrid Laurier, Mackenzie King, and Louis St Laurent, Diefenbaker was not from either Ontario or Quebec. He also had a healthy distrust of central Canada's political and economic elites.[81] Furthermore, he had strong political ties to the Maritime region. Hugh John Flemming moved Diefenbaker's nomination at the party's national leadership convention, and Robert Stanfield, the newly elected premier of Nova Scotia, delivered the convention's keynote address. Diefenbaker's Conservatives had garnered 121 seats in the June 1957 general election, 16 more than the party had in the previous general election. He went on to form a minority government, having won only seven seats more than the Liberals. In forming his government, he appointed a twenty-two-member cabinet, including four ministers from Atlantic Canada. For the first time in Canadian history, there were more ministers from Atlantic Canada and the West than from central Canada.

Diefenbaker had included an 'Atlantic Manifesto' as an important part of his 1957 election platform. The manifesto borrowed heavily from Flemming's Fredericton conference of Atlantic premiers and the Gordon Commission. It urged federal government aid to electrical-power development in the region, further freight-rate adjustment, capital projects, adjustment grants to the provinces, a Canadian coast guard, and a national resource-development program.[82] Though the federal Department of Finance was quick to recommend a 'go-slow' approach to Atlantic Canada, Diefenbaker had, within a year of coming to power, implemented several significant measures for the region, including a loan to help develop the Beechwood dam in New Brunswick and a $25 million special adjustment grant to Atlantic Canada.[83] In addition, measures to promote economic development on the Prairies would indirectly help the Maritime provinces. As we will see in the next chapter, the 1960 budget speech unveiled the first of many measures Ottawa has developed to combat regional disparities.

Looking Back

The reader can appreciate why Maritimers consider Confederation to be the origin of their economic woes and underdevelopment. There is *some* truth to this view. The drive for Confederation did not come from the Maritimes but from Ontario and Quebec, which could see the economic advantages of union for the Canadas. Historians will agree that the requirements of Confederation have not been kind to the Maritime provinces. Maritime political leaders feared in 1867 that the larger provinces, notably Ontario, would come to dominate national institutions, and their fears have been realized. The suggestion that the Maritime provinces could always count on Quebec in any conflict with Ontario has not been borne out, and no economic historian would ever make the case that Canada's National Policy has favoured the Maritimes.

Things have been different for Ontario. Ian Drummond et al. write that 'between 1890 and 1913 the Ontario industrial economy experienced its heroic age.'[84] They credit Ottawa's National Policy for at least part of the reason for Ontario's growth, writing: 'Many of Ontario's big firms were intended to serve the domestic market. This orientation was obvious with service-producing firms, such as Bell, Toronto Power, and the Canada National Railway. But the large manufacturing firms, such as Canadian General Electric, were oriented wholly or largely towards the domestic market, in which they enjoyed tariff protection.'[85] Businesses were able to look to tariff protection and to a fully developed national railway system to exploit economies of scale by locating new capacity in the centre of the country, in Ontario.

It would be wrong, however, to look only to Confederation to explain all of Ontario's economic successes and all of the Maritimes' economic woes. Ontario was ideally located to capture opportunities as east-west trade took shape. There were firms, notably in the automotive sector, such as General Motors of Canada and Ford, that located their activities in southwestern Ontario because of its proximity to Detroit. More generally, many large U.S. firms decided to locate their Canadian subsidiaries as close as possible to their head offices and southern Ontario, which was in many cases the closest geographically, became the logical choice.[86] Ontario is fortunate to be located on top of the American triangle that has witnessed strong economic growth for well over a hundred years. Sir John A. Macdonald cannot be held responsible for this, though his National Policy did favour development in southern

Ontario. As well, some domestic industries had begun to flourish in Ontario by the time of Confederation, especially the agricultural implement industry. This, combined with national political institutions that by design favoured Ontario's economic interest, made the province 'the first and only imperial province ... By far the most emphatic expression of that imperialism was the National Policy.'[87]

With or without Confederation, the Maritime region would have had to adjust to the end of 'sea and sail,' and the adjustment would not have been easy without Confederation. The region's economic prosperity depended on trade. The failure of the reciprocity trade agreement with the Americans would force the Maritimes to look for new markets. The sea would be less attractive to Maritime producers than in the past because new trade patterns would emerge. The railroad would in future have a profound impact on economic development and trade, and it would favour central Canada, much as the sea had favoured the Maritime provinces. The Maritimes also lacked a hinterland to provide a strong domestic market, and so the region became central Canada's hinterland. New means of transportation would favour central Canada because goods produced at that time were much heavier than they are today and transportation costs much higher. Businesses from central Canada began to buy up Maritime firms and to build new plants where the population and markets were concentrated. As a significant transfer of capital and human resources from the Maritimes to central Canada took place, the region became a hinterland to the economy of central Canada.

The federal government did not help matters with its decision to concentrate its investment in infrastructure facilities in central Canada. Nor did the Maritime provinces help matters. Although sensing that they were losing economic ground, they did not put aside traditional rivalries to strengthen their economic base. Competition between Halifax and Saint John, for example, inhibited the development of a strong metropolitan centre to compete with Montreal and Toronto.

That said, it is important to recognize that the federal government, since the late 1870s, had been preoccupied with building a national economy and fostering a manufacturing sector to resist the pull of the United States. C.D. Howe, who was the key architect of this strategy, had no interest in regional balance. His goal was to build a modern economy capable of competing with the Americans, and if this meant favouring central Canada, then so be it. For C.D. Howe, the national interest was what mattered, and this has been true for many of Canada's political leaders ever since. They would deal with regional interests only after the national interest was secured. However, the national interest has never been fully secured, at least to the full satisfaction of 'national' political leaders.

Thus, to sum up, it is an oversimplification for the Maritime provinces to single out Confederation as the sole architect of their economic misfortune. To be sure, Confederation has not helped matters, but the region's comparative advantages, based on sea, sail and trade were in any case starting to give way by the time Confederation was born. Nevertheless, a pattern was established early on that efforts should be concentrated on building a national economy. The National Policy, the work of C.D. Howe, and the need to strengthen national unity has served to concentrate Ottawa's attention on Ontario and Quebec. Canada's national unity is always fragile and the American threat to the south, in whatever form it may take at any one time, is always on the horizon. Still, there have been occasional bursts of interest on the part of the federal government to focus some of its economic development activities in the Maritime provinces. The question, at such times, has always been what to do? Policy makers could well look to the economic development literature for guidance. The literature has had some modest and sporadic impact, as the next several chapters reveal.

3 Theories Matter Less

What to do? How can governments promote economic development in the Maritime provinces? What lessons does the literature offer to policy makers? What advice does the spate of books and articles on regionalism, regional economic development, and economic dependency theory offer them? This chapter seeks to answer these questions and to provide an overview of the various approaches that have been suggested to promote development in slow-growth regions. We go back in history to trace the evolution of new thinking in regional development, and, in doing so, we focus on theories and approaches that are relevant to the Canadian context and that have had some influence on Canadian policy and efforts. For this reason, we do not discuss the literature on regional science, circular and cumulative causation, and bi-modal production and regional dualism. These and the neo-Marxist literature exude an aura of other-worldliness to Canadian policy makers, and their influence has been either non-existent or at best very modest. A survey of the literature not directly connected to the topic in hand has been produced elsewhere.[1]

One of Canada's leading economists, Richard Lipsey, once observed that 'for all the concern about regional area development and regional problems in Canada, we don't really have an underlying theory. We don't know what we would have to do, what are the conditions under which we would have regional equality, however we define equality.'[2] In an uncharacteristic fashion, the Economic Council of Canada summed up the situation this way: 'Doctors used to try to cure syphilis with mercury and emetics. We now know that mercury works but emetics do not and, moreover, that penicillin is best of all. We suspect that the regional disparity disease is presently being treated with both mercury-

and emetic-type remedies, but we do not know which is which. Perhaps one day an economic penicillin will be found.'[3] The Economic Council did not discover such an economic penicillin, nor has one been discovered to date. The point here is that regional economic development remains a relatively new field. It also does not have its own home in academe – it has never been fully accepted as a full partner in the departments of economics or political science, though it does have some link to the departments of geography and urban studies. For this reason, it has not enjoyed the level of resources and support other mainstream academic disciplines have in recent years.

Still, the search for an economic penicillin has given rise to many theories and suggested approaches to regional development. Some of these theories are home grown but others have been imported. Some have had influence in shaping Canadian public policy on regional development while others show some promise in explaining the pace and location of Canada's economic development.

Theories of Regional Development: The Canadian Variety

Well-known Canadian economic historian, Harold Innis rejected any thinking that suggested universal applicability. He argued that any theory could be formulated only on the basis of a thorough analysis of a given situation. He maintained that theories developed in, say, Europe could not easily apply to Canada, given its distinct historical, political, and economic development.[4]

Innis developed a staples theory of economic development in Canada, which his associates subsequently refined. He argued that Canada's development has been shaped by the export of 'staples' to the heartlands of Europe and the United States, insisting that 'concentration on the production of staples for exports to more highly industrialised areas in Europe and later in the United States has broad implications for the Canadian economic, political, and social structure. Each staple in its turn left its stamp, and the shift to new staples invariably produced periods of crisis in which adjustments in the old structures were painfully made and a new pattern created in relation to a new staple.'[5]

The staples theory seemed to fit the Canadian setting well. Indeed, the premise of this theory is that Canada's poorer regions were at one time prosperous, which, in fact, explains why they were populated in the first place. The staple that gave rise to this prosperity began to decline in importance, either because it was over-exploited, because of changes in world demand, or because of competition from lower-cost producers elsewhere. This decline, in turn, led to a decline in the region's fortunes. This theory has a strong appeal, if only because it appears to be a succinct explanation of Canada's economic history. New Brunswick's forest industry, for example, accounted for that province's prosperity at the turn of the twentieth century. With the decline of the forest sector, New Brunswick's economic prosperity took a downward turn. More recently, Alberta's economic strength, which became evident in the 1970s, is due in large measure to its oil and gas reserves. In short, once marketable resources are discovered, an inflow of capital and firms will follow. This inflow brings higher incomes and a growing demand for labour. Once the resources are depleted or no longer marketable, however, capital leaves the area. As a result, income falls, and the more mobile sector of the labour force leaves. Labour out-migration is excluded as a cure for alleviating regional disparities. Rather, stimulating production of other marketable products through subsidization becomes a viable alternative. Alternatively, transport costs may be subsidized. The important point is that if growth is to be sustained after staple exports decline, a shift in resources into more diversified economic activities will be required.

In short then, the economic fortunes of a region, according to the staples theory, depend on the availability and marketability of its natural resources. On the face of it, the theory seems to explain the changing economic fate of the Maritime provinces. James Bickerton writes: 'The application of the staples model to the case of the Maritimes led to the widely accepted thesis that the economic stagnation of the region within Confederation was the outcome of inexorable technological changes that left its resource endowment marginal to the pattern of growth in twentieth century North America.'[6] However, it does not explain the high unemployment rate in British Columbia, an area richly endowed with marketable resources.

By the 1940s and 1950s, several scholars schooled in the work of Innis began to study Canada's resource-dependent economy from different perspectives. One looked at resource development and its impact on provincial economies, another on foreign investments, and yet another on government planning for economic development.[7] By the 1960s, however, the staples theory was being challenged, and its sweeping historical generalizations were being subjected to empirical scrutiny. The Economic Council of Canada, for instance, argued that 'the absence of resources in Switzerland does not prevent economic access, and their presence in Argentina does not guarantee it.'[8] For another, the theory itself was being undermined by new approaches and methodologies in the social sciences, including behavioural and systems approaches.[9] E.R. Forbes has made the case that the staples theory has, if anything, contributed to the misunderstanding of the Maritimes: 'The view of Canada's history as the story of the development of a series of staples for export ... contributed only slightly more to understanding of the Maritimes. Accounts of the fur trade touched on the Maritimes only in the earliest period; those on the timber trade largely petered out with confederation. Harold Innis' *Cod Fisheries* devoted but two of fifteen chapters to the Atlantic fishery after 1867, and studies of the wheat economy ignored the Maritimes entirely.'[10]

Under the title *Living Together*, the Economic Council of Canada produced in 1977 an ambitious study on regional disparities in Canada. The study reviews theories of regional disparities, including the staples approach and the development, neo-classical, Keynesian, and the regional science approaches. The authors find none of these totally satisfactory. One senses, however, an underlying faith in neo-classical economics. One also senses that the authors regard the persistence of regional disparities as an affront to economic science. Thus chapter 4, 'The Anatomy of the Problem,' begins with a sidebar asking, 'Do regional disparities exist?' The team tried very hard to make the problem go away. For one thing, they offered several alternative measures of regional income disparities; if one looks at average family disposable income, for example, the range was only from 9 percent above the national average for Ontario to 26 per cent below the national average in Newfoundland. Quebec's average family disposable income was only 2 per cent below the national average.[11] If these figures were the measure of the problem of regional disparities, one might ask, 'What's all the fuss about?'

The council argued that the main explanation for differences in per capita output and income among Canadian regions lies in differences in productivity in given occupations. Differences in structure of output and employment were accorded a relatively minor role. The council added that aggregate demand and urban structure also explain the existence of regional disparities.

Turning to policy, the authors express their preference for non-discriminatory monetary and fiscal policies, with some degree of regionalization of these policies, in contrast to any kind of federal policy that would deliberately discriminate in favour of people in some regions and against those in others. They find that fiscal policy does have a differential impact by region. Ontario, the country's richest region, benefits most during periods of fiscal ease, but is also most affected by a tightening of fiscal policy. The poorest region – the Maritime provinces and Newfoundland and Labrador – neither benefits greatly during a period of fiscal ease nor suffers much during periods of fiscal tightness. Quebec and the Prairies fall somewhere between Ontario and the Atlantic region, while British Columbia 'exhibits the most erratic behaviour.'[12]

The authors offer some mild criticism of neo-classical theory – that it does not deal effectively with distance and geographical dispersion. They also suggest that international trade theory offers only limited help, that location theory has remained highly formal, and that 'while it is useful to know that properly functioning relative prices and free mobility of factors may be helpful in curing a region's problems, it is more useful to know why some regions' problems persist so long, despite equilibrating market forces.'[13] They also note that for residents of an affected region, out-migration is regarded more as a problem than as a solution. Nonetheless, there is throughout the study an underlying theme that market forces and mobility of factors of production *ought* to be able to eliminate regional disparities.

The Two Sides of the Dependency Debate

Notwithstanding the council's criticism, neo-classical theory came in fashion in the early 1980s and remains dominant to this day. One of its main proponents, Thomas Courchene, has argued that Canada approached regional policy with 'a concept of gap closing rather than a policy of adjustment accommodation. We see disparity out there ... and we rush to remove it with one set of funds or another rather than letting it adjust itself on its own.'[14] Courchene's argument has been vigorously debated among Canadian academics and policy makers over the past twenty years. Increasingly, one hears the view that a strong reliance on government transfer payments makes a region dependent on these to support current levels of consumption and services, which are much higher than can be sustained by the economic output of the region. It is this dependence that in the end serves to blunt or sterilize the required long-term adjustment that would bring production and consumption back into line. It is also dependence that makes the region unable to move towards self-sufficiency and to integrate itself more fully into the national and international economies.

The notion of dependency in regional development goes beyond what the neo-classical approach labels 'transfer dependency.' Some observers talk of a theory that attributes dependency 'to the systematic draining of capital and resources from one region by other regions.'[15] Ralph Matthews, a Canadian sociologist, contends that 'dependency theorists can legitimately argue that the eastern regions of Canada would not need today's transfer payments if they had not earlier been drained of their wealth.'[16]

Clearly, though both the proponents of the neo-classical approach and the dependency theorists talk about dependency, they do not share the same perspective. The neoclassicists would like to see 'natural' economic adjustments come into play to solve regional disparities. These adjustments would include a lowering of the minimum wage in slow-growth regions, a gradual reduction in federal transfer payments, and out-migration of workers or surplus labour so that the region can return to its natural balance. The dependency theorists argue the opposite. They contend, for example, that out-migration is simply a continuation of the 'systematic draining' of resources from one region by other regions.[17]

Dependency theorists also argue that governments and international economic forces, notably the multinationals, have made local communities and small entrepreneurs dependent on forces that they cannot control. Rather than providing a setting in which local initiatives can be defined and carried out, the 'system' does the opposite. Major economic decisions are taken in Washington, New York, London, Toronto, and Tokyo, and new economic plans and possible initiatives are defined in far-away Ottawa, in provincial capitals, or, worse still, in countless federal-provincial committees of officials that are often hardly visible to those outside government. Regional economic plans are formulated by officials tied to remote political and economic forces, and local communities are expected to comply with what they come up with, on the assumption that it is obviously in their best interests to do so. Communities and small entrepreneurs have no choice but to play by rules that are established elsewhere and that will make them dependent on policy makers or economic actors from away.

Students of Canadian federalism have in recent years asked some fundamental questions about the state of interprovincial relations that also speak to the dependency debate. Much has been written and said about the impact of globalization on the nation-state, particularly the federal nation-state. Regions are trying as best they can to integrate in the global economy, and in the case of Canada they are looking south to see how they can compete with neighbouring regions. Ontario has over one-third of Canada's population and about 40 per cent of the nation's gross domestic product (GDP). As Andrew Stark writes in his preface to Tom Courchene and Colin Telmer's book, 'Thirty years ago, Ontario was Canada's heartland. Whatever was in the interests of Ontario was in the interests of Canada. Whatever was in the interest of Canada was in the interests of Ontario. And both Ontarians and other Canadians believed this.' Courchene and Telmer go on to argue that 'Heartland Ontario is no more and the province is being transformed into a North American Region State.'[18]

Ontario now appears less certain about its place in the federation and in its relations with the federal government and the other provinces. One observer of Queen's Park remarked: 'Historically, Ontario was always the province most comfortable with Canadian federalism. Ontarians saw the government in Ottawa as their government, acting for a nation they saw as their own ... Ottawa took care of Canada for Ontario ... and it worked. Ontario is coming to the conclusion that Ottawa no longer works in its interest.'[19] There are increasing signs that Ontario may follow Quebec in adopting a policy of provincial economic activism. While it may have made economic sense to support transfer payments to slow-growth regions forty years ago, it is less clear that this is so today. The findings of the Ontario government's three-volume report entitled *Competing in the New Global Economy* is an excellent example of this thinking.[20]

As Ontario adjusts to the North American Free Trade Agreement and other global economic forces, it may well begin to question programs designed to maintain Canada's east-west links, whether in the form of transfer payments to individuals or of federal regional development programs. Measures to undercut Michigan's cost structure are more pressing for Ontario than are securing east-west links. Global economic forces will also have a major impact on the evolution of the political economy of Canada's regions. As these regions become inserted differently into the global economy, their links with the outside world will 'become more important relative to their economic linkages within Canada.' In this sense, Canada becomes less able to act as the giant 'mutual insurance company' that Saskatchewan premier Allan Blakeney once called it. In such a political economy, 'it may well become harder to sustain the political commitment in wealthier provinces to interregional redistribution.'[21]

Theories from Away

Entrepreneurship

Perhaps no concept has played so great a role in economic development theory as 'entrepreneurship': the capacity to introduce new technologies and new products, develop new resources, and improve business organization and management, and the ability to bring to life innovations of all kinds and bring together the required land, labour, capital, and management in an efficient and dynamic enterprise to make innovations succeed. Entrepreneurship has been analysed and discussed mainly in the context of development of national economics and societies, but the concept has certainly been no stranger to the theory of regional economic development. To the degree that subnational regions have distinct economies and societies, the need for entrepreneurship to promote development is just as pressing at the regional as at the national level. The lack of entrepreneurship in some regions and its concentration in others has been cited as an explanation of regional disparities in a good many countries besides Canada.

The presence or absence of entrepreneurship is frequently attributed to the culture of a society. We are learning that cultural differences among regions can persist even in highly industrialized countries. Thus, regional differences in the supply of entrepreneurship should come as no surprise. As recently as two decades ago, the role of the Roman Catholic Church was frequently cited as being responsible for the lack of French-Canadian entrepreneurship and the consequent lag in economic development of French Canada. But there is an element of chicken-and-egg circularity in much of the discussion of entrepreneurship. Do entrepreneurs bring development, or does development bring forth entrepreneurs?

While it is far from being 'operational,' the Weber-Tawney thesis regarding the rise of capitalism remains important for the enormous influence it has had on social thought. Translated more broadly into a theory of the relationship between a society's ideological framework and entrepreneurial endeavour, it remains highly germane to today's economic development problems, whether at the national, regional, or community level.

Max Weber's explanation of the 'rise of capitalism' in the sixteenth century is that the Reformation provided the proper philosophical and ethical setting in which the 'capitalist spirit' could flourish. The impulse

to acquisition is common to all times and all places, but Roman Catholicism held in check the pursuit of profit and the accumulation of wealth
that characterize capitalism. The problem is not the advent of capitalistic activity but the appearance of the sober bourgeois society in which
capitalism reached its apex. Even contemporary society gives us a clue
to the rise of this middle-class society, Weber argued, for in countries of
mixed religion, we find a dominance of Protestants among entrepreneurs, owners of capital, and high-grade labour. It was also true that the
more highly developed regions were those that gave most support to
the Reformation, finding its creed more suitable to aggressive and
progressive ways of life.

This concept is to be found in Luther's doctrines under the name of
the 'calling,' the idea that each individual is 'called' to do a certain job
and to do it as well as possible. The highest form of moral conduct is the
fulfilment of duty in worldly affairs. The ideal of monastic asceticism
was extended to worldly life: one should not indulge in luxury. Yet
Luther was opposed to monopoly and to usury, and cannot be regarded
as the apostle of capitalism. The real enemy of Catholicism was Calvinism. In order to become one of the 'chosen,' one must work hard and
spend little. One must accept one's lot as part of God's scheme. The
intensity of worldly activity alone dispels doubts as to one's being
among the 'elect.' In practice, the reasoning of the Baptist sects becomes
equivalent to Calvinism.

This explanation of the rise of capitalism was introduced to English
readers by R.H. Tawney. Although essentially the same as Weber's, his
treatment is more general and develops the thesis in relation to its
historical setting. Like Weber, Tawney points out that the Catholic Church
opposed usury and emphasized the sin of avarice. Catholic teaching
was an effective barrier to capitalistic development. Tawney attributes
less positive and more negative influence to Luther than does Weber.
Luther, he says, was opposed to the accumulation of wealth, usury,
monopoly, high prices, speculation, and the luxury trade with the East.
But Calvin's teaching was most characteristic and most influential of
the new doctrines. He saw economic life with the eyes of a peasant and
recognized frankly the need for capital, credit and banking, and large-
scale commerce and finance. Thrift, diligence, sobriety, and frugality
are the Christian virtues, and profit and interest are not necessarily evil
gains.

While few social scientists today believe that levels or rates of development can be explained by formal religion alone, there remains a
rough rank-correlation between dominant religion and per capita in-

comes. More important, many social scientists believe that development is aided and abetted by a generally held ideology of a sort that provides a unifying force and encourages entrepreneurship. Religious affiliation is fast losing its relevance in the modern secular world, but its influence lingers and this may well be more evident in the Maritime provinces than in other regions in Canada. The Maritime provinces have had little success in attracting new Canadians, and there is some evidence to suggest that traditional values remain more evident in the region.[22] In addition, it is likely no coincidence that some of the most economically disadvantaged areas of the Maritime provinces (Kent County and northern New Brunswick) are predominantly Roman Catholic and French speaking. A former senior official with the Atlantic Canada Opportunities Agency (ACOA), for example, always attached a great deal of importance to a community's religious affiliation and ethnic background when discussing its economic potential.[23]

Schumpeter

Joseph Schumpeter's career encompassed both the neo-classical and Keynesian periods. To these schools of thought he added something unique of his own, based partly on his knowledge of social sciences other than economics and partly on a range of experience unusually wide for his generation, including a term as minister of Finance in Austria and a sojourn as professor of economics in Japan. Out of this experience came a basic theory of entrepreneurship essentially interdisciplinary in scope.

Schumpeter ranks among the all-time greats in the history of economic thought and economic development. He has special interest for this survey because, virtually alone in his generation of economists, his main interest was in economic development. The German edition of his *Theory of Economic Development* was published in 1911, and throughout his career he continued to elaborate and refine his theory.[24] His eclectic and synthesizing approach was no doubt partly due to his wide range of experience. He leaned heavily on Marx, sharing his conviction that economic fluctuations and growth are inseparably intertwined. Schumpeter's own theory, however, was largely concerned with entrepreneurship, innovations, and their institutional setting. His ideas on these elements of development became stock-in-trade for all development economists.

Schumpeter maintained that the most important part of private investment is determined by such long-range considerations as technological change. He stressed innovation as the mainspring of this type of investment. Any 'doing things differently' that increases the productivity of the bundle of factors of production available is an innovation. The entrepreneur is not the inventor; he or she is the individual who sees the opportunity for introducing an innovation, a new technique or a new commodity, an improved organization, or the development of newly discovered resources. The entrepreneur raises the money to launch the new enterprise, assembles the factors of production, chooses top managers, and sets the organization going. Schumpeter believed that growth is associated with booms and recessions because successful innovations tend to bring 'clusters of followers,' with investment financed largely through new credit, resulting in a boom; then when the new plants are in place, debts are repaid and the money supply contracts just as output increases, prices fall, and the recession sets in. However, Schumpeter did not feel that deep depressions like that of the 1930s were necessary; like other neo-classicists, he believed such depressions represented mismanagement of the money system.

In Schumpeter's system, the supply of entrepreneurship is the ultimate determining factor of the rate of economic growth. This supply in turn depends on the 'social climate,' a complex phenomenon reflecting the whole social, political, and socio-psychological atmosphere within which entrepreneurs must operate. It would include the social values of a particular country at a particular time, the class structure, the educational system, the attitude of society towards business success, and the nature and extent of the prestige and other social rewards, apart from profits, that accompany business success in the society. A particularly important factor in 'climate' is the entrepreneur's understanding of the 'rules of the game,' the conditions under which he or she must operate. Sudden changes in the rules of the game are particularly deleterious to an increasing flow of enterprise. In general, the climate is appropriate when entrepreneurial success is amply rewarded, and where there are good but not too good chances of success. There must be a risk and a challenge to bring forth true entrepreneurial endeavour, but there must be some chance of high rewards. Schumpeter, however, does not tell us how to create entrepreneurs where they do not exist.

Creating Entrepreneurs

The conclusions of Harvard psychologist David McClelland and his colleague David Winter held promise for policy makers: if development is hampered by a shortage of entrepreneurs, it is possible to create them within a short space of time by appropriate training of carefully selected individuals, without operating on the rest of the society at all. In choosing methods for inducing technological change, many social scientists set store by the simple device of demonstration, which has had substantial results over the last two decades. But demonstration alone does not always succeed, say McClelland and Winter.[25] Some very poor fishermen in India, for example, were provided with nylon fishing nets by the government. These nets were stronger and held more fish than the fishermen's own primitive nets. Some men caught more fish with the new nets but stopped fishing when they had caught their usual number, while others fished longer but used the extra income to buy more liquor. Technical advance does not always produce the values and attitudes necessary to produce development. The purely economic tools to promote development (investment and technological advance) work too slowly. These tools should be supplemented by psychological education to accelerate development.

There is clearly a wide range of views among social scientists regarding entrepreneurship. At one extreme are those who argue that it is needed for development, and that it is a rare, delicate hothouse plant, requiring careful nourishment. At the other end of the spectrum are those who argue that it is necessary only to get something going – a major resource discovery, a new road, a factory – and entrepreneurs will spring up under every tree, or even in the desert. Between these extremes is a majority who say 'it depends.' But on what? No one has come up with the answer. Still, entrepreneurship holds considerable attraction for national governments because it enables them to shift the economic development challenge down to the regional or community levels and then say to them 'here, now you drive.'

Interregional and International Trade

What really interested the classical economists, from Adam Smith to John Stuart Mill, was international trade, which was thought to be an 'engine of growth.' The same was true later of the neo-classical economists, from William Stanley Jevons and F.Y. Edgeworth through Alfred Marshall to Paul Samuelson. Yet, it was clear that the same heterogeneity of space that gave rise to international trade could also give rise to interregional trade. Some economists have been logical enough in their analysis to draw attention to this fact. A few even found the theory of interregional trade a convenient way of approaching the theory of international trade. As early as 1752, David Hume pointed out that the theory of international equilibrium applied also to regions within the same country.[26] Adam Smith recognized that if all factors were perfectly mobile, the factors would move rather than goods and services; and since he believed such mobility to exist only within single neighbourhoods, he implicitly recognized that factor immobility could give rise to trade among regions of the same country.[27] John Stuart Mill reiterated this view.[28] Moving into the neo-classical period, J.E. Cairnes related interregional trade to his concept of 'non-competing groups,'[29] and J.S. Nicholson regarded interregional trade arising from internal immobility of factors of production as the general case.[30]

The person who thoroughly entrenched interregional trade into modern neo-classical theory, however, and made it ever since an integral part of general equilibrium theory was the Swedish economist Bertil Ohlin, in his classic work *Interregional and International Trade* (1933). Virtually all subsequent work on the subject owes a debt to him. Ohlin was not primarily interested in regional analysis, regional development and its relation to national development, or regional disparities. He was interested mainly in international trade theory as a device for explaining conditions under which trade took place and the distribution of gains from trade, and as a guide to foreign trade policy.

The classical economists contended that the volume and pattern of trade between two regions or two countries depend on the amount of labour required to produce various commodities in each region. To take David Ricardo's famous example, suppose that a certain amount of labour will produce twenty bolts of cloth or ten tons of wine in the United Kingdom and ten bolts of cloth or twenty tons of wine in Portugal. If there are no restrictions on trade, and transport costs are not exorbitant, the United Kingdom will specialize in textiles and Portugal in wine. Trade will take place at a rate of exchange of one bolt of cloth for one ton of wine, since the amounts of labour entailed in the producing country are the same, and transport costs are the same in both directions. In effect, Portugal and the United Kingdom are exchanging one person-day of British labour for one person-day of Portuguese labour. In this example, and in any other case where trade takes place, both countries or regions are better off than they would be if each tried to produce both commodities.

An important extension of the classical theory is the demonstration that trade is still mutually beneficial even if one region is more efficient at the production of all commodities, provided the superior productivity is more marked in some industries than in others. It is hard to imagine the United Kingdom being superior to Portugal at producing wine, but we can suppose that Portugal could introduce a modernized textile industry, so that the same amount of labour would produce twenty-five bolts of cloth instead of ten, whereas the United Kingdom textile industry is reluctant to change its ways. It will still pay Portugal to specialize in wine, and import its cloth; it can get cloth much more cheaply (in person-days) by exporting wine than by producing cloth at home.

Because the whole analytical system of the classical economist was built on the labour theory of value, it was natural and consistent for them to make differing labour costs the basis for interregional and international trade. But curiously enough, while attacking the labour theory of value in general, neo-classical economists continued to analyse interregional and international trade in terms of labour costs until well into the 1930s. P.T. Ellsworth, in a well-known book on international economics published in 1938, illustrates 'the modern classical position' using as an example Ohio and neighbouring Pennsylvania.[31] Ten days of labour will produce twenty tires or ten bolts of cloth in Ohio, ten tires or twenty bolts of cloth in Pennsylvania. So Ohio specializes in tires and Pennsylvania in cloth, and they exchange tires for bolts of cloth on a one-to-one basis. Some neo-classical economists even tried to justify building trade theory on a real-labour-cost foundation. The Harvard economist Frank Taussig, for example, argued that capital costs (interest rates) and wages for the same kind of labour did not vary much from country to country, and that prices equal costs of units produced at the margin, where there are no rents.[32]

Individuals have different capabilities and are better at doing some things than others. It is sensible and profitable for them to specialize in the things they are good at. In the same way, different regions have varying endowments of natural and human resources, and, because of varying economic histories, they also have different stocks of plants and equipment in existence and varying capacities to save and invest. These differences result in varying costs of production and varying demand for particular goods and services, and thus to varying prices. The differences in costs and prices among regions create opportunities for mutually beneficial trade among regions. They can also, however, result in differences in level of welfare among regions if there are barriers, natural or man-made, to movement of either factors of production or goods and services among regions.

Theoretically, differences in standards of living among regions could be eliminated, even if limits to movements of goods and services existed, making it difficult for a poor region to export the goods in which it has a comparative advantage, so long as there was perfect mobility of factors of production. People could move to the richer regions, or capital to the poorer regions to take advantage of relatively low wage rates, thus making wages higher. But perfect mobility does not, and basically cannot, exist. As Ellsworth puts it: 'It may be stated at the outset that the chief obstacle to movements of both labour and capital is psychological in nature. Human beings dislike change, and the changes involved in breaking home ties, leaving secure employment and a familiar environment for a strange locality and an uncertain economic future, are painful to make ... Owners of capital are likewise reluctant to transfer their wealth across national and regional boundaries to places where it is no longer under their direct supervision, and where the "real or fancied insecurity" is greater. To this psychological obstacle must be added another, the financial cost of moving. This often, in the case of labour, though rarely with capital, constitutes an obstacle of the first importance.'[33]

It might be noted in passing that when Ellsworth says that financial costs of moving capital are 'rarely' an obstacle to its movement, he is obviously thinking of capital in the form of money, or liquid capital. When an enterprise has built up plant and equipment in a particular region, the cost of moving it to another region may indeed be 'an obstacle of the first importance' to moving the enterprise to another region. The entrepreneur who wants to move has two choices: sell the enterprise for what he can get and establish a new plant and equipment in the other region; or wear out his machinery without replacing it (which could take years), sell it for scrap and sell his buildings for what he can get, and reinvest in the other region. Neither decision is one that entrepreneurs make lightly.

Where does this bird's-eye view survey of interregional trade leave us? What we have seen most clearly is that we are able to explain, in an *ad hoc* pragmatic way, patterns of location and interregional trade, and their impact on regional economic development, *after the event*. We can list the factors involved and perhaps rank them according to their importance in determining the course of events. However, we do not have, and we are unlikely soon to have, a general theory that can *predict* what *will happen* to a particular region. Accordingly, the theory has only limited value to those wishing to formulate measures to promote economic development in slow-growth regions like the Maritime provinces.

The Economic Base Theory

Closely related to theories of interregional trade is the economic base theory. It states that the development of any region, particularly of its urban centres, is a function of the growth of its 'base industries.' These, by definition, are export industries. They are not attracted to a particular region or city in order to exploit the market of that region or city. They are attracted because the location provides a favourable base from which to export to other regions; the location promises a comparative advantage to the base industry. In the case of 'smoke-stack industries,' proximity to natural resources is often the determining factor. The steel industry of the United States settled in Pittsburgh because of its proximity to coal mines and also to iron and industrial water. Pulp and paper mills settle near forests, aluminium mills near sources of hydro-electric power. Scientifically oriented enterprises settle where there are research institutes, universities, specialized consulting firms, and other sophisticated services. As services and scientifically oriented ('high-tech') industries come more and more to dominate metropolitan centres, and as both become more footloose, access to the most modern information and communications systems and amenities that make a city attractive become increasingly important factors in the location of economic activity. In the case of sophisticated services like consulting, top-level banking, trading desks, stock markets, insurance, and specialized accounting or legal services, access to clients and to information and technology are major considerations, which is why one finds the head offices of such enterprises in New York, Boston, Hartford, Connecticut, and Toronto rather than in Toledo, Ohio, Victoria, BC, or Moncton, NB.

Growth Poles

Of all the concepts utilized since the Second World War in the formulation of regional policy and the preparation of regional development plans, none generated so rapid a rise in popularity, nor so early and complete a disillusionment, as 'growth poles.' During the late 1960s and 1970s, there was scarcely a developed or a developing country that did not make use of the concept. In the form in which it was usually applied, the notion of growth poles made regional development seem so simple. All you have to do is to push or pull some industries into an urban centre in a retarded or disadvantaged region, through construction of infrastructure and incentives or regulations for private investment, and then sit back and watch the 'spread effects' of this investment eliminate the gap between that region and the more prosperous and dynamic ones in the same country.

Growth-pole theory is irrevocably associated with the work of François Perroux. Perroux was a prolific writer and remained so right up to his death at the age of eighty-six in 1987, as the volume of essays in his honour shows.[34] Perroux's notions about interactions in space first came to the attention of English-speaking social scientists through a lecture delivered at Harvard in 1949 and published under the title 'Economic Space: Theory and Applications' in the *Quarterly Journal of Economics* in March 1950.[35] Coming so soon after the war, it is not surprising that it expressed concern about European reconstruction and about mounting tensions – already – among European countries. Perroux thought that a false concept of space – 'territorial,' 'banal,' 'geonomic' – was contributing to these tensions. The idea of space as 'a container' holding a defined group of people ('the contained') gave rise to territorial demands and conflicts, including protectionism. It was essential to think instead in terms of abstract economic space, spaces as 'fields of force,' or as defined by a plan, or as homogeneous aggregates, rather than in terms of points, lines, surfaces, or volumes. It should be noted that when Perroux spoke of 'space defined by a plan,' he was thinking of plans made by private enterprises, not of regional development plans in the usual sense. As a firm might buy and sell all over the world, its 'planning' space need not be geographically contiguous. 'The topographical zone of influence of Michelin in France is inscribed in a region, but its economic zone of influence, like that of all large firms, defies cartography.'[36]

In the 1950 article the term 'growth pole' or 'growth centre' does not actually appear, but Perroux does speak of 'poles' and 'centres,' and it is clear that he thinks of them as concentrations of economic activity and as generators of growth. His idea that growth is always polarized (concentrated in particular centres or poles), leading to dominance and dependence, is also present in the article, although not yet spelled out in any detail.

Five years later Perroux published another article in English, although in a French journal, *Économie appliquée*, entitled 'A Note on the Notion of Growth Pole,' where the main outlines of his growth-pole theory are drawn.[37] A more thorough exposition of the theory was contained in his 1961 book *L'Économie du XXe siècle*. Even in the 1955 article, however, the basic concept of growth poles as constellations of dynamic, innovating enterprises, often but not always in urban centres, and generating 'effets d'entraînement' (propulsive effects) upstream and downstream, positive (spread effects) or negative (backwash effects), is already present.

Karen Polenske observes, 'As a number of previous reviewers, such as Darwent (1969) and Hermansen (1972) have noted, Perroux never made a clear distinction between a growth pole and a growth centre.'[38] That neglect was one of the reasons for the confusion surrounding the understanding and the application of Perroux's growth-pole theory. He also failed to provide a clear distinction between a growth pole and a development pole. His last effort to do so did not help much, particularly for those who wanted operational concepts as a basis of policy making and planning: '*The growth pole* is a set that has the capacity to induce the growth of another set; *the pole of development* is a set that has the capacity to engender a dialectic of economic and social structures whose effect is to increase the complexity of the whole and to expand its multidimensional return.'[39] In order to understand completely Perroux's theory of growth poles and development poles, it is essential to understand that it is just one facet, although an important one, of his running battle with the neo-classical system.

Neo-classical economics implies that the market will bring, among other pleasant things, an essential harmony in the distribution of economic activity through space, a kind of Pareto optimum of spatial equilibrium. It was precisely this comfortable conclusion that Perroux denied, contending that the natural tendency was towards polarization, dominance, and dependence, which was likely to become cumulative.

Perroux's own theory was imperfectly understood and still more imperfectly applied. But applied it certainly was, including in Canada. Many more governments have stated officially that they were pursuing a growth-pole strategy, at least in the urban and regional aspects of their development policy, than have claimed to be guided by any other philosophy, apart from laissez-faire; it became the guiding principle for regional planning in France, Belgium, Italy, and Canada in the 1960s and later in Spain, the United States, Japan, Latin America, Africa, and Asia.

As initially presented by Perroux, the theory was too complex, too abstract, and too non-operational to be used as a basis for planning. Indeed to apply the pure theory of Perroux would require global planning, if we take into account his insistence on planning transmission lines and receptors as well as generators of growth. Perroux's economic space, in which spread effects are felt, is global. He argues that Latin America's true growth poles still lie in Europe and, to some degree, in the United States. Such a concept is useless for regional planning, which is confined to a single country, let alone in a region such as the Maritime provinces in Canada. As a consequence, economists who found themselves involved in practical regional planning simply discarded the pure theory of Perroux. They converted it into a totally different theory, which treated growth poles as urban centres, and spread effects as being generated in a particular geographic space – namely, the region adjacent to the urban centre itself. Once this happy doctrine is accepted, it is possible to imagine that by pushing and pulling new enterprises (mostly industrial enterprises) into urban centres of retarded regions, it is possible to reduce regional disparities, decentralize urbanization and industrialization, and accelerate national development all at once.

It is here, of course, that the mistake was made. There are, to be sure, conditions under which industrial investment in a city will lead to increased income and employment in its peripheral region. In general, these conditions are that the industries in the city are natural-resource based and that the natural resources required are found in the peripheral region. When the concept of growth poles was first introduced, it should be remembered, many industries in western European cities were still natural-resource based, and many cities were based primarily on these industries. For such urban centres, the simplified theory of growth poles may hold. But there are many situations in which this theory – let us label it the Boudeville version of the original Perroux doctrine – simply does not hold at all.[40] One such situation is in the case of the propulsive region, in which the expansion of economic activities in the hinterland generates growth of its urban centre, rather than vice versa. Another is where the urban centre is too small and too unsophisticated in its economic activities to generate significant spread effects of any kind, as in the case of a small town with a cannery or some jiggery mills. A third is where industries are natural-resource based, but the natural resources are found outside the peripheral region. And the fourth, most common among major metropolitan centres today, is the situation in which the propulsive enterprises in the city are based not on natural resources but on human resources. In such cases, industry consists of scientifically oriented manufacturing and quaternary services; there is no link to the peripheral region at all, because the enterprises operate in a worldwide economic space.

The Boudeville version, however, simply took no account of these cases, which are certainly in the majority, until it had become abundantly clear that the application of this simple version of the theory was not working. In effect, the adherents of this theory behaved as though growth-pole theory and economic base theory were essentially the same. We learned in time the falsity of this premise. We found that it was indeed possible, although not easy, to lure new enterprises into urban centres designated as growth poles in retarded regions. Snaring them required a combination of investment in infrastructure, relocation of government enterprises, and incentives to private enterprise. But in most cases the hoped for and expected spread effects to the rest of the region did not appear.

Before we learned this bitter lesson, however, and once the door was opened to Boudeville's revisionism, all manner of policies regarding urban growth and regional development were justified as applications of the growth-pole doctrine. The urban centres labelled 'growth poles' ranged in population from many millions to a few thousand. In Japan they were vast industrial complexes requiring hundreds of millions of dollars of investment in each. In the Maritime provinces, growth poles consisted largely of a series of small cities and towns.

It is a long march from Perroux's theory to giving a capital grant to Volvo to make Halifax into a development pole, generating propulsive effects, in the form of higher employment and incomes, throughout the Maritime provinces. Indeed, Perroux is quite specific that it is 'untenable to reduce the theory of development poles to a mere instrument of regional policy.' One cannot implant any kind of productive activity anywhere one wishes, in any kind of environment. A rational policy involves both the choice of the motor and the management of the environment. Moreover, Perroux continues, 'Clearly, the market, full as it is of monopolies and various imperfections, is not up to these two tasks.'[41]

Statements such as these, together with Perroux's related theory of dominance/dependence, which is well analysed in Karen Polenske's chapter in the Higgins–Savoie volume,[42] make Perroux sound as though he were a radical political economist. But while he was a heretic in relation to his more purely neo-classical colleagues, in politics he was right of centre on the French political spectrum. He was conservative enough to have run into severe difficulties during the left-wing student riots in Paris in 1968, including the loss of his editorship of the journal *Tiers monde*, of which he was the founder. Perroux was certainly interested in politics at both the national and the international levels. Like

Keynes, he wrote a good many 'essays in persuasion.' He had limited faith in the free market and believed that dynamic capitalist economies need some degree of planning and management. Nonetheless, his political philosophy was basically eighteenth- and nineteenth-century liberal.

What remains of the growth-pole concept? Perhaps most informed observers would agree on the following conclusions:

- Development involves polarization.
- Growth poles are accordingly a 'good thing,' a source of dynamism in the economy, which generate spread effects *somewhere*, but not necessarily in their own peripheral geographic region.
- The principal role of growth poles is as a source and a diffuser of innovations.
- Therefore growth poles should be encouraged to form and to play this role, even if it involves some degree of domination/dependence relationship.
- A policy of selected decentralization, or creation of 'pôles d'équilibre,' is not in conflict with this Perroux-style growth-pole policy.
- As investment decisions in propulsive industries are risky and discontinuous, temporary subsidization can be justified in the same way that protection of 'infant industries' is justified. Growth-pole strategy might be regarded as infant industry strategy set in space and time, and should involve nurturing healthy infants for strictly limited periods, together with a refusal to run life-support systems for doddering geriatrics.
- There may be cases when small and middle-sized cities can serve as growth poles.
- What is excluded, or at least ought to be, from a Perroux-style growth-pole strategy is pushing and pulling enterprises at random into retarded and disadvantaged regions when the conditions for generation of spread effects are not present – in other words, the kind of strategy that was in fact pursued in many countries, including Canada, during the 1960s and 1970s.

Recent Literature

The reader by now is likely to conclude that regional development in general has been floundering in a theoretical quagmire. There have been numerous attempts to describe – and even some attempts to explain – what is occurring in individual regional economies. But the global picture is very confusing. What is happening in some regions seems to be the reverse of what is happening in others. Thus, we have theories of polarization, polarization reversal, and polarization-reversal-reversal; theories of agglomeration and theories of decentralization; diffusion models and theories of clustering; advocacy of small and middle-sized enterprises (SMEs) in small and middle-sized cities (SMCs); long lists of the qualitative advantages of metropolitan centres; factories in the fields; seedbeds and product life cycles.

The point is, however, that *all* these things are valid – somewhere or other – and, as we will see in the next several chapters, the government of Canada has tried some of them, among other approaches in one form or another, in the Maritime provinces. With recent trends in technological advance and in the managerial revolution, decision making has become a much more sophisticated and flexible affair, and there is no reason to expect that the management of one enterprise will make its decisions in the same way that another does. As Allen J. Scott and Michael Storper put it, 'The existing literature on the geography of high technology industry agrees on one point, i.e. that the classical Weberian theory of location with its emphasis on the individual decision maker is unequal to the task of accounting for the emergence and deployment of whole new sectors of production over the economic landscape. Most attempts to explain the spatial pattern of high technology industry have by contrast struggled to gain a systemic view of its concrete development paths in space and time.'[43]

When management is concerned not with maximizing profits but with maximizing growth, within constraints imposed by the need to avoid excessive fixed debt, stockholders' revolts, and takeovers – and when the president, the vice-president for finance with his or her MBA, the vice-president for marketing with his or her MBA, and the vice-president for production with his or her degree in industrial management all have different views on how to do that – there is no telling how they will decide on the location of a new plant and no reason to expect that they will make their decision the same way twice in a row.[44] The one thing the vice-presidents often have in common is the desire to be president. Yet, the individual entrepreneur has not disappeared, nor has the partnership, and they will presumably keep a closer eye on profits than will their corporate colleagues.

The decisions made by the management of a large corporation are in any case much more complex than they were even twenty years ago. Managers do not choose a location for producing a given product with a given technology. The product mix, the technique of producing it, and the location are chosen together. When the products and the technology are such that the products can be produced by a highly mechanized process, utilizing unskilled labour, they may very well choose a small town where labour is unorganized and consists in large measure of women and young people who accept low wages. When they need a large pool of highly skilled labour, especially with scientific, engineering, technical, and managerial skills, as in the start-up phase of a new product, they are likely to choose a metropolitan area, and the Maritime provinces have precious few centres left that would qualify as metropolitan areas.

During the 1960s and 1970s, some policy makers expressed concern at the seemingly irreversible tendency towards agglomeration and polarization in Western countries. Only the very large metropolitan centre seemed to have the requisite location factors for the new high-technology industries. As Scott and Storper express it, 'one of the currently fashionable accounts of high technology industrial location emphasizes the unique and exogenous locational factors alleged to be necessary pre-conditions of high technology development in particular places. A wide variety of such factors is commonly adduced in the literature: e.g. the presence of universities with major programs in science and engineering, accessibility to international airports, nearby military bases, the local availability of venture capital, a high proportion of technical/scientific workers in the local population, a superior quality of life and so on.'[45] However, they then add, 'In practice, these factors turn out to be little more than *ad hoc* lists hopefully masquerading as analysis. They miss entirely the central problem of the internal evolutionary dynamics of growth complexes.'[46]

Then, towards the end of the 1970s, it was found that there had been a 'polarisation reversal.'[47] Big cities like New York and Tokyo were actually losing population. Fu Chen Lo and Kamal Salih explained this phenomenon in terms of diseconomies of scale, pollution, congestion, high costs of living, high rents, and so on. But now it seems that the big cities are growing again. In Canada, it became evident by the turn of the last century that Toronto was in the ascendancy. No one need be surprised at this, once one realizes that all entrepreneurs do *not* behave in the same way and that, at any point of time, they may see the advantages and disadvantages of locating in small, middle-sized, and large cities differently, *for their own purposes*.

The Spatial Division of Labour

Philippe Aydalot begins his article 'La Division spatiale du travail' with this observation: 'In the general analysis of the forces which define the spatial inequality of regional development, the location of industry (enterprise) is a major chapter, because it is the enterprise which disposes of the dominant power of decision-making in this domain.'[48] He goes on to argue that the problem of location requires a single answer. It is a matter of determining for each agent the optimal location and making explicit the forms of the equilibrium that follow. Space must therefore be heterogeneous. If it were not, location would be a matter of indifference to the enterprise. In most neo-classical theory, space is treated as homogeneous, and location is therefore indeterminate. Homogeneity of space follows from the homogeneity of factors of production and the unity of markets.

The tendency is for transport costs to diminish and for products to become less heavy. Aydalot asks: 'Is this then the end of theory and the beginning of the era of indeterminacy? All that remains of the structure of space is labour; which, doubtless, one will say, is mobile and tends to become increasingly homogeneous. But such a viewpoint is too hasty; first because men wish to live where they were born, so that space is never completely homogeneous; and also because it is *men* who are displaced, and not the *labour force* ... Each environment has its own cost; the cost of reproduction of the labour force is not the same in all locations. The level of wages is only the most visible factor in choice of location. But the enterprise does not seek to minimise its wage cost alone; it seeks also a pattern of social relations which assures the security, regularity and perpetuity of its activity.'[49]

Hence, the enterprise will settle in a large city only if the efficiency of production offsets the higher costs. If possible, it will choose technologies that will permit it to employ non-industrial labour, which has a low level of unionization and which allows easy social relations. Only if the efficiency of the sophisticated labour force of the large cities is needed will the enterprise choose them as a location. If the technical processes can be sufficiently mechanized to permit the use of unskilled labour, the enterprise can seek a location where the cost of reproduction of the labour force is low.

Searching for Clusters

Michael Porter had advice for governments in his widely read *The Competitive Advantage of Nations*. The book became required reading in many government departments and essentially urged governments to create factors to establish competitive advantage tied to specific industries or industry group.[50] Porter also has specific advice for Canada. He writes: 'There is room for Canadian governments to ... support clusters, whether in providing specialized training and research institutions, specialized infrastructure, or incentives for related and supporting industries to co-locate. Governments should seek out cluster participants and proactively understand their needs at a time when early action can have a transformative impact ... Governments can and do promote the health and development of clusters by understanding their specialized factor requirements, determining which have such high levels of externalities involved that individual firms will not invest to create them, and proactively invest on behalf of the industry. Such investments can include specialized educational program, specialized infrastructure, or special regulatory regimes.'[51] As we will see in a subsequent chapter, Canadian government officials have embraced Porter's advice with enthusiasm.

Searching for the Creative Class

Richard Florida argues that a creative class has emerged to become the engine of economic growth at the regional and community levels.[52] He defines creative class as those whose function is to create meaningful new forms. This includes scientists, engineers, university professors, poets, artists, entertainers, think-tank researchers, and creative professionals employed in the high-tech sector, financial services, the legal and health care professions, and business management. Florida writes that many businesses understand what is necessary to attract creative-class employees – including relaxed dress codes, flexible schedules, and new work rules in the office, but that most civic leaders have failed to understand that 'what is true for corporations is also true for cities and regions.'[53]

Florida asks why some regions become destinations for the creative class while others do not. His answer: as economists speak of the importance of industries having 'low entry barriers,' it is similarly important for a place or a region to have low entry barriers for creative people – that is, to be a place where newcomers and creative people are accepted quickly into all sorts of social and economic arrangements. He maintains that regions 'that thrive in today's world tend to be plug-and-play communities where anyone can fit in quickly. These are places where people can find opportunity, build support structures, be themselves, and not get stuck in any one identity. The plug-and-play community is one that somebody can move into and put together a life – or at least a facsimile of a life – in a week.'[54]

Lester Thurow argues that recent developments in the information and high technology fields and, by ricochet, the capacity to generate new knowledge have had a profound impact on the location of economic activity. Capital and natural resources were the key factors. Coal could be mined only where it could be found, and capital-intensive products were more likely than not produced in resource-rich regions or close to markets. Today brainpower industries need not have pre-determined homes, and new economic activities are increasingly free geographically.

There is no doubt that the knowledge industries are reshaping the economy, much like the industrial revolution did a few hundred years ago. In the preindustrial era, people who owned land made the important economic decisions. In the industrial era, people who had the capital made the important decisions. In the postindustrial era, people who possess knowledge or can manage new knowledge will make the important decisions. Knowledge and some luck, not land or capital, made Bill Gates. Bill Gates is the world's wealthiest individual but, as Thurow points out, he owns nothing tangible – no land, no gold, no oil, no factories – he only owns knowledge. Knowledge made Silicon Valley, developments along Route 128 near Boston, and many new activities in the Carolinas. Thurow writes: 'Silicon Valley and Route 128 are where they are simply because that is where the brainpower is. They have nothing else going for them.'[55]

Tom Courchene, in his *State of Minds*, stresses human capital as key to economic competitiveness from a Canadian perspective.[56] He challenges policy makers to make Canada the world's foremost human capital society. He argues that we must rethink our machinery of government by moving away from a postindustrial production system and towards human capital production. He writes: 'It is inappropriate to tuck concerns relating to the information economy and human capital somewhere under the umbrella of Industry Canada. Rather, the reverse is appropriate for a GIR- (Globalization and the Knowledge Information Revolution) and social-cohesion-consistent approach – we ought to nestle Industry Canada, and industrial policy initiatives generally, within an overarching human capital and information super-ministry. Without such a conceptual rethinking and restructuring of our policy priorities, we will never make a fully successful transition capable of embracing the challenges and reality of the emerging GIR era, let alone embrace the societal mission statement. Phrased differently, without this accommodating shift in the mind of state, we will not make the societal transition to a state of minds.'[57]

Looking Back

A number of compelling messages emerge from our survey of the theoretical literature: we are in an era of extreme fluidity and flexibility regarding location of industry, agglomeration and deglomeration, integration and disintegration, polarization and 'polarization-reversal.' The only principles that seem to prevail are 'it depends' and 'anything goes.' We are also in an era of extreme fluidity and flexibility when it comes to shaping public policy in the regional economic development field.

Still, our review discovered no theory that is just plain *wrong*, in the sense of being internally inconsistent, disobeying the rules of logic, flagrantly conflicting with the known facts, or having been definitively disproved by standard empirical tests. For example, we argue that the 'base industry + export multiplier' (b.i.e.m.) theory could not be accepted as a *general* theory of regional economic development; somewhere, sometime, expansion must take place in a region where its growth cannot be traced to an increase of imports into another region. Once that happens, but only if that happens, a chain reaction may set in which affects many regions. However, if we combine b.i.e.m. with a theory of development through innovations, of the Schumpeter or Perroux type, and apply both types of theory at the regional level, we can certainly *explain* the development of some regions in some periods in that fashion. Expansion of the steel industry in response to growth of the automobile industry, bolstered by proximity to coal, iron, and industrial water, certainly goes a long way towards *explaining* the development of the Pittsburgh region in the first half of the twentieth century. The b.i.e.m. theory could also show how growth of the automobile industry in Detroit and Flint brought development to northern Sumatra, through expansion of rubber plantations and innovations in rubber planting and processing.

It follows that all the theories presented provide some understanding of how things are and why. Ultimately, however, we are interested in theories that help policy makers and regional development planners improve the outcome of measures taken to encourage the development of particular regions.

In the various cases that we have considered, very few carried any particular theory through to the prescriptive stage or provided a strong guidance to policy makers – except, perhaps, a somewhat bastardized version of the 'growth pole' or 'growth centre' doctrine and the literature on entrepreneurship. Does that mean that the theories are useless, or even wrong? Not at all. In the first place, the guiding principle behind all scientific investigation is pushing back the frontiers of knowledge, or contributing to the *understanding* of observed phenomena in the universe. When Einstein pieced together his theory of relativity, he was not thinking of the atom bomb or nuclear power plants. All the theories presented in this chapter contribute to our understanding of the functioning of a market economy. They also indicate how powerful are the forces at work that determine the geographical distribution of economic activity. The policy maker who would utilize these forces (if he or she considers them benign) or offset or alter them (if he or she considers them malign) must first understand them. Most of our cases indicate some dissatisfaction with the operation of the market – whether due to 'market failure' or 'government failure' – and constitute efforts to bring about better results through intervention of one sort or another. Our survey of Canada's regional economic development efforts reveals that one can see at least some traces of all theories outlined above. The federal government has, for example, tried Perroux's growth-pole concept in the Maritime provinces, a variation of the interregional and international trade theory (Department of Regional Economic Expansion and regional comparative advantages), and Schumpeter's entrepreneurship (Atlantic Canada Opportunities Agency).

The builders of neo-classical micro-theory were, for the most part, not really interested in application. They were devoted to the analysis and exposition of the manner in which the market functions. Many of them stopped there. Those who went on to consider policy split into two groups: those who thought that the market works very well in the absence of misguided government intervention, and those who thought that the market works rather badly in the absence of astute management and good policy. In his 1978 presidential address to the American Economics Association, Robert Solow commented on this fundamental split among mainstream economists. The policy recommendation of the first group was laissez-faire, and, as Joan Robinson explained, 'logical structures of this kind have a certain charm. They allow those without mathematics to catch a hint of what intellectual beauty means ... [but] apart from the advocacy of Free Trade there was not much to say on practical questions. The policy recommended was laissez-faire, and there was no need to describe in any detail how to do nothing.'[58] The other group proposed various kinds of intervention to deal with unemployment, inflation, economic fluctuations, inequalities, health, education, housing, and so on.

Because much regional economic development theory, particularly that produced in recent years, is derived from neo-classical theory, we should not be surprised that the same dichotomy should appear in regional theory as in general economics. The 'laissez-faire' school argues that the market, left to itself, will bring about a kind of 'Pareto optimum' in the distribution of economic activity in space and so has no recommendation beyond to 'leave the market alone.' For them, 'do nothing' is the application of theory to regional policy.

Putting aside Perroux and Schumpeter for a moment, one could easily conclude that too many theorists and practitioners have been working in isolation from one another. One could also conclude that many theorists, particularly since the late 1970s, have thrown up their hands and given up. The wave of neo-conservative thinking, the election of right-of-centre politicians, the disenchantment with the performance of public bureaucracies, and the difficult fiscal positions of most governments in Anglo-American democracies explain why a good number of theorists have given up and turned to the market to bring about the 'Pareto optimum.' As mentioned at the outset of this chapter, Richard Lipsey once observed that for all the political concern about regional disparities and regional development, we do not have an underlying theory.[59] Recently, Albert Breton went further and argued that every government in the world pursues regional development policies even when most economists say that they should not and should instead be encouraging mobility of people.[60] Quite a few theorists now appear to be asking, 'Why can't governments do like us and give up?' But politicians representing slow-growth regions are unlikely to give up, and they will continue to search for solutions. If they are unable to find some that suit, they are likely to invent them.

Underpinning the theories and approaches outlined in this chapter was the view that it is possible to separate governments and the market, to some extent even removing politicians from the task of defining optimal policy prescriptions. Theorists did not begin with the premise that politicians and politics matter, or that the challenge at hand was not one of economics but rather of political economy.

Perroux's concern was to explain patterns of economic development and what could be done to influence these patterns. The regional science literature, which embodies so well mid-twentieth-century techniques of economic analysis, seeks to explain why economic development takes place in certain areas at a given pace. The same is true for other theories, including the international and interregional trade theory.

It takes only a moment's reflection to appreciate that it was hopelessly naive to construct theories, particularly prescriptive ones, in isolation from how the public sector, broadly defined, would respond in implementing them. Keynes, Perroux, and others of like mind may well have been right in thinking that the operation of market forces did not guarantee a harmonious 'equilibrium' in space. To define a new theory to correct this without taking into account the 'behaviour' of the public sector in its implementation was simply a non-starter.

Proponents of the neo-conservative approach are 'equally' naive in thinking that governments would stand idly by and let the unfettered market call the adjustment tune.[61] One can hardly imagine a leader more ideologically committed to neo-conservatism than was Margaret Thatcher. Yet, even she balked at turning over the 'problem' of regional disparities to market forces. No doubt she had to contend with the political realities that government backbenchers continually brought to her attention. Handing over regional economic development to market forces would have meant foregoing funds from the European Economic Community earmarked for Britain's slow-growth regions. Having a political ideology and a neo-conservative agenda is one thing. Heroism, however, is quite another. Heroism would have been required of Thatcher to turn down funds with the risk of seeing them reallocated to a neighbouring country. Even the most ardent believer in market forces will admit that neighbouring countries and regions must play by the same rules for the rules to be effective.

Politicians representing highly developed regions are likely to argue for market forces, while those representing slow-growth regions more often than not support government intervention in the economy. Indeed, it is difficult to imagine many of the latter advocating pure national efficiency measures, at least publicly, even if there were long-term benefits for their own region. The length of political mandates is such that the long-term perspective holds little appeal.

Theorists, even those with a prescriptive bent, also paid little, if any, attention to the role public bureaucracies would be called upon to play to implement the policies and programs. We have precious little literature on how governments should organize themselves to support regional economic development policies. A former minister responsible for regional development in Canada once observed that how government organizes itself for promoting regional economic development efforts is as important as the policy itself.[62]

What can we conclude from all of the above? The literature on regional development has been of limited assistance to policy makers. Leaving aside the work of Perroux, Schumpeter, Courchene, and Florida, there has been a paucity of prescriptive theories and approaches recommended for practitioners to consider. There is all kinds of evidence to suggest that regional economic development policy and efforts have been sustained by politicians. It is not too much of an exaggeration to suggest that they have been left on their own to – as the Economic Council of Canada once argued – 'try this and that.' This, as the next chapters report, is precisely what they have attempted.

4 Trying This

Again, what to do? The literature, as we saw in chapter 3, is rather thin on the ground when it comes to policy and program prescriptions. The neo-conservative school can tell government to do nothing, but there is no need to describe how to do nothing. However, as long as there are politicians in Parliament from slow-growth regions, there will be pressure on government to do something. Perroux's growth-pole concept offered some promise to policy makers, and many tried it, at least for a while. We also saw in chapter 2 the negative impact the National Policy had on the Maritime provinces and that there was a willingness on the part of key policy makers in Ottawa to deal with a situation for which the region was not totally responsible. Yet, they too were not very clear on what ought to be done.

The federal government's response has been to experiment with regional economic development policies, to 'try this and that' in the Maritime region and elsewhere. This and the subsequent four chapters examine in some detail the various policies and programs attempted over the years. We will establish Ottawa's commitment to the Maritime region, discuss the success of the different endeavours, provide an understanding of Ottawa's motivation in the economic development field, and lay the groundwork for new approaches.

The federal government's venture into the field did not begin in earnest until the 1960s. Previously, there had been no overarching strategy and no explicit regional policy or even a consistent approach. Only on the occasions when the situation became over-heated, as with the rise of the Maritime Rights Movement, did Ottawa react to look for practical solutions to defuse the crisis.

It was only with the introduction of equalization payments in 1957 that Ottawa engaged in a concerted attempt to deal with regional disparities. Equalization payments held benefits for the have as well as the have-less regions. For the have regions, it meant that Ottawa would not tinker with where wealth was created. In addition, there was a quid pro quo in the case of Ontario, and, as one student of Ontario politics writes, the 'quo was worth more than the quid.' He writes, 'The time had come to build the St. Lawrence waterway, without delay. Not only would a deepwater canal open Ontario's ports from Cornwall to the Lake-head to international shipping, but the electricity produced by damming the St. Lawrence would satisfy Ontario's electrical needs for a generation. As part of the new spirit of cooperation ... the seaway was an awesome undertaking and [it] boosted the economies of every province and state that bordered it, lowering the cost of Quebec iron ore that now supplied the Hamilton and Sault Ste. Marie steel mills, and opening western grain to eastern exports. The railroads and Halifax paid the price. Ontario reaped the benefit of so much new power that, by the advent of the 1960s, virtually all the province's electricity was generated by water.'[1]

However, equalization payments were designed to help poorer provinces provide better public services, not to assist them with economic development. The latter was addressed by other federal measures that followed. It is important to remember that the mid- and late 1960s were years of strong if uneven growth in the national economy and, relatively speaking, a burgeoning federal treasury. The government moved towards explicit redistributive priorities, as seen in the Canada Pension Plan, the Medical Care Act (medicare), and the Canada Assistance Plan.[2] Keynesian thinking was clearly dominant in Ottawa.

National unity also became a priority with the federal government at this time. The Royal Commission on Bilingualism and Biculturalism tabled a series of reports from 1965 on intended to increase national unity and improve English-French relations. French Canadians, it pointed out, were disadvantaged not just from a cultural perspective but also from an economic one. The commission's report on official languages, published in 1967, concluded, 'We believe the notion of equal partnership connotes a vast enlargement of the opportunities for francophones in both private and public sectors of the economy.'[3]

The Beginning

The 1960 budget speech unveiled the first of many measures Ottawa has developed to combat regional disparities. The budget permitted firms to obtain double the normal rate of capital-cost allowances on most of the assets they acquired to produce new products, if they located in designated regions – that is, those with high unemployment and slow economic growth.[4]

Shortly thereafter, in 1961, Parliament passed the Agricultural Rehabilitation and Development Act (ARDA). This was Ottawa's first 'regional' development program on the spending side. ARDA began as a federal-provincial endeavour to stimulate agricultural development in order to increase income in rural areas. It aimed to do this by providing assistance for alternative use of marginal land, creating work opportunities in rural areas, developing water and soil resources, and setting up projects designed to benefit people engaged in natural-resource industries other than agriculture, such as fisheries. Later, in 1966, the program was renamed the Agricultural and Rural Development Act, and the program's objectives were adjusted. ARDA was expanded to include non-agricultural programs in rural areas, designed to absorb surplus labour from farming.[5]

The Fund for Rural Economic Development (FRED), introduced in 1966, applied only in designated regions – those with widespread low incomes and major problems of economic adjustment.[6] In the end, five regions were identified under FRED: the Interlake region of Manitoba, the Gaspé peninsula in Quebec, the Mactaquac and northeastern regions of New Brunswick, and all of Prince Edward Island. Separate 'comprehensive development plans' were then formulated for those five regions to develop infrastructure and industry.

In 1962 the federal government introduced the Atlantic Development Board (ADB).[7] Unlike other regional development programs, this board would be active only in the four Atlantic provinces, as its name implied. Largely inspired by the Gordon Commission and by the work of former New Brunswick premier Hugh John Flemming, the ADB was initially asked to define measures and initiatives for promoting economic growth and development in the Atlantic region. A planning staff was put together, mainly from within the federal public service. Considerable research was undertaken on the various sectors of the regional economy, and some consultations were held with planners at the provincial level.

Shortly after its creation, the board was given the Atlantic Development Fund to administer. By and large, the fund was employed to assist in the provision or improvement of the region's basic economic infrastructure. Over half of the fund, which totalled $186 million, was spent on highway construction and water and sewerage systems. Some money was spent on electrical generating and transmission facilities and in servicing new industrial parks at various locations throughout the region.

The fund did not provide direct assistance of any kind to private industry to locate new firms in the region. On this point, the ADB was criticized, notably by the Atlantic Provinces Economic Council, in a report published in 1967. It was criticized on other points as well. Some argued that ADB spending was uncoordinated, in that it was never part of a comprehensive plan gearing expenditures towards specific targets. Some said that spending was politically inspired and that in the end it simply became a tool of Jack Pickersgill, a powerful Liberal cabinet minister who represented a Newfoundland. The ADB never did deliver a comprehensive plan for the Atlantic provinces, despite its mandate to do so in 1962. There are a variety of reasons offered for this failure. Some observers suggest that the board was never given the political green light to deliver the plan, while others claim that when the ADB was disbanded in 1969, it was on the verge of coming up with a comprehensive plan.[8]

Other measures to promote regional development came in the form of the Area Development Incentives Act (ADIA) and the Area Development Agency (ADA) within the Department of Industry. Legislation establishing ADA was passed in 1963.[9] The central purpose behind these initiatives was to enlist the private sector in stimulating growth in economically depressed regions. This was to be done by enriching existing tax incentives and by introducing capital grants in designated areas.

ADA targeted regions of high unemployment and slow growth: only regions reporting unemployment rates above a specified threshold would become eligible. Manufacturing and processing firms were then invited to locate or expand operations in these regions. Three kinds of incentives were applied sequentially: accelerated capital-cost allowances, a three-year income-tax exemption, and higher capital-cost allowances. In 1965, a program of cash grants was introduced over and above the capital-cost allowances.

This brief outline of regional development initiatives by the federal government during the 1960s suggests that Ottawa was prepared to intervene directly to stimulate growth in lagging regions. Up until 1957, as we have seen, regional disparities had been analysed by royal commissions but had received little attention in terms of concrete federal action. Within ten years, Ottawa had moved in a very dramatic fashion away from its cautious, conservative, and frugal approach to economic policy to a preoccupation with slow-growth regions.[10] It stacked one initiative upon another in the belief that these would correct the country's substantial regional disparities. The initiatives were modest, provided carrots to the private sector to locate in slow-growth regions, and invested in infrastructure. However, they were all designed for slow-growth regions, and the Maritime provinces became a key target.

Trudeau and National Unity

In 1968 Pierre Elliott Trudeau made national unity his central preoccupation and described it as the single motivating force for his involvement in public life. National unity would dominate the agenda of his new government, and it would – at least initially – extend beyond English-French relations. He boldly declared: 'Economic equality ... [is] just as important as equality of language rights ... If the underdevelopment of the Atlantic provinces is not corrected, not by charity or subsidy, but by helping them become areas of economic growth, then the unity of the country is almost as surely destroyed as it would be by the French-English confrontation.'[11]

Shortly after assuming office, Trudeau called a general election and campaigned vigorously on the theme of national unity. The Liberal Party was returned to power with a strong majority after five years of minority rule. There was no doubt that the new government would give increased priority to regional development, but it was unclear how it would do so. Trudeau appointed Jean Marchand, his trusted Quebec lieutenant, as the minister responsible for regional development and Tom Kent, a powerful figure in Ottawa, as deputy minister. Kent had played a key role in the Liberal Party when it was in opposition and later became principal secretary to Prime Minister Pearson. Early in its policy deliberations, the cabinet decided to direct its regional development priorities towards eastern Canada. Jean Marchand stated that something like 80 per cent of the new expenditures should be spent east of Trois-Rivières. Only 'modest and controlled' expenditures should be directed to the slow-growth northern and northwestern areas of Ontario, Manitoba, and the northern parts of the three most western provinces. This decision was inspired not simply by the political thinking of the new Trudeau government, but also by economic circumstances. Even cabinet ministers representing constituencies between Windsor and Quebec City agreed that national unity was threatened when heavy and persistent unemployment plagued some regions at the same time that the economy in central Canada was buoyant, to the point of strong inflationary pressure.[12] It was relatively easy at the time to subscribe to the goal of dispensing economic growth widely, so as to bring the slow-growth regions as close as possible to those in the rest of the country without substantially slowing national growth.

The cabinet settled on François Perroux's 'growth-pole' concept to define the new policy.[13] The rationale was simple. The main difference between, say, Ontario and the Maritime provinces, according to Marchand, was that Ontario had major urban centres with vigorous economic growth to which people from northern Ontario could move. The Maritimes had few cities capable of strong growth and of providing employment; consequently, many people remained in economically depressed rural areas. The growth-pole concept, it was believed, could create new opportunities at selected urban centres. Economic growth would take place through movement and change within regions, rather than between regions.

Ottawa would implement the growth-pole concept through two new programs: the special areas program and the Regional Development Incentives Act (RDIA).[14] The two shared the same objective: to encourage manufacturing and processing industry in the slow-growth regions. Industrial centres with the potential for attracting manufacturing and processing firms would be chosen. A special area agreement with the relevant provincial government would then be signed. The agreement would provide for construction or improvement of the infrastructure – roads, water and sewer systems, and schools – within which industrial growth could occur.

With the infrastructure in place, the regional industrial incentives program, through cash grants, would be able to attract new manufacturing industry to the selected centres. The cash grants would lower the cost of setting up production, compensating the investor for locating in economically weak regions. The grant would be sufficiently large that the new production facility would generate the same return on investment that it would have had the firm located in southern Ontario without the grant.

Cash grants constituted a tried and proven approach (under the ADA program) and provided the entrepreneur a basis from which to determine whether the new facility would be economically sound. The new government discarded other possibilities because of significant shortcomings. Continuing government assistance – interest subsidies,

private-sector loans, or large transportation subsidies for finished goods
– was considered both too difficult to administer and politically unacceptable. The government also felt that income-tax credits or tax allowances were of limited benefit to new or smaller firms generating only
modest profits in their early years.[15]

Defining DREE: Central Agency or Line Department?

When Prime Minister Trudeau turned to Jean Marchand to spearhead
the government's regional development priority, he sent an important
message to his cabinet and the public service – regional development
was a key government priority. Trudeau, Marchand, and Gérard Pelletier
had all come to federal politics largely because of what they saw as
unacceptable cultural and linguistic inequalities and regional economic
disparities in Canada. Once he became prime minister, Trudeau turned
to Pelletier, his secretary of state, to oversee the government's language
policies and to Marchand to implement the new regional development
policy.

Marchand became minister of forestry and rural development after
the 1968 election but work began immediately on laying the framework
for a new department. Essentially, three options were considered. The
first was a super department of regional development with the necessary clout to get other federal departments to contribute to regional
development through their own programs, a program-delivery capacity of its own, and an ability to deal with provincial governments. The
second option would have brought together all the various regional
development agencies and programs into the Department of Manpower and Immigration, renamed Manpower and Regional Development. The third option was a typical line department, able both to
deliver programs and to negotiate with the provinces, but with an
uncertain ability to influence other federal departments and agencies.

Marchand later reported that the first option was preferred until the
very last moment. The proposal, not unexpectedly, met with stiff opposition from the Ottawa bureaucracy, more specifically from officials in
the Privy Council Office (PCO).[16] To a purist, the proposal was organi-
zationally untidy, since there would be two administrative structures
located in separate organizations, but with one reporting both to the
prime minister and to a cabinet minister.[17] This situation was simply
unheard of in Canadian public administration, and, given the traditionally incremental bias of PCO officials, it was viewed with a great deal of

suspicion. It is the conventional view in Ottawa that a minister cannot be responsible for programs and their fund seeking while at the same time having coordination authority over the programs of his or her cabinet colleagues. Such a situation would give the minister an unfair advantage over colleagues in that he or she could 'put on a coordination hat' to promote his or her own programs. It is precisely for this reason that the minister of finance and the president of the treasury board have had no programs to administer.

Marchand now reports that both the prime minister and he were prepared to overlook these administrative 'niceties' in order to ensure that regional development would be given the intended priority. In the end, they rejected the proposal for quite another reason. It was clear to everyone that Marchand would wield considerable power in the new administration without any kind of special coordination authority over his cabinet colleagues. Apart from assuming responsibility for regional development, he was named the regional minister responsible for Quebec.

Regional ministers have influence over political decisions and patronage. Cabinet ministers responsible for the two larger regions, Ontario and Quebec, are even more influential, not simply because of the political and economic weight of their regions, but also because of the number of seats they have. Trudeau's principal political advisers feared that adding still more to Marchand's prestige and power by having part of his department located within the PMO and PCO and by giving him a special coordinating role over the policies and programs of his cabinet colleagues would divide the cabinet. It would, in their view, place the prime minister in a very difficult position with his cabinet and lead to personality conflicts that would be particularly difficult for him to resolve. In the end, it was agreed that the new department would be a traditional line department.

There were other reasons why in the end Marchand and Kent favoured this option. A strongly entrenched and weighty line department would be better able to lead an interdepartmental effort than would a new central agency or partial central agency. What was envisaged was the kind of industry department that C.D. Howe had turned into the effective power centre in Ottawa and, indeed, in the Canadian economy. Moreover, an established department would provide a ready-made capacity and strength to plan and deliver programs quickly and avoid reliance on weak and diverse units of the old regional groups.

DREE – The Early Years

Marchand expected little difficulty from Parliament in getting new Department of Regional Economic Expansion (DREE) legislation passed, and on this he was correct. If anything, the opposition urged him to go even further than the proposals he presented to Parliament. The new Progressive Conservative leader, Robert Stanfield, was a former premier of Nova Scotia. He reportedly entered federal politics because of his commitment to regional development, much as Trudeau had entered politics to secure Quebec's place in Confederation. To the extent that one is able to do so in the usually highly partisan House of Commons, Stanfield was generally supportive of Marchand's proposals. He expressed concern, however, that DREE would be left alone to carry the entire load of promoting regional development, while other federal departments simply went on with their own sectoral responsibilities. Said Stanfield, 'There may very well be a tendency on the part of other Ministers to say "Let Jean do it" ... This bill does not assure anything like the degree of coordination which there must be among the departments of the government if regional disparity is to be attacked effectively.' The New Democratic Party offered little in the debate. Its leader, Tommy Douglas, lamented the lack of new and specific goals in establishing DREE. These ill-defined goals, he insisted, did not require a government reorganization. 'There is little advantage in talking about government reorganization,' he said, 'unless we know what it is the government is seeking to accomplish.'[18]

Both the prime minister and Marchand dismissed these criticisms. Trudeau argued that the establishment of DREE was necessary 'to achieve real coordination ... of our endeavours and undertakings in such a worthy and vital sphere in respect of our country's future.' Marchand added that his new department 'was the only way to secure the coordination of federal efforts' in regional development.[19]

Political criticism of DREE and its new policy direction came more often and with more conviction from government backbenchers than from the opposition. Members of Parliament representing economically depressed constituencies in rural Quebec and northern New Brunswick, many of whom were Liberals, feared that the emphasis on growth centres would leave their regions with little federal funding for development initiatives. The new approach represented a clear departure from the old regional development policy, in that ARDA and FRED had been designed expressly for their regions or for rural slow-growth regions. Marchand sought to allay MPs' concerns by arguing that his policy would put in place the urban and industrial structures required to give their provinces a new economic depth and strength. Once this was done, attention could then be given to the economically depressed rural areas or, more specifically, to their constituencies. In short, Marchand assured them that with time their turn would come.[20]

Two points in the DREE legislation need to be highlighted. Curiously, it said little about the goals of the new department. There was no indication, for example, of whether an increase in income levels in slow-growth regions, greater productivity, or even higher employment levels should be specifically pursued. The wording said merely that special areas could be designated when an area 'in ... [a] province is determined to require, by reason of the exceptional inadequacy of opportunities for productive employment special measures to facilitate economic expansion and social adjustment.'[21] The geographical dimension of special areas was not laid out, even in broad terms. There was no mention of the targets to be reached, or when the special-area designation would no longer be necessary.

Defining areas or regions, or, to put it more crudely, deciding who is 'in' and who is 'out' of development schemes, is always politically explosive. There was no doubt a political explanation for Marchand's not defining clearly in the legislation which regions would qualify for the special-areas program. He had already been told in no uncertain terms by many Liberal MPs that they were not pleased with his policy direction, given its focus on growth poles and, by ricochet, urban areas. A minister quickly discovers that such debates, particularly when they involve party colleagues, are more suited to the government lobby behind the House than inside, in full view of the opposition and journalists. Why then invite such a possibility by naming designated regions in a bill before the House? Doing so would serve only to force certain government members to defend the interests of their constituencies and thus openly speak against a government bill.

Similarly, ministers and permanent officials are never keen on laying out before Parliament or the general public specific indicators that reveal to what extent goals are being reached.[22] If results fall short of the stated goal, the minister and his or her department are politically vulnerable. Partisan politics being what they are, it is always preferable to be rather vague about objectives.

The DREE legislation provided flexibility – which was precisely what

Marchand was seeking. Special areas could be designated after simply 'consulting' the relevant provincial government. The format for federal-provincial consultation was not defined, and there were no restrictions placed on the kind of projects that DREE could sponsor in a designated area. Marchand had a free hand to set the tone for these negotiations and for the kind of projects deemed acceptable by DREE.

DREE was able to limit the number of designated special areas to twenty-three, and each became the subject of a federal-provincial agreement. Six of the special areas were expected to realize substantially faster industrial growth than the others, as a result of the incentives programs, and these were singled out in order to provide the infrastructure needed to support this growth. These six areas were St John's, Halifax-Dartmouth, Saint John, Moncton, Quebec City, and Trois-Rivières. Because of their locations, Regina and Saskatoon were also designated to assist in financing surrounding community development. In Newfoundland, the Burin Peninsula, Gander, Stephenville, Hawke's Bay, Come-by-Chance, and Goose Bay (Happy Valley) were designated in order to make them more attractive as 'receiving centres' under the Newfoundland Resettlement Program. The Pas and Meadow Lake in Manitoba and Lesser Slave Lake in Alberta were designated for industrial incentives to promote the development of resource industries and to improve community facilities, particularly to the advantage of the Indian and Metis populations. The Renfrew-Pembroke area in Ontario and Lac St-Jean in Quebec were designated for industrial incentives, for which they were not eligible under the regular incentives program. Finally, the Ste-Scholastique area, outside Montreal, was designated, as a result of the federal government's decision to construct a new international airport in the area.[23] In this case, assistance was provided to the province to put in place the extensive infrastructure that was required.

These special-area agreements sponsored a great variety of projects: highways, water and sewage systems, industrial parks, tourist attractions, servicing of industrial land, and schools. The federal government covered 50 per cent of the cost of certain projects, plus a loan for part or all of the remainder. In the case of highway construction, Ottawa paid up to 100 per cent of the cost. The great majority of projects involved infrastructure. A new industrial park was built in St John's, as were new water and sewer systems, a new arterial highway, and a new high school. Similarly, in other special areas of the province, nearly all the DREE funds were allocated to new water and sewer systems, roads, industrial parks, and schools. The pattern established in Newfound-

land was followed elsewhere. The Halifax-Dartmouth area, for example, saw some sixty-five projects exclusively for roads, sewer and
water systems, and school construction.

The Regional Development Incentives Program

The second major initiative developed by DREE was the new regional
development incentives program. This program would be discretionary and no longer automatically available to all new production facilities locating in designated areas. Grants would be available for selected
sectors only. The program would also be available over a much wider
area, providing incentives in growth centres and in selected urban areas.

Other features were added. The new program would confine itself to
development grants; would set a maximum level, but also provide for
offers at less than the maximum if circumstances warranted; and would
establish a two-part grant structure, one for capital costs and the other
according to the number of jobs created. Maximum levels for both were
more generous for the Atlantic provinces.[24]

The part of the grant calculated on the basis of jobs created would not
in any way be automatic: large discretionary power was left to the
minister. He could require a company 'to demonstrate' that a grant,
over and above what was available for capital costs, was necessary to
make the project 'viable.' He could also assess the project's contribution
to the economic development of the region and then decide whether or
not a grant should be offered. These provisions were to guard against
windfall profits for companies locating in regions for reasons other than
an incentives grant. In addition, they would permit the minister and
departmental officials to refuse aid to companies that, in their view,
could not stand on their own feet in the long term, regardless of whether
a grant was awarded or not.[25]

Not surprisingly, the most contentious issue confronting the new
program was its geographical applicability. Marchand and Kent were
adamant on two points: first, that the regions designated be sufficiently
limited so as not to dilute the effectiveness of the program to help slow-
growth regions, and, second, that unlike the ADA program, the new
program should apply in growth centres – Halifax, Moncton, Saint
John, and St John's, among others. Their reasoning was tied to the
thinking underpinning the growth-pole concept, which suggests that
'nothing succeeds like success.' New enterprises would have strong
economic reasons for preferring to locate where other firms already

existed, since these would help to finance all kinds of overhead for transportation and community service. A business, particularly if its technology is sophisticated, may run into difficulties by locating in an area with little other industrial activity. These obvious facts, argued Marchand, are the basis of the 'growth centre' or 'industrial centre' approach to development; the chances of starting a growth process that will become self-sustaining depends largely on whether industrial incentives can be concentrated on the stimulation of 'families' of projects at relatively few localities, rather than a series of projects spread over countless little communities.[26]

Regions designated for the program included all the Atlantic provinces, eastern and northern Quebec, parts of northern Ontario, and the northernmost regions of the four western provinces. Thus, regions were designated in all ten provinces, and this for a three-year period, ending 30 June 1972. The regions designated accounted for about 30 per cent of the Canadian labour force, and the average per capita income within them was approximately 70 per cent of the national average. On the face of it, this coverage may appear excessive in terms of the program's regional applicability, considering the purpose of the growth-pole concept.

However, initially at least, Marchand and Kent got what they wanted. They now report that they were successful in limiting the program's coverage to areas they had first envisaged. Parts of Ontario, Alberta, and British Columbia were designated more as a gesture to ensure that these provinces would not feel completely left out of a federal government program. Marchand and Kent feared that these provinces, given their relatively strong fiscal positions, might establish their own incentives programs, thereby greatly inhibiting the new federal initiative. In any event, the regional incentives program would be complementary to the larger, more expensive special-areas program. With the benefits of these two programs combined, it was felt, industrialists would dismiss smaller communities out of hand and opt for the growth-pole areas to locate new plants. Certainly, viewed with the benefit of hindsight, regional designation of DREE's industrial incentives program in 1969 was highly restrictive.

It was not long before strong political pressure was exerted on Marchand to extend the program's regional designations further. Cabinet ministers and MPs from the Montreal area frequently made the point that Montreal was Quebec's growth pole and that if DREE were serious about regional development, then it ought to designate Montreal under its industrial incentives program. Ministers from other regions did not share this view and did not hesitate to say so to Marchand and to the full cabinet.

Montreal's growth performance rate was not keeping pace with expectations, particularly those of the large number of Liberal MPs from the area. The city's unemployment rate stood at 7.0 per cent in 1972, compared with 4.6 per cent for Toronto. Further, Quebec's economic strength, Quebec MPs argued time and again, was directly linked to Montreal, and, unless new employment opportunities were created there, little hope was held for the province's peripheral areas. Montreal required special measures, they argued, to return to a reasonable rate of growth.

In the end, Marchand chose to designate Montreal as a special region, known as 'region C.' In this newly designated region, which consisted of southwestern Quebec, including what was then Hull (now Gatineau) and Montreal, and three counties of eastern Ontario, the maximum incentive grant was lower than elsewhere. The grant could not exceed 10 per cent of approved capital costs, plus $2,000 for each direct job created. Elsewhere in the designated regions of Quebec and Ontario, the maximum incentive grant was fixed at 25 per cent of approved capital costs and $5,000 for each new job created. A third level of assistance was established for the Atlantic region, which called for a maximum grant of 35 per cent of capital costs and $7,000 per job created. Finally, the changes stipulated that region C's special designation was to be for two years only. This, it was felt, would be sufficient to help Montreal return to a 'reasonable rate of growth.'[27] The changes, however, extended coverage of the designated regions to about 40 per cent of the population and almost 45 per cent of manufacturing employment and established a three-level hierarchy of incentive grants.

The two-year designation for Montreal quickly generated strong interest and a high number of applicants. During the 1971–2 fiscal year, the 360 incentive grants accepted by different firms in the new region C involved capital expenditures of over $225 million and the creation of some 14,000 new jobs. By comparison, 129 DREE incentives grants were accepted by firms in the four Atlantic provinces, involving capital expenditures of over $48 million and the expected creation of slightly less than 5,000 new jobs during the same period.[28]

The legislation for the incentives program provided for a termination date; projects had to come into commercial production by 31 December 1976. This was to ensure that a review of the program would take place no later than 1974. As has already been noted, the legislation did not establish the designated regions clearly. Changes could and in fact were introduced through orders-in-council, thus simply requiring cabinet approval. The minister had the same kind of flexibility in designating new areas that he had for the special-areas program.

In formulating the two new programs, DREE had to meet the requirements of Ottawa's central agencies and its expenditure-control process. This DREE did by providing some rather rough calculations of its financial requirements. 'Money was simply no problem in those days,' Marchand and former DREE officials report.[29] Marchand and Kent had secured from the Treasury Board all the funds they required – and then some.

In fact, it soon became obvious that the department would not be able to spend all its allocated budget. Special projects were approved from time to time to prop up the department's expenditure level. As we have already seen, special short-term agreements for highway construction were signed with the Atlantic provinces. This is not to suggest that such projects were supportive of DREE's growth-pole policy. They simply accommodated some concerns on the part of the Atlantic provinces and enabled DREE to spend its allocated budget. DREE, because of Marchand and Kent, could get projects through the government's expenditure approval process with relative ease and alacrity, because of who they were and because the prime minister had made it clear that regional development held a strong priority in the government's scheme of things. Money was simply no problem for DREE, and everybody in Ottawa was made aware of this. Moreover, DREE's spending gave the federal government a great deal of favourable visibility.

DREE's two major programs were designed in part to attract maximum public awareness to federal spending. In the case of the special-areas program, the federal government had clearly taken the lead, with the provinces adjusting their priorities to reflect the program's requirements. Marchand took an aggressive posture with the provinces, and which did not go unnoticed by the press.

The regional incentives program meanwhile lent itself quite readily to placing the federal government in a favourable light. It allocated grants directly to private investors, thereby bypassing provincial governments and enabling the federal government to occupy the limelight. The program also offered countless opportunities for government ministers and MPs to go back home on weekends to announce that X number of jobs would be created through a government grant and subsequently to attend ribbon-cutting ceremonies.

However, after three or four years, it became obvious that all was not well. In fact, by late 1971, a fair amount of public criticism was being hurled at DREE. Regions not designated as special areas were arguing more and more that they too could use federal financing for economic development. To many in the non-designated regions, it seemed that the federal government was, in effect, saying that only selected regions should grow and that Ottawa's economic development efforts would be concentrated there.

Policy makers concluded that Perroux had sold them a bill of goods. Rural areas and their MPs were angry, as there was little evidence that growth poles or centres were taking flight economically. For his part, Perroux must have concluded that policy makers were hopelessly naive. How could they possibly believe that designating Bathurst, New Brunswick, could generate propulsive effects? The result is that the divide between theory and practice grew. Policy makers worked feverishly to put in place measures that would work, that would have a positive impact in a relatively short period of time (less than four years). Theorists simply kept working at their own pace, on issues that mattered a great deal to them. They were not in the business of producing policy and program prescriptions.

Most, if not all, provincial governments were also critical of DREE. The no-nonsense 'take it or leave it' approach adopted by Marchand and Kent did not sit well with the provinces. The call for a closer form of federal-provincial cooperation was made time and again. Regional development efforts were being extended to cover more and more of Canada's regions. They would become part of Ottawa's effort to promote national unity and to show Quebec that Canadian federalism was rentable or viable to that province.

In brief, the early years of Canada's plunge into regional economic development would set the stage for what was to follow. It would become an important part of Ottawa's drive for national unity, no effort would be made to establish goals or objectives, and the important decisions for policy makers had more to do with the geographical application of the measures than anything else. There was also a sincere desire to come up with an approach that would finally crack the problem of regional disparity. This hope would continue to underpin future efforts, as the next chapters reveal. A new concern would, however, emerge – the need to protect the national economy, which came to be read as Ontario's regional economy.

5 Trying That

The Liberal government regrouped in Ottawa after the 1972 election, badly shaken and barely clinging to power. It had won 109 seats to the Conservatives' 107, losing over 40 seats in English Canada and suffering some humiliating defeats in traditionally safe Liberal seats.[1] Its clear parliamentary majority had been reduced to an almost untenable minority position. Regional economic development thus became a pivotal part of the government's strategy to win back the support of the electorate and, given its position in Parliament, to win it back in a hurry. Adjustments were required, and Trudeau quickly made them. During the campaign, much had been made of excessive 'French power' in Ottawa. In his new cabinet, Trudeau moved Gérard Pelletier from Secretary of State to Communications and Jean Marchand from Regional Economic Expansion to Transport. As well, the cabinet immediately called for new policy initiatives in regional economic development.

The 1972–3 DREE Policy Review

The prime minister appointed another powerful political figure to head DREE, Don Jamieson from Newfoundland and Labrador.[2] Jamieson decided to pursue an overhaul of the government's regional development efforts.

From an economic perspective, the growth-pole concept was now out of favour in Ottawa; the new password to DREE funds was 'developmental opportunities.' DREE would pursue 'viable' opportunities whether they were in urban or rural areas, though it would be preferable if they were located in slow-growth regions, and these would still be given priority.

Fifteen major policy papers were prepared. They were all written inside the federal government, under the guidance of a senior official. There were hardly any public consultations as the new approach took shape, and the bulk of the policy work was done in-house. The review reached several major conclusions and put forward a number of sweeping recommendations. The most important, and one that was stressed time and again, was that in regional economic development close federal-provincial cooperation was essential. In many ways federal policy was redefined to mean federal-provincial relations in economic development with an emphasis on have-less provinces. To promote this policy, the review recommended that DREE decentralize its operations to provincial capitals. The concept of 'identification and pursuit of development opportunities,' the policy review suggested, should guide DREE's new approach: each region was unique and required special measures formulated so as to take full advantage of the opportunities presented. Federal and provincial departments and agencies should also participate in a comprehensive fashion in promoting regional development.[3] The 'identification and pursuit of development opportunities' meant a kind of free-for-all, both in terms of projects that could be sponsored and where they could be supported.

Politically, the outcome of the policy review held strong appeal. Badly mauled in the west in the recent election, the Liberal government would be able to increase its presence there in the high-profile field of economic development. In fact, DREE prepared a number of background documents for the western provinces, and the department was deliberately associated with the highly publicized Conference on Western Economic Opportunities, held in 1973. Under the direction of Justice Minister Otto Lang (Saskatchewan's regional minister in the cabinet), the conference was designed to give Ottawa a better understanding of western opportunities and economic problems and to increase the Liberal Party's political visibility in the West.

A delivery mechanism, or a new administrative structure, was required to implement the new policy. It had to be flexible. Developmental opportunities would not, in some instances, provide long lead-time for planning purposes. They could surface spontaneously, and an ability to respond to them in a flexible manner was essential.

The General Development Agreements (GDAs)

DREE came up with a new decision-making approach with all the features the new policy required. It was remarkably flexible, capable of supporting any imaginable type of government activity. It provided for the participation of any interested federal department and for close federal-provincial liaison, with either level of government able to propose initiatives.

Negotiated by Ottawa with any province, a GDA provided a broad statement of goals for both levels of government to pursue, outlined the priority areas, and described how joint decisions would be taken.[4] GDAs were enabling documents only and did not in themselves provide for specific action; projects and precise cost-sharing arrangements were instead presented in subsidiary agreements that were attached to the umbrella-type GDAs.

No GDA was signed with Prince Edward Island, since that province had already signed a fifteen-year development plan with Ottawa in 1969. From a strictly administrative point of view, all nine GDAs with the other provinces were basically similar. Each had a ten-year life span; each stipulated that DREE and the provincial government in question would, on a continuing basis, review the socioeconomic circumstances of the province; and each outlined a similar process for joint federal-provincial decision making. They differed only in cost sharing for subsidiary agreements. Under the GDA approach, DREE was granted the following authority to share the cost of a subsidiary agreement: up to 90 per cent for Newfoundland, 80 per cent for Nova Scotia and New Brunswick, 60 per cent for Quebec, Manitoba, and Saskatchewan, and 50 per cent for Ontario, Alberta, and British Columbia.

Subsidiary agreements were presented in the same format as was the GDA. One section outlined the administrative-legal requirements of the agreement, another stipulated that both levels of government develop and implement a program of public information about projects and activities under the agreement, and yet another specified that the two levels of government must fully exchange information on 'any and all aspects of the work undertaken under the agreement.'[5] Moreover, all subsidiary agreements had a schedule (A) that presented the estimated cost as well as the federal-provincial cost-sharing arrangement, and some had a schedule (B) detailing the strategy of and the projects involved in the agreement.

The Decentralization of DREE

In announcing DREE's new approach in 1973, Don Jamieson stated that decentralization of DREE's operations and decision-making authority was not only desirable but indeed made necessary by the demands that the GDAs would invariably generate. The GDAs were to involve joint decision making and required DREE to participate in joint federal-provincial analyses of regional and provincial economic circumstances and opportunities. Such work, it was felt, would be superior, and economic circumstances better understood, if federal officials lived in the regions. Thus, the size of the Ottawa head office was substantially reduced, four regional offices were established, and the ten existing provincial offices were considerably strengthened. With only two assistant deputy ministers left in Ottawa – one responsible for planning and coordination and the other for administrative and financial services – the reorganization left the head office to 'coordinate and support field activities.'

With some modifications made for the Quebec and Ontario regional offices, as these two regions consisted of single provinces, a basic organizational structure was developed for the four regional offices. They had little in the way of programs to deliver and were simply to provide staff support to provincial DREE offices and to conduct general economic analysis and research of their regions.

Action and authority were delegated to the ten provincial offices. In fact, under the reorganization, these received nearly complete authority in program implementation and 'most of the responsibility for programme formulation.'[6] Unlike the early days of DREE, when the Ottawa planning division negotiated agreements directly with provincial governments and afterward delegated some implementing authority to the local offices, the provincial director-general and his office would represent the focal point of contact on 'all issues' involving DREE and the provincial government. In other words, DREE provincial offices would in future lead all DREE activities affecting their respective provinces. Regional and Ottawa-based DREE officials would have to channel their development relations or policy ideas through the provincial offices and refrain from contacting provincial governments directly.

The decentralization of DREE was designed to transform the Ottawa head office into a 'staff' one and to transfer much of the decision-making authority to the field offices, which were to assume 'line' responsibilities for developing and implementing the department's policies and programs. The intention was to reverse the ratio of head office staff to field office staff from 70:30 to 30:70. Such a massive decentralization was unparalleled in the history of Canadian public administration. DREE could not draw on past experience in establishing its new organizations. As one former senior DREE official observed, decentralization 'involved a move into uncharted water.'[7]

Implementing the GDA Approach

With the GDA concept approved by the cabinet and with the new procedures for federal-provincial cooperation defined, Don Jamieson began a cross-country tour to negotiate individual GDAs. Considerable consultation between DREE officials and provincial government officials had already taken place, and the substance of the proposed GDAs was fairly well defined. Provincial governments by and large reacted favourably to the new approach. They were relieved to see DREE move away from the special-areas concept and, at least publicly, commit itself to close federal-provincial liaison.

Nevertheless, the provinces foresaw potential problems. Those in the east feared that by moving into all regions of the country, DREE would lessen its commitment to Atlantic Canada. Jamieson sought to reassure them, stating both in public and in private meetings with the premiers that areas of naturally high growth will not be the concern of DREE. This of course did not exclude large areas of northern Ontario, Manitoba, and northern Saskatchewan, Alberta, and British Columbia. British Columbia and Alberta did not know quite what to make of DREE's sudden interest in the economic health of their provinces. DREE officials there have reported that initially they had considerable difficulty in starting a dialogue with provincial officials on the problems of the less-developed regions of their provinces, let alone bringing about intergovernmental cooperation and new program initiatives for these regions. In addition, a number of provincial governments, both east and west, at first were not quite sure what to make of DREE's intention to establish large offices in provincial capitals. Would it really lead, they asked, to joint efforts, or was it yet another federal attempt to dictate the priorities of provincial governments?

The minister of DREE signed six GDAs with the provinces in the eight weeks between early February and late March 1974. Three others were signed later that year. The premiers of Newfoundland and New Brunswick signed their respective GDAs; the other seven agreements were signed by a cabinet minister.

Virtually every economic sector was covered by the GDAs.[8] In Newfoundland, the GDA sponsored ventures in tourism, forestry, recreation, fisheries, highways, special projects for Labrador, ocean research, special projects for St John's, mineral development, industrial development, rural development, agriculture, and federal-provincial planning. Nova Scotia's GDA supported special projects for the Halifax-Dartmouth

area, the Strait of Canso, and Cape Breton; agricultural, mineral, industrial, forestry, tourism, energy, and dry-dock development; and special
measures for Sydney Steel Corporation and Michelin Tires.

New Brunswick signed subsidiary agreements in support of highway
construction, industrial development, tourism, urban development,
agriculture, pulp and paper and forestry, and so on. The province was
also able to sign subsidiary agreements to cover area or sub-regional
programming, including one for northeastern New Brunswick, the
Miramichi area, Saint John, and Moncton. It is not too much of an
exaggeration to write that for the New Brunswick government, the
GDA came to represent a kind of 'B' budget process from which it could
seek funding for virtually any new economic development.[9] Things
were not much different for several other provinces, as DREE came to
have ten economic development policies, one for each province.[10]

The GDA process continued in this vein right across the country. The
Quebec GDA, for example, led to some fifteen subsidiary agreements,
which in turn gave rise to numerous projects: establishment of news-
print mills, including one in Amos; industrial studies; mineral research
and exploration; construction of a number of industrial parks, including one near Mirabel airport; highway construction; and new tourism
facilities.

Ontario signed several subsidiary agreements. One was designed to
strengthen the urban system of northern Ontario by providing for new
industrial parks and new water and sewer systems in Parry Sound,
Timmins, Sudbury, and North Bay. Another promoted projects to improve forest management, accelerate reforestation, and construct new
forest access roads. Community and rural resource development became the subject of another subsidiary agreement: the Upper Ottawa
Valley and Kirkland Lake area benefited from industrial land development studies, geo-scientific surveys, and hardwood-forest renewal
schemes. A $180-million subsidiary agreement for strengthening the
competitive position of the province's pulp-and-paper industry was
also signed.

The western provinces set up a number of subsidiary agreements
with DREE. Manitoba's concerned development of the province's
northlands, its industrial sector, agriculture, tourism, water development and drought proofing, and the development of the Winnipeg core
area. Saskatchewan signed agreements for the northland, for development of a major tourist attraction in the Qu'Appelle Valley, for water
development and drought proofing, and for long-term development of

its forest industry. Alberta signed six subsidiary agreements with DREE. They involved the processing of nutritive products; attempts to improve incomes, living standards, and community facilities in northern Alberta; and further development of the northern transportation system. In British Columbia, the GDA gave rise to numerous initiatives in highway construction, support of the northeastern coal industry, industrial development, agriculture and rural development, tourism, forest management, and development of the Ridley Island port facility.

The list of GDA projects mounted. Over 130 subsidiary agreements were signed between 1974 and 1982, with a total financial commitment of close to $6 billion. The federal government's share was over $3.3 billion.

There is little doubt that the strength of the GDA system was in its flexibility. One senior DREE official remarked that the problem of regional economic disparity 'is economic and not constitutional.' 'Jurisdictional lines,' he went on, 'ought to be blurred so that appropriate, viable and coordinated measures to stimulate economic development could be brought forward.'[11] The GDAs certainly did this.

Provincial governments in time grew particularly fond of the GDAs. They liked their flexibility and the kind of cooperation that they promoted. They had every reason to do so. When an opportunity presented itself in Halifax for the possible development of a world-class dry-dock facility, DREE and the province simply got together and signed an agreement, and the project went ahead. No program limits existed to restrict their activities. Similarly, Quebec felt that a series of recreational parks would help its tourist industry. DREE agreed, and an agreement was signed involving $76 million of public funds. Ontario, wanting to diversify and stabilize the economics of single-industry communities, turned to DREE and signed a $20-million agreement to put in place a series of infrastructure projects.

Shortly after the introduction of the GDAs, it became clear that the relation between Ottawa and the provinces had been reversed. Unlike the situation under Marchand and Kent, when Ottawa had presented projects in a 'take it or leave it' fashion, provincial governments were now proposing initiatives, and the federal government was reacting. Admittedly, poorer provinces, contributing only 20 per cent of the cost, were never in a position to adopt a cavalier posture vis-à-vis the federal government. Nevertheless, even they were in an enviable bargaining position. If DREE refused to support a particular proposal, the province simply came back with another. Though the GDA system also allowed the federal government to make proposals, this did not occur often.

Another attractive feature of the GDA approach for the less-developed provinces was the cost-sharing formula. With Ottawa contributing 80 to 90 per cent of the cost, virtually any kind of economic initiative became viable. In many ways, Ottawa acted like the Treasury Board – it reviewed proposals from provincial governments, accepting some and rejecting others.

The one recurring criticism levelled at GDAs by the Atlantic provinces was that DREE had spread its efforts too thinly and had moved away from its firm commitment to that region. If one compared DREE spending with the pattern established by Marchand and Kent, then this criticism had some validity. By 1977–8, DREE was spending 39 per cent of its resources in the Atlantic provinces, 31 per cent in Quebec, 5 per cent in Ontario, and 21 per cent in the western provinces. By contrast, in 1970–1, the breakdown had greatly favoured the Atlantic provinces, which received over 50 per cent of DREE funds, with Quebec following at 23 per cent; Ontario received less than 5 per cent, and the western provinces about 16 per cent.[12]

Criticism of the GDAs was heard frequently in Ottawa. Many thought that provincial DREE officials had become too imbued with local attitudes. They were identifying with the interests of provincial governments and were unable to bring a national, or even interprovincial, perspective to their work.[13] They had, at least from an Ottawa stance, 'gone native.' How else could one explain the 'hodge-podge' of projects DREE was supporting? From an Ottawa view, not one of the GDAs pointed to an overall development strategy. They supported rural development if a provincial government favoured it, or tourism projects, or highway construction. Simply put, no one could discern a central and coherent purpose in any of the GDA strategies.

As viewed from Ottawa, provincial DREE and provincial government officials employed the concept of development opportunities to justify whatever project they wanted approved, rather than pursuing a strategy based on a region's strength. Over 50 per cent of DREE's expenditures in the Atlantic provinces went for the provision of infrastructure facilities, in particular highway construction.[14] This was hardly the kind of spending that Finance and Treasury Board officials had expected to see in DREE's pursuit of developmental opportunities or in its mandate to build on the strength of regional economic circumstances. GDA-sponsored initiatives in one province could also be in direct conflict or competition with another in a neighbouring province. Eugene Whelan, former minister of agriculture, put it this way: 'When I was ... in New Brunswick, one thing they [farm organizations] were raising Cain about was the fact that DREE was setting up another operation in another [province] of the Maritimes to produce cabbages ... when they already had a surplus of cabbages ... which they could not get rid of.'[15]

Ottawa-based officials believed that cost-benefit evaluation of proposed GDA initiatives rarely preceded an agreement. Evaluations of shortcomings and accomplishments of projects were also spotty and frequently incomplete. All agreements called for evaluation, but funds for this were often left unused. Some evaluations simply concluded that it was far too early to attempt assessment. Considerable time was necessary before the full impact of the projects could be felt in the economy, and thus a thorough evaluation would not be possible for several years.

The imprecise nature of the goals and objectives of the GDAs and subsidiary agreements further hindered evaluation. The BC GDA had as one of its objectives 'to promote balanced development among areas of British Columbia.' The New Brunswick GDA called for increasing 'per capita incomes while minimizing net migration from the province.' A subsidiary agreement with the Ontario government aimed 'to create a long-term expansion in employment and income opportunities in the Cornwall area.' Given these imprecise objectives, rigorous and clear-cut evaluations were practically impossible.

The hope that the GDA system would constitute a vital federal presence in the provinces was never fulfilled. Most subsidiary agreements were developed by provincial DREE and provincial government officials, with little contribution even from other DREE officials. DREE, and the GDA concept in particular, was also soon confronted with strong opposition from other federal departments, which charged that DREE was moving into their fields of responsibility with initiatives it was ill prepared to carry out. They claimed that interdepartmental consultation was not taking place. One federal minister maintained that DREE had signed a subsidiary agreement with a provincial government in a sector for which she was responsible, without having the courtesy to inform her or even her departmental officials.[16]

If federal-provincial agreements were required to promote growth in a given sector, line departments in Ottawa argued that the relevant sectoral department should negotiate the agreement. Some argued also that federal-provincial agreements were not always necessary and that the line departments could just as easily deliver the projects. On this point, departments were highly critical of DREE, and some of this criticism was voiced in public. For example, Roméo LeBlanc, federal fisheries minister, said: 'I resisted the DREE agreement in fisheries because I found it difficult ... to accept that ... what I could not do in my defined area of responsibility, I find another department ... doing.'[17]

Smaller provincial governments, however, looked at GDA planning differently. In fact, they criticized what they considered the overly elaborate planning involved in developing GDA initiatives.[18] The GDAs entailed more coherent planning than they had been accustomed to, given the size of their governments and the traditionally strong involvement of cabinet ministers in all aspects of government decision making. Provincial officials, unfamiliar with elaborate central agency requirements and processes, wanted to get on with projects and found the federal decision-making process too cumbersome and slow.

After the 1974 election that returned the Trudeau government with a clear majority, Marcel Lessard replaced Don Jamieson as the minister responsible for DREE. Lessard did not wield the kind of political clout that Marchand or Jamieson had done. He was not a regional minister, as were the first two, and he was new in the cabinet, and thus a 'junior minister.' This fact was significant in terms of DREE credibility in the Ottawa 'system.' The signal from Prime Minister Trudeau was that he no longer saw regional development in the same light as he had done when he first came to power. It is doubtful, for example, whether cabinet colleagues would have been as openly critical of DREE as LeBlanc and Whelan were had Marchand or Jamieson been in the portfolio. Lessard did not alter significantly DREE's policy direction or the kind of programs supported under the various GDAs. He was kept busy visiting provincial capitals to attend the annual GDA meetings and to sign new subsidiary agreements. While minister of DREE, Lessard signed more than ten subsidiary agreements each year.

The Regional Development Incentives Program

The regional development incentives program was revised slightly with the advent of the GDA approach in the mid-1970s to make it compatible with the new system. New regions were designated; the program was extended in Manitoba, Saskatchewan, Yukon, the Northwest Territories, Quebec (excluding the Montreal–Hull corridor), and northern Ontario and British Columbia. Provisions were made to offer specialized incentives through the GDA system to support developmental initiatives affecting non-designated areas. The 1972–3 GDA policy review also decentralized the administration of the program down to the provincial-office level. Provincial directors-general were given authority to approve incentive grants of up to $670,000.[19] By and large, however, the incentives program continued to operate much as it had in the past, and it never became an integrated part of the GDA approach.

By 1976, Montreal-area MPs were pressing Marcel Lessard to designate their city under DREE's incentive program. Unemployment in Quebec had risen to 300,000, half of it in the Montreal region. The election of the Parti Québécois in November 1976 resulted in a sudden downturn in private investment in the province and the widespread fear that head offices of major companies would leave Montreal because of proposed language legislation.

When Lessard first went to the cabinet with the proposal to designate Montreal, he met with stiff opposition. If DREE could justify a presence in Montreal, why could it not also justify one for Vancouver and Toronto? Fundamental questions were asked about DREE's mandate and its role in alleviating regional disparities. Cabinet ministers from the Atlantic provinces pointedly referred to Marchand's comment about the necessity of spending 80 per cent of DREE's budget east of Trois-Rivières. How would a Montreal designation affect other regions? Would it still be possible, for example, to attract firms into depressed regions if they could obtain a cash grant for starting new production in Montreal?

Lessard acknowledged that, with considerable help from seven ministers from the Montreal region, including the prime minister, he was finally able to convince the cabinet to designate Montreal under the RDIA program. The argument was simple: the country's unity was at stake and it had to look at its regional development policy from a different perspective. In June 1977, DREE introduced, under the authority of the DREE Act, a discretionary incentives program for selected high-growth manufacturing industries for the Montreal region, with only projects involving a minimum of $100,000 being eligible. Unlike in the Atlantic region, not every new manufacturing or processing facility was to be eligible. Only selected high-growth industries could qualify, including food and beverages, metal products, machinery, transportation equipment, and electrical and chemical products. Projects would be limited by a lower maximum grant than elsewhere: 25 per cent of total capital cost.[20]

In obtaining cabinet approval for Montreal's designation, Lessard gave in to some of his colleagues from other regions and agreed to look at the possibility of designating other regions, including northern areas of British Columbia and the Northwest Territories. He also committed DREE to undertake special development efforts in eastern Ontario, notably the Cornwall area.[21]

DREE Under Attack

By 1978, DREE was being assailed from all sides in Ottawa. The provinces were still generally supportive, although even from them some criticism could be heard. Smaller provincial governments were still finding the GDA process highly bureaucratic and cumbersome and probably better suited to a large bureaucracy like the federal government.[22] In any event, even if provincial governments had been fully supportive, DREE needed the financial support of central agencies in Ottawa and the political support of the prime minister and cabinet. The fact that DREE had a junior and relatively weak minister did not help matters.

Canada was entering a difficult period, both politically and economically. Quebec had elected a separatist government in the fall of 1976. Firmly committed to political sovereignty, the new provincial government had views in direct conflict with those of the prime minister, who was equally firmly committed to a strong central government. The large Quebec Liberal caucus in Ottawa, with few exceptions, endorsed the views of the prime minister. The election of the Parti Québécois thus signalled an out-and-out 'battle for the hearts and minds' of Québécois.[23] DREE was to be caught in this political crossfire, as Quebec was an important client and DREE's major program in the province required close federal-provincial cooperation to be effective.

The country's economic picture had also changed dramatically since DREE was first established. Then few had doubted that the economy would continue to prosper. By 1976, however, the economy was stagnant; unemployment was high and so was the inflation rate. The term *stagflation* had crept into our vocabulary.[24]

Given modest growth, high unemployment, and inflation, some were already beginning to ask whether Ottawa should continue to prop up slow-growth regions through transfer payments and regional development. Were federal cost-sharing agreements inhibiting rather than promoting prosperity in these regions?[25] There was widespread concern in Ottawa that the GDAs had failed to present the national perspective to provincial governments. The GDAs seemed a one-way street; provinces got what they wanted, but not so the federal government. Calls came from some quarters to abolish DREE and find a new strategy more in tune with Canada's current political and economic circumstances. DREE, of course, was well aware of all these forces at play. In its 1978 annual report, the department noted 'Quebec's vulnerability to ... increasing competition from foreign manufactures' and 'the apparent softness of the Ontario economy.' The apparent softness of the Ontario economy became a DREE concern, and not an issue only for the Department of Industry. In 1978 DREE launched a policy and legislative review, setting the scene for 'another stage in the evolution of regional development policy.'[26]

One Review

'Regional economic balance,' DREE argued in its review, 'has been shifting ... particularly since the middle of this decade.'[27] This shift necessitated a fresh look at the federal government's regional development policy. DREE's last major policy review, in 1973, had foreseen a buoyant Canadian economy that would permit national policies to enhance economic development in slow-growth areas and reduce disparities between regions. Yet by 1978, despite considerable public funds invested in slow-growth regions, regional disparities seemed virtually unchanged. In fact, a marked shift in private investment towards the western provinces was apparent, and closing the disparity gap would now be even more difficult.

DREE officials looked south of the border for a better understanding of regional imbalance in Canada, on the assumption that similar historical patterns of regional growth and economic fortunes are found on both sides of the border. The New England states, excluding Massachusetts, were found to be remarkably similar to Atlantic Canada in their long-term decline in population and their below-average incomes. The western border states, it was determined, had grown at rates roughly comparable to those of Canada's western provinces. Finally, the Great Lakes states of Michigan and Ohio had exhibited a pattern similar to that of both southern Ontario and Quebec. These findings suggested that regional economic development was influenced more by the continental forces of resource endowment and proximity to markets than by government policy. DREE officials would now follow the lead established by central agencies, notably the Department of Finance, and look to the neo-conservative school rather than Keynesian economics for inspiration.

The policy review suggested that Ottawa should reorient its regional economic development policy, changing its basic approach. DREE had directed a relatively high proportion of its funds into various forms of infrastructure. Expenditures of this kind had been useful, and many of the requirements of slow-growth regions had been met. However, the policy review recommended that DREE should be highly selective in such support, tying it to specific investments with strong potential for growth and employment. Marcel Lessard, accompanied by senior DREE officials, explained this new emphasis to the Senate Standing Committee on National Finance: '[DREE is not] a welfare agency ... Our primary objective ... is to help each region of Canada nurture and cultivate those areas and prospects with the best potential for development.' This could be best accomplished by 'intensive analysis ... to identify the comparative advantages of each region.'[28] On the face of it, Lessard and his officials were embracing the economic development literature rooted in interregional and international trade theory. However, a closer look reveals that the measures being sponsored followed no set pattern.

DREE produced a review of Ontario's economic circumstances and concluded that sustained, strong economic growth could no longer be taken for granted.[29] The increasing cost of energy and the westward movement of investment capital had weakened Ontario's economic performance. During the 1970s Ontario's economy had not performed as well as the rest of Canada's. Though narrowing regional disparities was a noble objective, 'the fact that it is occurring more by means of Ontario's weakening position rather than through other regions' growing strength, with the possible exception of Alberta and British Columbia, should be a matter of national concern.' A weakened Ontario would 'have negative implications for the whole country.'[30] Senior DREE officials were part of the Ottawa system, and the thinking in central agencies was that it made little economic sense to promote economic development in slow-growth regions when Ontario's economy was ailing. The result was that DREE was now prepared to speak to the economic interests of Ontario in the hope that it could stave off its own demise.

DREE's review revealed that between 1970 and 1978, Ontario had one of the slowest growth rates of all the provinces: the third lowest in manufacturing investment and the lowest in residential construction and per capita disposable income. Ontario's share of the country's newly arriving immigrants declined from 58 per cent in 1974 to 49 per cent in 1978. Ontario's population growth rate exceeded the national average only once in the same period. The state of Ontario's economy became cause for concern for federal government departments, including DREE.

Clearly, continuing growth in Ontario could no longer be taken for granted. DREE stressed the difficult problems of industrial adjustment in southern Ontario. The provincial government had stimulated slow-growth areas within the province, but now, DREE insisted, 'Ontario must ... be even more conscious of the overall development of the province itself.'[31]

DREE maintained that significant elements of Ontario's manufacturing industry required adjustment and restructuring in light of changing demands and international competition. The manufacturing sector needed assistance to make the required adjustments on a timely and economically efficient basis and to seize new opportunities in a rapidly changing international market. In the automotive industry, product lines would have to be changed and plants be completely re-equipped. Farm machinery was facing an uncertain future, due, in part, to its international orientation and its vulnerability to wide cyclical swings. Because it is linked to these two industries, Ontario's steel industry would also need to adjust to changing circumstances. Ontario needed to seize new opportunities for its manufacturing sector, for example, by linking its capacity to major new energy projects in eastern and western Canada.

The prospects for three of the four western provinces looked promising. In line with North America's basic economic trends, the growth of the Canadian western economy had surpassed the national average. Personal income in the West had increased 57 per cent between 1971 and 1978, as compared to 46 per cent nationally; employment had grown by 33 per cent, and the labour force by only 30 per cent.[32]

The main economic challenge for the four western provinces was one of managing growth. The energy sector and associated pipeline projects would offer numerous opportunities. DREE outlined a number of these, including the development of northern oil and gas reserves in the Arctic and the Mackenzie Valley. Four synthetic and heavy-oil projects were planned for the mid-1980s, as was the development of Saskatchewan's high-quality uranium reserves. These projects and others, DREE concluded, would bring substantial private investment to the area and create employment.

All in all, the policy review revealed that Canada's regional economic circumstances had changed considerably since the review in 1972. DREE would seek to adjust its programs to reflect these changes, and Lessard so informed his cabinet colleagues. DREE also concluded that the GDAs still constituted the best possible delivery mechanism. The GDA's most important characteristic, Lessard insisted, was its flexibility. A wide range of approaches and initiatives was possible, and development measures could be tailored to circumstances and to the development priorities of provincial governments.[33] GDAs had proved effective as a tool for federal-provincial cooperation, as witnessed by the broad endorsement that they received at the First Ministers' Conference in February 1978.

DREE acknowledged, however, that the GDAs were not without 'possible drawbacks.' They had not, for instance, been successful in dealing with multi-province issues. All GDA programming was structured on a bilateral basis, and DREE had been incapable of promoting regional or multi-province solutions in areas such as energy, fisheries, and transportation. Also, other federal departments had not become involved in promoting regional development, and the GDAs remained essentially a DREE-only instrument.[34]

The Clark Government

The Progressive Conservative government of Joe Clark came to power in June 1979. Elmer MacKay, a popular Nova Scotia politician, was named DREE minister. Clark had talked about regional economic development throughout the election campaign, insisting that 'the fight against regional disparity will be central to our policy as it is central to the Progressive Conservative's concept of national unity.'[35] Curiously, however, MacKay was excluded from Clark's inner cabinet. Thus, changes to DREE were expected to be structural in nature and likely to involve other departments.

During the campaign, the Conservatives had been critical of DREE programs. DREE's difficulties, in the minds of Conservative politicians, were 'rooted in the obsessive concern with developing such infrastructure as sewer and water systems that do not offer continuing economic benefits.' MacKay had a different take from Lessard on regional economic circumstances and emphasis, and he made it clear to his cabinet colleagues and officials that he favoured a strong commitment to the four Atlantic provinces and to large projects. He also signalled to his colleagues and departmental officials that DREE efforts should be concentrated 'east of the Ottawa river.'[36]

The department gave MacKay essentially the same policy and program proposals it had presented to Lessard. Little had changed in terms of economic circumstances at the regional level, and DREE officials saw no need for significant change to their basic policy orientation. The GDAs still represented, in their opinion, the most effective tool for federal-provincial coordination and would be particularly well suited to Clark's vision of Canadian federalism. Before MacKay and the Clark government could reorient Ottawa's regional economic development policy, however, the country was plunged into yet another general election.

Another Review

First elected in 1968, Pierre De Bané made regional development his main field of interest in Parliament. Though never a resident of the area, De Bané had been parachuted into the Liberal stronghold of Matane in the economically depressed Gaspé region. He was first named to the cabinet as minister of supply and services in late 1978, only a few months before the Trudeau government was defeated. During that brief period, he sought to reorient that department's policies to promote regional development. He initiated a program to identify the eight poorest regions in the country and sent a team of specialists to those regions to find out what local industries produced that the government bought in its day-to-day operations. While in opposition, he had been shadow critic of DREE. In that capacity, he wrote a widely circulated paper on regional development policy. It called on DREE to evaluate the regional effect of all federal programs, to take a direct interest in community development, to establish a special regional development fund, and to develop special tax concessions for businesses locating in slow-growth regions.[37]

When the Liberal Party returned to power, De Bané specifically asked Trudeau for the DREE portfolio.[38] Immediately after his appointment, he called for a major policy review, feeling strongly that the government's regional development policy needed to be completely overhauled. The guiding principle of the review was that the federal and provincial governments could do more, a great deal more, in promoting regional development.

At the same time, De Bané sought to strengthen DREE's position in Ottawa. He declared that it was unrealistic for the federal government to expect DREE to 'alleviate regional disparities with a budget which in total represented less than 2 per cent of Ottawa's expenditure budget.'

He publicly informed the deputy prime minister and the minister of finance that DREE would need a great deal more money if Ottawa was serious about combating regional disparity.[39]

De Bané called a DREE staff conference, to which he invited every departmental official down to relatively junior levels, and he asked them to contribute suggestions for a stronger policy. Those reluctant to voice their views before senior management he invited to write him in complete confidence. At the conference, De Bané echoed the views on regional development that Prime Minister Trudeau had voiced some twelve years earlier: 'Unless the federal government can put in place measures to extend to those people living in slow-growth regions hope and opportunities to turn the economy of their regions and communities around, then the future of the Canadian federation will be bleak indeed.'[40]

De Bané informed the conference that he would not accept the review that the department had submitted to him – essentially the same review that DREE had submitted first to Lessard and then to MacKay. It merely confirmed the 'status quo,' which he rejected out of hand. He also urged the department to do likewise. He recognized, he said, that a great deal of opposition to DREE existed at both the political and bureaucratic levels in Ottawa. 'To preserve the status quo,' De Bané stated, 'I would have to devote all my efforts and energies over the next twelve months to convince my colleagues of the appropriateness of DREE as we now know it. A very fundamental problem here is that I am not prepared to do that.' He urged his officials to put aside their 'bureaucratic inhibitions' and to come up with new measures 'to alleviate regional disparities.' No effort should be spared to bring about regional balance in economic growth, De Bané insisted. In line with this thinking, he outlined again all the measures he had identified in his paper on regional development. In particular, he stressed community-level development.[41]

Senior officials at DREE, however, remained sceptical that De Bané could deliver a bigger budget and a stronger mandate for the department. Opposition to DREE in Ottawa was still strong, and they were reluctant to seek a broader mandate, especially if it gave DREE the authority to assess the regional policies and programs of other departments. They were well aware that De Bané was a junior minister with a reputation in the press for being unconventional, a 'party maverick' and a 'black sheep.'[42] De Bané certainly raised eyebrows in DREE when he publicly rebuked veteran cabinet minister Allan MacEachen, deputy prime minister and minister of finance, for holding DREE's expenditure budget down to what he felt was an unacceptable level.

Senior DREE officials also saw no evidence for De Bané's claim that regional development held a priority status in Ottawa. The prime minister had made it clear that constitutional renewal and a new energy policy were at the top of the agenda. As he had in 1968, Prime Minister Trudeau turned to two senior Quebec ministers to undertake these tasks. Jean Chrétien, a seasoned politician, was appointed to justice, and Marc Lalonde, the regional minister for Quebec and a long-time adviser to Trudeau, was named to energy. The DREE officials were trying as best they could to protect or save their department by looking to the economic interests of all regions, including Ontario. They saw only trouble in what they felt was De Bané's desire to turn back the clock to the days of Marchand and Kent, when DREE was concerned primarily with eastern Quebec and the Atlantic provinces. Central agencies in Ottawa, notably the Privy Council Office and the Department of Finance, were in no mood to return to the old DREE days, something that was well known to senior DREE officials.

Still, Pierre De Bané resisted anything less than a complete overhaul of the federal government's regional development policy. He remained convinced that a stronger mandate for DREE and a clear focus on slow-growth regions were both essential and possible. But there were other forces at play. His cabinet colleagues and government backbenchers were highly critical of the GDAs, which they viewed as instruments substantially financed with federal funds but clearly favouring the political profile of provincial governments. On this issue, the criticism of federal ministers and government MPs became more and more vocal.

The GDA approach was no doubt better suited to times of quiet federal-provincial cooperation, such as prevailed when it was first introduced. However, by the early 1980s, competitive federalism had come to replace cooperative federalism. A bitter referendum campaign over the future of Quebec had just been fought by both Ottawa and the Quebec government. In addition, not one provincial government was of the same political persuasion as was the federal government. It was thus difficult for government MPs to see DREE funds simply transferred to provincial governments that used them to put in place popular initiatives for which they took the credit. MPs went home to their ridings on weekends only to see members of the Parti Québécois highly critical of Ottawa, the Prince Edward Island government labelling

Trudeau un-Canadian because of his position on the constitution, or Premier Peckford of Newfoundland insisting that the policies of the federal government were working against the best interests of his province. They also saw these same governments claiming credit for a host of GDA-sponsored initiatives for which the federal government had financed up to 90 per cent of the costs. How then, they asked De Bané, can DREE turn around and agree to finance even more subsidiary agreements, which in the case of Quebec would serve to fuel the political ambitions of a sovereignist government?

Well aware of this opposition, and convinced that marginal improvements in DREE's activities would not suffice, De Bané wrote to the prime minister to ask for support for a complete review of federal policy on regional development. He suggested that 'DREE's responsibilities – to ensure that all Canadians have an equal chance to make a living with dignity – can't be handled by one department with one percent of the federal budget.'[43] Sadly, he reported to the prime minister, the DREE experience had been a failure because of DREE's inability to muster a concerted federal effort in promoting regional development.

Defining departmental mandates is the prerogative of the prime minister. He or she alone, not the cabinet, and certainly not the incumbent minister, must decide which minister will have authority to do what. Frequently mandates overlap, and ministers and their departments will jockey to enhance their positions and their spheres of influence. However, only the prime minister can resolve jurisdictional conflicts. Thus, when De Bané wrote to request a stronger mandate for DREE, the prime minister naturally turned to his own officials inside the Privy Council Office (PCO) for advice.

While the PCO was busy looking at departmental mandates, De Bané sought to make DREE's incentives program more proactive or *dirigiste* in relation to the private sector. The Bureau of Business and Economic Development was set up to identify, through such techniques as import substitution, export analysis, industry profiles, and corporate and economic intelligence, attractive investment opportunities for the private sector in slow-growth regions.[44] Attempts would be made to select only dynamic industries and manufacturing sectors with high growth potential, so that new activities would sustain themselves. Once it identified opportunities, DREE would go to firms to outline opportunities and offer federal assistance in the form of grants or tax credits. Such representations would always be done at the highest level.

The first sector looked at was high technology. And the first development opportunity the bureau identified was for Bouctouche, a small, rural, economically depressed community in Kent County in eastern New Brunswick. With much fanfare, DREE announced that Mitel, a Canadian high-tech company that had enjoyed tremendous growth during the 1970s, would locate two new manufacturing plants in Bouctouche. The plants were expected to create some 1,000 new jobs. DREE would contribute a $15.7-million incentive grant to the Mitel project, which involved a total capital investment of $48 million.[45] The project was strictly a federal initiative; the provincial government first learned of the project through the news media, as did the residents of the province. But that is not all – the federal Department of Industry also learned of it only as a *fait accompli*. Yet, the Department of Industry considered the high-tech sector to be its own, not to be shared with DREE. It was busy promoting the sector in such areas as Kanata, Montreal, Toronto, and Waterloo and it saw no reason why DREE should elbow its way in to bring new investment to areas not particularly suited to the high-tech sector, areas such as Bouctouche, a small Acadian village some 50 kilometres north of Moncton.

Meanwhile, De Bané and Herb Gray, the minister of industry, trade, and commerce, were exchanging strong words in public over Volkswagen's decision to locate a new parts plant in Barrie, Ontario, in order to take advantage of Ottawa's duty-remission program, under which the duty on automobile imports was waived if a company established a plant in Canada.[46] At De Bané's urging, a delegation of federal officials was sent to Germany to meet with Volkswagen. DREE selected two sites, Montreal and Halifax, and offered a cash grant to Volkswagen to locate in either one. The company rejected the one-time grant, arguing that it would need a yearly operating grant to compensate for the fact that parts suppliers were located mainly in southern Ontario.

De Bané suggested that the federal government should refuse the duty remission for Volkswagen if the company pressed ahead with its Barrie location rather than a DREE-designated region. If regional development were to be effective, De Bané had said many times, it requires many instruments. One of them clearly was the duty-remission program. Herb Gray rejected De Bané's argument, suggesting that it was better to have Volkswagen locate in Canada, even in southern Ontario, than to have the company pick a site in the United States.

When the De Bané–Gray exchange became public, the Quebec government jumped into the debate and urged Ottawa to insist on a Que-

bec site. Quebec cabinet ministers argued that the province never received its 'fair share' of the Canadian automobile-production industry.
Quebec's minister of industry, Rodrigue Biron, said that if Ottawa were
truly serious about regional development and the promotion of 'real'
economic growth in the province, it ought to insist on a Quebec site.[47]

Volkswagen was unmoved by this public debate and remained committed to Barrie. The president of Volkswagen Canada issued a statement that it would not locate anywhere else in Canada, notwithstanding
a generous DREE grant.[48] As for duty remission, Volkswagen simply
assumed that it would be available, regardless of where it chose to
locate in Canada. In the end, the federal cabinet sided with Gray and
did not choose to employ duty remission as a means of inducing
Volkswagen away from southern Ontario. With the economy in a deep
recession, a number of ministers were in no mood to call Volkswagen's
bluff.

For De Bané, the Volkswagen episode simply confirmed his view that
regional development should be the responsibility of all federal departments, not simply DREE, and that a great variety of regional development tools was necessary. Duty remission was but one of them. But
before De Bané and DREE could amend their regional development
incentives program and define new tools, the prime minister unveiled a
major government reorganization. DREE would be disbanded. Its policy
role and the GDAs would be transferred to a strengthened Ministry of
State for Economic and Regional Development. Its regional incentives
program would be incorporated into the programs of a new Department of Regional Industrial Expansion (DRIE). Herb Gray was named
minister responsible for DRIE, and De Bané was moved to a newly
created junior portfolio in external affairs.

New Policies, Structures, and Programs

On 12 January 1982, Prime Minister Trudeau unveiled a major government reorganization for economic development. The reason for doing
so, he pointed out, was that 'it is no longer enough that one department
alone is primarily responsible for regional economic development.'
Perhaps he forgot the answer he gave when Robert Stanfield expressed
concern during the Commons debate on the proposed DREE legislation
that DREE would be left alone to carry the entire regional development
load. Trudeau, at the time, had dismissed Stanfield's concerns, insisting
that DREE was what was needed 'to achieve real coordination.' Trudeau

also pledged that the government would review the regional application of existing national policies and programs. The re-organization also reflected the new policy direction described in detail by the minister of finance in his 1981 budget speech. At that time, Allan MacEachen had spoken about a new economic reality in Canada and consequent changing prospects at the regional level. Substantial opportunities now existed in every major region in the country, suggesting that the federal government should adopt a new policy orientation.[49]

During his 1981 budget speech, Allan MacEachen tabled a document titled *Economic Development for Canada in the 1980s*, which maintained that regional balance was changing as a result of buoyancy in the West, optimism in the East, and unprecedented softness in key economic sectors in central Canada. Underpinning this view were the economic prospects associated with resource-based megaprojects.

The Atlantic region, in contrast to historical economic trends, was expected to enjoy a decade of solid growth, largely as a result of offshore resources. The West, meanwhile, would capture over half of the investment in major projects. Ontario and Quebec would face problems of industrial adjustment, brought about by increased international competition. Yet, opportunities were thought to exist there as well. If properly managed, the economic spin-off from major projects could create numerous employment opportunities in central Canada. Some 60,000 person-years of employment would be created in Ontario from major pipeline projects in western Canada. Thus, the regional challenge in the 1980s would take a new direction. Regions that had previously enjoyed strong growth were confronted with special problems of adjustment, while those that had traditionally lagged behind were enjoying prospects for expansion. All in all, both problems and opportunities existed in all regions. Accordingly, the minister of finance stated, 'regional economic development will be central to public policy planning at the federal level.'[50]

The policy direction would take advantage of major economic forces working on the Canadian economy. The policy document pointed to some $440 billion of potential projects, predominantly in energy and resources, that would be launched before the end of the century. By and large, these major projects would be located in the West, in the North, and on the East Coast and were expected to bring about a new set of comparative advantages and economic growth not seen in these regions in the twentieth century. They would provide an important source of income, improve provincial revenues, and generate new economic activity. Cabinet ministers began to voice a similar message of economic optimism, notably for the future of the Atlantic provinces. The minister of energy, Marc Lalonde, commented: 'What offshore oil and gas provides [in Atlantic Canada] is the opportunity for an accelerated, more dramatic economic turnaround than would otherwise have been thought possible. The basic strength is here. And now we must build on that strength.'[51]

Added to this was an anticipated growth in income from grains and other food products, including fisheries. The Department of Finance's policy document noted that 'rapid population growth in the world is placing new demands on food, and in response to rising world prices further expansion and modernization of the agricultural and food sectors throughout Canada is in prospect.' This development, it was felt, would also favour the western and Atlantic provinces. In central Canada, the competitive pressure on manufacturing would require adaptation and regeneration. The policy document thus stressed reorienting and restructuring this sector. The restructuring 'must both reduce the pressure for costly support to less competitive industries and at the same time provide alternative employment opportunities in higher productivity and higher wage sectors.' Much like the argument in the policy document, ministers also suggested that megaprojects could help restructure Ontario manufacturing. Senator Bud Olson, minister of economic and regional development, maintained: 'There is a significant underlying base of major project investment that must be looked at, and the cumulative impacts of those projects will and are having significant beneficial impacts in many parts of the country, not only in the provinces where the mega projects are situated.'[52]

In summary, anticipated major projects would enhance the economies of the West, the North, and the Atlantic region. In economic terms, these regions would be able to 'take care of themselves.' The new regional problem was the weakening manufacturing sector in central Canada. It was there that new employment opportunities ought to be created. Many manufacturers producing standard products, such as automobiles and appliances, as well as clothing and footwear, were losing out to foreign competitors. Even if they substantially improved productivity, however, competition would remain strong.

The process of economic growth in central Canada and the peripheral regions would thus be quite different. In the latter, growth would result from the infusion of new capital and labour. Atlantic Canada had a large reservoir of untapped labour to draw from. All that was required for growth in the West and East, then, was a good investment climate, market access, and an adequate supply of labour. In central Canada, however, growth would come about only by drawing resources from declining industries and moving them into growth sectors – in other words, by managing both industrial decline and industrial growth.

In 1969, much had been said about alleviating regional disparities and focusing federal efforts east of Trois-Rivières, and about the importance of regional development for national unity. In 1982, the prime minister's lengthy statement and the finance minister's policy document said nothing about regional disparities. Although regional development would be central to policy making, it involved something significantly different from what it had been fourteen years earlier. Now regional development referred less to alleviating regional disparities than to development at the regional level. De Bané was able to secure an overhaul of Ottawa's regional development policy, as he had requested in his letter to the prime minister. But what he got was vastly different from what he had envisaged.

New Government Structure

Pierre Trudeau, on the advice of his PCO officials, decided that a central agency with no program of its own would be better able to influence other departments. It could assess changing economic circumstances and follow up on crucial policy and program decisions. And it could ensure that regional development became part of the whole fabric of government policies and programs.

Trudeau established a new central agency, the Ministry of State for Economic and Regional Development (MSERD), by adding regional policy and coordination to the functions of the existing Ministry of State for Economic Development. The ministry was established in late 1978 to coordinate and direct economic development policy and to manage the economic policy 'expenditure envelope.' The envelope system integrated into a single process the separate functions of setting priorities, establishing spending limits, and making specific expenditure decisions. Within the envelope system the ministry was to advise deputy ministers and ministers on Ottawa's economic development budget and recommend allocation of funds between programs.[53]

In addition, MSERD was to see that 'regional concerns are elevated to a priority position in all economic decision-making by Cabinet.' These included all regional concerns, not simply those from have-less regions.

Because of this added responsibility, the new ministry had to decentralize part of its operations. Offices comprising eight to twelve person-years were established in every province. These offices were directed by a senior executive, called the federal economic development coordinator (FEDC), who advised cabinet; coordinated the activities of the federal government in the region; promoted cooperation with the provincial government, labour, business, and other economic-development groups; ensured that information about government policy was available in the field; and worked with other federal departments. The ministry, whenever appropriate, was also to appoint special project directors in the region 'to cut red tape on mega projects and avoid undue delay in project planning, approval and completion.'[54]

The FEDC, however, would direct activities in his or her region, keeping federal officials in the field informed of the activities and decisions of the Cabinet Committee on Economic and Regional Development. He or she would also coordinate the federal presence in the region and serve as the chair of a committee of economic development departments in the region. Through this committee and from their own staff work, the FEDCs would propose economic development plans for their own provinces. In turn, these plans would be the basis for federal-provincial negotiations for economic development and also assist in making federal departments and agencies more sensitive to regional circumstances.

The importance of having all federal departments play a more active role in regional development was stressed by the prime minister and MSERD's minister, Senator Bud Olson. While announcing the appointment of the FEDC for Prince Edward Island, for example, Senator Olson declared that the Cabinet Committee on Economic and Regional Development had 'launched a process of review of all existing economic development programmes to determine if they can be further directed toward regional objectives.'[55] Olson also told Atlantic premiers that the government would review the application of all national policies and programs at the regional level.

Largely because of the expected role of the FEDC, the new ministry was described by Ottawa as a 'decentralized central agency.' It would provide the full cabinet with regional information developed by federal sectoral departments in the regions or by on-site research and analysis with MSERD. Thus, the information would not, as with DREE, be based almost solely on federal-provincial discussions under the various GDAs.

The agency would, however, remain largely Ottawa-based. The head office under the 1983 reorganization would increase its allocation of person-years (originally established in 1978 at more than 100) by almost 200, and the new regional offices received 100. The rationale for a substantial increase in person-years was built around the need for ensuring that the 'regional dimension' was incorporated in the federal government's decision-making process. To do this, MSERD required an enhanced information system on regional issues. Moreover, approval was given for the Ottawa office to establish a major-projects branch to facilitate a government-wide approach to the development and management of the various major projects.[56]

Nearly two years later, the MSERD legislation was finally amended to incorporate the regional responsibility that was added to MSERD's responsibilities. The legislation was no more explicit on objectives than was the old DREE legislation; it said nothing about goals. It was not clear whether regional balance in economic growth or reducing regional disparities was to be paramount. MSERD's concern, the new legislation stated, was 'expansion of the economy through the development of productive enterprise in every region of Canada.'[57]

Economic and Regional Development Agreements (ERDAs)

The prime minister declared at the time that he announced the new organization for economic development that 'existing General Development Agreements with the provinces will continue until their expiry date,' to be replaced thereafter by ERDAs, a 'new and simpler set of agreements with the provinces, involving a wider range of federal departments.' The ERDAs would be formulated under the direction of the relevant FEDC. The reorganization reflected Ottawa's new approach to federal-provincial relations in the regional development field. The policy paper tabled by the minister of finance during his 1981 budget speech made it clear that 'joint implementation of economic development programming may not always be desirable.' ERDAs would reflect this new approach. The most positive characteristics of the GDAs would be retained, and less desirable features discarded.[58] The less desirable features had everything to do with a lack of visibility for the federal dollars spent in regional development. The Trudeau cabinet became convinced that the federal government was not obtaining its share of recognition under the GDAs.

It is also important to recall in this context that bureaucrat bashing came into vogue in the early 1980s. The BBC television program *Yes*

Minister became an instant hit, and politicians, the media, and a number of academics became convinced that career officials had too much influence, if not power. The federal government also believed that the GDA process had given rise to a process that lacked political control and direction. GDA initiatives were prepared and agreed to through a host of federal-provincial committees staffed exclusively with permanent officials. By the time they surfaced at the political level, planning was so far advanced that little change was possible. Under the new ERDAs, Ottawa would directly deliver certain projects under the aegis of the various subsidiary agreements. The respective responsibilities of the federal and provincial governments were to be much clearer, which would enable ministers to exert stronger political control.

ERDAs were designed also to encompass all federal departments and agencies, which were invited to contribute to the various ERDAs either by signing new subsidiary agreements with the provinces or by delivering specific initiatives. ERDAs were to respect interprovincial considerations and the needs of the national economy. Federal line departments would thus be better able than DREE had been to counter overreliance on a provincial perspective of economic development.

ERDAs would also be developed under close political scrutiny. The legislation (Bill C-152) establishing MSERD spelled out the joint planning process: 'Detailed negotiations ... of any subsidiary agreement shall not be undertaken ... unless a plan for economic development to which the draft agreement relates has first been approved by the Minister in concert with other Ministers.' Federal ministers would not be asked to approve proposed agreements when it was too late to affect their contents.

Apart from these changes, the ERDAs were remarkably similar to the GDAs they replaced. Like the GDAs, they were ten-year umbrella-type agreements that did not provide for specific projects.[59] They simply offered a broad statement of goals, outlined priorities, and described how joint decisions would be taken. They were, in short, enabling documents, with projects to be presented in subsidiary agreements.

A Regional Fund

At the same time that he announced the new policy and the new government organization, Prime Minister Trudeau declared that a regional fund would be established, something first called for by former DREE minister Pierre De Bané. The prime minister stated: 'Money freed up as the existing GDAs expire will be used ... to create a regional fund.' This fund would 'support regional economic development efforts and should reach $200 million by 1984–85.'[60] Shortly after the new government organization was unveiled, several federal ministers spoke about the importance of the new regional fund to regional economic development.

Initially, at least, some confusion existed over the size of the fund and how it would be financed. Responsibility for the various subsidiary agreements was transferred to a number of federal line departments and agencies, which added to the confusion. Further, the new line department, DRIE, now responsible for the old DREE programs, was understandably reluctant to transfer part of its unallocated resources to a new regional fund over which it had little control.

The problems with the regional fund, however, were more fundamental. The term *region* had never been properly defined. Consequently, it was unclear whether the fund was to apply to sub-provincial regions, to provinces, or to multi-province areas. More important, it was not clear whether the fund was to apply exclusively to disadvantaged regions.

Could the fund be employed exclusively to support projects that would not otherwise be developed in a disadvantaged region? Those who advocated a regional fund had consistently warned that it should not support projects that a line department should initiate through its ongoing programs. Otherwise, line departments would simply turn to the regional fund for total funding whenever an initiative came forward from a disadvantaged region. The department's ongoing program and budget would finance projects from more developed regions, while the regional fund would finance those in other regions. More simply put, the question was whether or not expenditures from the regional fund should be above and beyond the normal program responsibilities of departments in all regions. Unless they were, the purpose of a regional fund would be negated. Equally important, the regional distribution of the fund was not made clear. Given that the fund was being financed from 'money freed-up as existing GDAs expire,' one could assume that its regional distribution would have been based on DREE's historical spending pattern under the various GDAs.[61]

These questions were never properly answered. Indeed, the fund fell below the radar screen shortly after it was announced. We know that, initially at least, some projects in Manitoba and Atlantic Canada were funded. But that is all we know, or for that matter anyone knows, including federal officials in the regional development field. No mechanism was put in place to ensure a proper accounting of the fund's spending pattern. With the arrival of John Turner as prime minister in June 1984, the fund disappeared, and nothing has been heard about it since.

As already mentioned, the 1982 government reorganization also established a new line department – DRIE – through the amalgamation of the regional programs of DREE with the industry, small-business, and tourism components of the Department of Industry, Trade and Commerce (IT&C). The trade component of IT&C moved to the Department of External Affairs.[62]

The integration of DREE and IT&C, it was hoped, would capture the most positive characteristics of both DREE's decentralized and regionally sensitive organization and IT&C's centralization and ability to gather industrial intelligence and conduct relations with industry and government. In short, DRIE would not be as decentralized as DREE had been or as centralized as IT&C. DRIE was to set up provincial and subprovincial offices to deliver its programs. These offices became the new department's principal contact point for DRIE clients applying for assistance under the department's programs. Unlike in DREE, however, they had little say in formulating policy or programs. These functions, along with gathering of industrial intelligence, became the responsibility of new sectoral branches in the DRIE Ottawa office. DRIE's Ottawa–region staff ratio was set at 6:4, compared with DREE's 3:7.

Nevertheless, compared to other federal departments and agencies, DRIE was highly decentralized and 'regionally sensitive.' It represented the 'leading edge' in Ottawa's new economic development orientation and the model on which other departments were encouraged to pattern themselves.[63] The new department was expected to integrate regional and sectoral interests, be highly visible in the regions, and emphasize efficient program delivery.

The Volkswagen case also had an impact. Shortly after the reorganization was announced, a PCO official declared that under the new structure public debates such as that between De Bané and Gray over the location of a new Volkswagen plant could no longer take place. As he explained, public debate between two ministers 'will never happen again ... DREE had its own ideas on VW and IT&C had different ideas. There was a lot of squabbling. Now that they're together, they'll have to resolve their differences internally and then go to cabinet.'[64] The point here is not whether national or even regional considerations should decide the location of a Volkswagen parts plant. Rather, it is that, with the reorganization, there was no longer anyone in the cabinet bringing regional considerations into discussions whenever new economic activities were proposed. Regional trade-offs were to be resolved at the official level.

The Industrial and Regional Development Program

The first DRIE minister was Ed Lumley, who rose in the House of Commons on 27 June 1983 to explain Ottawa's new industrial and regional development program (IRDP). Lumley cautioned that 'combatting regional disparities is difficult even in good economic times ... It is much more difficult in a period when, because of a worldwide downturn, Canada's traditional industries are suffering from soft markets, stiff international competition, rapid technological change and rising protectionism from the countries that make up our market.' A new program to meet these circumstances would have to be one that he could 'clearly recommend to the business community, to the Canadian public and to Members of Parliament.' DRIE, Lumley reported, had come up with such a program. It was a 'regionally sensitized, multifaceted programme of industrial assistance in all parts of Canada ... This is not a programme to be available only in certain designated regions. Whatever riding any Member of this House represents, his or her constituents will be eligible for assistance.' Federal regional economic development had come full circle and now could be found in all areas of the country, including downtown Toronto. The program was also able to accommodate a variety of needs, including investment in infrastructure, industrial diversification, the establishment of new plants, and the launching of new product lines.[65]

An important distinguishing characteristic of the new program was the 'development index.' First suggested by De Bané, the index established the needs of individual regions, as far down as a single census district. All regions were arranged in four tiers of need.[66] The first, for the most developed 50 per cent of the population, covered districts with a need for industrial restructuring. In this tier, financial assistance was available for up to 25 per cent of the cost of modernization and expansion. At the other end of the spectrum was the fourth tier, which included the 5 per cent of the population living in areas of greatest need (based on level of employment, personal income, and provincial fiscal capacity). In this tier, financial assistance was available for up to 60 per cent of the cost of establishing new plants.

The program could provide financial assistance to both business and non-profit organizations through cash grants, contributions, repayable contributions, participation loans, and loan guarantees. The assistance was available for the various elements of 'product or company cycle': economic analysis studies, innovation (including product development), plant establishment, plant modernization and expansion, marketing (including exact development measures), and restructuring. Tier 4 regions were eligible under all program elements; tier 1 regions were not. Financial assistance under tier 4 could amount to 70 per cent of costs, while tier 1 varied from 20 to 50 per cent.

Winding Up MSERD

In naming his cabinet in June 1984, Prime Minister John Turner announced that one of his most important objectives was to ensure a more streamlined and leaner federal government. The federal government, he insisted, had become 'too elaborate, too complex, too slow, and too expensive.' He unveiled several measures to 'streamline' cabinet decision making. The number of cabinet committees was reduced from thirteen to ten, and the number of cabinet ministers from thirty-six to twenty-nine. Two central agencies, the Ministry of State for Social Development and the Ministry of State for Economic and Regional Development, were 'wound up.' In announcing his new cabinet structure, Turner mentioned regional development only to say that 'steps [would be taken] to strengthen the regional development role of the Department of Regional Industrial Expansion.'[67]

Specifically, Turner transferred the FEDCs from MSERD to DRIE. Accompanying the FEDCs to DRIE were the various ERDAs. The Office for Regional Development was established within DRIE. A junior minister, for all practical purposes reporting to the minister of DRIE and operating under the aegis of the DRIE portfolio, was appointed minister of state for regional development. The industrial and regional development program was left untouched by the Turner reorganization.[68] There is no doubt that Turner's winding up of MSERD was prompted by a strong commitment to streamline government, not by any desire to strengthen or overhaul yet one more time Ottawa's regional development policy. Accordingly, little was said at the time by either Turner or any of his senior ministers about the federal government's reorienting its regional development policy.

But already a number of important lessons learned emerged from this period. Federal regional development policy was subject to sudden changes for reasons that had little to do with economic circumstances in the Maritime provinces. Securing political visibility for federal spending in the name of regional economic development was an important factor. National unity concerns and a perceived economic weakness in the manufacturing sector in southern Ontario had a profound impact on Ottawa's economic policy-making process and on Canada's regional economic development policy. Even DREE itself expressed deep concerns about Ontario's manufacturing industry, suggesting that adjustment and restructuring efforts were needed.

DREE made the case, in one of its policy reviews, that each region in Canada was unique. But the logic extended only to federal-provincial agreements, not to Ottawa's policy-making and decision-making processes. More specifically, it referred to cost-shared programs, which the federal government funded but had limited say in shaping. Moreover, they were bilateral agreements so that the multi-province, or in the case of the Maritime provinces, the regional perspective was lost. With DREE officials operating in provincial capitals essentially engaged in transferring funds to provincial governments, Ottawa-based officials became concerned that these officials had 'gone native' and were no longer able to bring an interprovincial or national perspective to their work. Given all of the above, something had to be done. In the end, that something was the end of DREE.

6 Mulroney: Inflicting Prosperity

Brian Mulroney led his Progressive Conservative Party to a sweeping victory in the 1984 general election. They won 211 seats, the largest number ever won in any general election in Canada. During the election campaign and immediately on assuming office, Mulroney served notice that his government had a new political agenda that represented a fundamental break with the Trudeau Liberal past.

The new agenda involved four broad policy fronts: national reconciliation, economic renewal, social justice, and constructive internationalism.[1] Regional economic development was a key feature of the first two. Indeed, Mulroney had mentioned regional economic development time and again during the election campaign as a necessary element in strengthening national unity. In one of his campaign speeches in the Maritime provinces, he announced that he would 'have no hesitation to inflict prosperity on Atlantic Canada.'[2] On federal-provincial relations, he explained that 'our first task is to breathe a new spirit into federalism. I am convinced that the serious deterioration of federal-provincial relations is not exclusively the result of the constitutional deficiencies. Centralistic and negative attitudes are much more to blame.'[3] In short, his government would look to the provinces for solutions to regional economic development rather than impose centrally designed policies and programs.

If one assumes that 'to inflict prosperity on Atlantic Canada' would invariably entail new spending, as many – at least in the Maritime provinces – surely did, then, Mulroney's regional development objective ran squarely up against another key objective of the new government. He himself had pledged while in opposition that, if elected prime minister, the federal government 'would get a better handle on government spending.'[4] And, indeed, within a few weeks of coming to office, his senior ministers brought the point home. The minister of finance, Michael Wilson, in his first major economic statement in Parliament, explained: 'In each of the past ten years, the expenditures of the federal government have exceeded its revenues ... Unless we begin now to put our fiscal house in order, the burden of debt will continue to mount rapidly.'[5] Turning to regional economic development policy, he added that 'we must also review the effectiveness of existing tax and grant incentive programs, particularly in terms of their impact on business investment decisions and their contribution to regional competitiveness. Their cumulative impact, and the expectations raised by their availability may retard rather than facilitate adjustment to market forces. They may be unduly blurring the market signals that the private sector needs for decision-making purposes.'[6] This statement and many others from several senior ministers may not have pointed the way for defining new measures for regional development policy, but they did make one thing clear – past policies and efforts had not worked, and something new had to be attempted.

Still, Mulroney and his party had taken a number of positions on regional development in the months leading up to the election campaign and again during the campaign. The Progressive Conservative Party issued a policy paper arguing that 'when the Liberals dismantled DREE in 1981, they left Canada's least developed regions without their traditional voice.' The paper also suggested that the winding up of Ministry of State for Economic and Regional Development (MSERD) 'further reduced the importance attached by the federal government to the task of combating regional disparity.' The Department for Regional Industrial Expansion (DRIE), it added, 'is likely to neglect Canada's poorest regions.' It also reported that two principles would guide the new government: consultation, and fair and equitable distribution of regional development funds. The paper, however, was less forthcoming on specific policy goals or directions. It spoke of offering 'rewarding careers' to young people in Atlantic Canada in their home provinces – or 'place prosperity' as opposed to 'people prosperity.' The paper referred specifically to 'regional disparities' more than the Trudeau government had, particularly towards the end of its mandate.[7]

Brian Mulroney had further outlined a number of new measures during the 1984 election campaign. DRIE would receive a 'specific legislative mandate to promote the least developed regions,' and 'every department will be required to submit to the Standing Committee of

Parliament on Economic and Regional Development annual assessments of the effect of departmental policies on specific regions.'[8] Trudeau,
it will be recalled, had made a similar commitment in 1982; now
Mulroney decided to go a step further and require departments to
submit their findings to Parliament. DRIE would also get a wide range
of new policy instruments, including tax incentives. In the Maritime
provinces, efforts would be made to improve the economic infrastructure, including facilities for transportation and communications, as well
as training programs and improved market research. Commitments
were also made to assist communities suffering from chronic unemployment and little economic activity.

Though the Progressive Conservative Party was highly critical of the
Liberals for having 'dismantled' DREE, it did not re-establish the department when it came to power. In naming his cabinet, Prime Minister
Mulroney appointed no one responsible for regional development. Despite having a record forty ministers in his cabinet, several of whom
were made responsible for specific fields, Mulroney dropped the regional portfolio that John Turner had introduced only a few months
earlier. He did, however, retain the ministers of state first introduced by
the 1982 government reorganization that did away with DREE, such as
those for trade and for external relations. He also introduced new
ministers of state for tourism and for forestry, among others.

The Mulroney government was also slow off the mark in introducing
new regional development measures, although it did move quickly
to limit the scope of industrial and regional development programs
(IRDPs), in line with the election pledge to direct DRIE towards the
least-developed regions. DRIE minister Sinclair Stevens announced,
within two months of his appointment, important restrictions to tier 1
regions, the most developed of the country: 'modernization' and 'expansion' projects would no longer be eligible for assistance. Stevens
also served notice of the government's intention to transfer to the
provinces the responsibility for much of IRDP. Ottawa would administer large grants to national or multinational firms and let provincial
governments deal with small and medium-sized businesses.[9]

Yet, after less than a year in office the government began to reverse its
position. The fear that Ottawa would lose all visibility in its spending
on such grants led to a change of heart, and the federal government
continued to deliver all facets of incentives to the private sector.

The change of government did not dampen the federal desire to sign
ERDAs with all provincial governments. Shortly after the Mulroney

government came to office, Sinclair Stevens signed an ERDA with Ontario. The format established for earlier ERDAs was not disturbed, and Ontario welcomed the opportunity to sign one. Larry Grossman, the provincial treasurer, spoke about coordinated efforts for 'economic growth and permanent job creation in Ontario.' Both governments agreed also to a $2-million planning project, designed 'to support co-operative decision-making and improved coordination.' In addition, they announced that they would shortly sign agreements covering forestry and tourism – and then went on to identify priority areas for future efforts: industrial revitalization, resource management and production development, service-sector stimulation, human-resource development, and community development.[10]

Soon afterward, Sinclair Stevens signed an ERDA with Don Phillips, British Columbia's minister of industry and small-business development. In doing so, Stevens echoed the sentiment of his Liberal predecessor, Donald Johnston, when he said: 'ERDA, unlike the former GDA, covers all the departments and ministries which influence economic development and is intended to make sure that a wider range of federal policies and programs will be tailored to the priorities of each province.' He added that '[we] intend to identify the initiatives and opportunities which will strengthen British Columbia's economy and help it reach its full economic potential.' Both ministers also outlined a 'course of action [that] was agreed upon for implementation.'[11]

Quebec was the last province to sign an ERDA, on 15 December 1984, and the provincial justice minister, Pierre-Marc Johnson, explained the delay: 'Negotiations had bogged down with the previous Liberal government, but things changed radically when the Progressive Conservatives came to power this fall.' The new government, he added, had 'a different way of looking at things and [respects] Quebec's jurisdiction.' Johnson and Sinclair Stevens announced that the two governments would commit $1.6 billion over five years to tourism, culture, forestry, and industrial development. New projects and possibly new sectors would be identified at a later date for the last five years of the ERDA.[12] The one difference between Quebec's ERDA and the others was that no provision was made for any joint planning agreement.[13] The Quebec government refused to enter into such a subsidiary agreement, arguing that it preferred to arrive at joint action through consensus rather than through joint planning.

Thus, one by one, the provincial governments signed ERDAs with the federal governments, whether under Trudeau or Mulroney. The

ERDAs and GDAs were identical in format and similar in objectives pursued and types of programs and initiatives sponsored. The ERDAs, however, did provide for the federal government to deliver directly initiatives that had been previously delivered by provincial governments under the GDAs.

The Mulroney government continued to sign ERDA subsidiary agreements with the same regularity that the Trudeau government had. All in all, Ottawa committed over $3.0 billion of its own resources to ERDA agreements. The focus remained a sectoral one, and there is a remarkable similarity between the types of subsidiary agreements signed under the GDAs and ERDAs. As some ERDAs expired, they were simply renewed.

It quickly became apparent, however, that all was not well. Indeed, the government's fiscal objectives led to serious new challenges on the regional development front. In his first budget speech, Finance Minister Wilson reported on the government's intention to close down Cape Breton's two heavy-water plants, which employed some six hundred people. The plants represented, the minister argued, 'a symbol of waste and mismanagement.' He explained that 'they cost the taxpayers of this country more than $100 million per year to produce a product for which there is no demand. We will move immediately to close the plants, but we will not abandon the people or the region of Cape Breton.'[14] In the same year that the minister announced the decision to close the plants, a fire at one of the largest and most productive mines of the Cape Breton Development Corporation (DEVCO) dealt a harsh blow to employment levels in the coal mines, resulting in the loss of 1,200 jobs.[15]

Cape Breton was plunged into a crisis, a situation it had experienced many times before. The federal government responded by appointing a private-sector advisory committee to recommend new initiatives to the federal and provincial governments to promote economic development and productive employment in Cape Breton. In addition, the minister of finance unveiled an enriched tax-incentive scheme for new investment in the area.

The advisory committee reported in September 1985 and presented thirty-four recommendations.[16] The great majority of these were approved and implemented. The committee called for the establishment of a new one-stop agency for business incentives (to be called Enterprise Cape Breton – ECB), for modifications to the tax-incentive program introduced earlier by the minister of finance, for the modernization of the steel mill at Sydney, and for amendments to several federal-provincial regional development agreements.

Enterprise Cape Breton was established in 1985. A program of special incentives was also quickly announced for the island, including a new investment tax credit and a new Cape Breton Topping-Up Assistance program. This program was designed to provide cash grants of up to 60 per cent of eligible capital costs, compared to a maximum of 30 per cent elsewhere in the country. ECB became a part of the Atlantic Canada Opportunities Agency (ACOA) in 1987.[17]

All in all, Sinclair Stevens took up the Cape Breton challenge with determination; he subsequently turned to other slow-growth regions with the same commitment. Stevens also led the charge with his provincial counterparts in developing an 'intergovernmental position on regional economic development' and chaired a meeting of regional development ministers on 21 January 1985, during which he sought to establish an agreement on a number of fronts. He and his colleagues agreed to promote equal opportunities for the well-being of Canadians, further economic development to reduce disparity in opportunities, and provide essential public services of reasonable quality to all Canadians.[18]

Stevens was also successful in getting all ministers to agree to a set of nine 'fundamental' principles to guide all governments in Canada in their efforts to promote regional economic development.[19] These principles stated:

- The federal and provincial governments view regional economic development as a high priority among national and provincial economic goals.
- The overall objective of regional development is to improve employment and income through sustainable economic activity based on realistic opportunities in each region.
- Initiatives should be developed through consultation and discussion to assist Canadians in the less-developed regions to achieve greater economic security based on economic opportunity.
- Closer federal-provincial cooperation should be achieved by harmonizing all regional economic development efforts.
- All major national policies should be judged, in part, in terms of their regional impact. And, so far as is possible, those policies should reinforce the goal of fair and balanced regional development.
- Particular emphasis by governments should be given to improving

the investment climate, to removing impediments to growth, and to creating opportunities for the private sector to contribute to maximum economic growth in all parts of Canada.

- Continuing consultation with the private sector should focus on policies in areas such as innovation, exports, marketing, productivity, and training, with the overall purpose of developing concerted strategies for growth and adjustment.
- Governments should explore opportunities for increasing inter-regional trade and eliminating barriers between provinces.
- Transportation is recognized as a key to regional economic development.

Though the guiding principles were quite general in nature and still hardly constituted a clear guide for action, one ought not to dismiss their importance. It was the first time all ministers reached an agreement, however broad, on regional development. Moreover, some participants at the meeting now report that Sinclair Stevens would have gone further and outlined specific measures but that some provincial governments resisted. As it was, Stevens was able to secure an all-government agreement that ERDAs would remain the key instruments to deliver regional development programming, that new efforts would be launched in support of small and medium-sized businesses, and that all governments would instruct their officials to prepare, among other things, a series of options that could attract investment in all regions of the country.[20] If nothing else, the intergovernmental agreement firmly established Stevens as a friend of regional development and the slow-growth regions.

Still, Stevens needed all the credibility he could muster. The Mulroney government, only eighteen months into its mandate, began to hear criticism from slow-growth regions about its regional development efforts. This was true not only at the provincial level, but also within the government caucus in Ottawa, notably from Atlantic and some western MPs.

The first signs of disenchantment involved the closure of the heavy-water plants in Cape Breton. This sent signals throughout Atlantic Canada that the region could no longer count on political heavyweights in cabinet, like Allan MacEachen or Roméo LeBlanc, to protect federal spending in the region. Moreover, some began to ask why the region was being singled out for spending cuts. In addition, while the country was coming out of the deep recession of the early 1980s, economic growth was concentrated largely in central Canada. Indeed, by the mid-1980s, some observers were already pointing to the likelihood that the economies of southern Ontario and Quebec would overheat. Meanwhile, the Atlantic economy, where unemployment rates had fallen only slightly, was still in the doldrums. To make matters worse, the four Atlantic provincial governments were now taking dead aim at Ottawa's regional development efforts, even though they were all partisan allies of the Mulroney Progressive Conservative Party.

The press was reporting that the bulk of spending under DRIE was being directed to Ontario and Quebec. For example, over 70 per cent of DRIE's spending under the Industrial and Regional Development Program (IRDP) was going to Ontario and Quebec. By contrast, at least 40 per cent of DREE's budget had been consistently spent in Atlantic Canada.[21]

DRIE had other problems. It was viewed as a large, cumbersome, and bureaucratic department, largely insensitive to the economic circumstances of the Maritime provinces and Newfoundland and Labrador. Both the local business community and provincial governments in the region became openly critical of the slowness and bureaucratic nature of the DRIE approval process. One official revealed that a decision under a *signed* DRIE subsidiary agreement on a given project had to go through some twenty-two federal 'vetting centres.'[22] In fairness to DRIE, it must be noted that there was a tendency to compare the effectiveness of DRIE to DREE, which was not just. It was much like comparing oranges and apples. One major difference, of course, was that DRIE did not have the clear unencumbered mandate to promote regional economic development that DREE had had. This difference probably explains the main criticism that was directed at DRIE: that it was essentially an industry department and not a regional development department.

Many federal officials were very candid about the seemingly inherent conflicts in DRIE's dual mandate to promote industrial and regional development. The 'shotgun wedding' of DREE and IT&C was often referred to, and many concluded that the marriage had not worked. One frequently heard about the pulling and shoving inside DRIE over whether to concentrate on high-growth industries and to build on Canada's existing industrial strength (often located in central Canada) or on regional development. Former IT&C officials in DRIE were convinced that DREE issues dominated in the department, while former DREE officials were equally convinced of the opposite.[23]

It did not take long for the Atlantic and western premiers to view

DRIE as part of the problem rather than as part of the solution. The point was even made that DRIE programming had, in fact, increased regional disparities rather than contributing to their alleviation. The programs for which DRIE controlled the funds, such as IRDP and the Defence Industry Productivity Program (DIPP), applied to a far greater extent in southern Ontario and southern Quebec than they did in either eastern or western Canada. A province like Prince Edward Island, for example, had virtually no hope of taking full advantage of these programs because it lacked the appropriate economic and industrial base.

Some provincial government officials in the Maritime provinces also began to report that on occasion, firms, thinking of establishing a plant in either their region or southern Ontario, received more generous offers from DRIE to locate in southern Ontario.[24] It was true that under IRDP's tier system, the slow-growth regions were favoured. Since the tier system only established maximum levels of federal assistance, however, it was possible for DRIE to offer a more generous grant to set up in a more developed region simply by offering the maximum level available under that particular tier and less than the maximum under other tiers that apply to slow-growth regions.

The Mulroney government attempted to respond to this criticism in several ways. It unveiled a new interest buy-down program, through the Atlantic Enterprise Program (AEP), as well as a commitment under the Atlantic Opportunities Program (AOP) to ensure that the federal government would buy more of its goods and services from Atlantic Canadian firms.[25]

No matter what new initiative the federal government introduced, it seems that it could never successfully divert the attention of the slow-growth provinces, the media, and even members of its own party away from DRIE and its ongoing programs. In addition, as more and more Liberals came to office at the provincial level, Mulroney cabinet ministers grew increasingly restless with DRIE, in particular with the ERDAs. Just as the issue of visibility had led Trudeau ministers to revise the GDA approach, many Mulroney ministers similarly began to question the ERDA process. Increasing numbers of them began to voice deep concern about the lack of visibility for federal spending and the inability of ERDAs to reflect 'federal' priorities. They were dismayed that the federal government appeared to be continually on the defensive in responding to provincially packaged initiatives. In addition, many officials in Ottawa, particularly those in the Department of Finance, increasingly questioned the value of ERDA-sponsored programs. These concerns came to a boil in the late fall of 1986, and the Cabinet Committee on Economic and Regional Development declared a moratorium on new ERDA initiatives.

At this time, the committee also directed DRIE to launch a review of its regional development efforts. The purpose of the review was to determine 'the extent to which ERDAs and their instruments address current federal economic development priorities and how ERDA implementation is proceeding.'[26] The review found a number of weaknesses, both with the existing approach and how it was being implemented.

It found that there was 'considerable preoccupation in simply responding to ERDA proposals put forward by individual provinces and using the ERDA as a vehicle to provide incremental funds.'[27] Several reasons were found to account for this situation. Federal officials who had negotiated the ERDAs admitted that 'the objectives contained in the ERDAs are very broad in nature, and in some cases vague.'[28] They added that Schedule A of ERDAs, which outlined strategic development priorities, was still sufficiently broad to support virtually any type of activity.

No internal review of federal regional development efforts would be complete without a close look at the issue of federal 'visibility.' This review was no exception. Indeed, the issue had been a key factor behind the moratorium on new ERDA activities. This, even though the Mulroney government had been elected only thirty months earlier on an agenda to promote national reconciliation and with a promise to do away with federal direct delivery of projects. The government had said early in its mandate that it was little concerned with the matter of visibility. By contrast, the Trudeau government had been so concerned that it had included a special clause in the ERDA legislation that read: 'The ERDA will provide for the development of a public information program that will provide, wherever possible and in a manner satisfactory to the Minister of DRIE, for the permanent recognition of the contribution of the federal government under ... any subsidiary agreement.'[29]

It did not take long for the Mulroney government to change its tune. In June 1986, it put together a new ERDA guide for public information. The guide reported that ERDA communications objectives should, among other things, 'seek to ensure that in two or three years time the federal government be clearly perceived in each province as having made a substantial contribution to regional economic development through the ERDA process.'[30] The DRIE review concluded that there was substantial room for improving federal visibility under ERDA programming. It revealed that – with some exceptions – subsidiary agreements were meeting 'minimum' public-information requirements.

There was little doubt that the public-information objectives laid out in the ERDA guide were not being met. The review claimed that the decision 'to revert to the conventional provincial delivery approach' had not helped matters. It echoed the same conclusion reached by Trudeau's ministers in the early 1980s: 'When provincial agencies deliver joint programs, there is a tendency for the public to develop the impression that the investment involved is exclusively provincial.'[31]

DRIE did not only look back to see what it had accomplished in regional economic development. Sinclair Stevens called on his provincial counterparts to join him in establishing a federal-provincial Task Force on Regional Development to plan ahead on what should be done jointly at the regional level. His provincial colleagues agreed.

The task force brought together seventeen federal and provincial officials to coordinate the work and a number of others to undertake specific tasks. The task force sought 'to identify approaches and measures which have been and will be effective in achieving the goals of regional development, in the past and for the next decade.'[32] The review was all-encompassing. The task force was asked to look at regional economic development programs, the effect of Canada-wide growth and investment policies on regional development, the regional impact of sectoral policies and programs, the influence of fiscal and personal transfers on regional development, and experiences from other jurisdictions.[33] It was asked to submit an interim report by September 1986 and a final report by the end of the year. The final report was submitted to a Conference of First Ministers in Toronto, but not until November 1987.

The task force made a number of sweeping observations, including the following:

- Despite regional development efforts, regional disparities remain much the same.
- The principal mechanism for reducing regional economic disparities has been personal and fiscal transfers from governments, but these are directed at symptoms, not causes.
- Fiscal and personal transfers are now so expensive that significantly higher levels (i.e., greater reliance on transfers) appear unlikely.
- Recipients of these transfers do not want more dependence (transfers or make-work) but more opportunity for self-reliance.

- Regional development efforts have been either insufficient or ineffective in increasing the capacity of lagging regions to generate wealth.
- Efforts to attract large-scale 'investment-in' have not been cost-effective, and benefits from such investment have generally been short-lived.
- Development efforts have been pursued in the absence of a 'level playing field' because national and sectoral policies tend to build on the economic strengths of wealthier regions; as those strengths become vulnerable to international competition, industrial-policy interventions exacerbate this problem.
- Development should be a long-term process; by contrast, development efforts have often been ad hoc and subject to frequent change in the absence of a regional development policy that focuses on specialization within and among regions.
- 'Ad-hocery' in development efforts encourages competition among regions in which economic and political factors are determinants.
- Expectations about what governments can achieve to reduce regional disparities are markedly out of line with economic reality and experience.[34]

The task force sought to wrestle with some key issues. One of the first was the resource-allocation process. It examined trends in allocating federal funding and also the European experience. It assessed the merits of funding on the basis of fiscal resources through such instruments as tax points, tax transfers to the provinces, and the equalization formula. The task force cautioned that, in allocating financial resources on this basis, one must first establish that regional economic need exists. The difficulty, of course, is that there is no single indicator of economic need that is widely accepted.

The task force also looked at whether historical allocations or trends could serve as a guide for allocating further regional economic development funds. It rejected this option, arguing that the approach simply begs the question of whether existing historical allocations conform to widely accepted criteria. Another option it considered was a regional-wide basis or a grouping of provinces. This approach was thought to hold some merit, particularly in the ability it afforded to set an overall regional planning framework with the flexibility that entails. The difficulty, however, was in defining an appropriate supra-provincial region. Ad hoc allocations, meanwhile, were thought to hold some appeal, because of their flexibility. The downside, however, is obvious. Ad hoc allocations always open up regional development funding to political pressure and the risk of seeing the bulk of the funding going to short-term crises in specific areas. The Europeans, the report argued, had not come up with what they considered to be a viable solution. The European Community's Regional Development Fund was allocated to the members on a 'needs' basis, involving the per capita GDP of disadvantaged regions and their population size. The task force saw little merit in this arrangement, insisting that, among other things, the process was not sufficiently flexible for funds to be moved around to support the most promising development opportunities.

Though the task force pondered the merits and disadvantages of various options, it did not come out clearly in support of any one approach. Instead, it recommended that governments keep an open mind and choose the criteria to correspond to the objectives at hand and policy choices.[35]

The task force was not the only body to have looked at economic development policy. It will be recalled that the former Trudeau government had established in 1983 a Royal Commission on the Economic Union and Development Prospects for Canada. The commission – commonly known as the Macdonald Commission because of its chairperson, the former minister of finance Donald Macdonald – reported in 1985. It did not spend much time on regional development policy, but when it did, it was hardly positive. It concluded that 'there has been no discernible progress with regard to regional development. This finding alone would appear to be a serious indictment of the many policy efforts, and very large public sector outlays that, it was argued, could achieve that goal.'[36] The commission also borrowed from the neo-classical school of economics and reported on the 'transfer dependency' syndrome. It argued that the syndrome creates 'a vicious circle in which economic misfortune begets transfers which, in turn, father poor economic policies which beget further economic misfortune ... This situation causes increasing expense to the economic union as a whole.'[37]

Despite the pessimistic conclusions on efforts thus far, the commissioners argued that 'regional development must remain one of Canada's primary policy goals.'[38] It approved the federal-provincial ERDA process and concluded that 'the total federal financial commitment to regional development, which would combine the Regional Economic Development Grants [sic] with funds spent through ERDAs should *increase* significantly over the next few years.'[39] The main public focus on the Macdonald Commission's report, however, was on its recommendation to move ahead with a free-trade arrangement with the United States. Perhaps as a result, the report had only a limited impact on the country's regional development agenda.

Attempts to strengthen federal regional development efforts received a major setback when Sinclair Stevens was forced to resign as DRIE minister over charges that he had been in a serious conflict of interest. To rescue the financially strapped family business, Nora Stevens, his wife, had obtained a $2.6 million loan at a favourable interest rate from a firm that had secured $68 million in incentives from DRIE while Sinclair Stevens was minister.[40] One of the first casualties of the Stevens resignation was the intergovernmental Task Force Report on Regional Development. The report had lost its champion, and by the time the final draft was submitted, it was hopelessly overtaken by a number of events, as we shall see. All indications suggest that, like the Forget report, it was quietly shelved.[41]

Stevens's resignation in May 1986 opened up a new wave of criticism about DRIE from slow-growth regions. Prime Minister Mulroney met the Atlantic premiers on his way to a special Priorities and Planning Committee meeting in St John's the following September. He heard firsthand the complaints about DRIE. Better to have no federal regional programming at all, he was told, than to have DRIE. With its programs favouring central Canada, it was argued, DRIE served only to exacerbate regional disparities.[42]

DRIE was criticized on other points. It was again widely condemned as overly bureaucratic. Atlantic Canada's business community publicly hurled accusations at the department's bureaucratic tendencies, suggesting that they had to wait months for the local office to get a reply from the Ottawa head office on their applications. The prime minister himself got into the act when he mocked DRIE's many layers of bureaucratic decision making before the New Brunswick Economic Council. The most widely heard criticism, however, was again that DRIE was not a regional development department at all but, rather, an industry department, mainly concerned with southern Ontario and southern Quebec.

The prime minister returned to Ottawa from his Atlantic tour resolved to revamp completely the government's regional policy. Shortly afterward, the federal government announced in the 1986 Speech from the Throne that it would establish the Atlantic Canada Opportunities Agency. The government declared: 'Regional disparity remains an unacceptable reality of Canadian Life ... It is time to consider new approaches, to examine how our considerable and growing support for Canada's regions can be used more efficiently, more effectively and with greater sensitivity to local conditions and opportunities.'[43] Mulroney wanted above all a 'new' approach, one that would constitute a complete break from the past.[44]

The new DRIE minister, Michel Côté, made a plea for DRIE to house ACOA.[45] It was quickly decided by the prime minister, however, that the new agency would not be a part of DRIE or associated in any way with the department. DRIE, with its tier approach to industrial development, had by early 1987 been largely discredited. To add to the department's woes, Treasury Board discovered that DRIE was going to overspend its 1986–7 grants and contributions budget by nearly $350 million. Two reviews were launched, one internal and the other by the accounting firm Price Waterhouse.[46] The bulk of the new financial commitments were made under both the various ERDAs and the department's incentive program – IRAP – when Stevens was minister.

To add still more to DRIE's woes, Michel Côté was also forced to resign from cabinet over a conflict of interest. He had secured an undeclared loan from a friend while in cabinet, which was in violation of the government's conflict-of-interest guidelines.[47]

The establishment of a new regional development agency outside its jurisdiction, combined with the department's financial and political difficulties, spelled the end of DRIE. Few would deny that it lived a rather tortuous existence from its beginnings. Special review committees, departmental task forces, and working groups had been set up to review departmental policies, mandates, programs, program cohesion, services, and so on. Some of these reported on the department's two distinct mandates, observing that 'many perceive DRIE's image as blurred, with its distinguishing competence eroded,' and virtually all reported on the dual and, at times, conflicting mandates of national industrial development and regional development.[48] Added to this was the fact that from 1982 to 1987 DRIE had had four ministers, four deputy ministers, and numerous other changes of senior-level personnel.

ACOA – Looking East

On his way to the September 1986 Priorities and Planning (P&P) Cabinet Committee meeting in St John's, Mulroney stopped in Fredericton to meet with New Brunswick Premier Richard Hatfield. Hatfield told him that, contrary to what was happening in central Canada, the region had been unable to bounce back from the deep recession of the early 1980s. He then gave the prime minister a brief calling for the establishment of a new economic development agency for Atlantic Canada.[49] The paper outlined how such an agency should be structured and what it ought to do. Discussions at the P&P meeting, as well as at other informal meetings with local business groups and regional associations, also confirmed what the prime minister had been hearing from his own Atlantic caucus about the plight of the Atlantic economy.

Mulroney returned to Ottawa with firm intentions of doing something for Atlantic Canada. To be sure, his government had already introduced some new measures for the region – notably, the Atlantic Enterprise Program and Atlantic Opportunities Program and a special initiative for Cape Breton. But it had not done much to change the way DRIE had been operating since its establishment in 1983 by the Trudeau government. Mulroney had not even made good on his election campaign promise to give DRIE a specific legislative mandate to promote the least developed regions, which was to entail every department's submitting to the Standing Committee on Economic and Regional Development annual assessments of the effect of their policies on specific regions. Shortly after the prime minister's visit to the region, the federal government held an open conference on economic development in Atlantic Canada. Labelled the 'Atlantic Focus Conference,' the conference was attended by federal cabinet ministers from the region, who heard a barrage of criticism directed at Ottawa's economic policies, which, they were told time and again, were in large part responsible for the region's underdevelopment. They were also told that past attempts to rectify the situation had not been successful, largely because they had been designed in Ottawa.

In response to this challenge, the prime minister decided to bypass DRIE. In addition to its political, policy, and administrative problems, the prime minister had become convinced, in light of what many people had told him, that DRIE was more of a problem than a possible solution for the Maritimes.

It is important to note that the prerogative to establish new agencies and departments or to abolish existing ones in the government of Canada belongs exclusively to the prime minister.[50] Some key cabinet ministers may be consulted, but it is up to the prime minister to decide who to consult and when. Full cabinet and even P&P are often briefed on government changes only after the decision has been made and often only after an announcement has been made. DREE was a good case in point. Trudeau consulted only his two most senior ministers, Marc Lalonde and Allan J. MacEachen, before deciding to abolish DREE. The minister of DREE, Pierre De Bané, and the minister of industry, trade, and commerce, Herb Gray, were simply informed the evening before the announcement that the two departments would be merged. Other ministers, including senior regional ministers, learned of the change through the news media like everyone else.

The Privy Council Office explains that it is necessary for the prime minister to have a free hand in such decisions because cabinet could never properly take on the task. Ministers and their departments could scarcely be expected to look at such matters in a detached and objective fashion. To put it briefly, they could not be expected to put aside their self-interest to look at the broader context in the interest of the government as a whole in organizing government departments or in reallocating program responsibilities between departments.

In any event, Mulroney decided that he would have a direct hand in shaping ACOA. To the extent possible, he did not want the public service involved in the planning process. He felt certain that, left to their own judgment, public servants would simply come back with a recommendation that would see ACOA integrated in some way in the DRIE apparatus. Mulroney went outside of government for advice on how to structure ACOA. He gave the adviser free reign on what issues to look at and what kind of recommendations to bring forward, and asked only that Atlantic Canadians be consulted. Over one hundred Atlantic Canadians were consulted, including provincial premiers, federal cabinet ministers from the region, senior provincial officials, and a cross-section of business people, labour, academics, and voluntary associations. The consultations confirmed yet again that DRIE was not well regarded in the region and that Ottawa was perceived to be far more concerned with promoting economic development in Ontario and Quebec than in Atlantic Canada.

The consultations, however, pointed to other concerns.[51] The region's business community was highly critical of the federal bureaucracy and, almost to a person, argued that they preferred working with their provincial governments rather than with the federal government. That said, they reported that provincial governments were often less likely than the federal government to make tough policy decisions and some also argued that all too often partisan political considerations guided the development of new projects. In addition, a number of business representatives, academics, and federal officials argued that the four Atlantic provinces were incapable of taking a broad regional view of economic development and invariably looked to their provincial respective interests first. Still, they argued, provincial bureaucracies could get things done quickly and competently at the program level. The federal public service, meanwhile, was considered to be overly bureaucratic and hopelessly inadequate in 'delivering the goods' and in getting things done.

When asked what was needed, the response – again, almost to a person – was that there was no need for any 'more cash grants programs and the government would do well to cut back or streamline existing ones.'[52] The business community did, however, acknowledge the need for *limited*, one-time cash grants to those wishing to start new businesses. They added a qualifier to the effect that any such program for would-be entrepreneurs should be delivered by the provincial – not the federal – government.

Apart from urging that cash-grant programs be moved over to the provinces, business people also made a strong plea for both orders of government to streamline existing programs, one remarking that existing programs constituted a veritable 'tower of Babel.'[53] He added that there was such a variety of federal, provincial, and federal-provincial incentive schemes that even a good number of senior government officials, themselves in the economic development field in Atlantic Canada, did not know the full range of government assistance available to the private sector. It should thus not come as a surprise, he observed, that the business community had lost track of what was available to them.

Meanwhile, most government officials consulted supported the ERDA approach, acknowledged DRIE's shortcomings, and urged that the proposed agency be given enough clout to deal effectively with large federal departments.[54] Provincial officials expressed the hope that the agency would have the capacity to review the impact of existing national policies and programs on the region. They insisted that many of the negative consequences of national policies in the region were inadvertent and that large spending would not be required to correct them.

Many business people spoke about the need for greater access to new technology, new knowledge, and new ways of doing things, and, more specifically, for a research capacity geared to new product development and packaging techniques. They reported that local businesses were too small to have such expertise in-house and that, frequently, they had nowhere to turn for assistance in the region. A number claimed that, by and large, the universities had not responded well to their research needs and that there was insufficient two-way communication between the universities' research facilities and the private sector.

The report on establishing ACOA submitted to the prime minister pointed to endogenous development as the key to the future of Atlantic Canada. Atlantic Canadians themselves, it argued, 'will have to provide the energy, the skills and the imagination to conceive and organize economic activity if the region is to prosper.'[55] The report provided an analogy to explain past efforts to promote economic development in the region. It read:

> During the Second World War, natives of some Pacific islands saw the arrival of American troops. The Americans cleared and leveled an oblong piece of the jungle, set lights along the edges, and, lo! after a while, a giant silver bird arrived, bearing all manner of valuable things. This gave rise to a 'cargo cult' among the natives, who, having seen what the Americans had done to attract the silver bird, similarly set about clearing portions of the jungle and then waited by their fires, patiently and reverently, for the arrival of the bird. In practice, our regional industrial policy resembles these cargo cults. In regions where it was wished to attract economic development, industrial parks were constructed and cash grants offered. It was then time to sit back and wait for the silver bird of industry. No one knows for sure where the mysterious bird was to come from. Rarely did it come and when it did, it seldom stayed for very long. This approach to regional industrial development, mechanistic in its instruments, thinks magically about outcomes. In the cargo cult magic, the population of the designated region plays a passive role, except for the government officials who simply prepare the runway. If the silver bird comes, the people will provide the labour but the organization and promotion of economic activity comes from the outside. In short, the motor of economic development is exogenous.[56]

The report made the case that this approach had limited impact in the past and that there was no reason to believe that it would have more success in future. It went on to suggest how ACOA should be structured and also to identify what new measures it should introduce. It recommended that ACOA should be a 'stand-apart' agency, completely divorced from existing federal departments and agencies.[57] The report considered whether it should have Crown-corporation status, thus enabling it to operate independently; however, while there were advantages to this model, the report concluded that the drawbacks were far more serious. It was felt that it would be unlikely that a Crown corporation could exercise much influence in the ongoing federal government policy and decision-making processes and that, in the long run, the inherent isolation of a Crown corporation would inhibit federal regional development efforts. It was difficult to imagine how the agency, if it were a Crown corporation, could gain easy access to central agencies and cabinet committees, which is necessary if it is to influence federal policy and decision making.

The report recommended an organizational model that sits on the boundary between a government department and a Crown corporation. The agency must have the capacity, it was argued, to bring its activities and policy recommendations into the mainstream of parliamentary and cabinet affairs. It must have the capacity to seek advice and guidance from Atlantic Canadians, particularly from the private sector. It must also be able to respond quickly, in tandem with the provinces, to emerging economic opportunities in the region. Accordingly, it was concluded, it must be a stand-apart agency operating in full autonomy from any other federal department and with easy and unencumbered access to effective decision-making authority in Ottawa – that is, to cabinet and cabinet committees.[58]

The agency, the report also insisted, itself should not operate programs.[59] Rather, it should rely on existing federal and provincial departments and agencies for program delivery. The reasons for this recommendation were varied. It was felt that the agency could not, on the one hand, manage a new Atlantic Canada Fund and, on the other, operate programs that would be eligible to draw resources from the fund. In addition, it was felt that the management of programs would likely consume too much time and energy of the agency's most senior officials and inhibit the emergence of the necessary multidisciplinary perspective on the region's economic problems and opportunities. To be involved in setting up a program-delivery capacity would entail unnecessary costs at a time when there were already more than enough such mechanisms in place.

The report borrowed from the work of Joseph Schumpeter, David McClelland, and David Winter, highlighted in chapter 3, and recommended a strong emphasis on entrepreneurship, the development of new endogenous companies, the enhancement of existing businesses, the development of new products, and the expansion into new national and international markets.[60] It called for the establishment of a small number of Centres for Entrepreneurial Development in the region. Their purpose would be to encourage universities in the area to develop entrepreneurship and small-business courses in their business schools, to put in place an outreach program and contact-referral services, and sponsor a series of seminars on entrepreneurship.

The report also urged the federal government to replace its IRDP programs with business-development agreements with all four Atlantic provinces. Through these agreements, the federal government could turn over to the provinces the responsibility for delivering incentives to the aspiring entrepreneurs and to the small- and medium-sized business community.

In addition, it was urged that the agency put a clear emphasis on market development for the region's business community, on research and development, on human-resources development, and on community development. It also recommended that the agency develop a strong capacity to ensure that national policies and programs be made more regionally sensitive. As a first concrete step, it was proposed that ACOA assess a selection of national programs from the perspective of their regional impact. In time, ACOA should be able to assess all new policy and program initiatives for their impact on Atlantic Canada. Lastly, it was recommended that the agency have the capacity to promote coordination between federal and provincial departments and the private sector to capture for the Atlantic Canada economy as many benefits as possible flowing out of large projects, such as the frigate-construction program in Saint John or the fixed-link crossing between New Brunswick and Prince Edward Island.[61]

Unveiling ACOA

Prime Minister Mulroney picked 6 June 1987 and St John's, Newfoundland, to unveil ACOA. He boldly declared, 'We begin with new money, a new mission and a new opportunity,' and went on to assert that 'the Agency will succeed where others had failed.'[62] He invited the four Atlantic premiers and a cross-section of Atlantic Canadians to attend his press conference, which was greeted with enthusiasm by the audience and the media. The *Fredericton Daily Gleaner*, for example, ran the headline 'Atlantic Canada Gets Big Boost' on its front page.[63] The local CBC wondered whether this would not end 'red tape' in economic development in Atlantic Canada.[64] The agency was even applauded by

Liberal politicians from the region. In New Brunswick, for example, opposition leader Frank McKenna warmly welcomed the announcement and observed, 'I believe with this composition of the Agency and terms of reference, there is reason to be optimistic.'[65] Nova Scotia Liberal leader Vince MacLean echoed McKenna's belief that the announcement was very positive for the region.[66]

While accepting many of the recommendations in the report, the prime minister also rejected a number of important ones. He did announce that the agency's headquarters would be located in Atlantic Canada (in Moncton); that it would be headed by a deputy minister; that it would have an independent advisory board of prominent Atlantic Canadians; that it would be more autonomous than a typical government department but that it would not enjoy Crown-corporation status; that it would assume responsibility for the ERDAs; that FEDCs would be transferred to it; that it would have as its main focus the promotion of entrepreneurial development; and that it would have three additional mandates – playing an advocacy role on behalf of the region before national policies and programs, promoting cooperation with the provinces through the ERDAs, and playing a coordinating role with other federal departments, the four provinces, and the private sector.[67] When it came to new financial resources, Mulroney proved very generous. He declared that ACOA would receive $1.05 billion in new money over five years.[68]

However, it became clear early on that, rather than relying on the provinces or other federal departments, the agency would have its own program-delivery capacity with regard to aspiring entrepreneurs and small businesses. Nor did the federal government accept the recommendation that funding for ACOA be found by cutting back regional development programming in the most developed regions of the country.

Still, Mulroney announced that 'two Maritimers' would lead the agency. Senator Lowell Murray, a Cape Breton native with strong ties to New Brunswick from having served as deputy minister to Premier Richard Hatfield, was appointed minister. Donald S. McPhail, a career public servant who was Canadian ambassador to West Germany at the time of the ACOA announcement, was appointed president, a deputy minister–level position. Both Murray and McPhail made clear in their first interviews that 'the Agency will have no Ottawa bureaucracy to answer to,' and both made it known that decisions, including policy decisions, would be made in the region.[69]

The legislation establishing ACOA gave considerable authority to the agency to plan, coordinate, and implement economic development measures in the region, including full authority to promote 'economic opportunities and development in Atlantic Canada over which Parliament has jurisdiction.'[70] It added that ACOA 'shall coordinate the policies and programs of the Government of Canada in relation to opportunity for economic development in Atlantic Canada.'[71] With regard to program authority, the legislation enabled ACOA to 'enter into agreements with the government of any province or provinces in Atlantic Canada respecting the carrying out of any program or project of the Agency.'[72] In addition, the agency 'may, by order, establish as a designated area, for the period set out in the order, any area in Atlantic Canada where, in the opinion of the Minister, exceptional circumstances provide opportunities for locally based improvements in productive employment.'[73]

The ACOA legislation was relatively well received both by members of Parliament and by outside groups invited to appear before the special house committee established to consider the proposed legislation. The bill did, however, run into some controversy when it sought to deal with the various federal regional development agencies operating in Cape Breton. Quite apart from DRIE, two other important federal agencies were operating in Cape Breton at the time ACOA was established. DEVCO had been established in the late 1960s to deal with the 'coal problem,' and it set about to close inefficient mines. At the same time it established a unit – the Industrial Division (ID) – designed to attract new manufacturing industries to the island. The ID division in DEVCO went through several phases – attempts, first, to attract footloose industries; next, to promote local development; and, finally, yet again, to encourage import replacements. Though few Cape Bretoners would argue that any of these initiatives had met with a great deal of success, fewer still wanted to see them stopped. The other federal agency operating on the island was Enterprise Cape Breton.

The ACOA legislation sought, however, to deal both with DEVCO's industrial-development efforts and with Enterprise Cape Breton. The legislation proposed to remove the former from DEVCO and to place it in a new Crown corporation to be named Enterprise Cape Breton Corporation (ECBC). The legislation laid out ECBC's purpose as follows: 'the objects of the Corporation are to promote and assist, either alone or in conjunction with any person or the Government of Canada or of Nova Scotia or any agency of either of those governments, the financing and development of industry on the Island of Cape Breton to provide employment outside the coal producing industry and to broaden the base of the economy of the Island.'[74] Significantly, the legislation reported that the head of ECBC would be the deputy minister of ACOA, with a vice-president located in Sydney, Nova Scotia, acting as chief operating officer. The opposition Liberals strongly felt that this reorganization was not necessary, that DEVCO should be left alone, and that ACOA should be established without reference to it. Many felt that the Mulroney government was simply emasculating the popular DEVCO mandate to get at the Allan J. MacEachen Cape Breton legacy.

The opposition Liberals in the Commons voted against the ACOA legislation because of the so-called DEVCO provision. The Senate, led by MacEachen, held the bill up for a few months and then attempted to split the legislation between ACOA and DEVCO. The Commons, however, succeeded in keeping it as one bill, and in the end the ACOA act not only established the agency but also created a new Crown corporation for Cape Breton (ECBC). The legislation was finally given formal assent on 18 August 1988.

The establishment of ACOA also raised questions about the future of Enterprise Cape Breton. It will be recalled that ECB was established by Sinclair Stevens as a result of recommendations from a private-sector advisory group to deal with the sudden closure of the two heavy-water plants on the island. It was hoped that it would become a 'one-stop window' for firms looking for assistance to locate in Cape Breton. ECB also provided, however, generous financial assistance to the private sector through its own programs. At the time it was established, it reported directly to DRIE Ottawa. However, under the new ACOA arrangements, ECB would report to the Nova Scotia ACOA office. This development added to concerns in Cape Breton that the changes brought about by ACOA would in the long run work against the island's economic interest.[75]

Legislation was only part of the challenge that senior ACOA officials faced. The pressure on them to come up with new measures was intense. Given the findings of the report that led to the establishment of ACOA, one thing was clear. Any new measures would have to be geared towards the private sector, with a strong emphasis on small businesses and established, as well as aspiring, entrepreneurs.

The agency thus went to cabinet to secure numerous changes to AEP. The first thing it sought was a new name for the program, recommending that it be called the Action Program. It then urged that the terms and contributions of AEP be radically amended:

- to provide grants and contributions to non-profit organizations, including municipalities and other agencies, that provide specialized services in support of entrepreneurship and small and medium-sized businesses;
- to provide contributions for a broader range of manufacturing, processing, and repair and maintenance activities, including primary or initial processing activities and contributions for those service industries already eligible for loan insurance and interest-rate buy-down;
- to extend eligibility to projects that attract intra-provincial, inter-provincial, and international tourists;
- to provide cash contributions towards eligible costs for business establishment, new product expansion, modernization, and expansion; for innovation projects, including financial support to innovators who license their innovative product or process; and for studies and technical assistance, such as the development of market and business plans, feasibility studies, and venture-capital searches, and for hiring a qualified person to implement a marketing plan;
- to provide a single maximum level of contribution by type of activity for the Atlantic region as follows: 50 per cent towards eligible capital costs for establishment, new-product expansion, modernization, and expansion; 60 per cent towards eligible costs for innovation projects and for financial support to innovators who license their innovative product/process; 75 per cent towards eligible costs for development of marketing and business plans, feasibility studies, and venture-capital searches; and 50 per cent towards the costs of hiring a qualified person, for a maximum of one year, to implement a marketing plan;
- to provide progress payments towards authorized contributions to eligible applicants for eligible activities under the program, so as to lessen the financial burden associated with bridge financing for small and medium-sized companies;
- to raise the maximum level of government support to 75 per cent for commercial operations and 100 per cent for non-commercial operations and modify the calculation procedure for tax credits so that only the cash-refundable portion – then 40 per cent for small and 20 per cent for large firms – is used;
- to remove the policy that makes provincial Crown corporations, their wholly owned or effectively controlled subsidiaries, and companies effectively controlled by provincial governments ineligible for federal financial assistance.

The basic tests applied by ACOA in reviewing applications under its Action Program were fairly straightforward. It first assessed a project's commercial viability to determine whether it had a reasonable chance of success. It then looked to see whether the project would result in economic benefit for Atlantic Canada, and finally it reviewed the need for assistance for the project to proceed. The only caveat was that those projects involving more than $20 million in capital costs would have to go through DRIE, which would retain responsibility for large industrial projects, even in Atlantic Canada.

The Action Program was formally introduced on 15 February 1988. The response was overwhelming – no doubt in part because so many types of economic activities became eligible, and in part because of the high-profile publicity campaign heralding its introduction, but also because the region was finally coming out of the deep recession of the early 1980s. It was also one of the most generous regional development programs ever introduced in Canada. For whatever reason, the Action Program was quick off the mark. After a little more than a year, ACOA had reviewed over 34,000 inquiries, processed 6,800 applications, and approved 2,700 projects under the Action Program.[76] Applications, initially at least, came in at ten times the rate of any predecessor programs, such as RDIA or IRDP.

The Action Program was in full swing by the fiscal year 1988–9, and during that year alone applications totaled 9,634, of which nearly 5,000 were approved. The greatest number of approved offers involved modernization and expansion, followed by the establishment of new facilities and studies. ACOA also reports that the program assisted over four hundred first-time entrepreneurs. Although only about eighty innovation projects had been supported, this level of assistance was reported to be five-fold the rate of support provided by previous programs.[77]

Over 15 per cent of approved projects fell under the Business Support element of the program or activities aimed at improving the quality of entrepreneurial skills in Atlantic Canada, including business-database improvement, Atlantic case studies, and counselling. About 80 per cent of all studies supported under the Action Program were valued at less than $25,000.[78]

On a sectoral basis, the manufacturing sector generated the greatest number of applications, and received the most significant share of assistance. On the basis of size, small projects – those valued at less than $200,000 – constituted the lion's share of applications approved. However, projects valued at more than $2,000,000 in eligible costs, while accounting for less than 5 per cent of the number of approved projects, received a relatively large share – about half – of committed funding.[79] In aggregate, ACOA's Action Program committed $523.5 million from its inception to March 1989 and is reported to have leveraged an estimated $1.3 billion in private-sector investment in the region. This, in turn, ACOA claimed, would support the creation of an estimated 12,500 full-time jobs and the maintenance of another 15,000 positions.[80]

The agency decided early on to place a strong emphasis on promoting greater cooperation with the four Atlantic provinces. Senator Murray went to his cabinet colleagues to lift the moratorium on new ERDA initiatives in Atlantic Canada. In doing so, he pledged that ACOA would do three things: first, it would approve new ERDA initiatives only if they were clearly supportive of broader ACOA efforts in promoting regional development; second, it would integrate initiatives within an agreed-upon financial framework; and third, it would strengthen its communications strategy to give proper visibility and recognition for federal spending. Murray acknowledged that there had been a tendency for the region's provincial governments to announce projects as being 'subject to obtaining federal participation,' thus placing federal ministers in the difficult position of either going along with the provincial demands or being pointed to as the reason the project could not proceed. This, he insisted, would stop in the next round of ERDA initiatives.[81]

Murray reported that a primary focus for new ERDA subsidiary agreements would be to strengthen the private sector and create new permanent jobs. He also reported that new initiatives would be required to stimulate entrepreneurship, which, he claimed, was becoming more evident in many parts of the region, and noted a need to ensure that new and existing entrepreneurs have access to a wide range of quality business services and advice in order to ensure as many as possible achieve success. Finally, new programs would focus on improving the ability of entrepreneurs to develop, adapt, and commercially exploit new technologies.[82]

Murray proposed that an Atlantic Cooperation Fund be set up to support new ERDA initiatives. He reminded his colleagues that in establishing ACOA the prime minister had given the agency over $1 billion of new money and all the funding available under DRIE's A base for Atlantic Canada for IRDP and for the ERDAs. This kind of funding amounted to about $973 million over five years, with spending expected to peak at $228.4 million in 1988–9. Murray proposed to allocate the bulk of the new money to the Action Program and to employ the old DRIE A base for ERDA agreements. He reminded his colleagues that the signed ERDA subsidiary agreements were for a five-year period and that the majority were scheduled to begin to expire in 1989. In the absence of a new arrangement, Murray pointed out, the expiry of the agreements would leave no provision for future funding of the ERDA initiatives of line departments within the fiscal framework. He proposed that the Atlantic Cooperation Fund eventually provide for the maintenance of around $1 billion in federal funding for new ERDA initiatives in the region, and that as they expired the name of the ERDAs be changed to 'Cooperation Agreements.' Funds would begin to accrue at the end of the 1988–9 fiscal year, with major new commitments possibly beginning the following year, when most existing subsidiary agreements would have expired. He reported that priority setting for new initiatives should begin and be guided by a predictable financial-planning framework. Interim financing that he and his colleagues were prepared to support could start right away and come from departmental A bases, the policy reserve, or ACOA itself, in the case of initiatives falling clearly within its mandate.[83]

In late 1987, cabinet agreed to lift the moratorium on new ERDA initiatives. Indeed, it decided to give the green light to sign new ERDA subsidiary agreements everywhere in the country. ACOA was quick off the mark and, within a few months, Murray had his senior officials initiate intense negotiations on a new round of ERDA subsidiary agreements. Agreement was reached with all four provinces that the key elements of future ERDA subsidiary agreements would be entrepreneurship, innovation and technology transfer, marketing and trade development, human-resource development, and the environment. The ERDA agreements would be renamed Cooperation Agreements, and these too would have a ten-year life span.

ACOA reported little success with its 'advocacy' mandate. Indeed, it acknowledged that it 'may appear somewhat unusual for an Agency that is part of a federal system to be given a statutory role in advocating the interests of a particular region within that system.'[84] It added, however, that past experience had shown that 'regional interests cannot be adequately protected without an effective ongoing direct link to the central decision-making structure.'[85]

The agency reported that it had little success on either the coordination or advocacy fronts because, it insisted, it was never given the resources to be effective in these areas. ACOA argued that obtaining new money was only part of the equation. It also required sufficient staff or, in the parlance of bureaucracy, a sufficient number of person-years, to carry out its four mandates. ACOA was given 320 person-years. This, the agency argued, was barely sufficient to implement the Action Program properly. Indeed, ACOA maintained, it had to hire some fifty people on special contract to deal with the backlog of applications under the Action Program. Central agencies, in particular Treasury Board, resisted time and again any attempt by ACOA to secure more staff. Treasury Board had another agenda to pursue. It had to implement a 15,000-person-year cut in the federal public service that the Mulroney government had announced as part of a broad policy of restraint in government spending.[86]

In any event, relations between central agencies in Ottawa and ACOA were rarely smooth. It will be recalled that, initially, some thought had been given to establishing a Crown corporation so that the agency could operate at arm's length from the bureaucratic requirements of the federal bureaucracy. Later, attempts were made to position the agency somewhere between a central agency and a typical government department. This is one of the reasons why the head of ACOA was called president rather than deputy minister and that the heads of the provincial offices were vice-presidents rather than assistant deputy ministers. But the differences between ACOA and a typical line department were only superficial, and ACOA had to deal with central agencies in the same way that all other federal departments do.

It is clear, however, that the 'Ottawa system' had had more difficulties dealing with ACOA than it usually has with a typical government department. Regional policy, as we already noted, has never been popular in Ottawa. This has been true dating back to DREE's early days. It appears, however, that the situation was worse with ACOA. For one thing, its headquarters were not in Ottawa. Many Ottawa-based officials felt that they had lost control and that several relatively independent regional agencies were operating outside of the national capital, often at cross-purposes or in direct competition with one another without regard for national policies. For another, the idea of establishing ACOA came from the prime minister, not from the public service. In addition, national departments like DRIE – later, the Department of Industry, Science, and Technology and more recently Industry Canada – viewed ACOA as somewhat of an upstart, often playing havoc with their national perspectives and national economic development efforts.

The return of a majority Mulroney government in the 1988 national election saw some changes to the Ottawa decision-making process. A new cabinet Expenditure Review Committee (ERC), chaired by the prime minister, was set up to 'ensure that the Government's expenditure control continues to contribute to deficit reduction.'[87] The committee had its first meeting only a few days after it was established and initiated a thorough review of the government's expenditure budget.

The ERC was assisted in its work by central agency officials from the Privy Council Office, the Department of Finance, and the Treasury Board Secretariat. These officials expressed deep concerns after reviewing ACOA's spending plans. They argued that the agency was quickly overcommitting its budget, much as DRIE had done a few years earlier. They also argued that the agency's spending was out of control, that the Action Program had not only generated far too many applications but, more seriously, far too many approvals. Indeed, they argued that AOCA had initiated 'indiscriminate' spending.

Their views had some impact. The committee directed ACOA to spend its $1.05 billion of new resources over seven years, rather than five.[88] This obviously played havoc with ACOA's spending plans, and agency officials were forced to rethink many of their initiatives. It meant, for one thing, that the ACOA budget was fully committed for the fiscal year 1989–90, thus leaving no room to approve new initiatives. As a result, ACOA announced in May 1989 a significant modification to its Action Program. The agency imposed a new ceiling of $200,000 – down from $20 million – in eligible costs under the Action Program.[89] In addition, the minister of finance announced in his budget speech that in future the federal government would make all cash grants and contributions to the private sector to promote industrial and regional development repayable.[90]

In June 1989, Donald S. McPhail was removed as president of ACOA and replaced by Peter Leseaux, a career public servant and long-time personal friend of the prime minister who attended Saint Francis Xavier University with him in the 1950s. Notwithstanding these changes, there were plenty of reasons for concern as ACOA celebrated its third anniversary in the summer of 1990. Some observers still felt that the agency was being employed as a political 'slush fund' by the Mulroney government.[91] There were lingering suspicions that 'ACOA had reemerged as a re-configured version of DRIE, staffed to its previous level by many of the same individuals who previously worked to make the system appear complicated and complex.'[92] Others expressed concern that ACOA was putting far too much of its effort and funding into cash grants. The Action Program, they felt, was too open-ended and supported far too many projects, creating an over-capacity in many sectors. Some new businesses supported by the Action Program, it was argued, simply put existing enterprises, which did not have government-supported modern facilities, out of business.[93]

Meanwhile, Dalton Camp, a well-known partisan and a columnist with the *Toronto Star*, took an opposite view. He argued that ACOA had become so successful operating outside of the Ottawa system that senior mandarins were out to do it in. He insisted that McPhail's firing was a result of 'a bureaucratic coup in the national capital.' He added, 'the small bores in Finance, Treasury Board and latterly in the Prime Minister's Office, who have opposed ACOA from the outset, should not be allowed to make McPhail the first victim in their long campaign to destroy the Agency.'[94]

Free Trade

Mulroney led his party to victory after a gruelling 1988 national election campaign over the recently negotiated Canada-U.S. Free Trade Agreement (FTA). In 1990 Mexican officials asked the United States to consider negotiating a free trade agreement. Mulroney initially decided not to join the negotiations but later changed his mind. The North American Free Trade Agreement (NAFTA) negotiations began in June 1991. The three countries hoped that they would come to an agreement quickly, given that FTA provided a model. NAFTA had a particularly difficult ride in the U.S. Congress, and President Clinton had to secure the support of former presidents Bush, Carter, and Ford to kick-start the NAFTA approval process. On 17 November 1993, NAFTA passed the U.S. Congress by a margin of 234 to 200 and three days later the Senate, 61 to 38. In Canada, the newly elected prime minister, Jean Chrétien, who had opposed FTA, promised during the 1993 election campaign to renegotiate NAFTA to obtain more favourable terms for Canada. Minor changes were introduced, falling short of what Chrétien said he wanted to secure regarding the dispute-resolution mechanism and energy protection. Chrétien signed NAFTA in December 1993.[95]

Mulroney's decision to pursue free trade agreements with the United States and Mexico promoted heated political debates in Canada. Economic nationalists felt that the Canadian economy was already overly integrated with the U.S. economy. They argued that Canada exported too much of its natural resources as raw materials to the U.S. and that free trade would make matters worse. Some observers feared the

'Maritimization' of the Ontario economy, arguing that U.S. interests would purchase Canadian firms, including financial institutions, and move the head offices and plants from Toronto to New York or Chicago, much as Ontario firms had done to firms from the Maritime provinces at the time Canada's National Policy took root.[96]

Continentalists took the opposite view, making the case that protectionist policies, including tariffs, had served only to inhibit economic development by limiting both opportunities for Canadian firms to expand in the United States and for U.S. firms to invest in Canada. Mulroney argued that free trade would create new economic opportunities everywhere in Canada, while Jean Chrétien voiced his opposition. Chrétien said, 'I opposed the Free Trade Agreement with the United States principally because I believed that an international trading policy for this country is preferable to a continental policy ... The more decentralized we become at home, the more difficult it is to resist the force of continental integration. That is why I insist that we have a national government strong enough to act on behalf of the whole country.'[97]

In December 1987, New Brunswick premier Frank McKenna jumped into the debate and, although he had reservations about certain aspects of the deal, declared his support for the proposed agreement. He observed: 'New Brunswick's economy is driven largely by its resource-based industries ... Our economy is dependent on export markets and, naturally, very dependent on our major trading partner – the United States.' He added, 'our view is that it is better to expend our energies preparing for the new liberalized environment than in resisting the thrust of the federal government's action in this area.'[98]

McKenna's support of the Canada-U.S. Free Trade Agreement meant a break in ranks with his fellow Liberals in Ottawa and elsewhere. John Turner, the federal opposition leader, made clear his opposition to the deal, as did Ontario premier David Peterson. Peterson explained, 'In 1980 and 1981, for example, we used the Auto Pact commitments to get Chrysler and American Motors to modernize and expand their Canadian operations ... The federal government gave away the option of extending auto parts status to offshore companies ... Ironically, the federal government which cooperated with us to attract Japanese assembly plants to Canada has now severely limited our ability to expand these facilities and attract new ones.'[99]

What is most ironic is that, some hundred years after the introduction of Canada's National Policy, the Ontario government would stand four square against the proposed free-trade agreement between Canada and the United States. The Ontario government approved the federal government's ability to shape public policy to favour central Canada and its promotion of the region's manufacturing sector. It now feared that these gains would be compromised under free trade. By contrast, the premier of New Brunswick was prepared to cross party lines to support the proposed agreement, convinced that it was in his region's economic interests.

Regional Development: Looking Everywhere

One of the most powerful regional ministers in the Mulroney cabinet was Don Mazankowski, the deputy prime minister, and one of his most important goals was to do for western Canada what Trudeau, Marchand, and Pelletier had done for Quebec. He was determined to place the 'western' agenda front and centre on the national political agenda. His agenda was an economic agenda, not a language one, as in the case of Quebec, and he sought to put in place measures to diversify the western economy. He, like other westerners, was convinced that the West needed to develop sectors other than agriculture, oil, and gas.

In addition, by early 1987, the Mulroney government was in serious political difficulty in the West.[100] Public-opinion polls showed that the government was struggling to maintain a narrow lead and that, at one point, it trailed the New Democratic Party. In 1986, the government nearly lost a by-election in Pembina, Alberta, hitherto regarded as one of its safest seats in the country. Worse still, that same year, the government had awarded the CF-18 maintenance contract to a Quebec firm, although a Winnipeg firm had submitted the lowest bid. The public outcry in western Canada against this decision still resonates in the region to this day. A general election was expected in 1988, and it was important for Mulroney to solidify his western base quickly if he was to have any hope of winning a second mandate.

Mulroney went to Edmonton to announce the details of the new Western Economic Diversification initiative (WD).[101] He said that the agency would administer a $1.2 billion fund of new money, and that, like its sister agency, ACOA, WD would assume responsibility for DRIE's A base in western Canada and for the western ERDAs. The prime minister explained that his government's regional policy was designed to provide 'federal leadership for each region, tailored to its unique potential and needs. At the same time, we want to ensure that regional perspectives are front and centre in the development of national priorities, and that regional economic development is backed by strong national centres of industrial and technological expertise.'[102]

Deputy Prime Minister Mazankowski explained that WD would be similar in many ways to ACOA, and that it represented in reality the second phase of a multi-step redefinition of Ottawa's regional development policy. 'We think it is very important,' he said, 'to develop economic programs that fit a particular region and for the decision-making to take place in that region. We believe that to establish a uniform policy across the country, administered out of Ottawa, is not the answer. Clearly, the approach we've had in the past, in terms of addressing regional economic expansion, has not worked.'[103]

On 15 July 1987, the federal government unveiled yet another special agency to promote economic development, this time in northern Ontario. In announcing Federal Economic Development Initiative for Northern Ontario (FedNor), the federal minister for the region, James Kelleher, pointed out that the government had consulted the business community and regional governments to determine what was needed. Although the reaction to the announcement was positive, it was much less so than that following the decisions to establish ACOA and WD. The Ontario government, for example, made it clear that it had not been involved in the consultations; indeed, a deputy minister declared 'there haven't been any senior level discussions yet, and it is not clear what FEDNOR is for.'[104]

What was clear, however, was that the federal government would make $55 million available over five years. Two years later, Ottawa allocated another $14 million in 'top up' funds to meet 'new commitments.' Shortly after that, the cabinet allocated $40 million to a Resource and Technology Development Program and then a further $40 million for priorities emerging towards the end of the five-year planning period.

When unveiling WD, the prime minister announced that DRIE would be disbanded and that a new Department of Industry, Science, and Technology (DIST) would be created. The new department would obviously lose direct responsibilities for regional economic development in Atlantic and western Canada. It would, however, bring together the parts of DRIE that were not being transferred to ACOA and WD, as well as parts of the Ministry of State for Science and Technology, which was also being disbanded.

The battle between the old DREE and the Department of Industry, Trade, and Commerce officials that had been waged in DRIE since its creation came to an end when the regional economic development agencies were established. In future, the national perspective would hold sway, and DIST was poised to take advantage of the restructuring to address the question of economic efficiency and Canada's ability to compete in a global economy. In short, efforts would be made to build on Canada's economic strengths.

One can easily trace recent federal regional economic development efforts in Quebec to the *Plan de l'Est* that DREE initially put together and DRIE later implemented. The federal government unveiled a major regional economic development plan for eastern Quebec in May 1983. The plan was directed exclusively to the area commonly referred to as Gaspésie–Bas-St-Laurent, which comprised about 5 per cent of Quebec's total population, or about 350,000 people. This was one of the last efforts of the Trudeau government in regional economic development. Because the Parti Québécois then held power in Quebec and, because of the importance placed on political visibility for federal-government spending, particularly during the later years of the Trudeau government, the *Plan de l'Est* was a federal direct-delivery initiative. The provincial government was barely consulted and was not asked to deliver the projects. The *Plan de l'Est* was given a budget of $264.7 million for the first five-year phase, which ended in March 1988. The plan concentrated its resources in seven sectors: agriculture, forestry, mining, transportation, fisheries, tourism, and industry. Its objectives were twofold: to create an environment favourable to the maintenance and development of job-creating industries and to remove the constraints that hamper economic development in the region.

After the *Plan de l'Est* ran its designated five-year course, the government of Canada signed a five-year $820 million ERDA subsidiary agreement with the Quebec government to develop the province's regions. Ottawa agreed to contribute $440 million and Quebec $380 million. The funding was increased by an additional $283 million in 1989. The agreement simply divided Quebec's regions into two broad categories: the central regions and the peripheral or resource regions.[105]

The above examples make the point that regional development policy was still designed to do many things: to promote 'national reconciliation' and national unity and to enable the prime minister to assure all regions that his government had measures to promote their economic development. As before, however, the Ottawa-based bureaucracy paid scant attention and provided little support to this agenda. For them, the agencies were all about politics and politicians, and the best they could hope for was to limit any potential damage to national policies, the national economy, and the national treasury.

7 Chrétien: Regional Economic Development Was All about Politics, Pragmatism, and National Unity

Jean Chrétien was a career politician, serving as a member of Parliament for forty years, and in the process he developed shrewd political instincts. He was a student of political power, and for him politics was essentially about winning and retaining power. As he explained: 'the art of politics is learning to walk with your back to the wall, your elbows high, and a smile on your face. It's a survival game played under the glare of light. If you don't learn that, you're quickly finished. The press wants to get you. The opposition wants to get you. Even some of the bureaucrats want to get you. They all may have an interest in making you look bad.'[1] His stock-in-trade was not political ideology or even firm political or policy positions, though one never doubted his commitment to the cause of federalism in Quebec. Yet, even here he was pragmatic. Canada's constitutional and national unity problems, he once explained, were like getting stuck in a snow bank. All you have to do is rock your car back and forth until you are free.

He decided to make regional economic development one of six major policy themes in his 1990 bid to lead the federal Liberal Party. His views on the issue were simple. His instinct was to resurrect the Department of Regional Economic Expansion (DREE). He became convinced that its abolition in 1982 had been a mistake, and he blamed its demise on the 'bureaucrats' in the Privy Council Office who, he felt, had no sense of the country. He was talked out of this position on the grounds that he was already fighting the perception in the media, current since the late 1980s, that he was 'yesterday's man.'[2] But he also had other ideas. He felt that the federal government should invest in infrastructure and tourism facilities in slow-growth region, notably the Maritime provinces, insisting that 'you can't go wrong with that.'[3]

He also felt strongly about making the decentralization of government departments from Ottawa to the regions an instrument of regional economic development. He often claimed that this had been one of his most important accomplishments as a member of the Trudeau cabinet. It also became a central theme of a speech he delivered in St John's during the 1990 Liberal leadership race.[4] Chrétien's 1993 Red Book devoted three pages to regional economic development, arguing that his government would 'work closely with provincial governments to ensure that the federal government is a partner, not a competitor, in the formulation of regional economic development policy. We will work with provincial governments to fulfil the priorities established in provincial strategic economic plans. Our efforts will concentrate on infrastructure, including tourism; commercial application of research and development through local institutions; and specific aid to small business.'[5] This, then, was Chrétien's thinking on regional economic development when he came to power in 1993.

Chrétien and Decentralization

In relaunching a program of government decentralization, Chrétien could draw on his own experience. In May 1975, as Treasury Board president, Jean Chrétien obtained cabinet approval to initiate a program for relocating units of the federal public service away from the National Capital Region and other major metropolitan centres. A key objective had been to strengthen federal commitment to regional economic development. As Chrétien explained at the time, 'It is ... logical that serious thought be given to the possibility of using the relocation of federal jobs and salaries as another instrument for the promotion of economic activity in the less advantaged regions of this country.'[6]

Chrétien established a task force to assist departments and agencies in identifying units that might be moved and to report on a detailed relocation program. The task force broke down its planning into two phases: the first for units that could be moved easily, and the second for major units with significant economic impact but requiring close examination and ministerial direction.

The first phase proposed relocation of twenty-four federal units; 4,600 full-time and 5,500 part-time jobs were to be moved from the National Capital Region to twenty-four communities in all ten provinces between 1977 and 1982. A substantial number of these jobs would be filled through local hiring in the receiving communities rather than through a transfer of personnel from Ottawa. Total capital spending was projected at $190 million. The jobs were to be distributed in this manner: 2,235 permanent and 630 temporary for the Atlantic provinces, 1,091 permanent and 1,900 temporary for Quebec, 626 permanent and 1,680 temporary for areas of Ontario outside the National Capital Region, and 551 permanent and 1,870 temporary for the western provinces.[7]

The task force sought to direct units to areas of slow growth within provinces. For instance, in New Brunswick, Bathurst in the northeast and Shediac in the east were allocated federal units involving some 880 jobs. In Quebec, Matane in the Gaspé area was given a unit with 260 jobs. In Nova Scotia, Yarmouth, Sydney, and Antigonish were all designated as receiving communities. In Ontario, a large number of jobs were earmarked for Thunder Bay, North Bay, and Sudbury in the north. DREE officials who were consulted strongly favoured communities in economically depressed regions. The relocation was planned over a long period so that employees occupying positions being moved from Ottawa would have sufficient time to find other work in the event they chose not to move. Staggered moves would also minimize the economic impact on the city of Ottawa.

A number of unforeseen issues surfaced that required resolution to ensure the program's long-term success. For one, Ottawa-based employees were resisting the moves. It had been hoped that enough workers would go to ensure continuity of service. Some employees, for example, were reluctant to move to communities that did not provide schooling for their children in both official languages. In addition, new management information and control systems had to be set up to provide access by ministers and senior officials in Ottawa to the relocated units.[8] While these issues and others were being resolved, decentralization was proceeding as planned. Units for Matane and Bathurst were operational on schedule. Others, like that for Shediac, were set up in temporary accommodation while construction of permanent quarters was undertaken.

The program became the subject of heated political debate. Opposition MPs charged that far too many units were being relocated in Liberal ridings and that the selection process was politically inspired. The government pointed out that some units went to cities with opposition MPs, including Charlottetown and St John's, and that the great majority of units went to Liberal-held ridings because economically disadvantaged regions tended to vote Liberal. A principal objective of the program, the government insisted, was to strengthen Ottawa's commitment to regional development.

When the Progressive Conservative Party was elected in 1979, the new government immediately announced a review of the decentralization program. The review, insisted Treasury Board president Sinclair Stevens, was prompted by government restraint: 'It was necessary to review the decentralization programme in the context of the government's expressed priority to restrain government spending and to eliminate all but the most urgent discretionary expenditures.'[9] He announced the cancellation or deferral of thirteen projects that Chrétien had already unveiled, and a resulting $76-million saving. Projects that were in advanced stages of development, with substantial monies already spent, were not affected.

When the Liberal Party returned to power after only nine months in opposition, the cabinet asked the new Treasury Board president, Donald Johnston, to make recommendations on the decentralization program. A few cancelled or deferred projects were reactivated, notably the transfer of the Revenue Canada Taxation Data Centre to Jonquière, Quebec. Johnston declared that the federal government was committed to the principle of organizational decentralization, which would continue, but subject to new guidelines.[10] Johnston, like Stevens, considered the program expensive in times of government restraint. Actual costs had proved considerably higher than projected in most of the relocations. The program also continued to meet stiff opposition from affected public servants and from unions and local associations.

In light of these considerations, Johnston announced that future relocations would be negotiated between individual line departments and the Treasury Board secretariat. The task force on decentralization was disbanded on 31 March 1981. There is no evidence that work continued on identifying new units for potential relocation or that the second phase of the original program, which had called for long-term planning, was ever taken seriously.

The Mulroney government, however, did invoke decentralization in May 1990 in its attempt to deal with the closure of the Canadian Forces base in Summerside, Prince Edward Island. It did not, however, transfer an existing government unit. Rather, it decided to establish in Summerside a new administrative unit to process the goods and services tax. The prime minister explained that this would 'create approximately 400 direct jobs and up to 100 indirect jobs in Summerside. It will be an accounting centre for the new goods and services tax where the returns of the business community will be processed.'[11]

The Summerside unit was not the only Mulroney decentralization initiative. Many government backbenchers pressed the government in caucus meetings, time and again, to reactivate the decentralization program. The government consistently refused to do so, arguing that it would be too costly. Still, some decentralization occasionally took place. The Canadian Space Agency was moved to Montreal and a medical laboratory from Ottawa to Winnipeg. The Quebec caucus and some key ministers in the Mulroney cabinet were adamant that the space agency be located in the Montreal area, in part, they argued, because the city was the natural choice but also to begin to shift some federal spending in science and technology away from Ontario, where it had been traditionally concentrated. The laboratory's move to Winnipeg, meanwhile, was widely perceived to have been part compensation for that city's losing the CF-18 maintenance contract to a Montreal firm, even though Winnipeg-based Bristol had submitted the lowest tender.[12] However, Mulroney never pursued government decentralization with any degree of enthusiasm and commitment. Decentralization became a convenient way to deal with a political problem, but he saw no reason to re-establish the program.

Chrétien, for his part, lost interest in decentralization shortly after he became prime minister and he too never re-launched the program, as he had promised. He did locate the newly created gun registry centre (the Canadian Firearms Processing Centre) in Miramichi (formerly Chatham) to assist the community in dealing with about a thousand job losses after the federal government decided to close CFB Chatham and move its activities to Quebec and Alberta air bases. The Miramichi gun registry office now employs about 200 workers, including casual and term employees.[13]

Chrétien's earlier commitment to decentralization was in part derailed by a fiscal crisis that took priority within two years of his coming to office. The government's focus turned to ways to cut spending. A second but no less important reason is that the large Ontario caucus was in no mood to embrace decentralization nor was the Ottawa-based bureaucracy keen on returning to the days of government decentralization. The 'Ontario factor' became extremely important to Chrétien. Indeed, Ontario was the single most important region politically for Chrétien in all three general elections he fought as Liberal leader. Chrétien knew, better than anyone, given his longevity in federal politics, that Ontario was invariably the 'key to maintaining a Liberal majority.'[14]

A former minister in the Chrétien government maintains that the reason Chrétien lost interest in government decentralization had everything to do with Liberal-dominated Ontario and the Ottawa caucus. He adds that decentralization was a 'complete non-starter' with John Manley, an Ottawa MP and Chrétien's powerful industry minister, and later deputy prime minister and finance minister.[15] In a pre-budget consultation session in Moncton in November 2002, Manley simply dismissed out of hand a suggestion by one participant that Ottawa should look at decentralization, insisting that 'it would not work,' without explaining why.[16]

The senior public service in Ottawa, meanwhile, also reinforced Chrétien's political instincts and Manley's strong opposition to anything that would hurt their community. It is well known in Ottawa that senior public servants have never had any interest in promoting government decentralization. Those who could remember Chrétien's earlier program would recall that it hurt the Ottawa real estate market, that many public servants simply refused to move to new communities, and that union representatives were strongly opposed to decentralization, as were Ottawa-based economic and community associations. The program was also plagued by charges of political patronage, with opposition parties claiming that only areas represented by cabinet ministers and government MPs were able to secure relocated government units.[17]

Still, there is evidence to suggest that the earlier decentralization program had been successful, at least in some aspects, and that it could make economic sense. It is important to note at the outset that determining the cost of the program was different. Sinclair Stevens claimed that he was saving the government at least $76 million when he cancelled ten relocating projects involving about 850 permanent positions and an undetermined number of casual positions. With these figures, the cost per permanent job created would be $89,400.[18] This figure can be misleading, in that it includes the capital construction cost of new buildings in receiving communities. A corresponding adjustment should have been made for the rental cost of existing accommodation in the Ottawa region. In addition, no cost figure has ever been established when the government creates a new unit or a new agency outside of Ottawa. Presumably, the added cost would be at a minimum.

In 1981 the task force on decentralization calculated the cost of jobs created under its program at $26,000 each (1977 dollars). This figure is an average of all jobs actually transferred under the program; it accounts for rental cost in Ottawa, had a particular unit not been transferred. Some units were relocated at substantially lower cost. For example, Rigaud, Quebec, was chosen as the site for a new training centre for Revenue Canada, with over one hundred new positions. The task force estimated that the total additional cost for locating the facility in Rigaud, as opposed to Ottawa, amounted to only $100,000 a year for added travel costs.[19]

Even the figure of $26,000 per job created set by the task force needs further comment. The amount is considerably higher than the estimated figure for jobs created under DREE's regional incentives program during about the same period. But the $11,000 figure for DREE should be adjusted to reflect the overhead costs involved in administering the Regional Development Initiatives Act (RDIA). The figure needs to be adjusted to reflect incrementality as well: if 30 per cent of the new jobs would have been created anyway, then the RDIA estimate is inaccurate. These two revisions would add about $7,000 to the figure.

Other factors also need to be considered in assessing the decentralization program. There are strong indications that the decentralized units function more efficiently in the regions than if they were located in Ottawa. The cheque-redemption control unit of the Department of Supply and Services, located in Matane, in the economically depressed Gaspé region, processes the same number of cheques with 275 employees that it processed with 300 employees when it was in Ottawa. The director of the unit explained that one reason for the increased productivity was that he was able to select the 275 employees from 3,500 applicants, while in Ottawa he had considerably fewer applicants to choose from. He added that staff turnover at Matane is practically nonexistent, compared to the high turnover experienced earlier in Ottawa. The director of the supply and services unit in Shediac, New Brunswick, reported similar findings, claiming that his unit was far more efficient than when it was located in Ottawa.[20] That said, Ottawa has never calculated savings realized from efficiency when establishing the total cost in decentralizing government units and jobs.

In any event, the Chrétien-Martin program review exercise would provide all the ammunition the Ottawa Liberal caucus, John Manley, and the senior public service needed to ensure that government decentralization would not resurface. In December 1994, Mexico was plunged in a currency crisis, and the Mexican economic miracle came to an abrupt end. Within weeks, the Canadian dollar came under attack.

Given its high accumulated government debt, Canada became the focus of scrutiny by international financial markets. In early January 1995, the *Wall Street Journal* described the Canadian dollar as a 'basket case,' and in an editorial on 12 January – called 'Bankrupt Canada?' – the *Journal* declared that 'Mexico isn't the only U.S. neighbour flirting with the financial abyss.' It went on to argue that 'if dramatic action isn't taken in the next month's federal budget, it's not inconceivable that Canada could hit the debt wall and have to call in the International Monetary Fund to stabilize its falling currency.'[21] This editorial had a major effect on those in the cabinet still hesitant to accept the general expenditure stance advocated by finance; indeed, the deputy minister of finance, David Dodge, later described it as a 'seminal event' in the politics of the 1995 budget, and an ambitious program review exercise was launched.[22]

The result of the program review and spending cuts contained in the 1995 Martin budget are well known. Suffice it to note that 45,000 public service and military positions were eliminated, as were long-established programs like Freight Rate Assistance and transportation subsidies for western farmers. Major reductions were implemented in various agricultural and industrial subsidies. A further $1 billion in spending cuts were made in defence and $500 million in foreign aid. And the list goes on. Spending cuts were introduced to the unemployment insurance program and to federal-provincial transfers in the social policy area. Seventy-three boards, commissions, and advisory bodies were shut down. All in all, $29 billion in cuts were announced. By 1996–7 program spending was reduced to 13.1 per cent of GDP, the lowest level since 1951.[23] Ottawa's financial position improved substantially as a result, but Chrétien showed no interest in relaunching the decentralization program.

Chrétien and Program Review

The 1993 Red Book made a number of election campaign commitments and provided a 'to do' list for Chrétien, his advisers, his cabinet, and the public service for several years. The Chrétien government did honour a majority of its Red Book commitments, though it fell down on a few important ones.[24]

Red Book spending commitments were soon overshadowed by the need to deal with the deficit. In any event, the Red Book had also pledged to bring the deficit down to 3 per cent of GDP. Finance Minister

Paul Martin met ministers individually in June 1994 to inform them of the target cuts for their departmental budgets. At the same time, finance, Treasury Board, and Privy Council Office officials were already discussing with departments the amount of cuts needed and how they could be realized. Departments knew by early June that they were expected to produce either 'large,' 'substantial,' or 'token' cuts. Arthur Kroeger writes that it was universally acknowledged by those who participated that the process was 'utterly unscientific.'[25] The reductions were broadly divided into three categories: large, being 25 per cent or in some cases more; substantial, 15 per cent; and token, 5 per cent. The assigned reductions were to be implemented over a period of three years.

Still, central agencies sought to establish criteria against which government programs could be assessed. Eventually six questions were settled upon and were distributed to departments as guidance. They subsequently became widely known because of their frequent inclusion in ministerial speeches and government documents. They were:

1. Does the program area or activity continue to serve a public interest?
2. Is there a legitimate and necessary role for government in this program area or activity?
3. Is the current role of the federal government appropriate, or is the program a candidate for realignment with the provinces?
4. What activities or programs should or could be transferred in whole or in part to the private or voluntary sector?
5. If the program or activity continues, how could its efficiency be improved?
6. Is the resultant package of programs and activities affordable within the fiscal restraint? If not, what programs or activities should be abandoned?

A number of line ministers and their departments did not, at least initially, take the proposed spending cuts seriously. Some felt that they were politically unrealistic and fully expected that the government would not go through with them. But by the end of June, it was a different story. At the last cabinet meeting before the summer break, Prime Minister Chrétien left 'no doubt whatsoever that he was four square behind Martin.' He made it clear that he would 'do whatever was necessary to reach the 3 percent deficit target.'[26] Though the prime minister did not participate directly in the work of the program review committee, he was always fully aware of its deliberations. Two senior staff, members from his office, and the clerk of the Privy Council attended the Coordinating Group of Ministers meetings, and they regularly briefed the prime minister on the status of the program review. In addition, it had been agreed early on in the process that no decisions would be considered final until the prime minister had 'signed off on them.' We now know that while the prime minister agreed with most of the decisions, he also did not hesitate to overturn some and modify others. We also know that he 'stood firm at all times when ministers came calling to ask that he overturn Martin's decision on the proposed spending cut for their department or to plead for a special project.'[27]

One by one, ministers came to accept that Chrétien would not allow any light between himself and his finance minister throughout the program review. Indeed, ministers came to recognize that the notional targets were not simply Martin's targets, they were also Chrétien's. And in many ways they were. After finance had come up with the targets, PCO reviewed them and made some relatively minor adjustments to them on behalf of the prime minister.

Departments spent the summer of 1994 working on program review submissions, and by September they began meetings with the clerk of the Privy Council and her committee. The committee of officials reviewed the proposals and offered advice to departments in preparing their ministers to appear before the program review group. It also enabled the clerk to see which departments would be able to put forward solid, well-thought-out proposals and which were simply going through the motions.

It became clear, for example, that John Manley and his Department of Industry officials would try to avoid the six questions altogether and make the case that their department should be spared. They felt that their department spoke directly to the economic health of the national economy and that cuts in industry programs would serve only to make matters worse. But finance had targeted the department for a 'large' spending cut. Manley took the unusual step of writing directly to the prime minister to inform him that finance and the ministerial group were about to 'make a major political mistake' in cutting one of his programs, the Defence Industry Productivity Program (DIPP).[28] Industry officials and Manley were convinced that DIPP (about $150 million in annual spending) was the government's most successful industrial development program. DIPP has assisted such 'national' firms as Bombardier, Spar Aerospace, and Pratt and Whitney Canada to grow. Manley fought hard for the program. The contest became, in the words of one finance official, a game of 'political chicken to see who would blink first. We knew that this was a critical moment in the exercise, and if we were forced to back down on this one, there was no telling where the exercise would end up. We stood firm. The prime minister supported us completely and Industry had no choice but to play ball. Cuts to its budget would be made with or without the involvement of the minister of Industry and his officials.'[29] As it was, the prime minister did not reply until budget day, and, when he did, he effectively supported the decision to strip the program in question of government funding. Manley's loss, however, was short lived. Within eighteen months, Industry Canada would have a replacement program – Technology Partnership Program.

The Atlantic Canada Opportunities Agency (ACOA), meanwhile, answered the six basic test questions and very quickly came to terms with the fact that it would take a 25 per cent hit in its expenditure budget. David Dingwall, ACOA's minister during the program review, like Manley at industry, did make a pitch to the minister of finance and the prime minister to reduce ACOA's target cut. In making the case before the program review committee, ACOA turned to article 36 of the 1982 Constitution Act, which commits the federal government to 'furthering economic development to reduce disparity in opportunities for the well-being of Canadians' and to its ability to work with provincial governments. ACOA officials reminded central agencies and the Finance Department that Chrétien had, in the Red Book, pledged to work closely with provincial governments. These two requirements enabled the agency, ACOA officials argued, to meet the tests of public interest, of the role of government, of federalism, and of partnership. They also argued that the ACOA programs were not costly, relatively speaking – hence its ability to meet the affordability test.

Chrétien, Martin, and the central agencies stood firm in their decision to impose the large-cut category on ACOA. To comply with the new expenditure target, ACOA ended all grants to private businesses and reduced its budget by $173 million over a three-year period. The agency also announced that it would no longer fund resource agreements with provincial governments under its cooperation agreements. Federal-provincial agreements in fisheries, agriculture, and mineral development had been part of Ottawa's regional economic development efforts going back to the GDAs in the early 1970s, but resource agreements came to an end under the program review.[30] The ACOA minister, David Dingwall, reported a victory of sorts in his battle to protect ACOA during the program review exercise. As he told the Gomery Commission, 'On the Atlantic Canada Opportunities Agency there was a full campaign inside the government to get rid of the regional agencies, and we had to fight very, very hard to maintain those agencies.'[31]

Chrétien and ACOA

Unlike earlier prime ministers, who have sought to leave their own organizational imprint on regional economic development policy, Chrétien decided to leave well enough alone and to work with the existing machinery. Politically, he saw no reason to open the regional economic development file, a veritable hornet's nest for his party, unless he absolutely had to. He felt that reinventing ACOA could well cost him seats in eastern Canada, and he had absolutely no reason to believe that it would win him new seats elsewhere in the country. So, why tinker with the machinery?

In any event, Chrétien, always the pragmatic politician, never saw much merit in government restructuring or reorganization. He had no patience with and little interest in reviewing the possible application of the various past approaches to economic development outlined in chapter 3. He felt that such an examination would be a waste of time and serve only to inhibit the government's ability to get things done. If any past approach supported what he believed needed to be done, such as his interest in tourism and infrastructure, then he might show some interest but, if not, he would simply dismiss the theories as too academic and impractical.[32] Unlike Trudeau, Mulroney, and also Kim Campbell, who unveiled a massive government restructuring during her brief tenure as prime minister, Chrétien was convinced that government reorganizations never accomplished what they were designed to do (he would often point to the abolition of DREE to make the case), and would invariably divert the attention of public servants from the important tasks at hand.[33] He concluded that he could just as easily pursue his Red Book commitments within the existing machinery as he could with any new organization. He argued that ACOA had the required legislative mandate to be sufficiently flexible to introduce new efforts in tourism, infrastructure, and close federal-provincial collaboration through Cooperation Agreements, so why try to reinvent the wheel?

Shortly after Chrétien came to power, ACOA concluded work on a pan–Atlantic Canada tourism-development plan. The Atlantic Canada Tourism Partnership (ACTP) brought together ACOA, four provincial governments, tourism industry associations, and the Canadian Tourism Commission to promote Atlantic tourism. Advertising was undertaken in New England, the Tri-State Area (New York, Pennsylvania, and New Jersey), England, Germany, and Japan. ACOA maintains that ACTP generated about $66 million in new tourism revenues for the four Atlantic provinces between 1994 and 1997.[34]

ACOA, in light of the program review exercise, also brought all business assistance measures under one program. As a result, a new Business Development Program (BDP) replaced the Action Program, measures under the Fisheries Alternatives Program, and business support initiatives under Cooperation Agreements with provincial governments. Assistance under the new program took the form of fully repayable loans.

Chrétien made an important decision in early 1996 when he decided that ACOA and the other regional agencies would become members of the industry portfolio and report through the industry minister. This meant that ACOA would be headed by a junior minister reporting to the minister of industry rather than being a stand-alone agency with direct access to cabinet and cabinet committees, including the Treasury Board. Though the change never achieved a high public profile, it was significant for the agency, and senior ACOA officials were well aware of its implications. Many inside ACOA felt betrayed, interpreting the decision as a clear signal of Ottawa's desire to get the agency under greater political and administrative control. To make matters worse, John Manley became the senior minister responsible for ACOA. Manley was widely perceived in the region and also by senior ACOA officials, who had a first-hand look at his priorities and his interventions inside the government, as parochial and largely concerned with Ottawa, its suburbs, and the high-tech sector.[35]

In any event, Chrétien became preoccupied with other more pressing issues than the state of ACOA or to whom the agency should report. Manley may not have been a popular sell in the Maritime provinces, but he was in vote-rich southern Ontario. He was also a safe pair of hands who rarely got the government or the prime minister in political trouble. As it was, Chrétien had an extremely busy political and policy agenda. He not only played a hands-on role in the program review exercise, signing off on all spending cuts before they could be implemented; he also fought a referendum in Quebec on Canadian unity and dealt with the political fallout resulting from the government's decision not to do away with the GST, as it had promised to do in 1993. Cuts in the unemployment insurance program – a program that was renamed the employment insurance program – were also a hard sell in the Maritime provinces and a much greater political problem for Chrétien than to whom ACOA should report.

In any event, Chrétien saw no reason to do more in regional economic development. ACOA was operating well, and, as he promised, his government made new investments to promote the region's tourism sector. He also launched a new infrastructure program and allocated about $150 million from it to the three Maritime provinces from 1994 to 1998, and here too ACOA was asked to play a lead role in implementing the program.[36]

Chrétien decided to call a general election for June 1997, some eighteen months before the end of his mandate. He returned to power with a much reduced majority, winning only 155 seats out of 301. The government suffered heavy losses in the Maritime provinces: it lost every seat in Nova Scotia and won only three out of ten in New Brunswick, although it retained all four PEI seats. Chrétien lost his senior regional ministers of health (David Dingwall) and defence (Doug Young). He also saw his own former New Brunswick riding of Beauséjour, which he held while he was leader of the opposition, go to the NDP, even though he named the incumbent MP to the Senate and then handpicked the Liberal candidate, Dominic LeBlanc. The media and political observers from the region were quick to point to cuts to the unemployment insurance program to explain Chrétien's losses in the Maritime provinces. Chrétien's majority was overwhelmingly based in Ontario, where he won 101 of 103 seats.[37]

Chrétien made it clear within days of winning a new mandate that his government would stay the course. He saw no reason to adopt new policies or to overhaul his government's approach to economic development in the Maritime provinces. Ever the politician, he knew that Ontario, not the Maritime provinces, would remain the key to a majority in the next election. As the Maritime provinces had turned away from his government, the best they could expect from this seasoned politician was benign neglect, and that is precisely what the region received until the dying days of Chrétien's second mandate. To be sure, he saw no political reason to reinstate ACOA's stand-alone status, and so it continued to report through the industry minister – one of fifteen agencies to do so – and it remained this way as long as Chrétien was prime minister.[38] ACOA would operate virtually unchanged for the next few years, as it continued to focus on tourism, entrepreneurial development, trade, and infrastructure.[39]

From Catching the Wave to Rising Tides

Liberal MPs and senators from the Maritimes became concerned that their region was falling off the government's radar. Budget speeches provided for new spending and new economic development measures but none seemed to resonate in the Maritime provinces. The 1999 budget, for example, added $200 million to the Canada Foundation for Innovation, $75 million to the Natural Sciences and Engineering Research Council, $16 million for the National Research Council, $55 million for biotechnology research and development, $50 million for Networks of Excellence, $150 million for Technology Partnerships Canada, and $430 million for the Canadian Space Agency. There was very little here that would benefit the Maritime region. The Technology Partnerships Canada program was viewed for what it was, a program designed for the economic circumstances of Ontario and Quebec, which always secured the bulk of the program's budget, while the Canadian Space Agency was seen as mostly benefiting Ottawa and Montreal.[40] Though few government MPs said so publicly, they were taken aback when Chrétien decided to continue to have ACOA report through the Industry Department and John Manley, even though they knew Chrétien and his capacity to send out political messages – in this case a sign to the region that he owed it precious little after losing two of his senior ministers and every seat in Nova Scotia in the 1997 general election.

The 2000 federal budget held no greater promise for the region. It established a $60 million Foundation for Climate and Atmospheric Sciences but located its head office in Ottawa, provided $46 million for national pollution enforcement and the Great Lakes Action Plan, and added $900 million to the Canadian Foundation for Innovation. It also gave the Montreal-based Business Development Bank an $80 million injection of new money to support its financing activities.[41]

The Atlantic government caucus met with Finance Minister Paul Martin in late 1998 and early 1999. MPs outlined their concerns about the political fortunes of the Liberal Party in their region and the difficult economic circumstances of their constituencies. Martin responded by asking, 'Do you want another billion for the unemployment program?'

If not, then, 'come up with ideas to develop the region and you will be able to count on my support.'[42]

In response, two Liberal MPs – Joe McGuire from Prince Edward Island and Charles Hubbard from New Brunswick – teamed up with Senator Wilfred Moore from Nova Scotia and Senator John Bryden from New Brunswick to produce a report on possible future economic development efforts in Atlantic Canada. They retained an outside consultant to work with caucus research staff to produce a report, *Atlantic Canada: Catching Tomorrow's Wave*, which they tabled on 31 May 1999. The report proposed an ambitious agenda for the government. It pondered how to position the region in the new economy and explored new opportunities in biotechnology, aquaculture, health sciences, food processing, and oceans technology and urged the government to look at promoting clusters in these sectors. But it also looked to more traditional sectors, notably shipbuilding. It pointed the finger directly at Industry Minister John Manley and reported that an analysis of the 'shipbuilding industries in the United States, Denmark, France, Germany and Spain' reveals that 'Canada is the only country to not provide any direct construction grants, loan guarantees, preferential rate export financing, research and development grants, preferential tax treatment, or customs duties on imported ship materials.'[43] When former New Brunswick premier Frank McKenna decided to get into the debate, he echoed the findings of the caucus report on shipbuilding. He claimed that, had the shipbuilding industry been located in Ontario, Ottawa would have hurried to define a shipbuilding policy.

> The auto industry makes sense for Ontario; it certainly makes sense now because they have the industry there. And I think that aerospace probably makes sense for the province of Quebec. But just as sensibly as those industries can go in those provinces, shipbuilding belongs to us on the Atlantic Coast of Canada. But friends, this is not an artificial creation, we've been building ships for hundreds of years; before this country was ever created we were building ships. This is the land of the *Marco Polo* and the *Bluenose*. This is the story of our civilization as we developed here. We build ships and we build good ships. Unfortunately, we live in the only country in the industrialized world that does not have a shipbuilding policy to support those who build ships. And I can tell you, if you could get ships in Oshawa, Ontario, or Ottawa, they would have a shipbuilding policy for this country ... What we're looking for is not subsidization and handouts which is the solution that people keep prescribing to Atlantic

Canada. What we need is solid, repayable financing for purchasers of our craftsmanship. That is what we need.[44]

After Manley left the department for foreign affairs, Industry Canada did come up with a shipbuilding policy that, on 19 June 2001, provided some assistance for the shipbuilding sector.[45]

If Paul Martin wanted ideas on how to promote economic development, *Catching Tomorrow's Wave* delivered a number of them. The document identified new ways to access capital (it identified the lack of capital for new and expanding businesses as a serious problem in the region), to access management skills, to develop physical and intellectual infrastructure, and so on. It called on provincial governments to promote interprovincial cooperation, insisting that 'tiny' provinces competing alone and against each other will be crushed in the global village. But it asked the federal government to assume 'leadership' and to develop 'long-term strategic planning' for the region.[46] For its part, the document borrowed a page from Michael Porter's work, pointing to the establishment of 'knowledge-based industrial clusters' as the key to strategic planning for the regional economy. Porter and clusters became the new fashion in political circles in the region, much like Perroux and growth poles had been some thirty years earlier.

Senior ACOA officials worked hand-in-hand with their minister and senior representatives of the Atlantic caucus in developing a proposal and in promoting the package within the Ottawa system. The Prime Minister's Office (PMO) began to take a strong interest in the proposal as it took form. The final proposal was put together by senior ACOA officials and negotiated with a senior official in the PMO and senior finance officials.[47]

Chrétien and a New Atlantic Investment Fund

Prime Minister Chrétien went to Halifax on 29 June 2000 to announce what he described as a 'fresh approach to regional economic development.' He explained: 'The Atlantic Investment Partnership is a bold plan designed to ensure not only that Atlantic Canadians can take their rightful place in the new economy, but that they can make their place at home – in Atlantic Canada.' In making the announcement, Chrétien applauded the work of the Liberal Atlantic Caucus and its report, *Catching Tomorrow's Wave*. He announced that $700 million would be committed to the region over a five-year period to strengthen its ability to compete in the global knowledge-based economy. He broke down the proposed investment as follows:

- $300 million for the Atlantic Innovation Fund (AIF), which would make strategic investments to strengthen innovation capacity, increase the region's competitiveness, and encourage the region's transition to a more knowledge-based economy. Investment was to be overseen by an advisory board made up of academics and business leaders in the R&D and high-technology fields;
- $110 million for the expansion of National Research Council facilities in Atlantic Canada; and
- $135 million for the Partnership for Community Economic Development to strengthen economic planning at the local level and improve access to funding for strategic community-level projects.[48]

The announcement, inspired as it was by the work of the regional caucus, did not embrace one particular approach. The government completely ignored what the document and the regional caucus had to say about shipbuilding. Rather, it looked to the new economy, made reference to economic clusters, but also looked to immediate political requirements by focusing on local economic development projects. Some MPs representing rural parts of the Maritime provinces insisted that the new economy meant little to them and their constituents. Dominic LeBlanc, defeated Liberal candidate in the 1997 election who had declared his intention to run again in the next general election, would often say, 'in my riding, people think that the internet is a hair spray; they know a great deal about wharfs, roads and community centres, but not about the new economy.'

The Chrétien initiative was otherwise at first well received in the region. However, it soon became clear that $300 million of the $700 million promised was recycled or old ACOA money, all of which was earmarked for the Atlantic Investment Fund. The other $400 million was simply reallocated from the existing ACOA budget to do different things. In addition, ACOA would continue to report through the industry minister.

The reallocation meant the end of federal-provincial agreements for economic development. It will be recalled that these were first introduced in 1972–3 under the General Development Agreements (GDAs), continued in 1982–3 under the Economic and Regional Development Agreements (ERDAs), and again continued by ACOA, this time under the

Cooperation Agreements. These agreements came to an end in 2002–3 in Atlantic Canada, following Chrétien's decision to reallocate the ACOA budget to other activities, notably community economic development and the expansion of National Research Council facilities in Atlantic Canada. There are two other agreements still in existence, one for tourism and the other for trade promotion. But both orders of government bring their own money and activities to these agreements and neither is cost-shared in the traditional manner. It is important to note that, under Chrétien, federal-provincial agreements for regional economic development came to an end in the Maritime provinces even though he had committed in his 1993 Red Book to promote close federal-provincial cooperation in economic development and 'to work with provincial governments to fulfil the priorities established in provincial strategic economic plans.' It is also important to note that the federal government, through its Western Economic Diversification (WD) agency, decided to sign new federal-provincial agreements with the four western provinces. WD received $100 million of new money in the February 2003 federal budget, which enabled the agency to sign four-year $50 million agreements with each of the four western provinces, cost-shared on a fifty-fifty basis. The Alberta partnership agreement, for example, is built around two themes, 'innovation and value-added industries and regional economic development and sustainable communities.'[49]

The Atlantic Innovation Fund (AIF) program, meanwhile, which operates separately from provincial governments, is designed to build a capacity for innovation, research and development that lead to technologies, products, and processes or services that will contribute to economic development in the region. The fund is guided by an advisory board that includes representatives from the private sector, the universities, and specialists in research and development who make recommendations on proposals and provide advice to the minister and staff at ACOA.[50]

If one were to assess AIF on the basis of interest and applications, one would conclude that it has been successful. Indeed, demands under the program have far outstripped the fund's capacity. In 2001, the first request for proposals under this fund generated 195 proposals seeking $810 million – almost three times the value of the fund – towards projects with a total value of $1.5 billion. In the summer of 2002, the results of round one were announced – forty-seven projects across Atlantic Canada with AIF funding of $155 million. In November 2002, the second request for proposals resulted in 174 proposals from the

region's research organizations and business community, seeking a total of $545 million towards total projected costs of just over $1 billion.[51]
It is difficult to establish, however, whether the quality and viability of
the proposals presented for funding were strong, and it is much too
early to establish the impact of those that received funding.

We do know, however, that ACOA spent a total of $1.6 billion be-
tween 1998 and 2003, and a review of the spending suggests that the
agency did respond to Chrétien's priorities, as defined in his June 2000
speech in Halifax. The agency spent $85 million under the Infrastruc-
ture Canada and Canada Infrastructure Work Program, $104.7 million
in tourism, $237 million in innovation, $100 million in trade, $206
million in community economic development, $600 million in access to
capital, and $42 million on statutory transfer payments.[52] As noted
earlier, not long after Chrétien came to office, a decision was reached to
make financial assistance to the private sector repayable. ACOA officials reported that repayments were coming in on schedule and that, in
this respect, they outperformed other regional agencies, as well as
Industry Canada,[53] which had not been nearly as successful as ACOA
in securing repayments from assisted firms under its Technology Partnership program. Unlike ACOA programs, repayments under the Technology Partnership program are conditional, in that the firm receiving
funding can tie it to profits or if the technology was successfully brought
to market. More is said about this below.

ACOA also insisted that its efforts have had a positive impact on the
region. It pointed out that total employment in the Atlantic region in
2002 compared to 1998 had grown by over 20,000. This growth, it
argued, resulted from its direct support of small and medium-sized
businesses (direct plus indirect and induced). The agency also estimated that, in constant 1997 dollars, the region's GDP was almost
$1 billion higher annually by 2002 than it would have been in the
absence of ACOA's expenditures in direct support of business. Over the
five-year period, it maintained that its direct support to business produced total accumulated annual increases of well over $5 in GDP gains
for every dollar it had spent.

The agency, employing a model developed by the Conference Board,
argued that the $500 million it spent in its business development pro-
gram (access to capital) generated $600 million in new tax revenues. It
added that the model did not include corporate income taxes, which,
for technical reasons, could not be calculated. Moreover, possible savings to the government in employment insurance payments, as a result

of the additional employment created by assisted firms, were not included. The agency also pointed to several sectors that enjoyed strong growth between 1998 and 2003. These included aquaculture, wood-products industries, aerospace, frozen food, and tourism, all sectors that it was active in. In the case of tourism, there was a 35 per cent increase in the number of visitors over the period; total non-resident expenditures grew 37 per cent, from $2.30 billion in 1997 to $3.16 billion in 2002. Within the accommodations component of this industry, employment increased by 2,500 over the 1997–2002 period.[54]

ACOA also pointed to its accomplishments in trade promotions. Its strategy here centred around four themes: promoting exports as a growth strategy to small and medium-sized businesses; skills development, including training; capacity building, including leading trade missions to selected U.S. and European markets; and promoting coordination, including establishing new partnerships in the areas of trade and investment development and policy. The agency also identified key priority sectors for trade purposes, including ocean industries, oil and gas, fish and aquaculture, information communications, technology, environmental industries, and life science.[55] It put in place a multi-year international business development agreement (1994–2004) involving three federal government departments and four provincial agreements. These agreements are not typical federal-provincial agreements, in that each partner brings its own resources and activities to the table so that the federal government is not sharing the costs of provincial government activities.

ACOA reported that exports from the region increased substantially from $6.7 billion in 1992 to $19.2 billion in 2002. The agency also reported that there were nearly 2,000 exporters from the region, compared with about 1,600 in 1993. New England and New York continued to dominate the export market, accounting for 55 per cent of the region's exports. Trade in goods and services accounted for nearly 40 per cent of the region's GDP, and exports created one out of every three new jobs in the region.[56]

Much less certain is ACOA's success under its mandates concerning coordination and advocacy. With regard to coordination, the agency has supported various research projects over the years, including participation in an Organization for Economic Cooperation and Development review of 'territorial development policy.' It was also involved in promoting the Voisey's Bay nickel development project with other federal departments. The agency's report described the objectives to be pursued under its advocacy mandate and how it went about fulfilling them. It has had, however, precious few successes in this area since its establishment.[57]

ACOA's accomplishments continue to be much debated, as we will see below. Chrétien, however, had some political success in the region in the 2000 general election, and some observers would attribute part of that success to initiatives following the *Catching the Wave* exercise. Chrétien won seven new seats, including Beauséjour, his former seat in New Brunswick, as well as four seats in Nova Scotia.[58]

Liberal MPs from the region sought to build on this political success. They were of course well aware that Chrétien's 1999 commitment to the region, including his $300 million in new money, would come to an end in 2004. They also believed that *Catching the Wave* had had a positive impact in political circles in Ottawa and in the region. Moreover, Paul Martin, as finance minister, kept up the message: give me viable ideas for economic development and I will support you. Once again, they took his invitation to heart. A Liberal Atlantic caucus sub-committee chaired by Shawn Murphy, MP for Hillsborough in Prince Edward Island, was established to come up with fresh ideas by building on *Catching the Wave*. The sub-committee produced another report, *The Rising Tide: Continuing Commitment to Atlantic Canada*, which it made public in July 2003.[59]

The document, as one could have predicted, applauded the findings of *Catching the Wave*, as well as the federal government's response to its findings. It argued that much had already been accomplished, but more needed to be done. *The Rising Tide* described the region's economic circumstances, referring to impressive gains in key urban areas. However, it also made the point that a large number of people in rural areas remain computer illiterate and thus have limited access to the new economy. The report made the case that older, unemployed, blue-collar workers who were once employed in traditional resource industries need particular help to enable them to find new employment. It boldly acknowledged that older and less-educated workers may find it particularly difficult to move or retrain for new jobs, adding that Atlantic Canada has thousands, maybe tens of thousands, of people who are not equipped and may never be equipped to benefit from a knowledge-based, wired economy.

The solutions? The report had several. It called for new investment in transportation infrastructure, communications, human skills infrastructure, research and development, and measures to attract new Canadians to the region. It also made the case, as *Catching the Wave* had done, that the region has insufficient access to capital, particularly risk capital. It explained: 'In part that is because we no longer have our own financial institutions or head offices in our region. In part that is because the scale of investment required in our region is often too small to interest national or international investors. In part that is because capital decisions are made in Toronto, New York, London or Tokyo where Atlantic Canada enjoys little presence. Capital in Atlantic Canada tends to be risk adverse and comes largely in the form of debt or risk-adverse investment. Loans advanced by ACOA or the Business Development Bank are judged by their payback ratios rather than by their performance as growth investments.'[60]

The regional caucus also believed it had lost an important friend in court – Paul Martin – and that no senior ministers from the region had the political clout necessary to sell the report. John Manley, again primarily concerned with Ottawa-Kanata, expressed little interest in or support for *The Rising Tide*. Chrétien was caught in a fight for his political life with his former finance minister and, as before, had more pressing issues to attend to than the Maritime provinces.

Shawn Murphy, chair of the caucus committee, was a well-known Paul Martin loyalist, and he and others from the region held out hope that things would improve with a new Martin government after Chrétien stepped down. Initially at least, he had some reasons for optimism. In swearing in his cabinet, Martin announced that ACOA would revert to its old status and become a stand-alone agency with its own minister in cabinet. The agency would remain a part of the industry portfolio in name only. Martin also appointed a popular veteran MP from Prince Edward Island, Joe McGuire, to be the new ACOA minister.

Members of the regional caucus lobbied the prime minister and his office hard to have the government's 2004 Speech from the Throne endorse *The Rising Tide*. The Throne Speech did make a passing reference to the document, but it was hardly what the MPs were looking for. Towards the end of the speech, it reads: 'We must ensure that Ontarians see their ambitions fulfilled; that the hopes and dreams of Atlantic Canada as reflected in the report "Rising Tide" are realized.'[61] The speech focused on several issues, including urban development, Aboriginal peoples, education and Canada's place in the world, and health care, but had precious little to say about economic development in the Maritime provinces.

Atlantic MPs then turned to the new minister of finance to pressure him to include *Rising Tide* funding in his first budget. They were disappointed. Ralph Goodale made no mention of the document in his budget speech and allocated no new money to pursue initiatives recommended by it. *The Rising Tide* ran into difficulty with the 'Ottawa system' for a number of reasons. Politicians from other regions had been clamouring for new government funding for their regions. Ontario MPs had pressed Chrétien and were now pressing Martin for their own ACOA-type agency for southern Ontario. A number of western MPs made it clear to Goodale that if new funding were to be made available for a regional agency, then it should go to western Canada. After all, they argued, they had been bypassed when Chrétien announced new money for the *Rising Tide* document. One MP argued that Westerners could easily produce a 'Wind in the Wheat' document if that was needed to generate new funding for western Canada.[62] Earlier, Stephen Owen, a Vancouver MP and minister responsible for Western Diversification, declared that it was important to review funding levels for regional economic development agencies and to consider the 'touchy issue of regional fairness.'[63] The message here was that ACOA was receiving too much funding compared to other regions.

Liberal MPs from the Maritime provinces held out hope that Martin would introduce stronger economic development measures for their region if he could secure a new mandate in the 2004 general election. Martin had maintained an interest in the work of the Liberal Atlantic caucus in economic development, and he declared in an election stop in Fredericton, New Brunswick, in June 2004 that the Liberal Party was the party of regional development.[64]

The 2005 budget allocated $2.1 billion in investments for 'regional and sectoral development over a five-year period.'[65] ACOA's share amounted to $708 million. However, a close look at the $708 million reveals that nearly $300 million was drawn from its existing budget allocation. Other funding elements included $220 million to the National Research Council of Canada and its activities in Atlantic Canada and new money for Community Futures Program. New funding for the agency amounted to $95 million over five years.[66] However, Ottawa's expenditure-review exercise also cut $84.1 million out of ACOA's budget over a five-year period. This compares with cuts of $46.9 million for Canada Economic Development for Quebec Regions and $35.5 million for Western Economic Diversification Canada over the same period.[67]

Senior ACOA officials report that their efforts to secure more funding to implement the *Rising Tide* document ran into problems with central agencies, notably finance officials, after Ottawa negotiated special arrangements with Newfoundland and Labrador and Nova Scotia to eliminate clawbacks of equalization payments because of non-renewable off-shore energy revenues. The value of the arrangements over an eight-year period amounted to $830 million for Nova Scotia and $2 billion for Newfoundland and Labrador.[68] The view in central agencies was that the 'region' had more than its share under these politically driven off-shore accords and nothing more needed to be done. ACOA officials made the case, with little success, that these offshore accords were tied to the equalization program and had nothing to do with economic development and, further, that both New Brunswick and Prince Edward Island would not derive any direct benefit from them.[69]

Challenging ACOA

ACOA has been criticised by the national media, by opposition parties, and by think-tanks. It has been accused of being little more than a political pork barrel, of picking losers, and in the end of hurting the region more than helping it. Some of the more high-profile criticisms are featured below.

Stephen Harper, the first leader of the newly amalgamated Conservative Party of Canada, has been highly critical of ACOA over the years. In his leadership bid, he tabled what he called 'an economic revitalization plan for Atlantic Canada,' in which he said almost nothing about ACOA. He did pledge to 'redirect inefficient corporate subsidies ... to lower taxes.' He also pledged to give the region 'full access to non-renewable resource wealth,' to invest in 'infrastructure,' and to support the military, which, he argued, would benefit the Maritime provinces.[70] Shortly after winning the leadership of his party, Harper declared that he had not 'decided what we do with ACOA per se ... You know, I think it's an open debate whether we would want to deliver legitimate federal programs through a regional agency or not. I'm not closed to that.'[71] This scarcely constitutes a ringing endorsement for ACOA or its programs.

At the 2005 Conservative Party policy conference in Montreal, Harper insisted that the party mirrors his own view on regional development by emphasizing 'general infrastructure development and delivering conventional programs through a regional agency.' The party rejected, in a plenary session, a proposal that would have abolished regional development agencies and replaced them with a targeted business-tax reduction in the designated regions.[72]

Harper has on several occasions made reference to the work of the Atlantic Institute for Market Studies (AIMS) in his economic revitalization plan for Atlantic Canada. AIMS, an independent think-tank based in Halifax, was established in 1994. It has produced important work, which has been widely reported in the media. AIMS and its founding president, Brian Lee Crowley, have brought a fresh perspective to the economic challenges facing the region by advocating market forces as the way ahead. Both Crowley and AIMS have consistently argued that ACOA and federal transfer payments of one kind or another have created a dependency from which the region must break away. The institute also covers a wide variety of policy issues ranging from education, energy, equalization, and fisheries to regulatory reform and health care.

AIMS has never sought to camouflage its view that ACOA's policies and programs are, for the most part, misguided. Indeed, Crowley created an *ACOA Watch* series, which challenged ACOA's job-creation numbers and its reported successes. He insists that 'the economy, not ACOA,' creates jobs and makes the case that job creation in the region has not been as strong under ACOA (1988–2003) as it was in the decade before the agency was established.[73] ACOA, meanwhile, has not always been effective in responding to the criticism. The ACOA minister, Gerry Byrne, responded to *ACOA Watch* by hurling accusations at some board members of AIMS and at Crowley, describing the report as 'useless, asinine and devoid of any benefit.' He wondered whether John Crosbie, an AIMS board member who had once been ACOA's minister, agreed with the institute's position. He added, 'I guess Brian Lee Crowley is smarter than the auditor general, is smarter than John Crosbie because he seems to be the only one that has got any answers around here.'[74] The work of AIMS has had a significant impact on public policy debates both in the region and at the national level, and it deserves far more serious consideration than that reflected in Byrne's comments. It has brought a neo-conservative perspective to the issue, forcing the region to question many things it had taken for granted or simply assumed were making a positive contribution.

AIMS and others have also charged that ACOA has been particularly sensitive over the years to the partisan political interests of the government of the day. It argued, for example, that, 'for ACOA ... political connections were all too often more important than business savvy, and political gain more important than competitive prospects.'[75] AIMS has made it clear that this applies to both Liberal and Progressive Conservative governments. The charges of using ACOA for political gain have given the agency 'bad press' in both the national and regional media.

The *Globe and Mail* ran an editorial on 16 October 1996, claiming that ACOA has long been 'used as a tool for furthering the electoral strategy of the party in power. The Liberals put respected public servant Norman Spector in charge. They billed him as the man who would henceforth disburse grants based on economic merit, not political connections. Then he started living up to the advance billing ... Mr. Spector is no longer with ACOA.'[76] While Ottawa bureau chief of the *Globe and Mail*, Ed Greenspon had earlier written a highly sympathetic article on Norman Spector. Greenspon wrote that 'Spector ... was fundamentally opposed to maintaining the status quo at ACOA, where lacklustre accountability measures and free-spending ways had attracted the ire of the auditor general.'[77] Greenspon neglected to point out that over the years every government department has at one time or another attracted the ire of the auditor general. Simply put, it comes with the territory.

What was remarkable about the Spector controversy was that everyone, including the Atlantic media, bought the *Globe and Mail* version of events hook, line and sinker. What is surprising here is not Spector's claim, as he left government, that as a non-partisan career public servant he was offended by the partisan politics surrounding ACOA, but that there was no mention of the fact that Spector had been chief of staff to former prime minister Brian Mulroney, a partisan appointment not traditionally occupied by career public servants. In any event, ACOA has had to live with the reputation that it is subject to political influence in its program delivery at least for the past several years.

The auditor general produced a chapter on ACOA for its 2001 report to the Commons but made no mention of suspected partisan political pressure. The report did, however, take ACOA to task for having loosely defined goals and only a vague understanding about expected results from partnership arrangements; moreover the report suggested that even the roles and relationships with partners were not always clear. The report study maintains that 'the accuracy and relevance of the employment impact reported for non-commercial projects is questionable.'[78] But, as far as auditor general reports go, this chapter was relatively positive. The assessment concluded, for example, that 'ACOA's programs are consistent with its mandate, objectives, and priorities.

The Agency's framework for controlling grants and contributions is appropriate [and] ... 'we found that the Agency has used due diligence in assessing, approving, and monitoring commercial projects. Its assessment of commercial project applications has become more rigorous since our last audit. The Agency has developed policies both to assess the project proponents' ability to repay their contributions and subsequently to monitor their repayment.'[79]

The C.D. Howe Institute entered the debate with its December 2003 study *Brooking No Favourites*. The authors decided to 'focus on ACOA because its expenditures in per capita terms for the Atlantic region exceed those made by other agencies and the federal government in other parts of Canada.' They never explained how they arrived at this conclusion. To be sure, if one simply looks at regional agencies on a per capita basis, ACOA spends more in Atlantic Canada (annual expenditure of about $450 million) than WD in western Canada or the federal economic development agency in Quebec. But that hardly tells the whole story. What about Industry Canada (annual expenditure about $1.4 billion spent largely in Ontario and Quebec and $440 million for the Economic Development Agency in Quebec)? What about Export Development Canada, which has little presence in the Maritime provinces? What about annual funding of about $130 million for Atomic Energy of Canada, concentrated as it is in Ontario?[80] The institute also made no reference to a study produced by the Atlantic Provinces Economic Council that by the late 1980s the rest of Canada had not only caught up, but bypassed, Atlantic Canada in business assistance, even when calculated on a per capita basis ($133 per capita in Atlantic Canada compared to $252 for the rest of Canada).[81]

The underlying theme of the C.D. Howe study is that ACOA programs should be replaced by tax cuts. It begins with perhaps the most tired cliché in the economic development literature: 'governments are usually not good at picking winners, but losers tend to be very good at picking governments.'[82] The authors offer no evidence to support this view, first heard over twenty-five years ago in Britain and making the rounds ever since in countless conferences and popular articles. The authors also make a number of sweeping observations with little evidence to support them. They argue that ACOA is 'hampered by politics' because governing parties 'seem to use spending to influence marginal ridings' (the authors do not explain why they employ the term *seem* to qualify their claim). They add, 'even if politics did not influence ACOA spending patterns, grant programs will not have much impact on economic growth if they are targeted at inefficient businesses that are more efficient ones.'[83] Again, they present little evidence to support this claim in their nineteen-page document. The economic development literature from which they draw to produce their paper is thin on the ground.[84] Still, they conclude that 'a regional development policy more likely to be successful, in our view, is a broad-based corporate tax cut in the Atlantic region – which would replace ACOA programs.'[85] The recommendation begs the question: if this is good medicine for Atlantic Canada, why not extend the prescription to other regions and abolish the Industry Canada program designed to assist the private sector, as well as Export Development Canada, the Business Development Bank of Canada, with its outstanding loans to Ontario and Quebec accounting for 71.5 per cent of the total portfolio, compared with 6.6 per cent for the three Maritime provinces, and other such government agencies and programs, and lower corporate taxes across Canada?[86] The authors had nothing to say about Industry Canada's Technology Partnership (TPC) program and whether losers were any better at picking ACOA than they were at picking Industry Canada. When one compares the level of repayment between ACOA and Industry Canada clients, one can only conclude that ACOA is much better at picking winners than is Industry Canada. Yet, the authors of *Brooking No Favourites* ignored such data completely.

The facts speak for themselves. ACOA's annual average collections have exceeded $50 million a year for the past several years. By early 2004, it had 'disbursed' a total of $998 million from all of its business-assistance programs dating back to 1995. It had collected $315 million, classified $188 million as amounts 'defaulted,' and had well over $400 million classified as 'outstanding,' which it expected to be repaid. The cumulative default rate stands at 13.69 per cent, and the annual default rate (annual defaults expressed as a percentage of the outstanding portfolio) stood at 3.88 per cent for fiscal year 2003–4. ACOA has an elaborate recovery process in place, which senior management monitors closely. The annual default rate for commercial banks is usually much better, between .5 to 1 per cent.[87]

The contributinon of Industry Canada's TPC program is conditional on the firm turning a profit from the project being financed. The bulk of the program spending is in Ontario and Quebec and, to a lesser extent, British Columbia and Alberta. The program's annual budget is about $363 million, which is larger than the money ACOA makes available to the private sector in the region. At the risk of repetition, ACOA assis-

..I repayable without conditions. TPC is
...y explain in part why Ontario and Quebec
... budget. The level of repayability has been
...industry Canada officials report that they hope
... generate about $50 million in collections every
...rogram was established in 1996, by late 2003 Indus-
...et to put in place an administrative process of collect-
ing   anywhere near as sophisticated as ACOA's. An internal
depar..   ..i audit found many faults with the program, pointing out
that 'opp../rtunities exist to strengthen project file documentation and
ensure that technical advisors have the business backgrounds and/or
business related experience needed to minimize the risk.'[89] One federal
official noted that the level of repayability under the Technology Partnerships program is about '2 to 3 per cent,' a far cry from ACOA's
record.[90] One observer writes that 'the federal investigation into the
lobbying fees is the latest controversy surrounding the Technology
Partnership Canada program, which its reports show has invested more
than $2.3 billion in the past eight years in high-tech projects with little
return.'[91]

But that is not all. In 1998 TPC decided to partner with the Industrial
Research Assistance Program (IRAP) of the National Research Council
of Canada to support a new *non-repayable* program for small and
medium-sized businesses. TPC contributes about $20 million a year to
IRAP's total of about $100 million. Again, the bulk of the joint TPC-
IRAP spending is in Ontario and Quebec. Industry Canada also had a
$72 million program (annual spending that ended in March 2005) to
assist those communities hard hit by the downturn in the softwood
industry. The spending was earmarked for British Columbia, Alberta,
Ontario, and Quebec. This money is not repayable.

The national media also got into the act, employing the same logic as
the C.D. Howe study. William Watson in a *Financial Post* article offered
advice to Ottawa on ways to cut taxes. He wrote, 'The Atlantic Canada Opportunities Agency ($360 + 35 in Cape Breton: $395 million),
Economic Development Agency of Canada for the Regions of Quebec
($367 million), and the Office of Western Economic Diversification
($247 million). That's a billion right there. Delete them all.' He too said
nothing about Industry Canada programs costing over $1.0 billion,
including FedNor, the agency for northern Ontario ($40 million).[92] He
did not bother to explain why he would exempt these agencies.

Dealing with a Bad Reputation

Regional economic development in the Maritime provinces and else-where no longer enjoys the kind of public support it once did. In brief, the field now has a bad reputation. Few voices were heard against Trudeau's decision to establish the Department of Regional Economic Expansion (DREE) in the late 1960s. Indeed, as we saw in an earlier chapter, opposition leader Robert Stanfield argued that DREE's mandate would not be sufficiently broad for the task at hand. Today, the opposition leader is not certain that he wants to keep ACOA. Along the way, regional economic development has lost its way as it was pushed and pulled into all areas of the country to pursue a variety of goals, from influencing the recurring debate about Quebec's place in Canada, to securing economic adjustments in ailing sectors, and to delivering special initiatives such as the government's infrastructure programs. No one is certain any longer precisely what regional economic development means. Perhaps for this reason, it has come to feed a kind of 'Me Too' federalism where every Canadian region is on the lookout for how much money Ottawa spends in different regions so they can insist on their share. A former adviser of Chrétien's now reports that one of his boss's important contributions to regional economic development was to resist strong pressure by Ontario MPs to have their own regional economic development agency for southern Ontario.[93] This, perhaps better than anything else, speaks to the state of the regional economic development field in Canada.

It is revealing that Prime Minister Jean Chrétien and his finance minister, Paul Martin, called on the regional caucus in the Maritime provinces and Newfoundland and Labrador to come up with fresh economic development ideas. No similar request was made for the other regions, for Ottawa's various research and development programs, for Industry Canada programs, for developing Ottawa's innovation agenda, or whenever a policy paper is required for, say, the automotive sector. For these measures, thousands and thousands of career officials in Ottawa are working on Power Point presentations to develop government policy and package new programs. In one sense, it is as if Canada's political and bureaucratic leadership has simply given up on the Maritime economy and passed the problem to the regional caucus, saying, let's see what you can come up with. The objective is always to deal with political requirements without creating major difficulties for national policies and the national economy. Chrétien's decision to have the agencies report through the industry portfolio speaks directly to this concern.

We now have over forty years' experience with federal efforts to promote economic development in the Maritime provinces. What impact have these efforts had? How does the region differ today from the way it was before they were attempted? The next two chapters seek to answer this question.

8 Heal Thyself

Are the Maritime provinces the 'bellyache of Canada'?[1] There is no doubt that the region has a long history of pressing Ottawa for a better deal. It has played the supplicant, asking for more generous equalization payments, and has warned Ottawa not to tinker with transfer payments to individuals, such as employment insurance. Stephen Harper may well have hit a nerve in the Maritime provinces when he said that the region suffered from a 'culture of defeat.' But the observation may have resonated in other parts of the country as well,[2] because such thinking absolves them of any responsibility for circumstances in the Maritimes. The implication is that the 'have' regions gained their superior status by picking themselves up by their own bootstraps – so why can't the Maritime provinces do the same?

The bootstraps analogy has also been voiced in the Maritime provinces. The report *Establishing the Atlantic Canada Opportunities Agency* argued that the region itself 'will have to provide the energy, the skills and the imagination to conceive and organize economically' if it is to prosper.[3] Frank McKenna became as popular on Bay Street as he was in New Brunswick with his message that 'ultimately, a province such as ours can be what it wants to be. With a flourishing work ethic and entrepreneurship, you can stay as wealthy as you want to be.'[4] McKenna wanted New Brunswick to become self-sufficient and to have a strong private sector. He would often say in speeches that he wanted to address central Canada 'not as a supplicant, but as an equal.' He insisted, time and again, that 'New Brunswick is not going to be the bellyache of Canada.'[5]

But how could the Maritime provinces go about picking themselves up by their own bootstraps, given their economic history? Maritime interprovincial cooperation and entrepreneurship would top the list of most people looking for an answer. The region has a long history of attempts to promote interprovincial cooperation, and in more recent years it has sought to foster entrepreneurship to promote economic self-sufficiency. This chapter focuses on both these endeavours.

Searching for the Holy Grail

Proposals to promote Maritime cooperation have been made time and again, going back to and even preceding Confederation. As discussed in chapter 2, the Charlottetown conference that led to Confederation was originally called to discuss Maritime political union. Suggestions for increased cooperation between the Maritime provinces have been made ever since, covering the full spectrum of possibilities from full political union to striking a common position in their dealings with Ottawa.

There were a number of attempts to promote Maritime political union from 1867 up to the 1960s. During the 1880s, for example, Nova Scotia raised the idea as a way for the region to leave the Canadian federation. This was because a number of maritime politicians felt betrayed by the terms of Confederation and the unwillingness of the new union to settle the region's outstanding claims. For these politicians, the solution was simply to withdraw from the federation and unite under one government. Some attempts were made to establish a Maritime union party, but these failed. While not suggesting that the Maritime provinces leave the federation, the *Toronto Globe* wrote in support of political union, suggesting that this would enable the provinces 'to pull together with greatly more effect than at present, would much diminish the cost and labour of governments and above all could lend a vastly increased weight to their voice in the counsels of Canada.'[6] Still, Maritimers opposed political union. After the premier of Prince Edward Island declared in 1910 that Maritime union was 'so impracticable it could not even be considered,' the call for political union was heard less and less.[7]

By the early 1920s one increasingly heard assertions that national economic policies were hurting the Maritime economy. More and more of the region's youth were moving elsewhere in the country or to the United States for employment, and many Maritime leaders accused Ottawa and national policies, which they believed favoured central

Canada, of being responsible for the region's slow development. Such view led to the Maritime rights movement.[8] The movement's energy was directed at misguided federal policies, and actual union was never an important feature of its agenda. The movement petered out when the Conservative Party 'appropriated' its agenda and became the political voice for the movement.[9] It did engender new cooperative efforts on the part of the three provincial governments and the region's business community. For example, they agreed in 1925 to create the Maritime Transportation Commission to attack the freight rate differential between the region and the rest of the country.[10] They decided in 1928 to establish a joint trade commission office in Ontario, which operated until 1933.[11] They agreed in 1934 to cooperate in promoting the regional timber industry and to establish the Timber Commission of Eastern Canada, the forerunner of the Maritime Lumber Bureau.[12] The three Maritime premiers went further in 1956, when, together with the premier of Newfoundland, they decided to establish the Atlantic Premiers' Conference. A leading proponent of the conference, New Brunswick premier Hugh John Flemming, explained that it would signal 'the resumption of a certain order of business which was interrupted in the city of Charlottetown in the year 1864.'[13] It was a formal organization in the sense that the four premiers met annually. Though the conference had no staff, the premiers did commission research papers from both government and non-government people. At their first meeting, they agreed to study jointly the following themes:

- the advantages of collaboration in securing better federal-provincial financial agreements;
- the possibility of cooperating to achieve cheaper electric power;
- the desirability of a joint drive to locate defence industries and place defence orders in the Atlantic provinces;
- the means to attack jointly the effects of the tariff on the regional economy;
- the possibilities of cooperation in the marketing of fishing and agricultural products; and
- the possibilities of maintaining joint trade representatives in the United Kingdom and elsewhere.[14]

The Atlantic Premiers' Conference also led to the establishment of numerous coordinating bodies of one kind or another. Interprovincial committees and working groups, bringing together officials from the three provincial government (or four, whenever Newfoundland agreed to participate), were established to deal with most areas of government activities.[15]

All in all, there is little doubt that some progress was made between the 1920s and the 1960s in promoting interprovincial cooperation in the Maritimes – and in Atlantic Canada from 1949 to 1960. But there were also some significant failures. A proposed Atlantic Institute of Education, though discussed many times, was never established. It had been hoped that the institute would bring together teachers' colleges and Departments of Education in the four Atlantic provinces to improve teacher education, promote research in educational planning, and establish standards of achievement in teacher education. The Atlantic Provinces Office in London,which operated from 1958 until 1969, sought both to promote trade with the United Kingdom and Europe and to attract European investment to the region. However, Nova Scotia and New Brunswick decided to send their own representative to London in 1969, while Newfoundland and Prince Edward Island opted out of the arrangement altogether. There is more than one story to explain why the office was closed, although everyone appears to agree that when H.W. Jamer, who had directed the office since its establishment, retired in 1968 the provinces began to back away from the agreement. As Newfoundland premier Joey Smallwood reported, 'Now that Mr. Jamer has retired, Newfoundland might not be very interested in replacing him. We have been unenthusiastic about it for several years.'[16] New Brunswick appointed its provincial deputy minister to represent its interests in London, and Nova Scotia soon followed suit. Those familiar with the situation reported that Jamer had always been in an impossible position, trying to serve 'four masters,' with the four provincial governments often pursuing different interests and different policies.[17]

And there were other failures. A proposed joint industrial commission was one. The New Brunswick industry minister had proposed in 1964 a coordinating agency that would direct industries to specific locations in the region. He had hoped that the agency would be able to balance industrial growth among the four provinces. New Brunswick, he reported, had already stopped negotiations with certain industries, in part because they were trying to play one province off against another.[18] None of the other provinces, however, expressed much interest in the matter, and it was soon dropped.

Contemplating Political Union Once Again

During the 1964 federal-provincial constitutional conference in Charlottetown, New Brunswick premier Louis J. Robichaud asked his Atlantic colleagues if there was any interest in their moving towards a political union. He said, 'Perhaps Premiers Stanfield, Smallwood, Shaw and I may get together today and, on this centennial of the first meeting in Charlottetown, decide to reduce the number of Canadian provinces from ten to seven. Should that occur, the focal point of progress and activity in the nation would unquestionably and rapidly take a marked shift to the east.'[19] Robichaud explained why he was issuing such a challenge: 'The new pressures of the mid-20th century, the problems of national unity, and the growth in governmental responsibilities, combine in calling for a re-examination of proposals for the union of these four Atlantic provinces.'[20] The next step, he suggested, was a 'serious' study to look into all facets of the matter, since 'the subject is too serious to permit the discussion of it to be clouded or subverted by prejudices or pettiness of any nature.'[21]

The proposal, initially at least, did not meet with much enthusiasm from Robichaud's Atlantic colleagues. Premier Walter Shaw of Prince Edward Island dismissed the idea and said that the chances for political union 'were extremely limited.'[22] Premier Smallwood pointed out that Newfoundland was not on the mainland, and so could not be considered a 'Maritime' province. In any event, he maintained that Newfoundland much preferred dealing directly with Ottawa and not as part of the Maritime provinces.[23] Perhaps for good measure, Premier Smallwood attended only one more Atlantic Premiers' Conference, and it was later disbanded. Premier Stanfield of Nova Scotia did not shut the door on the proposal but expressed some caution: 'We are prepared to consider it, provided provision is to be made for proper safeguards. On a per capita basis, we have a higher standard of income than the three other provinces and we wouldn't want to have that brought down. We would only be prepared to consider it on a basis of everybody else being pulled up rather than Nova Scotia being pulled down.'[24] Despite his reservations, Stanfield obviously saw merit in Robichaud's proposal, as he later suggested that Robichaud and he ask their respective legislative assemblies to decide through a free vote whether the two provinces should proceed with a joint study to determine the feasibility of a political union.

In early 1965, the Nova Scotia and the New Brunswick legislative assemblies unanimously agreed to launch 'a study to enquire into the advantages and disadvantages of a union of the Province of Nova Scotia and the province of New Brunswick to become one province within the nation.'[25] Though the study was slow in getting started, certain developments gave it a major boost. When Alex Campbell was elected premier of Prince Edward Island, he immediately announced that his province would like to joint in. John Deutsch, the chairman of the Economic Council of Canada and principal of Queen's University, agreed to head up the study. The media were highly supportive of efforts to promote more cooperation between the Maritime provinces. This was particularly so in central Canada – no surprise to many in the Maritimes, as 'a proposed union of Eastern Canadian provinces had been a creature of the Central Canadian press for a number of years.'[26] Newfoundland, however, showed no interest in participating in the study. Not only did its premier stop attending the Atlantic Premiers' Conference, but a pattern emerged in the 1960s in which Newfoundland was less and less willing to develop 'a regional' voice in federal-provincial relations or to promote an Atlantic perspective on sectoral issues.[27]

With Prince Edward Island now a full partner in the maritime union study, no one doubted the study's importance and its potential impact. The three premiers issued a joint statement in their respective legislatures, reporting their commitment to public consultation and to the 'direct participation ... of interested organizations and bodies.'[28] The study also received a number of 'public briefs' and commissioned some twenty studies.[29]

Not long after the Deutsch Study was formally launched, it became clear that it would shift away from the issue of political union towards identifying ways to promote greater cooperation between the three provinces. This is not to suggest that there was no support among the Maritime population for political union. A public opinion survey sponsored by the study 'indicated a favourable attitude to complete union of the three provinces ... on the part of approximately two thirds of the people 16 years of age and over. One quarter of the people are not in favour of such union and the balance, approximately 10 percent, is not sure ... The people of Prince Edward Island are the least in favour while those in New Brunswick are somewhat more in favour than those in Nova Scotia. English respondents favour union more so than do the French.'[30] Still, the officials directing the study concluded that to advocate cooperation that would lead to political union would be less threatening than to recommend outright and immediate union. Public opinion polls were one thing, but convincing politicians and the three bureaucracies was quite another. Moreover, for citizens to agree via a public opinion survey on some vague notion of what Maritime political union might be and what it could entail is quite different from doing so after a full blown debate in which the merits and drawbacks are fully aired.

The Deutsch Study was made public on 27 November 1970 by Premier Campbell and two newly elected premiers, Richard Hatfield of New Brunswick and Gerald Regan of Nova Scotia. There was little doubt that the study's ultimate objective was political union. However, it urged that the region move only gradually towards this goal by a series of new cooperative arrangements. Still, the study pointed to eventual political union as the preferred option because of the 'uncertainties' confronting the region 'which ... arise from two dangers – the possible political disintegration of the nation and continued substantial economic disparities in relation to the remainder of the country.'[31] The study also made clear why it did not recommend immediate political union despite the favourable response reported in the public opinion surveys: 'The historical and traditional loyalties to the individual provincial entities are strong; the attachments to local diversities and interests are more intense than elsewhere in the country ... The resistance to change in existing political structures is reinforced by the established relationships and interests that are associated with governments; these tend to be particularly intimate and strong. It can be expected that various influential groups, the holders of franchises and concessions, the bureaucratic apparatus, and many who have vested interests in the existing arrangements would be apprehensive of changes that might bring uncertainties ... There is no question that in the Maritimes many of these forces weigh heavily in the direction of the status quo.'[32]

New Machinery to Promote Cooperation

The Deutsch Study looked to new measures involving the machinery of government to encourage greater cooperation and eventually political union. The new machinery would be charged with the responsibility of promoting 'regional economic planning, regional negotiations with federal authorities establishing common administrative services, developing uniform legislation, co-ordinating existing provincial policies, preparing a constitution for a single provincial government for the

Maritimes and implementing steps leading to political union.'[33] Inspired by the European Economic Community, the study recommended three new organizations to undertake the various tasks. It urged the establishment of a Council of Maritime Premiers, a Maritime Provinces Commission, and a Joint Legislative Assembly.

The Council of Maritime Premiers would consist of the three premiers, meet at least quarterly, consider recommendations coming from the new Maritime Provinces Commission, approve joint submissions, and negotiate with Ottawa on behalf of the region.[34] The commission, meanwhile, which would consist of five members, would be responsible for preparing a long-term development plan for the region, for recommending common regional policies, and for preparing proposals for joint administrative policies and a unification of the three public services, a constitution for a single Maritime province, and a timetable for political union.[35] The Joint Legislative Assembly would bring together all members of the three provincial legislatures in a joint session once a year to review the work of the council and commission. It would also be charged with determining the method by which the final step of political union would take place.[36] The study urged that a thorough review be undertaken in five years on the progress being realized towards full political union. If it reported that progress is not being made and 'political union cannot be accomplished within a further five years, the entire program should be reconsidered.'[37]

The three premiers quickly declared their support for much of the Deutsch Study's recommendations. The director of the study explains: 'It was staggering to submit a report on November 21, 1970 in the Confederation Chamber in Charlottetown, and then have it adopted within two months. I do not think there has been a Royal Commission in this country that has ever had that happen. Taken further, within four more months there was a formal and enforceable agreement between the three provinces. Then, lo and behold, we even have it accepted by the Legislatures and formal institutions of regional cooperation were established.'[38] Premier Hatfield also gave his support to political union, as long as the federal government provided financial assistance to implement it. The other two premiers were much more lukewarm on the issue, with Regan arguing that cooperation was possible without union and Campbell suggesting that union was not necessary at 'this time.'[39] Though the premiers took immediate steps to establish the Council of Maritime Premiers, they put off a decision on the Maritime Provinces Commission and the Joint Legislative Assembly. The power to constitute the commission was built into the legislation establishing the council. However, the premiers have never pursued the matter. The power to constitute the assembly remains the prerogative of the three provincial legislative assemblies, and this too has not been pursued.

The Council of Maritime Premiers can point to a number of initiatives that have led to new regional institutions and cooperative measures.[40] There are now a host of regional institutions in place, including the Atlantic Veterinary College, the Maritime Provinces Higher Education Commission, and the Land Registration and Information Service, along with a wide array of interprovincial committees that operate joint programs or provide services. The council could also report that it successfully promoted a 'Maritime' position in dealing with Ottawa.[41] But this is often relatively easy to do. Indeed, it is scarcely difficult to get the three Maritime premiers to gang up on Ottawa, to agree that the federal government should be doing more in, say, regional economic development and transportation or that it should not be cutting transfer payments to the provinces.

Though the council has had some successes, it also has had its failures, including attempts to cooperate on trade and investment promotion, which were stymied by continuing competition. Also, in the aftermath of Canada's energy crisis in the 1970s, the three premiers agreed to put in place an energy agency to encourage regional planning, a pooling of capital, and the allocation of regional or Maritime energy resources. However, the proposed Maritime Energy Cooperation failed to get off the ground.[42] The reasons for this particular failure are not difficult to pinpoint: province building overshadowed region building. Indeed, in time each province found one reason or another to lose interest in a joint energy corporation. New Brunswick was able to secure federal financing to construct its own nuclear power plant; a new government in Prince Edward Island declared its firm opposition to nuclear power; and Nova Scotia saw coal-generated power as a way to create new jobs in economically depressed Cape Breton. The three provinces also accused the federal government of reneging on its initial commitment to support the Maritime Energy Corporation.

There was no thorough or public review after five years to assess the progress being made towards full political union, as proposed by the Deutsch Study. Had there been one, the entire program would have been 'reconsidered' because there were, of course, no indications that 'political union' could have been 'accomplished within a further five years.' Such a review, however, would have been unfair to the Council of Maritime Premiers, as two key recommendations of the study were never acted upon: the establishment of a Maritime Provinces Commission and a Joint Legislative Assembly.

The council did, however, commission a review of its own effectiveness in the late 1980s. The report, *Standing Up to the Future*, begins by declaring that the 'Council of Maritime Premiers has served the provinces of New Brunswick, Nova Scotia and Prince Edward Island well – very well indeed.'[43] A few pages later, however, it notes, 'in no fixed order,' that with its 'current structure and performance [, the council] ... lacks a clear regional agenda on major economic issues facing the Maritime Provinces and a mechanism to develop such an agenda [and] ... it lacks credibility ... as a delivery mechanism for programs within provincial governments and their line departments ... [It has] an almost non-existent policy research role conducted internally or funded externally, and no on-line database to strengthen coordinated policy making for the region and a "wait and see" attitude by Secretariat personnel towards specific agenda items.'[44] For good measure, the review added, 'In recent years, various organizational weaknesses have emerged at the Council.'[45] The proposed solutions lacked clarity and purpose, though the review was clear on the issue of political union. It stated: 'Maritime Union is not a viable option.'[46] It did not, however, go into much detail about why this must be so. It then outlined a series of recommendations with which few Maritimers could disagree. It recommended an 'emphasis on attainable targets over a fixed time period, say, five years. Assume the overall target is straightforward – to make the Maritimes a have region by the end of the decade, by the start of the 21st century.'[47] The review suggested that the way to achieve this target was '[to double] the level of entrepreneurial exports from the Maritimes in five years, double the level of start-ups in each province and develop the technology base of the Maritimes over five years.'[48] Yet, it was not clear on how this could be accomplished. It recommended that the Maritimes should 'use' the Canadian consulate in Boston more, 'should learn from the Scandinavian experience [and explore] what new opportunities are there for new alliances with them to mutual advantage.'[49]

Though the review made little reference to the Deutsch Study, it appeared to borrow from it when it recommended the 'establishment of a Maritime Premiers Advisory Board on a three-year basis ... to help the Premiers establish a collective strategic agenda and to serve as a sounding board.'[50] The review was not very clear on the precise mandate and operation of such an advisory board, but it seems to have been inspired by Deutsch's recommendations on the establishment of a Maritime commission. Still, the review cautioned that 'a bold vision of the Maritime Premiers cannot happen by executive fiat – Citizens must be involved.'[51] It argued for the establishment of a Maritime Savings Development Fund that would capture the resources available in the region's pension funds to assist local economic development. It also called for the abolition of all interprovincial trade barriers between the three provinces.[52] These suggestions were ignored.

Despite its drawbacks, the review did serve an important purpose in that it placed the issue of maritime cooperation front and centre before the respective policy agendas of both the region and the country at a critical period in Canada's history. Canada's national unity woes in light of the failed Meech Lake and Charlottetown constitutional accords would push Maritime cooperation back on the public policy agenda. In the fall of 1990, New Brunswick premier Frank McKenna issued a call for greater cooperation, which was widely reported and applauded in the national media. Premiers Joe Ghiz of Prince Edward Island and Donald Cameron of Nova Scotia in turn soon voiced their strong support. Newfoundland Premier Clyde Wells then joined in and made a plea for an Atlantic rather than a strictly Maritime perspective to regional cooperation, with press reports suggesting that he favoured full political union of the four Atlantic provinces. Premier Wells subsequently retracted his support, saying that he had been misquoted – and later shifted to the more traditional and cooler Newfoundland posture.

The Council of Atlantic Premiers

At one of its regular meetings, on 27 October 1999, the Council of Maritime Premiers extended a formal invitation to Newfoundland and Labrador to join the council as a full partner.[53] Several months later the four Atlantic premiers met in Moncton to sign a memorandum of understanding establishing the Council of Atlantic Premiers. The four premiers made it clear that the focus of the new council would be 'to promote Atlantic Canadian interests on national issues ... to establish common views and positions and work to ensure Atlantic Canadians and their interests are well represented in national debates.'[54]

A former senior official with the Council of Maritime Premiers reports that the three Maritime premiers agreed to extend the invitation to the premier of Newfoundland and Labrador to strengthen their hand with the federal government, based on a profound desire for more clout in Ottawa. He explains, 'There was deep frustration over their inability to influence the federal government. All three were Progressive Conservative premiers. They looked to Brian Tobin, a former Liberal Cabinet minister in Ottawa with Jean Chrétien and concluded that he could help a great deal in their dealings with Ottawa. The Council of Atlantic Premiers is a lot about dealing with Ottawa, not as much about regional cooperation.' He adds, 'Tobin, meanwhile, saw an opportunity to become spokesperson for all of Atlantic Canada rather than just Newfoundland and Labrador.'[55] A currently serving official with the council readily acknowledges that interprovincial cooperation is far more difficult with 'Newfoundland and Labrador in the mix.'[56]

The council's first meeting set the tone for what was to come. The four premiers discussed the upcoming annual Premiers' Conference. They also 'identified regional priorities,' notably 'securing adequate funding for health care, identifying and pursuing key investments to strengthen economic growth, including infrastructure and highways, and seeking improvements to the national fiscal transfer system.'[57] With respect to strengthening economic growth, the premiers 'called for the federal government to invest in a new shared-cost highways program for Atlantic Canada to further economic development to reduce disparity and increase opportunities.'[58]

The central purpose of the Council of Atlantic Premiers is to lobby the federal government on behalf of the four provinces and to influence national policies. The work of the council differs from that of the Council of Maritime Premiers in that the former is more of a lobby group. The council itself reports that 'the work of the Council of Atlantic Premiers will be in addition to the ongoing work of the Council of Maritime Premiers, which has been in existence for more than twenty-five years. All premiers have recognized the need for continued concerted cooperation on a Maritime basis. The Maritime provinces do have specific ties and interests which are distinct from Atlantic concerns. These range from interprovincial flows in postsecondary education and health to the development of closer economic relationships.'[59]

Typically, the Council of Atlantic Premiers will, in its own words, meet to 'bring a strong and united voice to a number of national issues.' At the end of one typical meeting, the four premiers issued a press release to highlight:

- the growing fiscal imbalance between the federal government and the provinces, which diminishes provinces' ability to deliver key programs;
- new federal investments in health, postsecondary education, and other social programs;

- the need for a more aggressive approach by the federal government in international trade relations; and
- the necessity of addressing climate change.

At the same meeting, premiers did discuss regional cooperation, but the discussion fell short of expectations, even by the standards set by the Council of Maritime Premiers. They spoke about closer regional cooperation to attract new Canadians but then quickly turned their attention to Ottawa. They reported that they would look to greater regional cooperation in order 'to press the federal government to promote increased competition in the airline industry by allowing foreign carriers greater air access to Atlantic Canada; and regional cooperation on security and transborder issues, including adequate federal funding arrangements.'[60]

That the Council of Atlantic Premiers sees itself as mainly a lobby association working Ottawa on behalf of the four Atlantic provinces is made clear by the list of accomplishments it has made public:

- advocating for the sustainability of health care;
- calling for reform of the federal equalization program;
- defending the Atlantic Canada–US softwood-lumber agreement;
- requesting that the federal government pass new airline regulatory legislation to encourage competition;
- urging the federal government to establish a national shipbuilding and marine-fabrication policy;
- harmonizing the framework for regulating the licensing and sale of insurance products in the region; and
- collectively building international trade opportunities for Atlantic businesses through the Team Canada Atlantic trade partnership.[61]

Having Newfoundland and Labrador in the mix has made it extremely difficult for the region to do much beyond forming a club to lobby Ottawa. But even in this capacity there have been some significant disagreements among the four provincial governments, notably on fishery policy and federal equalization payments. The four Atlantic premiers can agree that 'the fiscal capacity of the Atlantic provinces falls short of the national average even after equalization. These shortcomings in the Equalization Program must be corrected.'[62] They agree on little else about equalization.

It is important to stress that until Premiers Wells and Tobin came on the scene, Newfoundland and Labrador had consistently shunned closer cooperation with the three Maritime provinces – so much so that its government passed an order-in-council in the late 1970s prohibiting any government department from signing a regional agreement with the Maritime provinces without first securing full cabinet approval. Newfoundland and Labrador effectively killed the Atlantic Premiers' Conference when it decided in the mid-1960s to no longer attend meetings. The government of Newfoundland and Labrador also stopped its annual contribution to the operation of the Atlantic Provinces Economic Council in the early 1980s, arguing that its economy was so different that it made no sense to speak of an Atlantic economy. It later established its own Newfoundland and Labrador Economic Council. Patrick O'Flaherty of Memorial University recently explained that 'Newfoundland's economy is more tied into that of Central Canada ... I don't think maritime union represents any real alternative for Newfoundland. It is not a big issue here. I would say that if there is any kind of option that Newfoundlanders would entertain, if Canada does break up, the first one that they will want to explore will be independence. There is still a strong subterranean nationalist feeling in Newfoundland.'[63]

It is important to remember that Newfoundland has had a distinct political and economic history. The province was not populated by Loyalists and Acadians, and its ties to the rest of Canada are relatively recent. A former secretary to the Council of Maritime Premiers explains that 'it's hard enough to get three sovereign governments to cooperate on anything and that's in the good times. When you add a fourth, who is further away, whose history is different, whose culture is different and whose aspirations are different, it gets even harder to negotiate anything.'[64] Premier Wells, it will be recalled, quickly backtracked on his earlier call for greater cooperation, on the grounds that he did not know quite what 'economic cooperation and integration' mean. The *St John's Evening Telegram* ran an editorial at the height of the discussion entitled 'A Boat to Miss?' and argued that 'the real reason behind Mr. Wells' reluctance to get involved in the scheme may lie in the simple fact Newfoundland has little to gain by it ... This may be one boat the province will only be too glad to miss.'[65]

A Boat Everyone Missed

If the Maritime region were to heal itself through political union or even through close economic cooperation, then it has thus far failed to do so. To be sure, there are many reasons to account for this lack of success. Some of them are self-inflicted but others are not.

Provincial premiers are elected to promote the interests of their province. These interests are defined by provincial boundaries, by geography, and by voters living in a defined physical space. Province building is rooted in this political reality for all provinces but perhaps more so in the case of the Maritime provinces. Quite apart from the fact that tigers do not easily part with their stripes, the three Maritime premiers are unlikely to allow the region's voice to be attenuated without some lasting compensation. Relatively disadvantaged provinces enjoy all the privileges and responsibilities associated with provincehood within a competitive but also generous system of transfer payments.

A number of Cape Bretoners, for example, are convinced that their economy would be considerably stronger if their island enjoyed provincial status. The Cape Breton Regional Municipality commissioned a study in 2003 to consider broad options. The report, prepared by an economist and a political scientist from Memorial University, argued, 'With a population of 130,000, Prince Edward Island offers a useful comparison to Cape Breton in that the latter has a population of approximately 150,000. Province-hood appears to bring with it noble objectives, much power, and the capacity to build a self-reliant, political entity.' It added, 'While the status quo system of governance is an option, it is certainly not one that is desirable from the perspective of contributing to the long-term viability of Cape Breton. Cape Breton is not sustainable as a meaningful economic entity under the current governance arrangement. If nothing is done the long-term viability of Cape Breton is in question. In other words, Cape Breton, being a region of a province, does not have the kind of resources or fiscal instruments available to it to deal with its economic problems as would a separate provincial entity.'[66]

Equalization payments and a political and administrative infrastructure are only two examples of what full provincial status holds. Cape Breton could well have today an economy much like that found in Prince Edward Island if it had enjoyed provincial status over the years. Provincial status means, at a minimum, having a capital, an elaborate administrative structure with a large number of stable federal and provincial public-service jobs, a university, and usually a number of consultants. Moreover, by each having a seat at the First Ministers Conferences, provincial premiers enjoy not only a special status and high visibility in the national media, but they are also given a say in the future of the country. They can plead, often before a national television audience, for a better economic deal for their province.

One only needs to spend a few days in Ottawa to hear many politicians of whatever party and most senior federal officials report privately their full support for greater cooperation, if not full political union, among the Maritime provinces. Indeed, many quite readily admit bewilderment that three such small political entities, with the largest – Nova Scotia – having a population base not much greater than the National Capital Region, are not already united economically and politically.

The federal government has, however, made only a few tangible efforts to promote Maritime cooperation. For example, it shared the costs of the Deutsch Study and seconded Edgar Gallant, a senior federal bureaucrat, to set up the Council of Maritime Premiers. Such isolated gestures aside, and despite the vast number of individuals in Ottawa who favour Maritime political union or, at a minimum, greater cooperation, particularly in economic development, there is precious little evidence to suggest that federal policies are geared to assist this outcome. On the contrary, evidence suggests that they have, over the years, actually worked against it. Otherwise, how do we explain, for example, Ottawa's change of position with regard to the establishment of the proposed Maritime Energy Corporation? Such second thinking certainly did not help matters, and probably gave the three provinces a *porte de sortie* to back away from the proposed deal.

There are other examples, but perhaps none more telling than those found in federal regional development efforts that were overhauled in 1972, when the General Development Agreement (GDA) was introduced to implement regional development programs. The GDAs, as we saw earlier, were later replaced by a series of new generations of federal-provincial agreements. These agreements have sponsored programs and projects totalling billions of dollars in the three Maritime provinces since the early 1970s, including measures sponsored in agriculture, fisheries, transportation, industrial development, energy, minerals development, local development, forestry, ocean-related industries, rural development, pulp and paper, urban development and tourism – among other sectors and specific geographical areas. These programs were almost exclusively *provincial* in scope. Only in the case of tourism and trade has the federal government recently attempted to introduce a 'regional' focus. There have even been instances where local federal offices were in competition with one another to secure a project for 'their' provinces, much as provincial governments have been accused of doing.[67]

In short, the federal government, the one government with the necessary detachment to bring a 'Maritime' perspective to economic development, has failed to do so. The bulk of Ottawa's efforts in regional development over the past thirty years in the Maritime provinces has been channelled directly to the three provincial governments for programs designed and implemented by the provinces. This is not to suggest for a moment that Ottawa could easily ignore the fact that provincial governments are the effective agents of political power in the region. Still, it could have promoted a regional perspective in its dealings with them and at least indicated the advantages of signing 'regional' rather than strictly 'provincial' agreements for a number of sectors. This would have required a political focus on the Maritime region, establishing the issue in Ottawa as an important priority and encouraging the expenditure of political capital to pursue this priority.

The impact on the Maritimes of Ottawa's apparent unwillingness to encourage greater regional cooperation has been considerable. For one thing, given the status of the three provinces, the great majority of provincially designed measures to promote economic development have been, at least in part, federally funded. If the federal government does not follow a regional perspective in its dealings with the provinces, then provincial politicians and officials will naturally pursue provincially designed programs and seek federal funding for them. Moreover, the pervasive local federal presence – and its ready funding – has encouraged the three provinces to turn to it rather than to one another to promote economic development.

It is no coincidence that the issue of Maritime political union or cooperation will surface on the public policy agenda only when national unity is threatened. In 1964, it was Quebec's Quiet Revolution and the pressures of the mid-twentieth century that accounted for Louis Robichaud's call for a 'serious' look at political union of the four Atlantic provinces. The issue again gained currency immediately after the Parti Québécois came to power in Quebec in 1976. Frank McKenna issued a call for greater regional cooperation in the aftermath of the failed Meech Lake and Charlottetown constitutional accords. The point is that outside forces, not those from within, have put Maritime union on the public policy agenda. The same can be said of economic cooperation. Progress on this front has been extremely modest. When the federal government decided – after pressure from the provinces – to look to bilateral agreements to promote economic development, the three Maritime provinces were only too happy to agree.

Growing a Private Sector

For many, the best way for the Maritime region to move ahead is through entrepreneurship and a stronger private sector. The idea is hardly new. John Stuart Mill wrote about the importance of entrepreneurship to economic growth and argued that risk taking was the main function distinguishing the true entrepreneur from the manager.[68] As noted earlier, Joseph Schumpeter maintained in his 1934 book, *The Theory of Economic Development*, that the entrepreneur is the mainspring of growth and development. For Schumpeter, the entrepreneur is the innovator who 'does something differently,' introducing a new product, a new resource, a new technique, combining land, labour, capital, and management in new ways so as to get more product from a given bundle of resources. The entrepreneur then finds the necessary resources and brings them together under a new management. He hopes to establish a monopoly, and usually does – for a time. But then, once the success of the new venture is assured and demonstrated, a 'cluster of followers' appears, and some degree of competition occurs.[69]

Policy makers, and their advisers, charged with promoting economic development in the Maritime provinces have, particularly since the mid-1980s, looked to entrepreneurship and the private sector to grow the economy. The report that led to the establishment of the Atlantic Canada Opportunities Agency (ACOA), it will be recalled, stressed the importance of these factors. ACOA has made entrepreneurship the centerpiece of its efforts from the moment it opened its doors. Former New Brunswick premier Frank McKenna, among others, also pointed to the private sector as the way ahead for his province. Yet, for all the talk, we have very little literature on the issue from a public policy perspective. For example, the Atlantic Institute for Market Studies (AIMS), which produced a number of studies about the region and its economic development challenges, has had little to say on the issue. AIMS is not the only research institute or group to focus their research on other topics.

We have seen, since the late 1980s, a number of government programs introduced by both orders of government designed to promote entrepreneurship and to stimulate the local private sector. Though the federal government abandoned all cash grants to businesses in the mid-1990s because of its difficult fiscal position, governments still have a variety of measures designed to promote entrepreneurship and a stronger private sector in the region. In any event, the debate – if one ever existed – whether entrepreneurs are 'good guys' or 'bad guys' is *passé*. As local, regional, national, and international economies are becoming increasingly market economies and as government activities and expenditures are reduced, the Maritime region needs entrepreneurs. In brief, entrepreneurs and small and medium businesses have become the new panaceas for the region.

Within five years of its establishment, ACOA sponsored over 400 Entrepreneurship Development projects and activities. These included small-business and self-employment counselling initiatives; development of university enterprise centres; entrepreneurship awareness and promotion projects, which build entrepreneur role-models (through the use of television and entrepreneurship awards programs); self-employment and entrepreneurship training projects for start-up, survival, and growth; entrepreneurship orientation and education activities; network-building activities, entrepreneurship-related research and publications; and intergovernmental meetings and other forms of consultations.[70]

Entrepreneurs and small and middle-sized enterprises (SMEs) have attracted the most attention in recent years: much more has been written about them than about large enterprises, and there are now many organizations providing support to them of one kind or another or defending their interests. This situation arises partly from the simple fact that the vast majority of enterprises are small or middle sized; but it also reflects a wide-spread feeling that SMEs are somehow more desirable for social or economic reasons than large ones. We know that over 95 per cent of Canadian enterprises have less than a hundred employees. Thus when we speak of SMEs in Canada, we are speaking of virtually all enterprises. However, despite their preponderance in numbers, the SMEs account for less than 60 per cent of gross domestic product (GDP). The feeling that SMEs are somehow 'better' than larger enterprises springs from a conviction that they are more likely than large enterprises to produce a situation closer to the ideal of pure competition, and from the belief that economic power is likely to be reflected by political power, so that SMEs are more 'democratic' than large enterprises.

The Canadian Federation of Independent Business and Scotiabank teamed up in the fall of 1997 to survey Canadians on their views on small business. The survey revealed that farmers and small businesses were among the most respected groups when compared to other types of organizations or institutions in society. This was true even when the findings were broken down by regions. In brief, Canadians' levels of respect for major types of organizations (on a scale of 1 to 10) breaks down as follows: 8.3 for farmers, 8.2 for small businesses, 7.0 for the education system, 6.8 for health care, 6.6 for religious organizations, 6.5 for large Canadian companies, 5.9 for the legal system, 5.9 for multinational corporations, and 5.5 for government.[71]

Whether or not these convictions are justified is a matter that needs careful study. If hundreds of small enterprises are organized into a cooperative, for example, as the dairy farmers in the United States used to be, they can exercise a good deal of monopoly power. Conversely, if the managers of a huge corporation are not owners of the corporation and are more interested in growth of the firm than in maximizing profits, their policies may add up to a situation that is closer to pure competition than to monopoly. Indeed, the divorce of management from ownership has gone so far that it is difficult to tell what the management of any large corporation is trying to do, or even whether all members of the management team have the same objective. Very few of them seem to be endeavouring to maximize profits by restricting output to the level that equates marginal cost to marginal revenue. Many seem to be maximizing market share, perhaps in the hope that success in outselling rivals will result in maximizing their salaries. In any case, SMEs and large firms are not two entirely separate categories. There are many interdependencies among them. The policy should be not to have SMEs rather than large firms, but rather that each firm should attain the optimal size for the kind of goods or service it is producing and the technology it is using. One cannot produce steel with a small firm, as the Chinese found out in their experiment with backyard foundries.

The private sector in the Maritime provinces is made up of a handful of locally owned large firms, some large firms from away, and a great number of SMEs. Some of the region's largest firms are family owned and unwilling to reveal information. The Irving Group and the McCain Food empires are two prime examples. Harrison McCain decided not to take McCain Foods public largely because he wanted to keep his business activities private. When asked to explain his business success, McCain, never one to waste words, simply answered, 'right place, right time.' When asked to talk about the state of his business, he told a journalist, 'my business is none of your business.'[72]

Atlantic Progress magazine published a survey that gives a good picture of 'big entrepreneurs' in the region. The editor describes it as 'a hard look at ourselves by an economist who compares what he finds on the list with large trends sweeping through the economy of the region and the nation.'[73] It confirmed that the region's largest companies are family owned and reticent about making business information public. It pointed out that 'it remains a strong characteristic of business in Atlantic Canada that some of the biggest companies are more or less closely held by single families. This pattern ranges from the Irvings and Jodreys, who permit no outsiders to have an interest in their companies, through to the McCains, who went outside the family in 1995 to hire a new president and CEO, to the Sobeys whose Empire company stock is publicly traded, but where family holdings still predominate.'[74] In this light, one can appreciate why governments would focus on entrepreneurs and SMEs as the most promising way for Maritimers to pull themselves up by their own bootstraps.

ACOA published several reports on the state of small business and entrepreneurship. Together, they provide a valuable picture of the recent evolution of SMEs, the vast majority of enterprises in the region. As stated in one of the first such reports, 'the small enterprises, particularly the new ones, have created more than half the jobs in the course of the last decade, and the entrepreneurial culture, which is flourishing in the small enterprises, shows the way to rejuvenation of all sectors of the economy.'[75] Continuing in the same vein, the executive summary states that for a long time, Atlantic Canada has benefited from 'a panoply of precise measures taken to close the chronic gap between the economic possibilities which presented themselves and those which the rest of the country offered.'[76] These policies have not attained their ambitious objectives. Despite good intentions, the report acknowledges, aid to the region seems to have given birth to a spirit of dependence rather than favouring a spirit of initiative. Henceforth, the objective should be to cultivate this spirit of initiative. Priority will be given to the training of people, the most important resource of the region, 'so long attached to fishing, forests, and mines.'[77] During the 1980s, the report asserted, entrepreneurship came to be considered one of the most promising means of increasing employment. Yet, the report adds, we should not confuse entrepreneurship and small enterprises. *Entrepreneurship implies a commitment to growth, whereas small enterprises are happy to remain small.* They are most at ease, ACOA points out, if big companies have difficulty in competing with them.

Interestingly, the sector subjected to the market economy has grown faster in the region (in terms of employment) than the subsidized (government) sector, while in Canada as a whole the reverse is true. During the 1980s, employment has grown by 23 per cent in the subsidized sector and by 24 per cent in the market-economy sector in the region; in Canada, it has grown by 36 per cent in the subsidized sector and by 28 per cent in the market-economy sector. Between 1979 and 1988 small enterprises with less than a hundred employees created 99 per cent of the employment in Canada as a whole, but only 96 per cent in the Maritimes. In the same period, large private enterprises, with more than five hundred employees, reduced their staffs by 6.3 per cent in Canada, but only by 2.6 per cent in the Maritimes.

New enterprises, rather than small enterprises in general, the report pointed out, contributed most to employment during the 1980s.[78] Yet, new enterprises are vulnerable, and many do not survive for long. In fact, the average life of an enterprise in Atlantic Canada is only 6.75 years. An inquiry revealed that 10 per cent of the enterprises in the Atlantic provinces that ceased their activities in 1987 failed, and 44 per cent quite simply closed their doors or had their activities suspended by their·owners. Between 1978 and 1988 the new enterprises represented, each year, on average, 20 per cent of the total enterprises in existence.

In the 1994 *State of Small Business and Entrepreneurship*, ACOA begins by stressing the continuing structural change taking place in the region: 'The Atlantic region is in the midst of an unprecedented process of sustained restructuring that is simultaneously eroding its traditional economic base and developing the infrastructure of the new economy that will take its place.'[79] It provides figures of the changes that have taken place between 1951 and 1991, the most important of which is a decline in employment in the primary sector. In 1991 the structure of the Atlantic Canada economy resembled somewhat the structure of the Canadian economy as a whole, except that Atlantic Canada still had 12 per cent of its labour force in public administration, compared to 8 per cent for Canada as a whole. In terms of rate of change, however, ACOA notes one other important difference: 'Among the changes in the private sector, it is notable that manufacturing lost only two percentage points in the region over the forty years, falling to 13 percent from 15 percent. In Canada as a whole, manufacturing's share fell to 15 percent from 20 percent over the same period.'[80] Two generations ago, having a large share of the labour force in the manufacturing sector was a sign of a strong economy; now, with the 'new industrial revolution,' it is a sign of weakness. Turning to 'the secrets of growth' in chapter 2, the 1994 report states that 'over the 10 years from 1979 and 1989, the total number of firms in the region grew by 56 per cent, but it was not a smooth ride. There was unprecedented activity in firms with fewer than five employees – the number of startups alone was 34 percent more than the *total* number of firms of that size that existed in 1979.'[81]

The report distinguishes 'growers' from 'sliders' (firms that have declined to a smaller size category by the end of the period). The results are reproduced in table 8.1, which shows turnover within each size category of firms, from start-ups, cessation of business, growing into larger size categories, declining into smaller size categories or coming *into* the size category. The impact of 'growers' and 'sliders' on total employment is shown in table 8.2.

ACOA then cites at considerable length a survey made by John Baldwin for Statistics Canada, entitled *Strategies for Success: A Profile of Growing Small and Small and Medium-sized Enterprises in Canada*. ACOA describes the purpose of Statistics Canada in undertaking the research as follows: 'Given scarce resources, an important question is which programs are more useful and effective in helping SMEs succeed and grow? These are the areas in which government is likely to receive the greatest return for its investment of time, energy, and resources in the future. To answer this question, the Statistics Canada research team has examined three aspects of the SMEs – their strategies, their activities, and their characteristics.'[82]

Statistics Canada found that 86 per cent of Canadian SMEs are in-dependent and 14 per cent are affiliated with a parent firm. Owner-op-erators run 84 per cent of the SMEs while 16 per cent have outside owners. Nine factors, listed in table 8.3, were considered by respondents to have been important in their growth. ACOA comments: 'The manage-ment skills SMEs have developed and the skill levels of their workforces are seen as being important as are access to markets, capital and tech-nology.' This statement would seem to be tautological: one could have arrived at such a list without ever consulting the SMEs; it is obvious that firms having those qualities will grow while those lacking them will fail. While expenditures on research and development ranked only eighth in the list of nine factors, it seems likely that it has been more impor-tant than the weight accorded by the respondents. ACOA comments that 'the average level of R & D to sales for SMEs performing R & D was 3.1 percent in 1991. However, using R & D as a proxy for innovativeness in SMEs tends to give an inaccurate picture because innovation comes from many other sources in the company besides R & D.'[83]

Chapter 3 of the 1994 ACOA report is devoted to the effort of various

TABLE 8.1
Turnover with firms by size (as percentage of firms at beginning of period),
Atlantic Canada, 1979–89, 1989–91

Type of change	No. of employees						
	<5	5–19	20–49	50–99	100–499	500+	Total
1989–91							
1989 firms	100	100	100	100	100	100	100
Went out of business	38	14	20	25	21	16	32
New entrants	41	15	21	29	27	19	35
Inflow[a]	4	21	25	35	16	6	8
Growers[b]	3	5	9	14	4	0	4
Sliders[c]	0	18	20	17	11	7	4
Net change by 1991	3	(2)	(4)	8	6	2	2
1979–89							
1979 firms	100	100	100	100	100	100	100
Went out of business	60	46	48	54	53	44	56
New entrants	134	73	65	65	48	26	112
Inflow[a]	3	54	83	108	40	22	20
Growers[b]	12	21	45	61	20	0	16
Sliders[c]	0	13	14	11	5	4	3
Net change by 1989	64	46	41	48	10	0	56

Note: Totals may not coincide with the sum of some columns due to rounding.
[a]*Inflow* for a particular size category counts the sliders and growers from other size categories that end the period in the size category in question.
[b]*Growers* are firms that existed in the base year (1989 or 1979) and grew sufficiently to be classified in a larger size category by the end of the period.
[c]*Sliders* have declined to a smaller size category by the end of the period.
Source: *Growing and Declining Business Report, Atlantic Canada, 1989–91* (Ottawa: Small Business and Special Surveys Division of Statistics Canada, 1993). This is a special run of *Employment Dynamics*, the data base used extensively elsewhere in this report.

government agencies to advise and assist SMEs. It begins with the observation that 'the critical role of new and small business in the growth of the economy has led government and other agencies to provide services to aid in their development, especially during the pre-start-up and survival stages. These services are being provided through a variety of government departments, crown corporations, industrial and economic development commissions, university and community-based small-business development centres, and other publicly-funded agencies ... It is estimated that there may be upwards of three thousand people employed in these governments and publicly funded agencies in the region.'[84]

TABLE 8.2
Distribution of firms by status and corresponding net gains and losses in employment,
Atlantic Canada, 1989–91

Status	Firms in each status		Net change in jobs	
	Number	As a % of 1989 firms	Number	As a % of total loss[a]
Exits	27,988	32	(55,300)	−473
Unchanged	51,355	59	(8,300)	−71
Growers	3,423	4	31,700	271
Sliders	3,893	4	(36,000)	−308
1989 firms	86,556	100	(67,900)	−580
Entrants	30,063	35	56,200	480
Net change[b]	2,075	2	(11,700)	−100

[a]Employment loss is expressed as a negative percentage to aid understanding if not
mathematical precision.
[b]Net change in firms is entrants less exits. Net change in employment is the overall
change in jobs in the Atlantic region.

TABLE 8.3
Average rankings by respondents of the contribution made to the growth of their firms
by specified factors

Factors	Mean value[a]	Proportion (%) responding with a ranking of 4 or 5
Management skills	3.3	55
Skilled labour	2.9	43
Marketing capability	2.9	43
Access to markets	2.8	43
Access to capital	2.7	33
Cost of capital	2.7	33
Ability to adopt technology	2.5	33
R & D innovation capability	1.4	16
Government assistance	1.4	14

[a]On a scale of 1 to 5, with 1 being not important, 2 slightly important, 3 important, 4
very important and 5 crucial.
Source: Canada, ACOA, *The State of Small Business and Entrepreneurship in Atlantic
Canada* (Moncton: ACOA, 1994), 23.

Despite their significance, little is known about the general make-up
and characteristics of these service providers.[85] To find out more about
them, ACOA mailed 'an extensive survey questionnaire ... to eight
hundred and four people employed in agencies or organizations which
provide business support services to small businesses.' ACOA found

that the respondents (the response rate was 31 per cent) divided themselves among seven types of offices and mainly among six types of services. The types of service provided were: business-advisory services (19 per cent), financial assistance (14 per cent), self-employment or management-development training (13 per cent), marketing assistance (12 per cent), technical support (9 per cent), expert assistance (6 per cent).[86] With regard to fees, 61 per cent of respondents did not charge, 17 per cent always charged, and 21 per cent sometimes charged. Of the 249 respondents, 74 per cent were male and 23 per cent were female, while 3 per cent did not indicate gender. Almost three-quarters of the respondents were under the age of fifty. Almost 81 per cent had been to a university, and 63 per cent had one or more degrees. The vast majority of those with degrees undertook studies related to business (such as an MBA). A small minority had degrees related to engineering. The work experience of some 83 per cent of the respondents was 'directly applicable to small business practice.' More than one-third had been business counsellors for four to ten years, another 30 per cent had more than ten years of experience.[87]

The way in which the respondents spend their time is varied. ACOA remarks: 'Most counselling appears to be done in the initial up-front stage of business creation with relatively new, inexperienced entrepreneurs.'[88] It then proceeds to deliver a mild rebuke to the respondents for not showing enough interest and expertise in the use of computers. 'It is becoming difficult to conceive a business of any significant size operating efficiently without the use of computers ... The percentage of respondents who indicated a high degree of proficiency in use of computers is low.'[89] ACOA asked its respondents to indicate 'the areas in which they felt it was most important to acquire new information or knowledge in order to be more effective in their counselling work. They assigned a weighting from 1 to 5 (1 = not important; 5 = very important) to each of these areas.' ACOA has this to say about these results: 'While there appears to be an incongruity between the finding that innovation/new product development ranks tenth on the list when ... innovation is the major differentiating factor of higher growth SMEs, this is a reflection of the fact that almost half of the small business counsellors' time is reported to be spent with pre-start-up entrepreneurs.' The report adds: 'Only three of the top ten items chosen by respondents addressed the critical elements for growth and success identified, namely market research, innovation, and new product development ... This sounds a warning bell for the future as businesses grow and develop.'[90]

In its 1998 *State of Small Business and Entrepreneurship in Atlantic Canada*, ACOA noted that both Canada and the region experienced an economic downturn for much of the 1989–95 period, but that the 'region managed an increase of 5 per cent in the number of firms operating, approximately twice the rate experienced nationally.'[91] It added that from 1989 to 1995 'firms with fewer than five employees were responsible for all of the total increase in the number of firms in the region. This category experienced the highest number of entrants and exits and had the highest increase in number of firms (10.8 percent) of any size category.'[92]

This report, like earlier ones, stressed the importance of education to entrepreneurship. The agency devoted several chapters in its *State of Small Business* reports to education. It also sponsored numerous measures over the years designed to link entrepreneurship to education. The thinking here is that entrepreneurship can be created, a point made in chapter 3 in discussing the work of Harvard psychologist David McClelland and his colleague David Winter. ACOA officials embraced this view and looked to education from high schools to universities to create entrepreneurship and to develop an entrepreneurial culture and society. The agency reports that there were 'no entrepreneurship teachers in Atlantic Canada in 1990' but in 2005 there were about five hundred teachers with the knowledge and capacity to teach entrepreneurship in high schools throughout the region.[93]

It is difficult, however, to evaluate the work of ACOA in this respect because the objectives of the various measures have been so sweeping. How does one create an entrepreneurial society and, if one is able to do so, how could one possibly isolate the reasons that led to its development? One could speculate that our educational system is much better at teaching people to be good managers, good engineers, and good lawyers than at teaching them how to be successful entrepreneurs.

We know from anecdotal evidence that some highly successful entrepreneurs (K.C. Irving and his sons, for example) had limited post-secondary education. We also know from anecdotal evidence that sending sons and daughters to the world's best universities and business schools does not guarantee that successful entrepreneurs will be created. For generations the Fairfax family of Australia had owned one of the most prestigious group of newspapers in the country. The family sent young Warwick Fairfax, heir to the newspaper chain, to Oxford and later to the Harvard Business School, where he earned an MBA. He came back to Australia, took over the management of the papers, and within months had bankrupted the Fairfax Corporation, forcing the family to sell the newspapers. In Australia, people told the following riddle: 'Do you know how to create a small business? Give a large one to Warwick Fairfax.'[94]

The 1998 report contained a chapter on regional competitiveness in which it argued that the region had a strong basis for competitiveness and growth, particularly vis-à-vis the United States. The report listed some of the region's competitive advantages:

- initial investment costs are lower in the region for every industry, largely as a result of lower land-acquisition costs and lower construction costs;
- operating costs are lower in the region for every industry, primarily as a result of lower labour and benefits costs;
- the region's cost advantage holds over a wide range of exchange rates;
- wages are lower in the region than in the United States and the cost-of-living index and housing prices are also lower; and
- crime rates and homicide rates are lower in Atlantic Canada than in U.S. jurisdictions.

The report also highlighted serious drawbacks that had to be overcome if the region's competitive position was to improve. These included a high rate of unemployment, decelerating population growth, and the out-migration of highly educated young people, all of which were having a negative impact on the region's human-resource potential. These problems are compounded in the technology area by comparatively low rates of innovation and technology adoption and a low level of private-sector investment in research and development and related human resources.

ACOA produced yet another report on the state of small business and entrepreneurship in 2004. The report revealed that the region generated more new businesses during the 1990s than the national average. All three Maritime provinces experienced a gain in the number of firms during that decade. However, the region also reported the highest exit rates (see table 8.4).[95]

The report's overall theme is that 'small business is big business' in Atlantic Canada. It reports that over 60 per cent of all new jobs created in the region in recent years occurred in small firms or those with fewer than a hundred employees. In addition, micro firms or firms with fewer

TABLE 8.4
Average annual entry and exit rates for businesses: Canada and the Maritime provinces, 1990–8 (%)

Region	Entry rate	Exit rate	Retention rate
Prince Edward Island	21.4	20.2	1.2
Nova Scotia	19.0	18.4	0.6
New Brunswick	18.0	17.4	0.6
Canada	15.4	14.8	0.6

Source: Canada, *The State of Small Business and Entrepreneurship* (Moncton: ACOA, 2004), 21.

than five employees generated more new jobs than large firms with more than five hundred employees.[96]

If the public policy goal was to create an entrepreneurial culture in the Maritimes, then there is some evidence to suggest that the measures have had a positive influence. More Maritimers are establishing their own businesses than ever before. Self-employment grew faster than total employment in both New Brunswick and Nova Scotia throughout the 1990s. The region, however, continues to *trail* the national average in self-employment as a percentage of total employment (see table 8.5).

As it had in previous reports, ACOA again decided to survey the intentions of Atlantic Canadians with regard to starting a new business. The number of males with the intention to start a business within two years increased in each age category until 1997, and then declined somewhat until 2001 except among the younger (18–34) age group, which continued to reflect high levels of intent. In 2001, 26 per cent of this age group reported they were very or somewhat likely to open a business, up from 18 per cent in 1992. Males in the 35–54 age category experienced a slight decline in intent to open a business over the decade, falling from 15 per cent in 1992 to 12 per cent in 2001. This was the only age group for either gender to experience a decline.

The overall trend for females was similar to that of males, increasing through the mid-1990s then declining towards the end of the decade. Levels of intent among females were, however, lower than males in the same age category. Interestingly, as with males, it is females in the 18–34 age group who reflect the highest levels of intent. The intention to start a business for young females doubled from 7 per cent in 1992 to 14 per cent in 2001. While a significant increase, intent levels among young females remained considerably below that of young males in 2001 (26 per cent as compared to 14 per cent).[97]

TABLE 8.5
Self-employment as a percentage of total employment, Canada and the Maritime provinces, 1989–2000

Region	1989	1990	1991	1992	1993	1994	1995	1996	1997	1998	1999	2000
PEI	19.9	19.0	18.9	19.6	19.3	19.0	18.5	17.7	17.6	19.2	19.1	17.7
NS	13.1	13.1	12.6	12.8	13.7	13.5	14.1	15.1	15.6	15.2	14.7	13.9
NB	11.3	12.0	12.5	12.3	12.5	12.3	12.6	13.6	14.6	14.0	13.1	12.4
Canada	13.9	14.1	14.7	15.0	15.8	15.5	15.7	16.1	17.1	17.2	16.9	16.2

Source: Canada, The State of Small Business and Entrepreneurship (Moncton: ACOA, 2004), 41.

Reasons for Failure

As small businesses are by far the greatest number of all businesses in the Maritime provinces, there is good reason to try to find out why many of them fail. We do not have an abundance of studies on this issue, but Wayne T. Vincent, territory manager for Atlantic Canada of Western Union Financial Services, produced a thorough and useful study, *Reasons for Failure of Small Retail Businesses in Atlantic Canada*. He confined himself to retail businesses for three reasons: it is the sector he knows best; so many of the small enterprises in Atlantic Canada are in retailing; and 'there is not a wealth of information in publication, on the small retail industry.'[98] For the purpose of his research, he defines a small business as 'a company with fewer than 100 employees and sales of less than $5 million.'[99]

He had more difficulty in defining 'failure.' He cites the Dun and Bradstreet definition, with its distinction between bankruptcies and closings for other reasons, such as merger or takeover. In the end, however, he settled for an easier definition: 'the closing of the doors of the retail operation.'[100] He justifies his choice as follows: 'These failures may or may not entail loss to suppliers or creditors, but do affect the community in which the business operated. The services provided by the firm are no longer available, or must be attained somewhere else, and there is a loss of employment for some people.'[101] He adds that 'business failure is not an event but a process. It may take place over a few months, or a few years, the culmination being the closing of the doors.'[102] He states that 'the most commonly cited reason for failure was managerial incompetence.'[103] That term, he insisted, was too general to be of use in determining causation. Instead, he looked at the more specific reasons noted for small-business failure.

From the literature, Vincent gleaned a list of 107 'apparent causes of failure in small retail firms.' In running over this list, it is apparent that many – if not most – of the items listed under 'planning' or 'financial' are clearly the fault of the owner, and could just as well be listed under the category 'owner.' Many entrepreneurs are incompetent, have education unrelated to their task or lack specialized training, don't do careful advance planning, are over-eager or too optimistic, don't seek advice or get inexpert advice, don't have accountants at all or have the wrong kind, and so on. It is *too easy* to start up a small enterprise, and too many people start them simply because they are unemployed or want to be their own boss. They hire employees who don't have the requisite skills for the job. The enterprise should never have been launched in the first place. There are seldom only one or two reasons for failure. The entrepreneur who makes a few mistakes usually makes a host of them.[104]

This last point is well illustrated by the six cases of unsuccessful small businesses whose owners were interviewed by Vincent. Of the causes of failure compiled by Vincent, these persons 'could find no factor ... that they found inappropriate,' and indeed had committed most of the 107 mistakes themselves. To be absolutely sure that no bias existed, 'a distinguished panel of successful business people was selected to review the reasoning ... In reviewing the list ... none of the entrepreneurs could find any factor that they felt did not belong on the list.'[105]

While placing the blame for failure squarely on small-business owners, Vincent does allow himself one complaint against the banks: their policies are inconsistent and change from area to area, and person to person. Not only do the institutions treat entrepreneurs differently, individuals in the financial institutions seem to use different guidelines. They often use their own interpretation of the rules, leaving no consistency from area to area. Banks have some unqualified account managers who are less familiar with small business as a whole, forcing customers into counterproductive business arrangements.[106] 'In the United States,' Vincent says, 'the bank manager is most often considered a resource, or advisor, like a lawyer or accountant. Yet in the research I have done in Atlantic Canada the opinion of the bank manager is much lower, and they are not considered an advisor. That is unfortunate. To avoid failure there must be a strong relationship between the entrepreneur, who does the work, and the banker, who provides the capital.'[108]

Vincent also has a complaint against suppliers. 'The issue of discrimination by suppliers is not a new one, [but] the fact that it happens because of the region rather than the size of the business is new. Retailers in Atlantic Canada have always faced difficulties in getting supplies of the product.'[107]

Yet, on the whole, Vincent considers shortcomings of the entrepreneurs themselves the main cause of small-business failure. There are, he argues, 'three issues that emerge that I would suggest require further study. The first issue is the tendency of the entrepreneurs to minimize the number of reasons for failure of their businesses, typically citing two or three significant factors. In reviewing the failures with the entrepreneurs more factors became apparent than had originally been obvious ... It is only when all the factors and the impact of interaction between these factors are considered, that a true picture of the reasons for failure emerges.'[109] The second issue is the relationship between the entrepreneur and the bank, discussed above. The third is the relationship between the entrepreneurs and their accountants. 'More specifically, were the entrepreneurs getting the information necessary to help them make informed decisions in running the business? Given reasonable financial information, were they able to interpret the information given to them, or was at least part of the reason for failure, the ignorance of the entrepreneurs?'[110] Good question!

Vincent raises one more question regarding the capacity of small entrepreneurs to run their businesses successfully. He quotes a 'successful retailer' as saying, 'there was very little skill necessary to open a small retail operation ... If the entrepreneurs were forced to make a bigger commitment to the business, would they be as likely to undertake the venture? If there were a more significant initial capital investment necessary before the entrepreneur could begin, would the failure rate be as high?' The final sentence in the report notes that, while 'all retailers experience at least some factors in the list [of reasons for failure], the difference between successes and failures is their ability to handle the adversity when it arises.'[111]

Looking Back

The message to heal thyself holds a lot of appeal. Those who sing the virtues of self-help and believe regions like the Maritime provinces have been treated too softly by misguided government programs are convinced that a sharp dose of market discipline can solve their economic problems. One is thus left to assume that strong economic regions in Canada became strong on their own merit, with little government intervention. To be sure, the economically comfortable regions want to believe this. That assumption, as we already noted, not only lets them off the hook, but also confirms their belief that market forces and their own abilities explain their economic success. This view, however, overlooks the historical factors that have accumulated to produce the current economic plight of the Maritimes and that explain at least some of the economic successes of other regions.[112] Still, the view has become embedded in the national media and in the Ottawa bureaucracy that Maritimers are considered less entrepreneurial and less productive than Ontarians. More is said about this in a subsequent chapter.

What this chapter attests, however, is that the Maritime region has not been able to heal itself through political union or close economic cooperation. The competition between the three provinces is as intense today as it was forty years ago. Moreover, the federal government has hardly helped. Indeed, it has made matters worse by focusing its efforts on federal-provincial agreements, thereby leaving the regional factor largely unattended. Former Nova Scotia premier John Savage argued that one of the biggest obstacles to promoting economic development and attracting new investment to his province was interprovincial competition with New Brunswick. He said, 'When I go to Toronto to meet with Chief Executive Officers to promote Nova Scotia as a place to invest, I very often discover that Frank McKenna has already been there. We need to coordinate our activities better.'[113] Not much has changed in recent years.

Entrepreneurship and small business became the new panacea, the instrument through which the region would pull itself up by its own bootstraps. Progress has been made on this front, though one can hardly state with certainty that it is because of government intervention. The October 1999 survey sponsored by the Canadian Federation of Independent Business and Scotiabank reveals no sharp difference between the Maritime provinces and other regions in Canada when respondents were asked if business ownership was a desirable goal. The level of respect for small business is as high in the Maritime provinces as it is in Ontario and higher than in the Prairie provinces, including Alberta. When asked if they would approve if a son, daughter, or a close relative decided to start a business, the approval rate was higher in the Maritimes than any other Canadian region.[114] However, promoting an entrepreneurial culture is one thing. Generating economic activities and development is quite another. In the next chapter, we paint two economic pictures – the Maritime provinces in 1961 and again in 2001. The chapter documents the economic progress the region has made over a forty-year period. The data will provide some insights on the impact of forty years of federal regional development measures and various efforts by the region to pull itself up by its own bootstraps.

9 The Region Then and Now

How is it, John Kenneth Galbraith once asked on a visit to New Brunswick, that strong economic development did not occur in the Maritime provinces in the last century?[1] The region, he pointed out, is strategically located between western Europe and New England and the eastern seaboard of the United States. How could it be, he wondered, that economic activity simply jumped over the Maritimes, to the eastern seaboard of the United States, on to the edges of western Europe and to central Canada? Why could the region not take advantage of its strategic geographical location? That question has become even more pressing in light of the many federal forays in the field since the early 1960s.

In earlier chapters, we presented the size, scope, and cost to the public treasury of various efforts to promote regional economic development in Canada, with a focus on the Maritime provinces, and table 9.1 outlines the evolution of Canada's regional development programming. We now want to assess their impact. We know, however, that it is virtually impossible to determine, with any degree of certainty, the number of firms established, new jobs created, and the part of a region's earned income that can be tied directly to the federal government's economic development measures or to attempts by the region to pull itself up by its own bootstraps. These efforts have not been sufficiently large to enable us to assess their impact in relation to other economic forces such as interest rates, the value of the Canadian dollar, the state of the American economy, and even other federal expenditures such as transfer payments to the provinces and individuals. In any event, there have been so many different federal approaches to the problem that a comprehensive evaluation is not possible. No sooner had a program

TABLE 9.1
Evolution of Canadian regional development programming

Year	Program	Regional application
1960	Tax incentives	regions with high unemployment and slow economic growth
1960	Agriculture Rehabilitation and Development Act (ARDA)	economically depressed rural areas
1962	Atlantic Development Board	Atlantic Canada
1963	Area Development Agency and new tax incentives	economically depressed areas
1965	revisions made to the 1963 changes to make them more generous	economically depressed areas
1966	ARDA renamed Agricultural and Rural Development Act	alleviating rural poverty and non-agricultural measures
1966	Fund for Rural Economic Development (FRED)	selected regions with low income and major economic problems
1969	Department of Regional Economic Expansion (DREE) and two new programs, Special Areas (Growth Poles) and Regional Development Incentives Act (RDIA)	focus on Atlantic Canada and eastern Quebec
1973–74	Introduction of General Development Agreements (GDAs) and revisions to RDIA. GDAs subsequently renamed Economic and Regional Development Agreements (ERDAs) and later still Cooperation Agreements	focus became more national in scope
1982	DREE abolished. Ministry of State for Economic and Regional Development (MSERD) and Department of Regional Industrial Expansion (DRIE) established. A new program, Industrial and Regional Development Program (IRDP) based on a 'development index' was also introduced	national and a shift away from 'need' to 'opportunity.' The development index covered all of Canada
1984	MSERD abolished	
1988	DRIE abolished and a new Department of Industry, Science and Technology established. Three new regional agencies established (ACOA, WD, FedNor) and a special fund established for Quebec	national
1991	A regional agency established for Quebec (FORD-Q) and renamed Canada Economic Development for Quebec Regions (1998)	
1993	Department of Industry, Science, and Technology (DIST) renamed Department of Industry	

been in place for four or five years than it was replaced with a new one with the promise that this one would be better. Career officials are more interested in assessing an ongoing program than one that is already history. Changing course often may make for good politics, in that it enables prime ministers to put their own personal stamp on a high-profile policy field, but it doses not make for sound public policy. Professors Kydland and Prescott, Nobel laureates in economics, make the case that 'if government cannot commit themselves credibly to a course, their policies may be futile.'[2] The inability of government to establish a direct link between federal regional programs and jobs created and the number of new firms established has led research institutes, outside economists, and the auditor general to challenge ACOA and its predecessors in their claims that their programs created x number of new jobs and y number of new businesses. We do not attempt to settle this debate. What we propose instead is to determine, broadly speaking, whether the Maritime provinces made economic progress between 1961 and 2001, both within the region itself and also in relation to the progress of other regions in Canada. As well, we invoke key economic indicators to suggest what the future holds for the region.

In this chapter, we compare the state of the Maritime economy in 2001 with that in 1961. We have used a variety of sources, especially census data from Statistics Canada, to assess the economic progress the region has made over this forty-year period, a period that captures the full range of federal measures in the field, as outlined in this book. In some instances, however, we could secure data only from five, ten, or twenty years ago. We stress once again that it is not easy to establish a direct link between federal efforts in the region and its economic health, even from a comparative perspective. But, *faute de mieux*, a comparative perspective will enable us to assess whether the region made economic progress during a time when the federal government invested billions in economic development programs in the Maritime provinces. In addition, a comparative perspective will enable us to determine to what extent the region remains dependent on federal transfer payments.

To be sure, the Maritime economy has made significant economic progress, as anyone who visited the region in 1961 and again in 2001 would recognize. However, this progress can tell only part of the story, and a small part at that, since one could make the same observation about other Canadian regions. Accordingly, benchmarks are established to determine if the region is less dependent on federal transfer payments in relation to other Canadian regions and if it has kept pace with the national average in terms of such standard indicators of a region's economic health as unemployment rates, labour force participation rates, per capita income, and earned income. Trade patterns are also compared. We use a series of tables and graphs to paint a detailed picture of the Maritime economy from a comparative perspective, both in terms of time (1961 and 2001) and in relation to the national economy.

Visiting Grandparents

Maritimers who 'went down the road' to other parts of Canada thirty or forty years ago, returning to visit, will see huge improvements. They will notice new or modernized airports in Moncton and Halifax, the four-lane highway that now cuts through New Brunswick and Nova Scotia, and the Confederation Bridge that links New Brunswick to Prince Edward Island. They will see new hospitals and new consolidated secondary schools in all three provinces and a new university catering to the Acadian community in Moncton. Returning Acadians would see their community transformed. In 1961 their society was economically backward and their education standards were very poor. Rural poverty, widespread in all the Maritime provinces, was particularly prevalent in Acadian communities, and there was a near total lack of any kind of private-sector investment. Indeed, one could easily draw a parallel between Acadian society, circa 1961, and some depressed Aboriginal communities in New Brunswick and Nova Scotia today.[3]

Acadian communities now draw economic strength from a growing entrepreneurial class, from institutions of higher learning, from numerous professionals in law, accounting, and medicine, and from a sense of confidence that has seen Acadians excel in business, politics, public service, and the arts. It is not much of an exaggeration to suggest that Acadian society in New Brunswick was transformed by a single historical event in 1960 – the election of the Louis Robichaud government. As Michel Cormier details in his biography of Robichaud, *Louis J. Robichaud: A Not So Quiet Revolution*, the Robichaud government overhauled virtually every aspect of New Brunswick society.[4] Its Program of Equal Opportunities had a profound impact on the entire province, but most notably on the Acadian community. The impact is still apparent today and will continue to be so for years to come.

The level of public service, particularly in health care, social services, and education, is infinitely better throughout the Maritime provinces today than it was forty years ago, and provincial bureaucracies are considerably stronger than they were in 1961. The visitor would see that small villages and hamlets still dotting the coast in all three provinces are much better off today than they were in 1961. One needs only to look at housing to see that the level of poverty is not what it was. Halifax and Moncton, meanwhile, are doing very well, and their employment levels are not much different from other cities of similar size in Ontario. We know, for example, that the unemployment rates in Vancouver, Calgary, Regina, Winnipeg, Gatineau, Fredericton, Moncton, Saint John, and Halifax usually vary between a fairly narrow range from 4.8 per cent in Calgary to 9.1 per cent in Saint John.

David Alexander once argued that the Atlantic provinces should search for 'new notions of happiness' rather than pursue the goal of attaining a North America lifestyle based on standard indicators of economic well-being.[5] There is evidence to suggest that Maritimers have a stronger sense of community than do other Canadians. The region has lower divorce and crime rates, and Maritimers are more likely to own homes that are mortgage free than are people in Ontario, Quebec, or western Canada.[6] A study produced for *Health Canada, Where to Work in Canada: An Examination of Regional Differences in Work-Life Practices*, reports that Atlantic Canadians work the longest and hardest and are the happiest with their employment and lives.[7] Living in small towns and cities has, it seems, its advantages. One of the authors of the report, Linda Duxbury of Carleton University, adds that 'if I had a business looking for hard-working and committed workers, I'd go to the Maritimes.'[8] The report, based on a survey of 32,000 workers, reveals that, by comparison to workers in Ontario, Quebec, the Prairies, and British Columbia, Maritimers work the longest hours, have the most unpaid overtime, take the most work home, yet have the lowest intent to change jobs or to leave for a more balanced lifestyle, and find more time to volunteer for community activities.[9] Employed Maritimers may well be highly grateful that they have employment and will go the extra mile to hang on to their jobs.

Maritimers may well have discovered new notions of happiness, and their sense of community may well be the envy of some residents in other regions. To be sure, the Acadian community has made substantial progress, particularly in relation to other Maritime communities. But this hardly constitutes the full picture. There is plenty of hard evidence to suggest that the economy of the Maritime provinces has not kept pace with other regions of Canada. Indeed, visitors would likely return to their homes elsewhere in Canada or the United States convinced that the Maritime region offers few jobs outside of Halifax and Moncton and that economic prospects for their grandchildren are limited.

The People Factor

There does not exist a widely accepted single indicator to establish the economic health of communities, provinces, regions, and nations, but we have seen in recent years the use of a variety of indicators in an attempt to gain a comprehensive picture. The Economic Council of Canada has acknowledged that, despite there being no single all-encompassing indicator, a wide variety of facts suggests that individual well-being does differ from one region to another.[10] The people factor, including the number of people in the workforce, levels of unemployment, population growth, and dependence on unemployment insurance, stands at the top of most lists of factors gauging a region's economic health.

Communities, provinces, and regions themselves will often look first to population gains or losses to take the pulse of their economic health. Decline in population is particularly worrisome, not only because it points to a host of economic difficulties but also because it means a loss of political influence. Size of population matters for a variety of reasons, not least because the composition of the House of Commons and some federal transfer payments to provinces are tied to population. In our system of government, the composition of the House of Commons decides who gets to exercise political power at the national level.

Population growth is vital for regional economies because the workforce, from unskilled labourers to highly skilled knowledge workers, remains an important factor of production and economic growth. Population adjustments take place at all levels from the hamlet to the city, and from intraprovincial, interprovincial, to international levels. We know that population has grown at different rates in various regions and that migration patterns have been more pronounced at the sub-provincial level than at the provincial and regional levels. Northern New Brunswick and Cape Breton, for example, have a much lower population-growth rate than the rest of the Maritimes.

That said, the Maritime region, as a whole, scores poorly on the people factor. The region is not able to attract many new Canadians and loses population to other regions. Its population age structure is cause for concern, and the degree of urbanization is low when compared to other regions. We present below a series of figures and tables on the people factor in the Maritime region in relation to Canada. One is hard pressed to tease out something positive for the region from the data.

Many of the region's major economic challenges can be found in tables 9.2 to 9.6. An inability to attract new Canadians or Canadians from other regions speaks directly to a region's economic weakness and to its inability to create jobs and entice newcomers. We know that Canada receives about 200,000 new Canadians each year and that 54 per cent of them have professional skills or have met specified business criteria. We also know that the government of Canada believes that new Canadians will likely account for all labour force growth by 2011.[11] There is also a growing body of literature pointing to the important role new Canadians play and will increasingly play in promoting economic development.[12]

The natural rate of population growth in the Maritime provinces has been relatively close to the Canadian average. However, because Maritimers have been leaving the region and because of its inability to attract new Canadians, its population growth since 1961 is about a third of the Canadian average (see table 9.2). New Canadians may well prefer to go where others from their home countries already live, but they also will wish to go where employment opportunities exist. Maritimers, too, will move in search of new jobs, and there is plenty of evidence to suggest that they have done just that. New Brunswick lost 10,566 residents to interprovincial migration between 1981 and 2002, Nova Scotia lost 5,175, while Prince Edward Island lost 1,022 during the same period (see table 9.3). Ontario gained 197,000 and Alberta 141,400, while Quebec lost 273,300.[13] The outmigration of Maritimers to other regions has a further cost: a large number of those leaving are highly educated: over 30 per cent have a university degree; only 2 per cent have Grade 9 education or less and about 15 per cent have Grade 9 to 12 education.

Maritimers are well aware of this demographic trend. Recently, New Brunswick premier Bernard Lord embarked on a cross-country tour to 'repatriate' New Brunswickers who had left the province for better job prospects. The tour, however, brought few home.[14] The need to attract new Canadians was also one of the key themes at the fiftieth anniversary of the Atlantic Provinces Economic Council conference held in Moncton in September 2004.[15] Harry Bruce, a well-known Maritime columnist, writes that 'the only hope for population growth will be newcomers from across Canada and around the world. But for nine

TABLE 9.2
Population growth, Maritimes and Canada, 1961–2001

	1961	Share of Canada 1961	1971	1981	1991	2001	Share of Canada 2001	Change, 1961–2001
Prince Edward Island	104,629	0.6%	111,641	122,510	129,765	135,294	0.5%	29.3%
Nova Scotia	737,007	4.0%	788,960	847,445	899,942	908,007	3.0%	23.2%
New Brunswick	597,936	3.3%	634,557	696,405	723,900	729,498	2.4%	22.0%
Maritimes	1,439,572	7.9%	1,535,58	1,666,360	1,753,607	1,772,799	5.9%	23.1%
Canada	18,238,247	100.0%	21,568,311	24,343,180	27,296,859	30,007,094	100.0%	64.5%

Source: Statistics Canada, Census of Population.

TABLE 9.3
Interprovincial migrants, Maritimes and Canada, 1966–2001

	1966	1971	1976	1981	1986	1991	1996	2001	Change, 1966– 2001 (%)
Canada									
Total interprovincial migrants	408,569	405,299	376,970	380,041	302,352	315,659	284,484	280,408	−31.4
Prince Edward Island									
In-migrants	3,732	4,205	4,307	3,471	2,496	2,888	2,727	2,671	−28.4
Out-migrants	4,719	4,334	3,998	4,254	2,989	3,303	2,326	2,403	−49.1
Net migration	−987	−129	309	−783	−493	−415	401	268	−127.2
Nova Scotia									
In-migrants	23,381	23,186	22,990	19,273	17,061	18,961	16,033	15,511	−33.7
Out-migrants	29,875	23,941	22,629	21,738	17,800	17,922	17,097	17,457	−41.6
Net migration	−6,494	−755	361	−2,465	−739	1,039	−1,064	−1,946	−70.0
New Brunswick									
In-migrants	19,897	21,636	18,934	13,843	11,395	12,845	11,067	10,878	−45.3
Out-migrants	26,692	19,838	17,294	18,609	14,292	12,924	11,977	12,792	−52.1
Net migration	−6,795	1,798	1,640	−4,766	−2,897	−79	−910	−1,914	−71.8
Maritimes									
In-migrants	47,010	49,027	46,231	36,587	30,952	34,694	29,827	29,060	−38.2
Out-migrants	61,286	48,113	43,921	44,601	35,081	34,149	31,400	32,652	−46.7
Net migration	−14,276	914	2,310	−8,014	−4,129	545	−1,573	−3,592	−74.8

Source: Statistics Canada, Estimates of Population, CANSIM II, table 051-0017; compiled by the author.

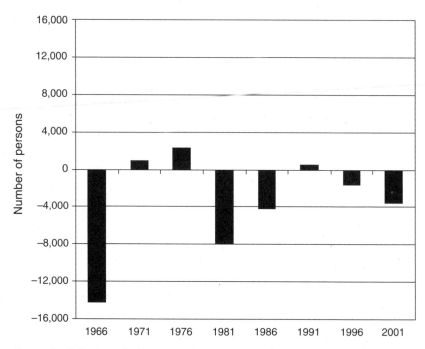

Source: Statistics Canada, Estimates of Population, CANSIM II, table 051-0017; compiled by the author.

Figure 9.1
Net interprovincial migration, Maritime provinces, 1966–2001

years now, immigration to Nova Scotia has been in steep decline. To make matters worse, Nova Scotia is lousy at hanging onto the few foreigners who do come here. Between 1991 and 2001, it managed to keep only 40 per cent of its immigrants.' The same can be said about New Brunswick and Prince Edward Island.[16] Bruce adds that the region's inability to attract new Canadians or Canadians from other regions comes at a great cost, pointing out, for example, that 'after the 2001 census reported, Nova Scotia had to return to the federal government $193 million in equalization and transfer payments.'[17] The Nova Scotia government meanwhile produced a discussion paper on demographic challenges, which notes that 'if these demographic trends continue, the province will experience lost economic opportunities, competitive disadvantages, declining opportunities and ever-increasing fiscal pressures and may experience labour market shortages.'[18] Bruce's advice?

TABLE 9.4A
International immigrants, all ages, both sexes, Maritimes and Canada, 1976–2001

	1976	1981	1986	1991	1996	2001	Change 1976–2001
Canada	170,028	127,238	88,657	221,382	217,478	252,533	48.5%
Prince Edward Island	222	146	129	149	127	190	−14.4%
Nova Scotia	2,004	1,271	974	1,542	3,397	1, 761	−12.1%
New Brunswick	2,241	963	625	738	646	883	−60.6%
Maritimes	4,467	2,380	1,728	2,429	4,170	2,834	−36.6%

TABLE 9.4B
International immigrants, all ages, both sexes, Maritimes and Canada,
as a share of total immigrants, 1976–2001

	1976	1981	1986	1991	1996	2001
Canada	100.0	100.0	100.0	100.0	100.0	100.0
Prince Edward Island	0.1	0.1	0.1	0.1	0.1	0.1
Nova Scotia	1.2	1.0	1.1	0.7	1.6	0.7
New Brunswick	1.3	0.8	0.7	0.3	0.3	0.3
Maritimes	2.6	1.9	1.9	1.1	1.9	1.1

Source: Statistics Canada, Estimates of Population, CANSIM II, table 051-0011;
compiled by the author.

The region needs to open up to newcomers because 'in the long run a
closed society is a stupid society.'[19]

As table 9.4B shows, the Maritime region has consistently been able
to attract only about 2 per cent of new Canadians. Also significant is
that the working-age population has shrunk (see tables 9.5 and 9.6) and
will likely continue to shrink in future years. The elderly dependency
ratio (population over sixty-five divided by working-age population) is
higher in the Maritimes than the national average. The data also suggest that the dependency ratio is poised to grow to between 25.7 and
27.6 per cent for the three Maritime provinces by 2016 compared to 23
per cent in Ontario and 24.3 per cent for Canada as a whole.[20]

Joe Ruggeri and Yang Zou carried out a review of labour supply in
Atlantic Canada in 2005 and their findings point to important challenges ahead. They conclude that employment growth similar to that
experienced over the past twenty-five years cannot be sustained, that
maintaining employment growth of 1 per cent in the region (equal to
the projected national average) will require large increases in annual

TABLE 9.5
Population by age, Maritimes and Canada, 1961 and 2001

1961

	Total population (n.)	0–14 (n.)	%	15–29 (n.)	%	30–44 (n.)	%	45–54 (n.)	%	55+ (n.)	%
Prince Edward Island	104,629	37,701	36.0	20,904	20.0	16,771	16.0	10,501	10.0	18,752	17.9
Nova Scotia	737,007	256,328	34.8	157,506	21.4	132,978	18.0	75,881	10.3	114,314	15.5
New Brunswick	597,936	227,187	38.0	124,554	20.8	103,665	17.3	56,676	9.5	85,854	14.4
Maritimes	1,439,572	521,216	36.2	302,964	21.0	253,414	17.6	143,058	9.9	218,920	15.2
Canada	18,238,247	6,191,922	34.0	3,825,502	21.0	3,661,695	20.1	1,878,504	10.3	2,680,624	14.7

2001

	Total population (n.)	0–14 (n.)	%	15–29 (n.)	%	30–44 (n.)	%	45–54 (n.)	%	55+ (n.)	%
Prince Edward Island	135,295	26,645	19.7	26,830	19.8	29,915	22.1	20,120	14.9	31,775	23.5
Nova Scotia	908,010	165,025	18.2	172,425	19.0	213,140	23.5	138,280	15.2	219,130	24.1
New Brunswick	729,500	130,100	17.8	143,115	19.6	171,290	23.5	113,160	15.5	171,835	23.6
Maritimes	1,772,805	321,770	18.2	342,370	19.3	414,345	23.4	271,560	15.3	422,740	23.8
Canada	30,007,090	5,725,530	19.1	5,907,335	19.7	7,198,360	24.0	4,419,290	14.7	6,756,565	22.5

Source: Statistics Canada, Census of Population.

TABLE 9.6
Net change in population by age, Maritimes and Canada (%), 1961–2001

	Total population	0–14	15–29	30–44	45–54	55+
Prince Edward Island	29.3	−29.3	28.3	78.4	91.6	69.4
Nova Scotia	23.2	−35.6	9.5	60.3	82.2	91.7
New Brunswick	22.0	−42.7	14.9	65.2	99.7	100.1
Maritimes	23.1	−38.3	13.0	63.5	89.8	93.1
Canada	64.5	−7.5	54.4	96.6	135.3	152.1

Source: Statistics Canada, Census of Population.

immigration flows, and that it will prove increasingly difficult for the region to maintain the pattern of convergence of living standards witnessed in the region over the past twenty-five years.[21]

Figure 9.2 strikingly illustrates the degree to which the Maritime region remains rural (nearly 50 per cent) compared to Canada as a

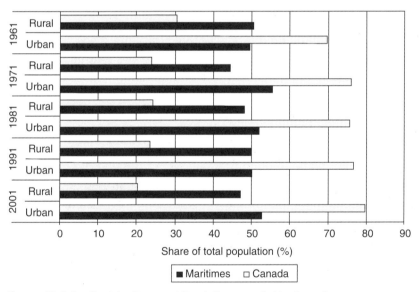

Source: Statistics Canada, Census of Population; compiled by the author.

Figure 9.2
Urban and rural populations (as a share of total population), Maritimes and Canada, 1961–2001

TABLE 9.7
Unemployment rate, Maritimes and Canada, 1966–2001

	Maritimes	Canada	Gap
1966	4.8%	3.3%	1.5%
1971	6.4%	6.2%	0.2%
1981	10.9%	7.6%	3.3%
1991	12.7%	10.4%	2.3%
2001	10.5%	7.2%	3.3%

Source: Statistics Canada, Selected Economic Indicators and Labour Force Survey.

whole (20 per cent). Ontario is now only 13 per cent rural. We need to underline the importance of the urban-rural split for several reasons: for one thing, 93 per cent of all new Canadians went to large cities in 2002, and 73 per cent of them to only three cities – Toronto, Montreal, and Vancouver, with Toronto alone attracting nearly half of all new Canadians. But that is not all. Urban regions have a higher standard of living than rural areas as measured by per capita income, and average GDP per capita is higher in urban areas. The unemployment rate is higher in rural areas: in Moncton in 2001 it was 8.1 per cent, as compared to 16.8 per cent in Campbellton, and 7.2 per cent in Halifax, as compared to 19.7 per cent in Cape Breton.[22]

The Employment Factor

During his tenure in office, New Brunswick premier Frank McKenna made employment a top priority for his province and, by his own admission, 'pursued job creation with a missionary zeal.'[23] He ran three election campaigns on 'jobs, more jobs and still more jobs,' and insisted that the 'best form of social assistance was a job.'[24] Ultimately, economic development is about creating jobs and creating jobs is the best way to lessen dependency on federal transfer payments.

The employment factor encompasses several facets: number of jobs, participation in the workforce, quality of jobs, number of full-time and part-time jobs, and whether the jobs being created are in growth sectors. Tables 9.7 to 9.10 provide a detailed account of the employment factor in the Maritime provinces from a comparative perspective.

The employment and unemployment tables report modest economic gains for the Maritime provinces over the past forty years. The region's

TABLE 9.8
Total employment, Maritimes and Canada, 1966–2001

	Maritimes	% change	Canada	% change
1966	460,000	–	7,242,000	–
1971	490,000	6.5%	8,104,000	11.9%
1981	636,000	29.8%	11,398,000	40.6%
1991	732,000	15.1%	12,916,000	13.3%
2001	824,000	12.6%	15,077,000	16.7%

Source: Statistics Canada, Selected Economic Indicators and Labour Force Survey.

TABLE 9.9
Labour force, Maritimes and Canada, 1966–2001

	Maritimes	% change	Canada	% change
1966	484,000	–	7,494,000	–
1971	526,000	8.7%	8,639,000	15.3%
1981	713,000	35.6%	12,332,000	42.7%
1991	838,000	17.5%	14,408,000	16.8%
2001	920,000	9.8%	16,246,000	12.8%

Source: Statistics Canada, Selected Economic Indicators and Labour Force Survey.

TABLE 9.10
Participation rate, Maritimes and Canada, 1966–2001

	Maritimes	Canada
1966	58%	63%
1971	57%	63%
1981	65%	73%
1991	70%	76%
2001	74%	76%

Source: Statistics Canada, Selected Economic
Indicators and Labour Force Survey, Tables 051-6026
and 051-0026.

unemployment rate drew closer to the Canadian average in 1971 but
widened in 1981 and the gap has remained relatively stable since then
(see table 9.7). Table 9.8 shows that the Maritimes have not been able to
keep pace with the Canadian average under the 'total employment'
indicator. Though not to the same degree, the same can be said for size
of the labour force (see table 9.9). That said, table 9.10 reveals an
important convergence trend in the participation rate between the Mari-

time region and the Canadian average. In 1966 the gap between the Maritime provinces and the Canadian average stood at 5 percentage points, but narrowed to 2 percentage points by 2001. To be sure, the participation rate is a crucial indicator of a region's economic strength, but it does not mask the fact that the employment tables reveal modest convergence on the employment front.

Other employment data also show limited progress for the Maritime region. For example, the Maritime provinces had 42,200 seasonal workers in 1997, representing 6.6 per cent of the workforce, but the number increased to 50,600 by 2003, representing 6.8 per cent of the workforce. By contrast, Canada had 328,100 seasonal workers in 1997, representing 2.9 per cent of the workforce and 391,800 in 2003, still representing only 2.9 per cent of the workforce.[25]

Much has been written of late about the importance of knowledge workers to economic development, and we made reference to some of this literature in chapter 3. Knowledge workers made up 7.7 per cent of total employment in Canada in 1984 and 11.1 per cent in 2002. Ontario saw a significant increase in the number of knowledge workers during the same period, from 8.4 per cent to 12.4 per cent of its workforce. In the case of the three Maritime provinces, however, the figures for the same years are much less impressive: in Prince Edward Island, the numbers are 3.2 per cent and 5.1 per cent; Nova Scotia, 5.5 per cent and 7.7 per cent; New Brunswick, 4.1 per cent and 6.8 per cent.[26]

We have seen solid progress on the educational front over the past forty years in the Maritimes, though the Maritimes still lag behind other regions. Ontario leads the way, with 19 per cent of its labour force holding one university degree. Only about 12 per cent of the workforce in the Maritimes has a university degree. Still, there has been undeniable progress compared to 1961, both in terms of where the region was and in relation to other regions (see table 9.11 below).

The work of Richard Florida introduced in chapter 3 looks to human capital as the key to successful regional economies. His argument is that we live in a creative age and that the ability to attract talented people – not the existence of materials or natural harbours – is the engine of economic growth. Creative people, he argues, are not spread equally across regions. Regions need to come up with ways to attract immigrants, highly educated and creative people, as well as people of different ethnic, racial, and lifestyle groups.

Florida and others have come up with various indexes to assess a region's capacity to attract and retain a creative class. They include: the

TABLE 9.11
Percentage of the population over 15 who have a bachelors degree or higher,
Maritimes and Canada, 1961–2001

	1961	1971	1981	1991	2001	% change 1961–2001
Canada	2.9	4.8	8	11.4	15.1	420
Prince Edward Island	1.5	3.2	6.1	8.5	11	633
Nova Scotia	2.3	4.1	7.4	10.4	13.5	486
New Brunswick	1.8	3.4	6	8.4	10.8	500

Source: Canada, Census of Population.

talent index (population over eighteen years with a bachelor's degree or higher), the bohemian index (employment in artistic and creative occupations), mosaic index (proportion of the population that is foreign born), and tech-pole index (a region's share of national employment in high-technology industries). A recent study assesses the performance of Canadian city-regions under the four indexes. Under the talent index, the Ottawa-Gatineau region leads the country (first out of twenty-five), followed by Halifax and Toronto. Under the bohemian index, Vancouver, Toronto, Victoria, Calgary, and Ottawa-Gatineau lead the way, with Saint John third from last of the twenty-five city-regions surveyed. Both Halifax and Saint John score very poorly under the mosaic index (Halifax ranks nineteenth and Saint John twenty-first). Under the tech-pole index, Montreal leads the pack, followed by Toronto and Ottawa-Gatineau, which, in the words of the authors of the report, 'dominate all other city-regions.'[27] Halifax ranks tenth and Saint John seventeenth. What this suggests is that the Maritime provinces are not poised to experience strong economic growth when compared to other regions. It also suggests that there does not seem to be a strong correlation between a lower cost of living, shorter commute times, lower crime rates, and long-term economic growth.

It is revealing to note that four cities (Toronto, Vancouver, Montreal, and Ottawa) dominate in the number of high-paying jobs in the service sector. Together, they account for 38 per cent of Canada's population, but are home to 56 per cent of Canadians employed in the top decile in terms of remuneration in the service sector (see table 9.12).[28] Halifax, with 1 per cent of Canada's population, has 2 per cent of these jobs. In contrast, with only 4 per cent of the population, but with its large public service population, Ottawa is home to 12 per cent of the top-paying jobs in the service sector.

TABLE 9.12
Percentage of population and employment in top decile
in relation to Canadian total

City	Population (% of Canada)	% of jobs in top decile
Toronto	16	22
Vancouver	7	9
Montreal	12	13
Ottawa	4	12
Total (TVMO)	38	56
Halifax	1	2

Source: Statistics Canada, AEEEH and 2001 census.

Income

Economists have long looked to both per capita and earned income to gauge a region's economic health. We know that there was some progress in reducing regional disparities in Canada in per capita income between 1961 and 1981, and again between 1981 and 1988. The effects from personal income, transfers from governments, income received by family earners (average family income), and taxation of personal income (average family disposable income) have served to reduce regional income inequalities. The largest reduction in income disparity occurred in average family disposable income – where income disparities appear smallest – while the least reduction was with respect to earned income per capita – where they are widest. In short, the lowest-income provinces have made substantial progress in closing the gap with the Canadian average over the past forty years when employing the income indicator.

In 1961, the three Maritime provinces, Newfoundland and Labrador, Quebec, Manitoba, and Saskatchewan received considerably less than the national average income, while Ontario, British Columbia, and Alberta were above average. By 1981, Ontario was still leading the nation, followed by Alberta. Between 1961 and 1981, however, Saskatchewan gained a great deal in relation to the national average, while Quebec and Manitoba stalled. The Maritime provinces, together with Newfoundland and Labrador, however, still ranked last by 1981. Newfoundland and Labrador and Prince Edward Island remained the lowest-income provinces, despite showing the best performance in all income measures in the four Atlantic provinces. New Brunswick moved closer to Nova Scotia, which, in turn, moved closer to the national average. Some important changes, however, occurred between 1981

TABLE 9.13
Personal income per capita, selected years, 1961–2001:
Relationship to national average (Canada = 100)

	1961	1965	1971	1975	1981	1985	1991	1995	2001
Newfoundland and Labrador	62.0	61.4	67.7	71.6	72.5	73.3	82.8	80.6	81.1
Prince Edward Island	62.2	64.7	66.3	70.8	73.5	74.9	82.0	86.8	83.2
Nova Scotia	78.0	74.5	78.0	78.8	81.9	86.7	86.4	90.0	91.1
New Brunswick	68.4	69.0	74.6	75.6	76.4	79.6	82.6	87.9	87.3
Quebec	91.2	91.6	91.5	91.0	89.6	91.0	92.4	91.9	91.4
Ontario	116.5	114.6	115.2	110.6	104.1	108.1	108.8	107.8	106.8
Manitoba	94.2	94.4	93.9	95.9	95.7	98.2	93.2	94.4	92.8
Saskatchewan	72.8	90.4	84.3	103.9	102.2	89.5	85.8	88.0	86.7
Alberta	101.3	97.8	96.5	102.0	115.9	110.8	102.1	103.2	115.1
British Columbia	115.2	112.8	105.7	107.0	112.6	102.7	103.6	103.2	96.1

Source: Statistics Canada, Provincial Economic Accounts – 2002.

and 1991. Ontario once again led the nation, with British Columbia second (see table 9.13). Quebec moved up during this period, ranking fifth among the ten provinces, while Saskatchewan ranked seventh, trailing Nova Scotia for the first time since 1961. The three Maritime provinces, however, continued to make progress during the 1981–8 period. By 2001 they had made significant progress, compared to 1961, on a per capita income basis. Alberta also gained and by then led all provinces by a relatively wide margin.

Some have suggested that earned income per capita provides a better measure of a region's economic performance than per capita income. The former excludes relative gains from interregional transfer payments. According to this measurement (wages, salaries, and supplementary labour income), regional disparities were more pronounced, narrowed from 1961 to 1981, but not to the same extent as they did under the personal per capita income indicator. Still, moving from 72.9 per cent of the Canadian average in 1961 to 77 per cent by 2001 is no small achievement (see table 9.14).

From UI to EI

It is hardly possible to review Ottawa's regional economic development efforts in the Maritime provinces without looking at transfer payments to individuals. Data in table 9.15 reveal that the region – leaving aside

TABLE 9.14
Per capita (18+) wages, salaries, and supplementary labour income,
1992 constant dollars

	Maritimes	Canada	Maritimes as % of Canada
1961	7,387.7	10,140.2	72.9
1965	8,728.9	12,332.9	70.8
1975	13,581.2	17,853.6	76.1
1981	13,809.0	18,651.8	74.0
1985	13,755.8	17,794.5	77.3
1991	14,376.2	18,244.9	78.8
1995	14,303.0	18,153.4	78.8
2001	15,778.5	20,486.9	77.0

Source: Statistics Canada, Provincial Economic Accounts.

TABLE 9.15
Personal transfers from governments as a percentage of personal income,1961–2001

	1961	1965	1971	1975	1981	1985	1991	1995	2001	1961–2001 change (%)
Newfoundland and Labrador	19.0	17.8	23.1	27.5	25.1	22.5	24.1	25.1	21.6	13.7
Prince Edward Island	17.1	14.5	20.4	22.1	21.6	21.4	21.7	21.0	20.1	17.5
Nova Scotia	11.9	12.0	15.0	17.4	16.6	15.5	16.9	18.2	17.1	43.7
New Brunswick	14.1	12.8	15.9	19.7	18.8	19.8	20.1	19.2	18.6	31.9
Quebec	9.6	8.6	11.6	14.0	14.8	14.9	15.2	16.2	15.1	57.3
Ontario	6.9	6.6	9.4	10.4	10.0	9.6	12.5	13.5	11.8	71.0
Manitoba	9.7	8.7	11.5	11.4	12.0	12.4	15.2	17.0	16.4	69.1
Saskatchewan	13.1	9.3	12.8	11.1	12.7	14.8	16.5	17.8	17.8	35.9
Alberta	8.7	8.6	11.5	10.0	9.0	10.1	11.1	11.2	9.8	12.6
British Columbia	9.9	8.8	10.7	12.7	10.6	13.2	13.7	13.7	14.1	42.4

Source: Statistics Canada, Provincial Economic Accounts.

Newfoundland and Labrador – is more dependent than other regions on personal transfers from government. All provinces, however, became more dependent on such transfers as a percentage of personal income between 1961 and 2001. It is important to note, however, that the increase for the Maritime provinces was less than it was for Ontario, Manitoba, and Quebec.

There has been no shortage of reviews of Ottawa's unemployment (later, employment) insurance program over the years, and we have seen some politicians taking aim at the concept. Frank McKenna, for example, often quoted Félix Leclerc, who wrote 'the best way to kill a man is to pay him to do nothing' and insisted that 'passive support programs are destroying our spirit and our soul. We are the only nation in the world providing such generous support with such inadequate reorientation toward training, education and work.'[29] The size of the money under the program flowing to the Maritime provinces dwarfs regional economic development investments under the Department of Regional Economic Expansion, the Department of Regional Industrial Expansion, and the Atlantic Canada Opportunities Agency.[30]

The national media, think-tanks like the C.D. Howe Institute, and academics have all been critical of the employment insurance program and its impact on regions. There is now a consensus in the literature and among policy analysts that the scheme is much more an income redistribution program than an employment insurance program. As the C.D. Howe Institute points out, 'Over time in [a] pure insurance model, the premiums paid by members of an occupation or residents of a region would roughly balance the unemployment benefits the occupation or region received.'[31] This is not the case for the UI-EI program. William Watson goes to the heart of the issue when he writes, 'UI may have started out as insurance, and it probably should be insurance, but at the moment it functions very much as an income support for Atlantic Canada – and other economically laggard regions. Unfortunately, Atlantic Canada in general and Newfoundland in particular have such serious problems that, unless the rest of Canada wants to inflict a second economic and social disaster on the region (UI being the first), it will have to continue to provide net income transfers, that is, it will have to send the region more money than it pays in federal taxes for some time to come.'[32] There are few voices being heard anywhere, including in the Maritime provinces, making the case that the UI-EI program is an employment insurance program.

Doug May and Alton Hollett carried out an extensive review of the impact of UI-EI on Atlantic Canada and concluded that it was a particularly bad way to deliver federal transfer payments to the region. They pointed out that the program frequently pays out more money to high-income than to low-income earners (this maldistribution is particularly evident in the fishery) and that the program's 'approach to income redistribution wastes scarce tax dollars on a grand scale.'[33] They added that the program may well encourage young Atlantic Canadians to make inappropriate choices about careers or to remain in communities or industries where there will continue to be severe job shortages.[34]

The May and Hollett study makes the case that the desire of 'Ottawa policymakers' to deal with Atlantic Canada as a region 'masks underlying variations across the provinces.'[35] In aggregate, Nova Scotia shows UI-EI and social assistance numbers that are not much different from those for Canada as a whole. UI-EI dependency is much greater in Newfoundland and Labrador than in the Maritime region, and new policy prescriptions should reflect this difference.

The May-Hollett study, moreover, produced specific policy and program prescriptions. They include the following:

- Basic education would be required of, and offered to, repeat users of UI, while UI payments would be geared to performance in, rather than attendance in, such programs.
- New entrants to the labour force would require 150 weeks of work over five years to qualify for UI.
- The UI benefits of repeat users would be clawed back at a rate of 40 per cent if their family income were above the poverty line and 100 per cent if it were above the national median income.
- Responsibility for basic income redistribution, including welfare, would gradually be made the responsibility of the federal government, with provincial governments providing hands-on services for workers who had experienced chronic difficulty in getting or keeping work.[36]

The government of Canada has often been accused of playing politics with the UI-EI program. It will be recalled that the federal government decided to cut about $2 billion in UI benefits as part of its 1995 program review. The government made the case that the cuts were introduced not just to fight the deficit but also to give workers the incentive to find employment and upgrade their skills. The changes hit seasonal workers, notably fishermen, tourism, and construction workers hard. In consequence, the Chrétien government lost nineteen seats in the four Atlantic provinces in the 1997 general election, including those of senior cabinet ministers. Shortly before the 2000 general election, Chrétien restored some EI benefits to seasonal workers, and his party went on to make significant electoral gains. Paul Martin also decided shortly before the 2004 general election to further improve EI benefits to seasonal workers.[37] No mention, however, was made of the need to give workers

TABLE 9.16
Total regular EI benefit payments (millions of $), selected years, 1972–2001

	Maritimes	Percentage of total	Quebec	Percentage of total	Canada
1972	136.1	8.0	521.7	30.7	1700.2
1975	282.6	9.7	1011.8	34.8	2907.7
1981	497.3	12.1	1643.4	39.9	4115.8
1985	938.5	10.5	2885.0	32.1	8975.3
1991	1475.6	10.0	4716.5	31.9	14783.3
1995	1157.5	11.8	3337.4	33.9	9838.2
2001	1078.7	13.3	2665.0	32.9	8089.4

Source: Statistics Canada, Employment Insurance Statistics, CANSIM II, table 276–0005.

greater incentive to find employment when the government made the 2000 and 2004 changes. Jeffrey Simpson insisted that Liberals 'know how to bribe voters or at least try to impress them with their own money as an election draws near. So it was yesterday that a clutch of Liberal MPs from eastern Quebec and New Brunswick announced yet another rollback in the brave but contentious changes from the first Chrétien government, which had tightened requirements for seasonal workers' employment-insurance benefits.'[38] The purpose, it seems, had more to do with winning seats than with sound public policy. A senior government official explained that the 2004 changes had everything to do with winning support in Quebec, where there are more rural seats than there are seats, urban and rural, in the Maritime provinces.[39] It is also important to point out that the three Maritime provinces' share of UI-EI benefits has grown over the years, as table 9.16 indicates. In addition, Quebec's share of EI benefits went from 30.7 per cent (1972) to 32.9 per cent (2001) of total EI benefits paid.

Transfers to Government

On leaving a meeting with fellow premiers held to discuss possible changes to Ottawa's equalization program in October 2004, Ontario premier Dalton McGuinty expressed opposition to adding substantial new funding to the program. He explained, 'My concern is that it's very important that the provinces understand that they have to protect the golden goose here. If there is more money available from the federal government, we'd rather that it be distributed in such a way that it benefits all of us, including supporting, for example, postsecondary education in the province of Ontario, which contributes to the strength of our economy and increases our capacity to make contributions to the federal government.'[40] The next day a new federal-provincial agreement on equalization was struck, and McGuinty quickly expressed his approval.[41] The media reported that the Ontario premier gave his support to the agreement only after he was 'reassured that any increases in their obligations would be incremental.'[42] McGuinty later explained that he was satisfied that the agreement would not hurt Ontario, which he described 'as Canada's economic engine.'[43] Later still, McGuinty would have second thoughts about the agreement and launch a high-profile campaign to secure a greater share of federal transfers for Ontario. More is said about this later.

For their part, the three Maritime premiers were disappointed that future increases would be capped at 3.5 per cent annually. Nova Scotia premier John Hamm explained: 'If you look at the escalator of 3.5 per cent, that is destined to fail. We have replaced a failing program with one that is destined to fail.' Hamm was also highly critical of Ottawa's decision to shift half of the program's funding formula to a per capita basis. Quebec pushed Ottawa to adopt the per capita formula because it stood to gain far more than the other receiving provinces, and Ottawa chose to support Quebec's position. Hamm argued, 'That's absolutely the wrong way to go. I didn't agree with that. The one program that must never go to per capita funding is equalization.'[44] New Brunswick premier Bernard Lord maintained that 'per capita goes against the fundamental principle of equalization.'[45] Jim Travers provides an explanation for Ottawa's position on the debate: 'Martin's federal Liberals share with Jean Charest's provincial Liberals a pressing interest in securing for Quebec the best possible arrangement. After effectively losing a majority to the Bloc Québécois in the last election, Martin is determined to do everything possible to recover it and throwing money at Quebec never hurts.'[46] The federal government never explained how the per capita criteria relate to equalization or answered Andrew Coyne's charge that per capita 'by a happy coincidence raises Quebec's share of the total (i.e., paid under the program), but obviously has nothing to do with equalization.'[47]

Ottawa placed its equalization program on a downward track in 1982, when it decided to drop the ten-province formula in favour of a five-province formula that excluded Alberta, thereby saving billions over the years for the federal treasury. But this was not the only reason for Ottawa's decision to move to a five-province formula. Escalating resource revenues pushed the ten-province formula so high that all provinces, with the exception of Alberta, would have qualified to receive equalization payments. In addition, Ottawa decided to take the four Atlantic provinces, those with the weakest tax bases, out of the formula, which would serve to soften the blow to all the receiving provinces. By at least one estimate, the five-province formula reduced revenues to the receiving provinces to about 92 per cent of what they would have received under the ten-province formula.[48]

As McGuinty suggested, Ottawa's equalization program is hardly the only federal transfer program to the provinces. Ontario, for example, received 11.4 per cent of its revenues from Ottawa in 2004–5, compared to 36 per cent for New Brunswick and 16.3 per cent for Quebec.[49] It will also be recalled that Ottawa overhauled its transfers to provinces for health care, postsecondary education, and social services in 1996–7 as part of its program-review exercise. Ottawa merged two existing programs – the Canada Assistance Plan (CAP) for social assistance and Established Program Financing (EPF) – to create the Canada Health and Social Transfer (CHST) program. The CHST included both a transfer of cash and tax points, and the initial transfers were below levels established in earlier programs. In addition, EPF and CAP had an equalization component that provided additional cash to have-less provinces. The new program, which once again divides funding between health and social transfers, moved to an equal per capita payment, which favoured provinces with expanding populations, notably Alberta and Ontario. New funding adjustments were subsequently made ($11.5 billion over five years announced in 1999, $21 billion in 2000, and a further $35 billion in 2003).[50] In addition, a high-profile First Ministers Conference on health care, held in September 2004, added $41 billion of new money over a ten-year period under CHST. All these adjustments translated into $16.5 billion in federal transfers for health care in 2005–6, an amount that is to grow to $24 billion in 2009–10.[51]

Tables 9.17, 9.18, and 9.19 suggest that all provinces are dependent on federal transfers, some more than others.[52] The three tables reveal that federal transfers to the provinces dropped significantly between 1961 and 2001. This is true for all provinces. Ontario saw a drop, while Alberta's share went from 33.8 to 8.7 per cent and British Columbia's from 34.4 to 12.3 per cent. Nova Scotia saw a drop from 51.1 per cent to 37.9 per cent; New Brunswick, from 50.0 to 36.2 per cent; and Prince Edward Island, from 60.0 to 42.5 per cent (see table 9.17). In brief, all provincial governments in the country became less dependent on fed-

TABLE 9.17
Federal transfer payments as a percentage of provincial revenues, 1961–2001

	1961	1965	1971	1975	1981	1985	1991	1995	2001
Newfoundland and Labrador	63.0	60.8	58.5	52.8	48.4	49.4	44.0	43.0	43.1
Prince Edward Island	60.0	54.3	59.6	59.6	52.4	49.6	42.5	39.7	42.5
Nova Scotia	51.1	45.8	46.0	49.7	47.1	40.3	36.9	40.3	37.9
New Brunswick	50.0	49.7	48.2	49.7	44.3	42.9	36.0	35.1	36.2
Quebec	23.3	21.7	28.9	25.3	23.0	24.3	17.7	19.9	16.3
Ontario	25.9	16.0	19.5	22.1	16.9	16.9	14.5	15.4	11.4
Manitoba	44.2	30.9	34.7	38.9	33.5	31.0	31.6	29.7	27.4
Saskatchewan	34.4	24.6	37.5	34.6	28.3	29.9	33.8	33.5	34.0
Alberta	33.8	19.0	22.6	15.8	7.9	12.2	13.7	11.6	8.7
British Columbia	34.4	15.3	19.9	18.6	15.0	18.8	12.2	11.5	12.3

Source: Statistics Canada, Provincial Economic Accounts.

TABLE 9.18
Equalization payments as a percentage of provincial government revenue

	1961	1965	1971	1975	1981	1985	1991	1995	2001
Prince Edward Island	25.0	28.6	22.5	26.2	31.5	28.3	26.0	23.5	24.7
Nova Scotia	19.5	21.9	20.2	25.2	27.0	20.5	20.0	23.8	21.8
New Brunswick	21.1	22.1	19.5	21.7	25.4	22.6	22.2	20.7	21.6

Source: Statistics Canada, Provincial Economic Accounts and ACOA.

eral transfers. With respect to equalization, the Maritime provinces' share has remained constant from 1961 to 2001 (see table 9.18). The shift to the per capita formula, however, will change this. On a per capita basis, Prince Edward Island received $1,776 in 2004–5, New Brunswick $1,537, and Nova Scotia $1,223, while Quebec obtained $500.[53] With part of the formula now based on a per capita basis, Quebec stands to receive more money from the equalization program in future. Table 9.19 reveals that the Maritime provinces' share has remained relatively constant at 26.8 per cent in 1961 and 2001, while Quebec's share has gone from 35.6 per cent in 1961 to 45.6 per cent in 2001.

Productivity and Capital

Capital and productivity numbers should be cause for concern for the Maritime provinces. In contrast to the region's relative improvement on

TABLE 9.19
Equalization payments, current dollars

	PEI	NS	NB	Maritimes	Maritime's % of equalization payments	QC	Quebec's % of equalization payments	Canada
1961	5	26	24	55	26.8	73	35.6	205
1965	10	44	40	94	29.6	133	41.8	318
1971	20	108	93	221	23.5	453	48.2	940
1975	48	252	187	487	26.0	1,049	55.9	1,875
1981	107	528	445	1,080	24.6	2,490	56.6	4,396
1985	134	596	604	1,334	25.9	2,728	53.1	5,142
1991	187	850	967	2,004	26.1	3,464	45.1	7,673
1995	192	1,140	976	2,308	26.9	4,037	47.0	8,592
2001	256	1,316	1,190	2,762	26.8	4,690	45.6	10,288

Source: 1957–91 taken from Department of Finance statistics presented in Martin Budget Speech 2001, Table A1); 1992–2000 taken from Department of Finance's Calculation booklets for Provincial Fiscal Equalization; 2001–4 from Department of Finance's Web site.

TABLE 9.20
GDP per person, 18 years and older, as a percentage of Canadian GDP, 1961–2001

	1961	1965	1971	1975	1981	1985	1991	1995	2001
Canada	100	100	100	100	100	100	100	100	100
Prince Edward Island	51.2	52.8	53.8	55.4	58.9	59.7	68.9	73.3	72.2
Nova Scotia	66.3	63.3	68.9	65.1	64.9	76.4	78.8	74.5	77.3
New Brunswick	64.9	65.5	67.4	65.2	63.2	69.5	75.7	78.3	76.3
Maritimes	64.7	63.4	67.2	64.4	63.8	72.3	76.8	76.0	76.5

Source: Statistics Canada, CANSIM II, tables 051-0001, 051-0026, 384-0035, and 384-002.

the income front over the past forty years, output per worker is on a downward track. Productivity, as is well known, is the key driver of GDP per capita and self-sustaining economic growth.

The one set of data that suggests that the region has made solid gains since 1961 is GDP per person (see tables 9.20 and 9.21). GDP per person in Prince Edward Island as a percentage of the national average was 51.2 per cent in 1961, but shot up to 72.2 per cent in 2001. New Brunswick and Nova Scotia experienced similar increases (see table 9.20). GDP per person, however, is hardly a solid measure of a region's growth or productivity, but rather speaks to a region's standard of living. Indeed, one can speculate that the gain is due at least in part to out-migration.

Labour productivity in the region remains well below the national average and continues to slip. In Prince Edward Island, manufacturing productivity fell from 64.2 per cent of the Canadian average in 1990 to 60.0 per cent in 1999. Nova Scotia's productivity declined from 75.1 per cent of the national average in 1990 to 69.7 per cent in 1999. In New Brunswick, productivity fell from 84.4 per cent of the Canadian rate in 1990 to 74.0 per cent in 1999. Ontario, Quebec, Alberta, and Saskatchewan led the country by a wide margin (see table 9.22).

In a detailed study of levels of productivity in Atlantic Canada, Andrew Sharpe of the Ottawa-based Centre for the Study of Living Standards concluded that the average output per worker in 2001 in Atlantic Canada was 80 per cent of the national average. He identified only three industries in the region that had output per worker above the national average in the same year: public administration, at 110.5 per cent of the national average; finance, insurance, and real estate at 107.7 per cent; and information and cultural industries at 101.3 per cent.[54]

TABLE 9.21
GDP per person, 18 years and older, 1961–2001

	1961	1965	1971	1975	1981	1985	1991	1995	2001	Percentage change, 1961–2001
Canada	3,669	4,802	6,855	10,951	19,881	24,936	32,069	36,602	46,339	1,163
Prince Edward Island	1,879	2,535	3,690	6,069	11,715	14,897	22,093	26,846	33,478	1,682
Nova Scotia	2,434	3,039	4,722	7,130	12,908	19,056	25,257	27,284	35,822	1,372
New Brunswick	2,383	3,145	4,624	7,137	12,574	17,323	24,266	28,667	35,354	1,384
Maritimes	2,373	3,045	4,608	7,057	12,683	18,039	24,622	27,826	35,457	1,395

Source: Statistics Canada, CANSIM II, tables 051-0001, 051-0026, 384-0035 and 384-002

TABLE 9.22
Manufacturing labour productivity, defined as value added divided by total hours worked, 1990–9 (Canada = 100)

	1990	1991	1992	1993	1994	1995	1996	1997	1998	1999
Newfoundland and Labrador	65.3	73.3	69.8	73.7	67.8	82.7	82.7	75.4	73.4	68.8
Prince Edward Island	64.2	68.0	65.5	59.4	64.0	61.5	56.7	55.2	73.4	60.0
Nova Scotia	75.1	74.8	72.3	74.4	71.7	67.7	67.4	67.7	72.5	69.7
New Brunswick	84.4	80.0	79.4	81.1	88.4	91.4	83.6	80.8	83.9	74.0
Quebec	97.6	103.1	100.2	100.4	101.0	100.2	102.4	101.3	103.7	100.6
Ontario	102.5	101.1	103.9	103.7	101.5	101.2	102.6	103.4	103.0	106.6
Manitoba	88.6	86.1	82.0	77.3	75.8	72.4	73.5	76.7	78.3	59.7
Saskatchewan	111.4	96.6	91.7	85.0	85.9	90.2	89.5	99.5	102.3	80.1
Alberta	119.0	111.8	113.2	107.0	119.5	129.4	120.9	116.1	108.7	107.4
British Columbia	98.7	96.5	91.4	96.5	99.0	96.3	88.5	88.3	84.8	90.5

Source: Statistics Canada, Annual Survey of Manufacturers.

There are also several other indicators that suggest cause for concern. They include: low level of research and development activity, slower rates of technology adoption, a weaker exposure to international markets, modest levels of foreign investment, and highly educated young people leaving the region. These are all key factors necessary to a knowledge-based economy.[55]

As noted earlier, research and development (R&D) is a crucial component of the new economy. Statistics Canada defines R&D as creative work undertaken on a systematic basis to increase the stock of scientific and technical knowledge and to use this knowledge in new applications. Expenditures on R&D are thus an important indicator of the effort devoted to creative activity in science and technology. In provinces with strong R&D performance (Ontario, Quebec, Alberta, and British Columbia), the business sector and governments are both very active. The private sector in the Maritime region does not invest nearly as much, even in per capita terms, in R&D activities as do private firms in Ontario and Quebec. This is also true for the federal government, which, while being a major player in Ontario and Quebec, is hardly present in this sector in the Maritime provinces. It may well be that one influences the other, and that federal programs designed to encourage R&D are tied to private-sector participation. This would explain at least in part why federal R&D programs have had so little impact in Atlantic Canada. In other words, we may well be dealing with a catch-22, a kind of vicious circle from which the region cannot escape. Whatever the reason, in 2001, 78.6 per cent of federal government spending in the natural sciences, engineering, social sciences, and the humanities went to Ontario and Quebec while 2.6 per cent went to the three Maritime provinces. In 1981 the Maritime provinces had secured 3.1 per cent of the funding (see table 9.23).

The Maritime provinces also score poorly on the supply of venture capital. Table 9.24 reports that in 2003 Quebec led the country, with 52 per cent of the supply of venture capital. Nova Scotia and New Brunswick trail all provinces, with the exception of Prince Edward Island and Newfoundland and Labrador. All in all, the Maritime provinces secured less than 1 per cent of venture capital in 2003.

Though one can debate their merit in contributing to a more competitive region, the Maritimes now also trail other regions on business subsidies – defined as cash transfers to businesses for current operations. Business subsidies in the Maritime provinces have been declining for the past fifteen years. In addition, about half of the subsidies in the

TABLE 9.23
Provincial distribution of total R&D expenditures in natural sciences, engineering, social sciences, and humanities, 1981–2001 (Canada = 100)

	1981	1985	1991	1995	2001
Newfoundland	0.9	1.0	1.0	0.7	0.6
Prince Edward Island	0.2	0.1	0.1	0.1	0.2
Nova Scotia	2.1	2.4	2.2	1.9	1.7
New Brunswick	0.8	1.3	1.1	1.0	0.7
Quebec	18.6	22.8	26.6	26.8	27.8
Ontario	37.8	44.5	42.9	44.7	46.6
National Capital Region	8.3	6.4	6.8	5.9	4.2
Manitoba	3.1	2.9	2.6	2.2	2.0
Saskatchewan	1.9	2.5	2.0	1.8	2.8
Alberta	10.7	8.9	7.3	7.1	6.8
British Columbia	6.0	7.0	7.3	7.8	7.6

Source: Statistics Canada, table 358-0001.

TABLE 9.24
Supply of venture capital (VC) in Canada by province, 2003

	VC under Mgt ($000's)	% of Canadian supply	% of Canadian population	$VC per capita
Canada	22,424,018		100	708.86
Quebec	11,700,434	52.0	23.7	1,562.73
Ontario	7,710,533	34.4	38.7	630.03
British Columbia	1,227,050	5.5	13.1	295.67
Saskatchewan	673,033	3.0	3.1	676.52
Alberta	588,096	2.6	10.0	186.48
Manitoba	318,231	1.4	3.7	273.68
Nova Scotia	122,141	0.54	3.0	130.49
New Brunswick	73,500	0.3	2.4	97.92
Newfoundland	12,000	0.05	1.6	23.10
Prince Edward Island*	–	–	–	–

* No numbers for Prince Edward Island are reported by Macdonald & Associates. The number is thought to be very small.
Source: Macdonald & Associates Limited for VC numbers and Statistics Canada for population figures.

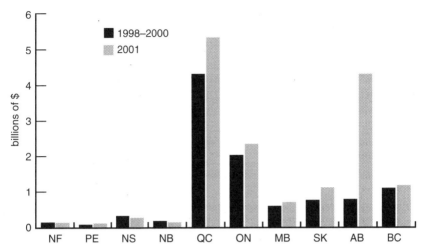

Source: Reproduced from, Atlantic Provinces Economic Council, *Subsidized to the Hill* (Halifax: Atlantic Provinces Economic Council, September 2004).

Figure 9.3
Total business subsidies, annual average, 1998–2001

region are now targeted to non-commercial objectives, such as transportation in remote areas and special adjustment measures resulting
from a plant closure. The Atlantic Provinces Economic Council (APEC)
carried a thorough review of business subsidies in September 2004 and
concluded that the vast majority of subsidies in Canada are paid to
firms in central and western Canada. It reported that between 1998 and
2000, almost 42 per cent of Canadian business subsidies went to Quebec, about 20 per cent to Ontario, with the western provinces receiving
31 per cent of the total. Within the Maritime region, Nova Scotia received the largest amount of business subsidies during the 1998–2000
period, with an annual average of $317 million, followed by New
Brunswick with $172 million and Prince Edward Island with $77 million (see figure 9.3). The termination of subsidies for coal mining in Cape
Breton will contribute to a sizeable drop in total business subsidies in
Nova Scotia after 2001. Provincial subsidies are particularly important in
Quebec. Provincial and local subsidies are at relatively low levels in the
three Maritime provinces (figure 9.4).[56] Thus, federal business subsidies
are relatively more important in the Atlantic provinces.

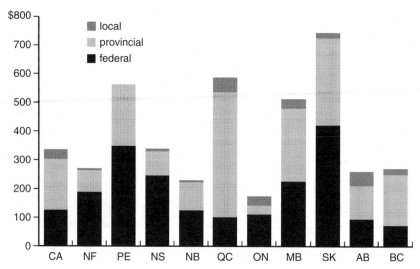

Source: Reproduced from, Atlantic Provinces Economic Council, *Subsidized to the Hill* (Halifax: Atlantic Provinces Economic Council, September 2004).

Figure 9.4
Total business subsidies, per capita, 1998–2000

Trade

Trade agreements between Canada and the United States (FTA) and later between Canada, the United States, and Mexico (NAFTA) have altered trade patterns and the dynamics of economic integration. They have also created new transborder regional alliances. Examples include the Cascadia region, involving the British Columbia, Washington, and Oregon triangle on the west coast and the New England Governors and Atlantic Premiers Council on the east coast.[57] International trade, and in particular trade with the United States, has grown faster than interprovincial trade in recent years, particularly since the FTA and NAFTA signings.[58] In 2002, for example, total Canadian exports accounted for about $470 billion, which represented 41 per cent of total GDP, while interprovincial trade accounted for 20 per cent of total GDP ($224 billion).

The same trend holds true for the three Maritime provinces. The region exports more to the United States, in particular to northeastern United States, than ever before. Key export sectors include food manu-

TABLE 9.25
Exports to the United States, as a percentage of national or provincial GDP

	1976	1981	1991	2001	Percentage change 1976–2001
Canada	12.7	15.1	15.3	31.9	151.2
Prince Edward Island	1.9	3.7	4.3	17.3	810.5
Nova Scotia	9.1	9.7	8.4	17.9	96.7
New Brunswick	10.6	22.3	14.8	36.8	247.2

Source: Statistics Canada, Provincial Economic Accounts and Catalogue 65-003.

facturing and crop production (Prince Edward Island), the plastic and rubber products manufacturing sector and paper manufacturing (Nova Scotia), and paper manufacturing, food processing, and wood product manufacturing (New Brunswick). But this list suggests that since a large proportion of the region's exports remains closely linked to its natural resources, the region has not been successful in making a transition away from resource-based activities. This fact explains why rural exporters in the four Atlantic provinces outperform urban exporters. The opposite is true in other regions of Canada.[59] Table 9.25 reports on the region's exports to the United States since 1976 from a comparative perspective and shows that the growth of such exports from New Brunswick and Prince Edward Island was greater than the Canadian average from 1976 to 2001.

Table 9.26 makes the point that growth in trade is now centred more on international trade than interprovincial trade in all regions of Canada except Yukon, where a sharp decline in gold mining had a profound impact on one of the territory's key exports. International exports accounted for 25 per cent of the GDP of Nova Scotia and 43 per cent of New Brunswick's in 2002 compared to 17 and 26 per cent respectively in 1992. The federal government has always kept a close watch on Canada–U.S. trade relations and, particularly since the signing of FTA and NAFTA, there has been a constant flow of studies on such trade relations coming out of Ottawa. The federal Department of Industry, for example, produced an exhaustive study in 2002–3 on a variety of issues ranging from growth sectors to research and development and productivity. All the issues were reviewed from a 'national perspective,' and nothing was said about issues of special concern to the Maritime provinces.[60] The same can be said about numerous other studies prepared or

TABLE 9.26
Interprovincial and international exports as a share of GDP,* Canada, provinces and territories, 1992, 2000, and 2002

	Interprovincial exports/GDP			International exports/GDP			Total exports/GDP		
	1992	2000	2002	1992	2000	2002	1992	2000	2002
Newfoundland and Labrador	10	15	20	19	41	40	29	56	60
Prince Edward Island	30	26	26	14	29	28	44	55	55
Nova Scotia	19	21	21	17	26	25	36	47	45
New Brunswick	26	31	32	26	39	43	52	71	75
Quebec	19	20	20	21	40	35	40	60	55
Ontario	19	19	19	31	51	46	50	70	64
Manitoba	25	32	32	19	29	28	44	61	60
Saskatchewan	23	27	28	28	42	37	51	69	65
Alberta	23	24	24	27	41	35	50	65	59
British Columbia	13	15	14	24	33	27	37	48	42
Yukon	11	17	15	47	15	13	58	32	27
Northwest Territories and Nunavut	19	25	22	20	30	29	38	55	51
Canada	19	20	20	26	43	38	45	63	58

*Ranking of provinces varies when import content of exports is taken into account.
Source: Input-Output Division, Statistics Canada.

sponsored by Industry Canada in recent years, which frequently ignore the regional dimension.[61]

Convergence and Problems

The findings in this chapter point to several general conclusions: disparities in income between the Maritime provinces and the rest of Canada have been reduced over a forty-year period, but even here the regional convergence has slowed down in recent years. The region has made significant gains in human capital accumulation, and Maritimers have made substantial strides in living standards. There have also been major improvements in the region's physical infrastructure and in the delivery of public services. The region now has modern industrial infrastructure facilities, notably industrial parks, though some of these stand near empty and others have been abandoned.[62] Federal transfer payments in one form or another have been instrumental to the parks' construction.

That said, the data in this chapter suggest that forty years of federal involvement have had only a modest impact. About all that can be claimed is that the economy of the Maritime region might be worse off today had it not been for federal activity. The fact is that several economic indicators confirm that the gap between the Maritime and other regions has not narrowed. Specific initiatives sponsored by DREE, DRIE, and ACOA may well have helped the region in promoting its economic development, but the numerous evaluation reports of consultants over the past thirty years or so have told us very little, if anything, in this regard.

It is worth repeating what we observed in the introductory paragraphs to this chapter: federal government efforts at promoting economic development in the region have not been sufficiently large in relation to other economic forces, such as interest rates and the value of the Canadian dollar or even other federal government spending programs, to permit a credible assessment of their impact. When there were economic gains, they were concentrated on the income front, in large part as a result of Ottawa's redistributive policies, which took form in the early 1960s. In most other areas, however, the region has underperformed. Not only has it not kept pace with Canadian averages on a number of key economic indicators, the region also scores poorly on several indicators that predict future economic growth. The Maritime region has serious problems to address in productivity, accessing venture capital, and attenuating further the dependency on federal transfers. The region is losing population at a rapid rate, its populations remain substantially rural compared with other regions, it is unable to attract new Canadians, and its working-age population is shrinking. Although the region has made strides in rediscovering its traditional export markets, the eastern seaboard of the United States, even here the bulk of its exports remain tied to natural resources.

We saw in earlier chapters that the Maritime provinces 'missed the boat' in the development of Canada's manufacturing sector. There is now every indication to suggest that this pattern will be repeated as North America continues to shift to a knowledge-based economy. The Maritime region is once again left out in the cold as research and development take place elsewhere in the country and as knowledge workers select communities in which to work.

It is often overlooked in our ahistorical world that the federal government played a major role through tariffs and the establishment of Crown corporations in promoting the country's manufacturing sector. Ottawa is now assuming similar leadership in the development of the new economy through its investment in research and development, which had totalled $13 billion since 1997.[63] When decisions are made in Ottawa on where to locate a new research foundation, the space agency, or a government unit engaged in R&D, the debate nearly always turns on whether it should be located in Ottawa, other parts of southern Ontario, or Montreal. Only rarely will the Maritime provinces get, in the words of a former clerk and secretary to the cabinet, a 'breakaway' and draw the attention of Ottawa-based decision makers.[64]

The mindset of Canada's national political and administrative institutions is to promote the country's economic engine (here, read southern Ontario) and to monitor national unity concerns (here, read Quebec). The Ontario and Quebec governments and opposition caucuses matter to the prime minister and the leader of the opposition because the two provinces are key to securing political power in Ottawa. It is hardly possible to appease the demands of those wishing to assist Canada's economic engine to compete in the global economy and with the United States or of Quebec federalists in Ottawa wishing to make the federal government more relevant in Quebec. Our national political-administrative institutions by design give weight to these two appetites, appetites that are rarely satisfied.

10 The Problem: Big Dogs Eat First

In May 2002, Stephen Harper, leader of the opposition, had this to say about the Maritime region's economic problems: 'Because of what happened in the decades following Confederation ... there is a culture of defeat that we have to overcome.'[1] A few months later the *National Post* declared in an editorial, 'Through equalization, regional development, overgenerous employment insurance, welfare and a welter of inefficient government make-work programs, we transfer billions from rich provinces to poor provinces. Albertans and Ontarians are getting awfully tired of subsidizing the buggy-whip makers of Canada's backward regions.'[2] Similar observations can readily be found in the *Globe and Mail*. John Ibbitson, a *Globe and Mail* columnist, writes, 'Ontario is a have province, subsidizing most of the rest of the country. That subsidy was tolerable when high tariffs guaranteed that other Canadians would be forced to buy Ontario wares in return. But the arrival of free trade made the rest of Canada economically irrelevant to Ontario.'[3] It is now widely argued in many circles, including academic ones, that federal policies and programs, notably transfer payments to the Maritime provinces in one form or another, are not only unfair to the more prosperous provinces, but that they actually explain the region's lack of economic development.[4] Some, however, argue quite the opposite. For example, Stéphane Dion, the intergovernmental affairs minister in the Chrétien government, insists that 'the Atlantic provinces benefit from federal policies, the federal effort for the Atlantic provinces is justified [and] federal policies are not inhibiting economic development.'[5]

Among the reasons offered for the relative underdevelopment of the Maritime provinces are their locational disadvantages, as a tariff wall under the National Policy threw open Maritime markets to Ontario and

Quebec; the region's apparent inability to promote a single metropolis; the transfer of capital and human resources to a more established industrial base in central Canada; and substantial growth in parts of western Canada flowing from energy development. We saw in chapter 2 that there was a deliberate attempt by national political powers to promote the interests of the industrial centre at the expense of the Maritime provinces. Some historians, for example, specifically point to changes made to the freight-rate structure to explain the rapid de-industrialization of the Maritime provinces in the 1920s.[6] Other historians argue that the region itself also failed to tackle new economic challenges and opportunities and changing trade patterns.[7] We do not propose to settle the debate in this chapter.

The point is that market forces alone can never fully explain the pace of economic development in Canada's regions. Public policies also count a great deal, and they are the focus of this chapter. We need to ponder this question: can Harper and Dion both be right, given that one insists that federal policies are responsible for the region's relative lack of economic development while the other maintains that these very policies benefit the region? We also need to look at the problem from a Maritime perspective. In doing so, we focus on history and on the workings of Canada's national political-administrative institutions.

Political Institutions Matter

Many practitioners agree that at least part of the problem for regional development in the Maritimes lies in how federal policies and programs are designed and implemented. Harper said as much when he spoke about 'the decades following Confederation' to explain the region's 'culture of defeat.' He is hardly alone. Paul Martin has also referred to 'Canada's unique and highly differentiated regional economic structure' and to the need for a 'high degree of regional flexibility and sensitivity in terms of federal policies, programs, services and communications.'[8] Even career officials in Ottawa recognize that there is a problem with program coordination on the ground. The Task Force on the Coordination of Federal Activities in the Regions reported in 2002 that there was not only a 'weak federal ability to respond nationally to key regional issues,' but also 'real delivery frustration on the ground [and that] regional realities are not sufficiently reflected in policy and program design.'[9]

Roger Gibbins, some twenty-five years ago, pointed to the 'majoritarian bias of parliamentary government' and the 'exaggerated contemporary role of the provincial premiers [caused] by ineffectual territorial representation within the national government.'[10] Provincial premiers may no longer enjoy the exaggerated role they once held, but our national political institutions operate much as they did twenty, thirty, or forty years ago. If anything, political power has become even more concentrated in Ottawa in the hands of the prime minister.[11]

We have repeatedly noted that our national political institutions were designed and took form in a unitary state. One of the very first things that a student of Canadian political institutions observes is the conflicting principles of federalism and parliamentary sovereignty. The House of Commons dominates Parliament, cabinet dominates the House of Commons, and the prime minister dominates cabinet. The Senate remains unelected and largely ineffective, and few observers have even tried to make the case that it constitute a voice, important or otherwise, on behalf of the regions. Ontario dominates the Commons (it has 106 out of 308 seats) followed by Quebec (75 seats). The lead article in the *Globe and Mail* on 29 June 2004 – 'Ontario Rescues Martin' – summed up well Ontario's influence in the Commons. The CBC's *The National* similarly observed: 'Win Ontario: Win the Election.'[12] The *Globe and Mail* explained, at least in part, the loss of support for Harper during the 2004 national campaign in this fashion: 'Harper's last day pledge to westerners that they would have substantial influence in a Conservative government spooked some Ontario voters.'[13] Leaving aside Joe Clark's brief stay at 24 Sussex in 1979, and Kim Campbell's in 1993, the prime minister since 1963 has come from either Ontario or Quebec.

Politics in Canada is more about who wins and who loses than it is about the finer points of public policy: longevity in office is its own reward. If one cannot win in Ontario or Quebec, or both, one simply does not win national political power. There is an old saying among political organizers in Canada: you need to win Ontario to win an election and you need to win Quebec to win a majority of seats. Ottawa, the seat of political power and bureaucratic influence, is also located in Ontario, on the very border that joins Ontario and Quebec. When the prime minister and cabinet have to deal with regional competition for projects or initiatives, they will look to Ontario and Quebec because that is where their main political interests lie. Such decisions are far more common than one assumes or the high-profile cases would sug-

gest (the CF-18 maintenance contract; the location of Crown corporations, museums, and new federal government agencies; and funding
for specific projects).[14]

It is revealing to note that immediately after Martin presented his
new cabinet in July 2004, regions began assessing if they had won or
lost. John Ibbitson, in a front page *Globe and Mail* article, boldly declared
that: 'Ontario is the loser,' and went on to ask whether Martin was
'punishing Ontario for not giving his party every single blessed seat.'[15]
He neglected to mention that Ontario was given sixteen cabinet ministers, which is more than western and Atlantic Canada combined received. The three Maritime provinces secured five cabinet posts. The
ministers of finance and industry are not from Ontario, but the ministers of agriculture, defence, social development, human resources development – infrastructure and communities, and immigration, among
others, are. We know that immigration, human resources development,
and cities are key elements of the new economy. It makes one wonder:
what would the cabinet have to look like for Ontario to be declared the
winner?

The *Ottawa Citizen* also ran a front-page story under the headline 'A
Capital without Clout.' They argued: 'If cabinet meetings can be seen as
important family gatherings, then Ottawa is now sitting at the kids'
table - far away from the grownups who make important decisions.' It
quotes an Ottawa city councillor who remarked that 'it's quite a come-
down considering we had John Manley, who was the big heavyweight
for Ottawa in the Chrétien cabinet ... We are missing our champion.'
The article concludes by noting that former defence minister David
Pratt, representing an Ottawa constituency, had been 'able to persuade
colleagues to come up with a $600-million expansion' for the city's
O Train.[16] Days before calling the 2004 general election, the Martin
government announced that it would provide $200 million in assistance
to extend Ottawa's public transportation system.[17]

Meanwhile, ministers from the Maritime provinces represent a de-
creasing percentage of the total number of cabinet members. For a long
time the three Maritime provinces accounted for about a third of the
cabinet. Indeed, as we saw in chapter 2, in the pre-Confederation discussions, it was agreed that the Maritimes would have one-third of
cabinet posts to compensate for the representation by population in the
Commons. As late as the 1957 Diefenbaker government, the region
accounted for about 20 per cent of the federal cabinet. The number has
dwindled down to about 12 per cent over the past thirty years. In

addition, there are departments traditionally given to Maritime MPs (e.g., fisheries and oceans) and others that are not (e.g., finance, immi-ᵗion, and industry).[18]

ᵗᵉral cabinet has traditionally played a key regional role. How- ᵢle is less effective today than it once was. For one thing, ᵢ become so large (there are now about forty members) that it dominates the government's policy and decision making in One member of the Chrétien government described cabinet as ᵢ group' for the prime minister.[19] As well, the influence of re- ᵢ ministers has waned in recent years. Christopher Dunn writes there was a period in Canadian history (1917–1957) when strong ᵢisters were the primary representatives of their provinces or re- ᵢns.' He explains that 'the rise of the power of the Prime Minister and arious efforts by the PMO to supplant the influence of these ministers ᵢed, if not to an extinguishment of their power, then certainly to a signifi-cant diminution of it.'[20] More is said about this in the next chapter.

The Public Service Also Matters

Our constitution is silent on the role and responsibilities of the civil service. Indeed, Canada's consolidation of its Constitution Acts does not have a great deal to say about the machinery of government. It reads: 'The Executive Government and Authority of and over Canada is ... vested in the Queen ... [and] ... there should be a Council to aid and advise in the Government of Canada, to be styled the Queen's Privy Council for Canada; and the persons who are to be members of that Council shall be from time to time chosen and summoned by the Governor General and sworn in as Privy Councillors, and members thereof may from time to time be removed by the Governor General.' It says little else on the matter and nothing at all to guide the work of the prime minister, ministers, and permanent officials. Even the Constitu-tion Act of 1982 has nothing to say about the bureaucracy. The Fathers of Confederation thought that they had settled the matter once and for all when they wrote in the British North America Act that Canada should have 'a government similar in principle to that of the United Kingdom.' In brief, they wrote the constitution according to the British notion of responsible parliamentary government and grafted to it a federal structure based on the American model.

It is important to stress that the British civil service took shape in a unitary form of government. Regionalism, though important in any political system, has never dominated British politics to the same extent it has in Canada. It is also important to recognize that, though the civil service may well have been an institution of limited importance in 1867, this is not the case today. Indeed, one can now hardly overstate its importance. The role of the federal government now extends to virtually every sector of Canadian society. The Canadian civil service is the country's largest employer and it is present in the daily lives of all Canadians. It houses the country's largest public policy advisory capacity, and the prime minister and cabinet depend on its work to strike new policy measures, to make decisions, to deliver programs, and to carry out operations. Yet, we have paid little attention to its role in dealing with regional issues. Even the literature on intrastate federalism in Canada has paid scant attention to it. One of the most widely read studies on the topic devoted all of three pages to the role of the civil service in Canadian regionalism.[21]

No one disputes the point that today the public service exerts considerable influence on the policy process and on program decisions. Dalton Camp, senior adviser to Prime Minister Mulroney, reported that he opposed awarding the CF-18 maintenance contract to a Montreal-based company rather than to the one in Winnipeg that had submitted a better bid. Yet, 'Quebec always loomed large in the minds of Ottawa bureaucrats ... [and that] senior bureaucrats lobbied strenuously in support of Montreal [partly] because they were anxious to reinforce Montreal's aerospace industry.'[22] There is no need to remind senior public servants in Ottawa of the economic interests of the two central provinces, Ontario and Quebec. For the most part, they are from these two provinces themselves and live there.

J.E. Hodgetts designates the period 1841–67 as the 'formative years' of the Canadian civil service, insisting that few students of government appreciate the extent to which historical decisions, both by ministers and by officials, determine many present practices.[23] These formative years had their roots in Britain and Lower and Upper Canada – and nowhere else. The early architects of the machinery of government sought to replicate British forms and processes in the colony. Indeed, developments in Britain very often directly affected Canada's civil service and machinery of government on both large and small matters. The result is that 'British influence informed virtually every major development in the rise of the Canadian civil service,' including the implementation of the departmental structure.[24]

Still, the North American colonies and their bureaucracy had to deal with something that British civil servants did not. Because they had to come up with ways to provide services over a vast territory, they had no choice but to experiment with decentralization. This is difficult enough in mature governments with well-oiled administrative and financial processes already in place. For the pre-Confederation civil service to decentralize operations while creating a departmental structure was an extraordinary challenge. The fact that they were unable to look to Britain for guidance did not help matters. As a result, major problems surfaced in regional and local offices. Hodgetts writes that 'it would be a tenable thesis that the history of the developing federal civil service reveals a gradual curtailment of powers delegated to local agents ... and has tended to place a few key officials under an unbearably heavy burden.'[25] The political and administrative difficulties associated with this decentralization gave rise to an institutional memory that lingers still.

Within months of Canada's being born, it became clear that Ontario and Quebec would dominate the new civil service. The British North America Act provided for the transfer of some officers and clerks of the United Province of Canada 'to the service of the Dominion.'[26] We now know that the new civil service consisted of 'little more than' the old bureaucracy of the old United Province of Canada.[27] This fact became important for residents of New Brunswick and Nova Scotia: they became convinced that the federal government could never appreciate, for example, that harbours were as critical to many maritime communities as roads and canals were to central Canada. Nor, it was felt, would the civil service give proper attention to trade issues affecting the region.[28]

It is important to underline the fact that the Canadian civil service has been designed to serve the government of the day in a Westminster-style parliamentary system. Accordingly, the civil service has no constitutional personality or responsibility distinct from the government of the day. The government can turn to the civil service knowing that civil servants have exchanged overt partisanship, some political rights, and a public profile in return for permanent careers, or at least indefinite tenure, anonymity, selection by merit, and the promise of being looked after at the end of a career in return for non-partisan obedience and professional competence. The prime minister and ministers can also take comfort in the knowledge that they will never be challenged publicly by career officials, or those who have an intimate knowledge of the relevant policy or administrative issue.

It is not possible to delineate in clear terms the power and influence of Canada's political and administrative institutions. But this much we do know: it has not been possible for a long time to state that politicians decide all policy issues and career civil servants look after only administrative matters and implement ministerial decisions.

Indeed, the growing influence, if not power, of career officials has been a major public policy issue in Western governments for the past thirty-five years. By the mid-1970s politicians began to voice their criticism publicly about the work of their civil servants. Richard Crossman, a prominent minister in Harold Wilson's Labour government in Britain, led the charge from the political left, the traditional ally of the civil service. His concerns had more to do with what he felt was unresponsiveness than with management. In his widely read diaries, which began to appear in 1975, he claimed that 'whenever one relaxes one's guard the Civil Service in one's Department quietly asserts itself ... Just as the Cabinet Secretariat constantly transforms the actual proceedings of Cabinet into the form of the Cabinet minutes (i.e., it substitutes what we should have said if we had done as they wished for what we actually did say), so here in my Department the civil servants are always putting in what they think I should have said and not what I actually decided.'[29] Crossman opened a floodgate of criticism, and it has not abated. The criticism came as no surprise to the political right: it believed that the bureaucracy has been subverting its policy objectives all along.

Crossman's *Diaries of a Cabinet Minister* spoke of his exasperation with a bureaucratic machine that had taken on a life of its own, like an uncontrollable monster. The diaries gave rise to the popular BBC television series *Yes, Minister*, which attracted some nine million regular viewers in Britain and became the favourite program of the permanent secretaries. The series gained a worldwide audience and became highly popular with some politicians and civil servants in Canada, the United States, and Australia. The not-so-subtle message was that public servants were running the country and that the Sir Humphreys of the bureaucratic world wielded considerable power.

The public administration literature has long acknowledged the influence of career officials on both policy and administration. Every textbook published in public administration since the early 1980s deals with the influence of career officials in shaping public policy and delivering government services. Even Max Weber, who sang the praises of the bureaucratic model, identified the problem a hundred years ago when he observed, 'The political master finds himself in the position of the dilettante who stands opposite the expert, facing the trained official who stands within the management of administration.'[30] Today, students of government recognize the influence, if not the power, of the bureaucracy, and some report that the civil service projects 'an image of autonomous powers, more important than the powers of political and participative organs in determining the behaviour of the state and the course of public affairs.'[31]

The Canadian civil service has, over the years, initiated a number of affirmative action programs to hire more francophones, women, Aboriginals, members of visible minorities, and persons with disabilities. Although the Employment Equity Act does not set quotas, it does refer to 'numerical goals' to be achieved through 'reasonable progress.'[32] Some efforts may have been made in the past to have the civil service reflect Canada's regional composition, but these have never enjoyed the same degree of visibility or commitment as other affirmative action initiatives. There is an unwritten deal between the federal government and the province of Quebec going back to the Trudeau years that 25 per cent of federal public servants in the national capital region should be located on the Quebec side.[33] No such deal, written or otherwise, exists between the federal government and the Maritime provinces, western Canada, or Newfoundland and Labrador. Unless one equates francophone civil servants and Quebec, and clearly one should not, the government of Canada has never publicly stated its intention to hire career officials on the basis of regions. The Canada West Foundation recently tabled an action plan to address western discontent, arguing that it is more difficult to determine the 'regional composition of staff ... [than] linguistic, gender or visible minority composition [since] regional identities are often very fluid in a country where people move around a great deal.' The foundation, however, urged Ottawa to undertake a 'restricted' review of the regional composition of staff of a 'small handful of horizontal central agencies that have a uniquely important role to play in ensuring that regional perspectives and interests are brought into play in the design of national policy.'[34]

Donald Gow writes that the unresponsiveness of the federal government to regional interests has a great deal to do with the way the government is organized. Departments generate demands on policy and resources based on their responsibilities for sectors or clients. Gow explains, 'Unless a minister was very clever, the problems which got identified and had their "issues" stated were those within the department's own frame of reference. Since the frames of reference of normal departments are drawn on the basis of industries or social categories, those problems which come up within a regional or cultural context are ignored, or are not seen clearly. With an eye to the integrity of their "little society" almost any bureaucracy will resist answers to cultural and regional problems which may involve loss of functions.'[35] Thus, a proposal or advice that bubbles up from government departments and agencies to ministers and central agencies has a sectoral, national, or client-specific focus, rarely a regional one.

In December 2003, we consulted the Privy Council Office (PCO) and the Web sites of twenty-nine government departments to determine the place of birth of deputy ministers in the federal government. We did not survey associate deputy ministers or other senior federal officials that PCO does not consider to be members of the deputy minister community. Nine of the twenty-nine deputy ministers we surveyed were born in the province of Quebec, eleven in Ontario, five in Western Canada, two in Atlantic Canada, and two abroad. Eighteen of the twenty-nine received their first university degree in Ontario, four in Western Canada, three in Quebec, two in Atlantic Canada, and one abroad. We were not able to establish whether or where one deputy minister obtained a university degree. Ontario and Quebec, the two largest provinces with a particularly strong presence in the House of Commons and in cabinet, also dominate the upper echelons of the Canadian public service.

No Maritimer has occupied the key public service position of clerk of the Privy Council and secretary to the cabinet since Arnold Heeney transformed the post into the top public service job in the 1940s. Public servants from Ontario and Quebec have occupied the position for twenty-eight of the past thirty years.[36] The same can be said, for the most part, about other key posts in Ottawa, including deputy ministers of finance and industry and secretary to the Treasury Board.[37] These individuals influence government policy in many ways: they help shape the policy agenda and offer strategic policy and program advice, and they have, better than other public servants, the capacity to move files and projects forward. They are also very busy people and must pick files or projects they wish to influence. For example, Jean Pelletier, former chief of staff to Prime Minister Chrétien, told the Gomery Commission that he regularly worked ten hours a day and had to put in place a process to identify priority issues on which to focus. He spoke about meeting bank presidents and taking an urgent phone call from Laurent Beaudoin, the head of Bombardier, from his home province, to deal with an important issue concerning Embraer, Bombardier's competitor from Brazil.[38] One can easily speculate that Maritime firms do not have such easy access to key policy makers in Ottawa, given their size and their relative lack of contacts at the most senior levels at court.

Where one stands on policy depends on where one sits. The Canadian civil service has offices in many communities and in all provinces and regions. So where do federal civil servants actually sit? Table 10.1 reports on the location of work of federal civil servants, by province. We decided to present the findings on a yearly basis starting with 1996, the year after the Chrétien-Martin program review was launched, up to 2003. We also tried to secure reliable data on federal government employment by census metropolitan area. However, the data did not square with the provincial breakdown presented in table 10.1. That said, the metropolitan data suggest that the number of federal public servants in Ottawa-Gatineau went from 93,640 in 1996 to 112,234 in 2003 (an increase of 18,594). This compares with a decrease in Halifax of 920 (from 17,448 to 16,528) an increase of 3,334 in Montreal (from 23,210 to 26,544), an increase of 2,447 in Toronto (from 19,724 to 22,171), and an increase of 499 in Calgary (from 6,049 to 6,548).[39]

Table 10.1 reveals that Ontario added 13,353 federal civil servants between 1996 and 2003. This compares with a gain of 2,316 for Quebec during the same period, a loss of 346 for Manitoba, a loss of 46 for British Columbia, a loss of 853 for Saskatchewan, and a gain of 344 for Alberta. Ontario was home to 42.8 per cent of federal civil servants in 2003, Quebec 21.2 per cent, Atlantic Canada 13 per cent, and western Canada 22.5 per cent (see table 10.2). Ontario represented 38 per cent of Canada's population in 2001 while Quebec had 24.1 per cent, Atlantic Canada 7.6 per cent and Western Canada 29.9 per cent (see table 10.3).

Numbers tell only part of the story. For the most part, civil servants operating in local and regional offices deliver government programs and services. They do not play much of a policy advisory role. Line departments and agencies have regional operations to manage and services to deliver, but central agencies do not. In addition, the senior executive category is concentrated largely in Ottawa. Deputy ministers (with four exceptions) are all located in Ottawa; even the four located outside of that city do not spend a great deal of time away from the capital. One senior Treasury Board Secretariat official reports that 'now over 70 per cent of the Executive category is located in Ottawa.' He adds that this trend can be traced back to the program-review exercise of the mid-1990s.'[40] Moreover, an important part of the policy work of

TABLE 10.1
Employment in federal general government minus uniformed RCMP, annual averages, 1996–2003

Province	1996	1997	1998	1999	2000	2001	2002	2003*	% change, 1996–2003
Newfoundland and Labrador	8,077	7,124	6,555	6,320	6,495	6,446	6,451	6,560	-18.8
Prince Edward Island	2,941	2,994	2,997	3,023	3,234	3,441	3,440	3,414	16.1
Nova Scotia	24,902	23,907	22,799	22,260	21,918	21,832	22,177	22,521	-9.6
New Brunswick	12,664	11,797	11,850	12,121	12,472	12,375	12,485	12,633	-0.2
Quebec	70,987	67,722	65,643	66,037	68,069	69,961	72,935	73,303	3.3
Ontario	134,959	128,160	126,997	127,713	132,093	136,971	143,069	148,312	9.9
Manitoba	15,416	13,962	13,584	13,937	14,506	15,140	14,671	15,070	-2.2
Saskatchewan	8,433	7,868	7,745	7,578	7,622	7,623	7,576	7,580	-10.1
Alberta	23,614	22,513	22,185	22,164	22,629	23,187	23,652	23,958	1.5
British Columbia	31,222	29,309	28,563	28,487	29,176	30,230	30,883	31,176	-0.1
Yukon	869	708	667	675	695	697	721	531	-38.9
Northwest Territories	956	876	858	854	866	888	906	938	-1.9
Nunavut	0	0	0	79	146	229	258	251	–
Outside Canada	3,097	3,003	2,905	2,969	3,105	2,998	3,016	3,110	0.4
Total Canada + outside	338,137	329,943	313,348	314,267	323,026	331,838	342,240	349,357	3.3
Total Canada only	334,040	316,940	310,443	311,298	319,921	328,840	339,224	346,247	3.3

*Average for 2003 is based on data from January to September.
Source: Statistics Canada, 'Public Sector Employment, Wages and Salaries,' Cansim II, table 183-0002, special order; compiled by the author.

TABLE 10.2
Employment in federal general government minus uniformed RCMP, annual averages, 1996–2003 (%)

Province	1996	1997	1998	1999	2000	2001	2002	2003*
Newfoundland and Labrador	2.4	2.2	2.1	2.0	2.0	2.0	1.9	1.9
Prince Edward Island	0.9	0.9	1.0	1.0	1.0	1.0	1.0	1.0
Nova Scotia	7.4	7.5	7.3	7.2	6.9	6.6	6.5	6.5
New Brunswick	3.8	3.7	3.8	3.9	3.9	3.8	3.7	3.6
Quebec	21.2	21.4	21.1	21.2	21.3	21.3	21.5	21.2
Ontario	40.3	40.4	40.9	41.0	41.3	41.6	42.2	42.8
Manitoba	4.6	4.4	4.4	4.5	4.5	4.6	4.3	4.4
Saskatchewan	2,5	2.5	2.5	2.4	2.4	2.3	2.2	2.2
Alberta	7.0	7.1	7.1	7.1	7.1	7.1	7.0	6.9
British Columbia	9.3	9.2	9.2	9.2	9.1	9.2	9.1	9.0
Yukon	0.3	0.2	0.2	0.2	0.2	0.2	0.2	0.2
Northwest Territories	0.3	0.3	0.3	0.3	0.3	0.3	0.3	0.3
Nunavut	0.0	0.0	0.0	0.0	0.0	0.1	0.1	0.1
Total – Canada only	100.0	100.0	100.0	100.0	100.0	100.0	100.0	100.0

* Average for 2003 is based on data from January to September.
Source: Statistics Canada, 'Public Sector Employment, Wages and Salaries,' Cansim II, table 183-0002, special order; compiled by the author.

the federal government continues to be contracted out to consultants and policy research groups. One senior Treasury Board Secretariat official speculates that 'something like 70 per cent of cabinet documents are now prepared by outside consultants,'[41] a practice that would have been unthinkable forty years ago.[42] The great majority of consultants and think-tanks advising the federal government are located in Ottawa, not in the regions.

Both the United States and Australia have elected Senates that are able to give life and credibility to a regional voice at the centre of government. Accordingly, there is probably less of a need to have the civil service speak to regional circumstances and interests in those countries, and a greater need for such a role in Canada. In the case of the United States, over 80 per cent of all federal civil servants (non-military) are located outside of the District of Columbia, Virginia, and Maryland.[43] In Australia, close to 70 per cent of all federal civil servants are located outside Canberra.[44] One senior Treasury Board official re-

TABLE 10.3
Population count for Canada, provinces, and territories, 1996 and 2001

	1996		2001	
	no.	%	no.	%
Newfoundland and Labrador	551,792	1.9	512,930	1.7
Prince Edward Island	134,557	0.5	135,294	0.5
Nova Scotia	909,282	3.2	908,007	3.0
New Brunswick	738,133	2.6	729,498	2.4
Quebec	7,138,795	24.7	7,237,479	24.1
Ontario	10,753,573	37.3	11,410,046	38.0
Manitoba	1,113,898	3.9	1,119,583	3.7
Saskatchewan	990,237	3.4	987,933	3.3
Alberta	2,696,826	9.3	2,974.807	9.9
British Columbia	3,724,500	12.9	3,907,738	13.0
Yukon	30,766	0.1	28,674	0.1
Northwest Territories	39,672	0.1	37,360	0.1
Nunavut	24,730	0.1	26,745	0.1
Canada	28,846,761	100.0	30,007,094	100.0

Source: Statistics Canada, "Population and Dwelling Counts for Canada, Provinces, and Territories," 2001 and 1996 censuses.

ports that the percentage of federal civil servants located in Ottawa has gone up further in recent months and that it is now close to 40 per cent.[45]

The National Media also Matter

The national media – concentrated as they are in Toronto, Ottawa, and Montreal – also tend to define national issues from an Ontario-Quebec perspective. Ottawa-based officials read the *Globe and Mail*, the *Toronto Star*, and the *Ottawa Citizen*, and, if they should happen to be bilingual, perhaps *Le Devoir* or *La Presse*. They do not as a rule read the *Cape Breton Post*, the *Saint John Telegraph Journal*, *L'Acadie nouvelle*, or the *Winnipeg Free Press*. We saw earlier that the media regard Trudeau, Mulroney, Chrétien, and Martin as national politicians while Diefenbaker, Harper, and Manning are described as regional politicians. As Stephen Tomblin writes, 'regional stereotypes have drawn national attention to peripheral regions, rather than to Central Canada.'[46] One would be hard pressed to find a positive stereotype in the national media in recent years about the Maritime provinces. Harry Bruce's *Down Home* documents the 'cultural imperialism' of CBC Toronto and the 'insistence' that stories from the Maritimes deal with 'Anne of Green Gables, Highland games, national parks, and fishermen in rubber boots.'[47] Jeffrey Simpson, one of Canada's most widely read columnists, writes, 'Atlantic Canada has a bit of an image problem. It's been down, economically speaking, for so long that people in the rest of Canada think of the region as nothing more than four provinces full of friendly people looking for handouts. You know the image. Unemployment insurance. Seasonal workers. Make-work projects. Regional development agencies. Pork-barrel politics. Equalization.'[48] As Robert Young explains, 'there can also be comfort in the old images of politics in the Maritimes – the snake-oil salesmanship, the rival cliques fighting for the spoils of office, and the politicians who stride across small stages like petty princelings – for these images elicit, especially among Upper Canadians and the more jaded elements of the regional society, that soothing sense of bemused condescension so gratifying to those who can afford to be above the fray.'[49]

Edith Robb, a leading Maritime journalist, was asked to survey the national media during the 2004 election campaign for Moncton's daily newspaper, the *Times and Transcript*. It is worth quoting her at some length:

> Hardly anybody had anything at all to say about us. And if they did, it was in reference to us as a poor, rather backward, Ottawa-dependent province full of people working in the fishery or on the farm and collecting pogey most of the year. Here are some examples: CTV came to New Brunswick to report on the election and ended up writing about our 'horrible' roads. The *Toronto Star* focused on 'fishing families' of the east coast, along with potholes and gas prices. They described eastern voters as 'wearing overalls and jeans,' noting picturesquely 'the hands [the candidate] shakes spend a lot of time in warm red dirt or cold ocean water.' The *Star* also described our region as a place where Employment Insurance is used as an industrial subsidy. The *National Post* had us all as cagey strategists who liked to be 'on the winning side,' presumably to protect our pogey. The Canadian Broadcasting Corporation described us as a region where 'the Liberals remain popular where a benevolent Ottawa is a matter of the region's very survival.' The Canadian Press described us as 'an area with chronically high unemployment and major reliance on economic props.'[50]

What the national media reports about the Maritime provinces matters for two reasons. Media stereotypes are like codes that give the reader a ready understanding of a region or a group of people. Stereotypes can also become realities in the eyes of the region itself and of policy makers. As Edith Robb explains, 'Stereotyping can also impact on a region's self-image. We start to think that if this is the way others see us, then perhaps that is the way we are. The confidence to trust yourself when others doubt you is not in great supply.'[51]

One of Frank McKenna's most important contributions to economic development in New Brunswick during his term as premier was to instill in New Brunswickers a sense of pride and a 'can-do attitude.' McKenna asked an outside firm to assess New Brunswickers' views of themselves and their province and to get a feel for the perceptions other Canadians had of New Brunswick. The report card was not positive. It revealed that New Brunswickers' pride focused on their local community, their cultural heritage, and on being Canadians; pride in their province trailed behind almost everything else. Perceptions of New Brunswick in the rest of Canada were dominated by the 'have-not' image. Except for those who had a personal connection with the province, the rest of Canada, the wealthier provinces in particular, viewed New Brunswick as a place they had to subsidize.[52]

McKenna decided to attack this problem in many different ways. The government adopted a new visual public relations symbol for the province that it employed 'widely, extensively and consistently.'[53] It launched new publications such as *Trade Winds*, which was circulated widely to embassies and corporations around the world and reported on success stories in business and in university research in New Brunswick. McKenna himself accepted numerous speaking engagements outside the province to sell the assets of New Brunswick and to report on 'the diversity and strength of its people and its successes.'[54] He went to major economic centres to promote the province and to 'aggressively market New Brunswick to the world.'[55]

At home, McKenna took a comprehensive approach to improve the image New Brunswickers had of their province and of themselves. For example, he turned to local firms to handle tourism promotion and other public relations work for the provincial government, rather than using Toronto-based companies, as had been done in the past. The thinking here was that, given a chance, New Brunswickers would, in the great majority of circumstances, be as creative and productive as any out-of-province firm. He was proved right, and today New

Brunswick is home to several highly successful public relations and communications firms. Many of these have gone on to secure contracts in other parts of Canada and abroad and to win high-profile work with leading New Brunswick firms, such as McCain and Irving.[56]

What the national media report about the Maritimes also matters in Ottawa. It matters because key policy makers read the *Globe and Mail*, the *Ottawa Citizen*, and *Le Devoir*, watch the national news and constantly monitor CBC-Newsworld and CTV to have a sense of what the media have to say about their departments. Deputy ministers meet most weeks at the 'DM breakfast,' which is always held in Ottawa, to compare notes and to arrive at common understandings.

The national media matters because the policy process in Ottawa is much more porous today than it was, say, forty years ago. Leaving aside policy issues that are of direct interest to the prime minister, policy making in Ottawa is the product of many hands. It is also less evidence based than was the case forty years ago.[57]

Policy by Announcement

Up to the early 1970s, deputy ministers commonly rose through the ranks of their departments and stayed in that position until retirement. They knew their sector, their department, its personnel, its policies, and its programs extremely well, which gave them considerable influence. They were, thus, able to use their strong knowledge to speak truth to power.

Today, deputy ministers are appointed for their familiarity with the interdepartmental policy process, their ability to network, and their capacity to keep their ministers out of political trouble. As former fisheries and oceans minister Roméo LeBlanc observed, 'You now have deputy ministers and assistant deputy ministers of Fisheries who have never been on a wharf.'[58]

Central agency experience is *un droit de passage* for a potential deputy minister. Deputy ministers now find that consultative and interdepartmental work takes up about 30 per cent of their time. Two of them estimate that they spend 75 to 95 per cent of their time on 'horizontal' management, defined broadly. They characterize horizontal management as 'fuzzy, nowhere and everywhere, but increasing significantly.' Their work seems more and more tied to 'networks' designed to get things done. One reports, 'Whether we want it or not, everything is now horizontal.' Many also report a larger legal component to their work, thanks to the Charter of Rights and the North American Free Trade Agreement. They also made numerous references to access-to-information legislation and to its impact on their relations with their ministers and the clerk of the Privy Council.[59]

Senior public servants are 'careerists' with an eye to the next promotion, whether the position is in their department or not.[60] Deputy ministers can expect to head three or four departments in both the economic or social policy fields before they retire. Between 1984 and 2004 there were twelve secretaries of the Treasury Board, twelve deputy ministers of fisheries and oceans, seventeen deputy ministers of industry, and twelve deputy ministers of citizenship and immigration.[61]

The objective, as Mike Prince points out, is now less one of speaking truth to power and more one of 'sharing truths.'[62] Deputy ministers are less willing today to give fearless and forthright policy advice, not only because the policy environment is less conducive to doing so than it once was, but because policies are increasingly the product of many hands. The goal of public servants is to get things through the policy process and serve their ministers by avoiding errors and steering the minister clear of blame for any possible mistakes. This explains why today 'ministers prefer a deputy minister who has intimate knowledge of the system, can work well with the centre of government, and has the ability to get proposals through the consultative decision-making process over one with sectoral expertise or who knows intimately the department, its policies, and its history.'[63]

It is also a world where policy consultants and lobbyists have come to exert influence. Consulting firms have grown substantially in number and size in Ottawa over the past forty years. The Yellow Pages in the Ottawa telephone directory now contain listings for hundreds of consulting firms in economics, program evaluation, and various aspects of public policy. Many of these firms employ former federal career officials and do work once performed by them.

There is another breed of consultant that, according to Jeffrey Simpson, has grown 'like Topsy in the last two decades' in Ottawa. They are the lobbyists, or - if one wants a more dignified term - 'government relations experts.'[64] From a dead-start thirty-five years ago, there are now forty-two lobbying firms listed in the Ottawa directory, and by one count there are now 1,500 lobbyists in Ottawa. Policy consultants and lobbyists have several things in common, not the least of which being an Ottawa perspective. They have few reasons to look to the regions to influence policy, particularly in the case of the Maritime provinces. The federal government, with the exception of the Atlantic Canada Opportunities Agency (ACOA), which has a modest policy capacity in the region, has virtually no policy specialist in the Maritime provinces. Natural Resources Canada, for example, has one policy adviser located in the Maritime region who covers 'energy' matters; Agriculture and Agrifood Canada has one policy analyst/economist; Transport Canada has three policy officers; and the Department of Fisheries and Oceans has seventeen officers employed in policy and statistics units.[65] In brief, national policy is shaped in Ottawa, not in the regions, and no one knows this better than policy consultants and lobbyists.

The above, together with the perverse impact of access-to-information legislation and the role of the new media, including twenty-four-hour news channels, has pushed the federal government to make policy by announcement. That is, the prime minister simply delivers a major speech, makes an announcement or asks a minister to do so, and then the machinery of government scrambles to put the pieces together. Examples abound. They include Mulroney on constitutional renewal and Hibernia, Chrétien on foundations and the Kyoto Protocol and Martin on subsidies to the automotive sector.

Things National Really Matter

Nick Mulder, a former senior deputy minister in Ottawa, maintains that the Canadian government has had the most successful regional development policy anywhere. He argues, 'Look at Ontario and its history of economic development. Ottawa has done a pretty good job at regional development.'[66] Our national political institutions, as we have already pointed out time and again, with no effective second House acting as a voice for the regions and smaller provinces, favour the most populous provinces, notably Ontario and Quebec. The national media are concentrated in these two provinces, as is the senior federal public service. All of these combine to speak to the national perspective. But there are also powerful political and economic forces that favour a national perspective. The Quebec factor has had and continues to have a profound impact on Ottawa and national policies. Many issues and policy and program proposals are put through the national unity prism. In his comparative study of Canadian and Australian foreign affairs, Andrew Cooper writes, 'A tell-take sign of how Canada's economic and diplomatic strategies were subordinated to political tactics in agricultural trade was the routing of all important decisions in this issue area in the later stages of the GATT negotiations through the central agencies of the Prime Minister's Office and the Privy Council Office. The decisive impact of the constitutional issue in this matter inevitably stymied the government's ability to perform effectively in the concluding phase of the Uruguay Round.'[67] Cooper's example is hardly an isolated one. Quebec concerns, because they are seen in Ottawa as vital to national unity, matter in most things national or not. It will be recalled, for example, that Canada's regional development efforts were adjusted in the early 1970s, and several times after, so that they would resonate better in Quebec and cast Ottawa and the federal government in a more positive light in that province.

The economic pull of the United States also pushes federal policy makers to focus on how Canada deals with developments south of the border. One only needs to consult a few government documents in Ottawa to see the federal preoccupation with keeping up with the Americans. Policy makers and their advisers in Ottawa are constantly comparing Canada-U.S. productivity gains, participation in leading-edge manufacturing and services, and investments in research and development. They constantly monitor developments and economic progress in the United States and those in Canada's key economic engine located between Montreal and Windsor. A front-page article in the business section of the *Globe and Mail* with the headline 'Canada Slips Again in Global Ranking' focuses the minds of senior officials in the Privy Council Office, finance, and industry on ways to strengthen Canada's competitiveness through national policies.[68]

A national perspective, however, means different things to different regions. In the Maritime provinces, a national perspective is a code phrase for the regional interests of Ontario and Quebec. While any issue affecting Ontario and Quebec is inevitably regarded in Ottawa as a national concern, requiring the close attention of the national government, the same cannot be said of the Maritimes. An example makes this point clear. The Supreme Court of Canada's decision in the *Marshall* case, which gave broad fishing rights to the Mi'kmaq nation, had far-reaching political and economic consequences in the Maritimes. For some unexplained reason, Atlantic Canada's representative on the Supreme Court did not participate in the *Marshall* decision. One can hardly imagine a case before the Supreme Court having a strong impact on one of Ontario's key economic sectors (e.g., the automotive or financial services sector) that would not have all of Ontario's representatives on the court participate in the decision. In addition, by all accounts, the government of Canada had no contingency plan in place to deal with any political fallout resulting from *Marshall*. Contrast this to the federal government's setting up of a special ad hoc unit in the Privy Council Office to deal with any political fallout at the time the Supreme Court tabled its decision on the Quebec referendum. Yet, Ottawa has jurisdiction over both the fishery and Aboriginal affairs.

From the time of John A. Macdonald's 'National Policy' through to C.D. Howe's policies during and following the Second World War, the goal of Canada's economic policies was to build a national economy, not regional ones. This mindset has been fed over the years by Canada's national political-administrative institutions. It would lead to concern, as we saw in chapter 6, about the 'Maritimization' of the Ontario economy in light of NAFTA, but would accept the 'Maritimization' of the Maritimes as the price to pay to strengthen the national economy. Viewed from Ottawa, market forces are fine when it comes to the Maritimization of the Maritimes but not, it seems, when they mean the Maritimization of central Canada.

The introduction of the National Energy Program (NEP), for example, brought home the difference between the interests of Ontario and Quebec, defined as the national perspective, and the interests of the outer provinces. Western Canadians saw little merit in using its energy profits to subsidize both exploration in frontier regions controlled by the federal government and energy consumption in Ontario. At the same time the Atlantic provinces saw little merit in Ottawa's deciding that offshore energy developments were within national jurisdiction and in its refusal to give up any jurisdictional powers over these oil and gas resources. Peter Leslie, a well-known observer of Canadian federalism, writes that Ottawa's positions were viewed in both western Canada and the four Atlantic provinces as a central Canadian strategy rather than a national one.[69] More recently Ottawa's decision to invest $13 billion in research and development activities, with little attempt to tailor them to Canada's regional economic circumstances, speaks to the same mindset.

Policy matters in Ottawa have long resisted a regionally differentiated approach because of the perception that focusing on regional interests would be at the expense of national policy. In the early 1980s, Jean Chrétien applauded Ontario premier Bill Davis when the Ontario premier summed up the challenge of Canadian federalism as a choice between 'province-building or nation-building,' urging Canadians to embrace 'national loyalties and a national spirit.'[70] But therein lies the rub.

The automotive and auto-parts sectors have long been regarded as a national initiative, while, for example, the fishery is viewed as regional. Ontario-based newspapers have taken editorial positions urging Ottawa to support 'Canada's vital auto industry.'[71] The Martin government unveiled plans to give the auto sector $500 million to support the development of Ontario auto plants.[72] The aerospace sector concentrated in Montreal is also regarded by Ottawa as a key economic area and it enjoys financial support (in the form of loans) worth $9.3 billion from the Export Development Canada (EDC).[73] Senior policy makers in Ottawa see no reason why elements of the aerospace sector would wish to locate in other regions. Against the advice of its former chair, EDC has also provided financial support totalling $750 million to Nortel Networks. Patrick Lavelle reports that he 'strenuously argued against having EDC provide Nortel with a proposed $500 million line of credit at a time when the company was in financial trouble.' He explained, 'It isn't the role of EDC to back up private sector companies that have run into some financial problems.'[74] EDC, meanwhile, has scarcely been visible in the Maritime provinces, providing little financial support to its high-tech firms.

Rather than tailor national policies to accommodate regional economic circumstances, the federal government has, over the years, introduced a veritable alphabet soup of regional development programs, described in chapters 4 to 8. The programs have been a model of inconsistency. Never regarded as part of national economic policy and never fully accepted by the Ottawa bureaucracy as true economic development investments, the programs have been nevertheless subjected to major adjustments for reasons that have had little to do with the economic interests of the Maritimes. They were overhauled in the 1970s to contribute to Ottawa's national unity efforts in Quebec, in the 1980s because of concerns over the perceived softness in the Ontario economy, and again in the 1990s because of a lack of political visibility for federal government spending. Jean Chrétien pledged in the 1993 election campaign to 'work with provincial governments to fulfil the priorities established in provincial strategic economic plans.'[75] A few years later, he declared that the federal government would no longer enter into federal-provincial agreements for regional development in the Maritime provinces, a practice that began in the 1960s.

Key policy makers and their advisers in Ottawa place a premium on pursuing the national interest and a national policy agenda. Regional and local considerations are frequently viewed as political preoccupations and constraints to be managed or overcome. This is particularly true when economic investment and emerging economic opportunities are at play. Efforts are made to isolate government initiatives from regional (in Ottawa, read political) considerations. Janet Atkinson-Grosjean carried out a study of Ottawa's Network of Excellence Program, in which she explored the regional distribution of the program. She concluded, 'When the program was being planned, the "network" component appealed to politicians because it offset the elitism implied by "excellence." To a Canadian politician, elitism means geographical concentration. According to a federal informant, the program was sold to Cabinet "as an economic development package – a regional economic package. But Cabinet was sold 'a bill of goods.'"'[76]

Programs Are National

Ever since Woodrow Wilson wrote his seminal paper on the division of politics and administration in 1887, public administration literature and practitioners have been struggling with what properly belongs to politics and what to administration. Wilson maintained that politicians should establish policies and that the administrators should run government programs.[77] This view has been challenged time and again, but the myth that one could separate politics from administration was born, and career officials have found it useful ever since. Their message to ministers is straightforward: you take care of politics and establish policy, and we will look after administration.

Provincial public servants prefer implementing province-wide programs with no political or geographical bias. Similarly, federal public servants prefer implementing national programs with no political or geographical bias. Still, there are some federal programs that have a regional bent, ranging from equalization and employment insurance to regional economic development programs outlined in earlier chapters. In every instance, one can easily discern the hand of politicians in shaping these measures – more often than not against the advice of their public servants.

The federal government had an expenditure budget of $178.3 billion in the fiscal year 2003–4. Public debt charges amounted to about $36 billion in that year – some 20 per cent of the total. Transfers to persons and other orders of government – including old age security, Canada health and social transfers, and equalization payments – represented 40 per cent of the total budget, or $71.4 billion. Direct program spending totalled $70.7 billion, again about 40 per cent of the total. There have been some trends in the expenditure budget in recent years: public debt charges have fallen by 28 per cent, from almost $50 billion in 1995 (when the first program review was launched); major transfers have increased by almost 20 per cent, from about $60 billion in 1995; and direct program spending has increased by over 40 per cent, from about $50 billion in 1995. The federal government hands out $18 billion in grants and subsidies, including $6 billion in business subsidies. According to a senior federal Finance Department official, the overall growth in direct program spending since the program review (between 1994–5 and 2001–2) can be accounted for by a 30 per cent growth in operating expenditures, an 8 per cent increase in transfer payments, and a 23 per cent decrease in capital expenditures.

On the human-resources side, the total number of employees in the public service was about 385,000 in 1995. After reaching a low of 335,000 in 1999 (in the immediate aftermath of the first program review), the number had grown to about 365,000 in 2003. When uniformed RCMPs are excluded, the public service employment level is now the same as at the pre-program-review level. As we saw earlier, growth in employment has also varied widely by region. In the National Capital Region (1996–2003) it was over 20 per cent, while in Ontario (including Ottawa) it was nearly 10 per cent and 33 per cent in Quebec. In Saskatchewan the change was −10 per cent, −2.2 per cent in Manitoba, 1.5 per cent in Alberta, −9.6 per cent in Nova Scotia, and −0.2 per cent in New Brunswick. These differences, officials in Ottawa explain, were largely the result of a greater emphasis on policy work and centralized service delivery, both of which take place largely in the National Capital Region. This may well explain why Ottawa was the city of choice for migrant Maritimers between 1996 and 2001 (see figure 10.1). More recent data reveal that Ottawa continues to do well. A report released in September 2004 found that staffing in the National Capital Region 'hit a record 121,600 in the second quarter of this year ... As it turned out, the federal hiring binge saved the region from an overall employment loss offsetting declines in manufacturing, construction and commercial services.'[78]

Some federal ministers have recently suggested that Ottawa is looking at relaunching the program to relocate government offices outside

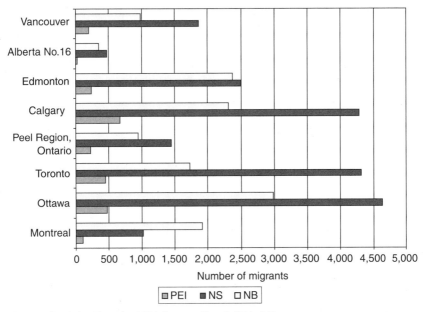

Source: Statistics Canada, 2001 Census, Special Tabulation.

Figure 10.1 Canadian destinations of migrants from the Maritime region, in 1996–2001

of the National Capital Region. Andy Scott has insisted that a 'study of the superannuation directorate ... has confirmed that there are economic gains to be had in pursuing such a program.'[79] No sooner had Scott made clear his views than a public service union (the Public Service Alliance of Canada) issued a press release, arguing that 'moving jobs from Ottawa doesn't save money through salaries because, as opposed to moving jobs overseas, federal employees in Canada receive the same salary.'[80]

Martin's decision to move the Canadian Tourism Commission to Vancouver met with stiff resistance inside the federal public service. The tourism commission, a Crown corporation, has eighty-five employees. The commission's vice-president wrote a memo arguing that it was best to keep the organization in Ottawa, insisting that 'nothing would be gained' by moving to Vancouver and that Canada's 'tourism industry is concentrated in Montreal-Toronto.'[81] Jim Watson, the commission's former head and subsequently an Ontario provincial minister, also did not see any economic or strategic reasons for moving the commission, arguing that its mandate is to promote all of Canada and that 'from an economic point of view, that's 85 jobs from Ontario and it's part of the overall concern that we have the $23 billion gap' between what Ontario sends Ottawa and what it receives from the federal government.[82]

Ottawa has never produced a study to compare the cost of operating a unit in Ottawa as opposed to in a region. Some outside studies have suggested that there are cost savings in locating new government units outside of Ottawa.[83] I put the following question to a deputy minister in Ottawa in the summer of 2004: 'Why not relaunch the decentralization program to promote economic development and perhaps better public administration?' The response: 'Think about it. Officials in Ottawa are more concerned about the real estate market in Ottawa than in Timbuktu.'[84]

One can easily compare the region receiving the most federal cash transfers with the one that receives the least, and thus the accounting is highly accessible to the media. Federal transfers also matter a great deal to provincial premiers and their bureaucracies and they will make every effort to place them on the political agenda. Ontario premiers can easily claim, as they have on many occasions, that their province contributes billions more to the federal treasury than it receives every year. It is a great deal more difficult, however, to document how much Ontario receives annually in federal tax expenditures or from the activities of Crown corporations, the great majority of which have their head offices in that province. Atomic Energy of Canada Limited (AECL), for instance, not only has its head office in Ontario, but virtually all of its research and development and most of its activities are located there as well. It has also been handsomely supported by Canadian taxpayers since it was established in 1952. However, neither Crown corporations (including AECL), nor the economic development programs of federal departments and agencies figure in 'fair-share' federalism or in debates or discussions about 'closing the gap.'[85]

Ontario's fair-share federalism campaign took a new turn in February to May 2005. Premier Dalton McGuinty embarked on a high-profile campaign to close the '$23 billion dollar gap' between what Ontario pays in taxes to Ottawa and what it receives from the federal government. McGuinty wrote that Ontario is 'Canada's economic engine and the heart of Canada.'[86] He told Ontario MPs in Ottawa to 'smarten up' and Ontarians that their 'tax dollars help pay for training in Sydney Mines and St. John's, surgeries in Montreal and Regina, and post-secondary education in Whitehorse.' He added that Ontarians should be very concerned, as 'Ontario exports are more likely to run North-South than East-West.'[87] In the ensuing debate, the national media was largely supportive of McGuinty's position. Mary Tonigan, for example, wrote in an article titled 'Yes, Ontario Is a Victim' in *Maclean's* that 'equalization is now the Energizer bunny of transfers, endlessly shuffling funds, even when needs decline ... Such generosity was fine when Ontario was rich.'[88] Writing in the *Globe and Mail*, Eric Reguly points out that Ontario has about '40 per cent of Canada's population, and generates about 44 per cent of GDP. Yet it gets only 37.2 per cent of the transfer payments to universities, 23.5 per cent of cash transfers to the provinces, and 32.6 per cent of the transfers to persons.' He adds, 'Ontario gives far more than it gets and the outflow is unsustainable. Mr. McGuinty has no choice but to pursue a mad-as-hell strategy. His leverage is the 74 federal Liberal seats in Ontario.'[89]

The Canadian Imperial Bank of Commerce published a report, *Killing the Golden Goose?*, supporting McGuinty's position. The report pointed out that the 'sheer magnitude (of the gap) weighs on an already burdened economy, taxing the Ontario government's ability to invest in a strong, vibrant provincial (and hence national) economy.'[90] It adds: 'Ontario looks to have missed out on the notable fiscal improvement enjoyed elsewhere in 2004–05.'[91] Neither this report nor McGuinty explored how Ontario became the Golden Goose in the Canadian economy in the first place or the role 'national' economic policies played in its development. No one in the national media or elsewhere wrote about closing the gap on the economic development front resulting from past and current federal economic development policies and programs.

Prime Minister Paul Martin initially resisted McGuinty's call for more federal funds from Ottawa, insisting that Ontario receives plenty from the federal government, including '39 percent of the monies being transferred' to provinces under the federal-provincial health care accord.[92] Martin's resistance, however, proved to be short lived. He subsequently agreed to transfer $5.75 billion over a five-year period (2005–10) to Ontario. McGuinty declared that progress was made as a result of Martin's decision, 'but there's still work to do.' He insisted that 'unfairness persists.'[93] McGuinty's campaign to close the 'gap' is not only ahistorical but also lumps all types of federal government spending in one all-encompassing category. There is quite a difference, for example,

between transferring money to individuals under Ottawa's employment insurance program and investing in research and development
initiatives. Transfer payments do not generate economic development –
indeed, they may well inhibit it and they have fallen out of favour in
many quarters.

My talks with Ottawa-based officials about economic development
in the Maritime provinces invariably centre around transfer payments.
Using the data to underscore their point that the region is the big
winner, they ask how it can possibly complain about federal policies
and programs. They add, however, that the region needs to break away
from such payments. They are less forthcoming when it comes to what
should replace them. Some insist that a good dose of market discipline
should help. Others endorse the Schumpeterian notion that entrepreneurship and technological innovation are the way ahead and that the
role of the state needs to shift away from supply-side services. They
refer to both investment to create the necessary Schumpeterian climate
for economic development and to the need to reduce the tax load in
every region in Canada. That, in a nutshell, is the view from Ottawa, at
the officials level, on the Maritime problem.

Federal investment in economic development came from direct program spending ($70.7 billion in 2003 and 2004) and from tax expendi-
tures. It is very difficult to secure a regional breakdown for either. Both
prime ministers Trudeau and Mulroney pledged to document the effect
of departmental policies and programs on the regions, but this has
never been done.[94]

The Canada West Foundation in its 'Action Plan to Address Western
Discontent' urged the federal government to 'conduct an audit of the
regional distribution of program expenditures.'[95] It is still waiting for
such an audit. The foundation also urged a review 'of the regional
composition of central agencies within the federal government.' It explained that 'while seats at the cabinet table provide political voice, so
too does an effective pressure within the public service. In fact, it can be
argued that the latter is essential if national programming is to reflect
unique regional challenges, assets and aspirations.'[96] It added that a
systematic review of the entire public service was impractical – hence
its call to limit the review initially to central agencies. Such a review is
still also waiting.

The data we obtained for the purpose of this study from several
federal departments reveal that the Maritime provinces do not fare well
under direct program spending. The Maritime provinces have about

6 per cent of Canada's population and 4.4 per cent of its GDP. Data from the Canadian International Development Agency (CIDA) reveal that Ontario and Quebec were able to secure the bulk of 'conditional transfer payments for specified purposes.' Indeed, the proportions accorded to Ontario (51.3 per cent) and Quebec (31.7 per cent) represented a total of 83 per cent of such transfer payment. Ontario leads all regions by a substantial margin under the heading 'transfer payments to conduct research or execute a project.' The region was able to secure about 83 per cent of the grants over $100,000, followed by Quebec (13 per cent) and western Canada (about 4 per cent). When all CIDA contracts and agreements are grouped together, the Maritime provinces were able to secure less than 4 per cent of CIDA funding.[97]

Data on national transportation funding reveal that the Maritime region received about 7 per cent of federal funding under its strategic highway-infrastructure program, less than 6 per cent of the funding 'to enhance quality and safety of passenger rail service (VIA Rail),' while Ontario received 31 per cent, Quebec 38 per cent, and the Western provinces 25 per cent. Ontario, Quebec and British Columbia received about 90 per cent of the funding under Ottawa's Border Infrastructure Fund (BIF).[98]

The Department of Fisheries and Oceans (DFO) has a budget of about $1.5 billion and employs 11,000 people. It is important to stress that the majority of jobs in and revenue from the fishery sector is in Atlantic Canada (about 70 per cent).[99] Yet the three Maritime provinces are home to only 2,843 DFO jobs. The department allocates 26 per cent of its budget to head office in Ottawa, 18 per cent to the three Maritime provinces, and another 4 per cent to the Gulf region, which covers both the Maritimes and Newfoundland and Labrador (for a total of $600 million).

Ottawa-based officials equate political interference in the management of national programs with political patronage, and many point to the establishment of the new public health agency to make their case. In May 2004 the federal government announced that the new agency would be located on two pillars, one in Winnipeg and the other in Ottawa. Politicians from all regions had lobbied hard for the new centre. Winnipeg was declared the winner after it was reported that Treasury Board President Reg Alcock, a Winnipeg MP, successfully lobbied on behalf of his constituency. *Maclean's* magazine later reported that 'the win is now bittersweet. Manitoba officials are privately complaining that few jobs will relocate. Health Canada officials in Ottawa have been told that no one will move. Loser B.C. got two collaborating centres: for Aboriginal and environmental health. And Ontario officials, who kept quiet because the PMO said few jobs would move, are fuming: they fear jobs will shift despite Ottawa's vows – and they're furious that Ontario's pivotal expertise is being tapped for only a collaborative centre on infrastructure, info-structure and new tools development. Whatever that means.' So what have we learned? Ontario Liberal Ross McGregor, a volunteer advocate for the Toronto alliance, is lethal: 'It is an example of our insistence on regional equity at any cost. Or, patronage usually trumps policy.'[100] Again, when the federal government locates a centre in, say, Manitoba, New Brunswick, or British Columbia (e.g., the Tourism Commission move to Vancouver), it will be called 'patronage,' but doing so in Ottawa or Toronto carries no such negative label. Historian Margaret Conrad put things in perspective when she wrote: 'Patronage remains a factor in the region's politics not because there is something in our history or genetic makeup that makes us more corrupt, but because it serves as a way of legitimizing a national policy that does not serve the region very well. Elsewhere in Canada, patronage is dressed up as national policy – the construction of the St. Lawrence Seaway ...'[101]

It is apparent that Ontario assumes that new 'national' research centres and 'national' economic development projects ought to be located in that province, while senior federal public servants will wish to ensure balance between Ontario and Quebec. The same applies to national museums. It seems that only central Canada can properly be home to national museums. New museums are established in the Ottawa-Gatineau area with some regularity (e.g., the Museum of Civilization [1980s], the National Gallery [1980s], and the War Museum [2005] with a minimum of political controversy in the national media. Things were different when the Asper family applied for federal government funding to help build a Canadian Museum of Human Rights in Winnipeg.[102]

The mindset is that when it comes to national initiatives, the focus should be on the Toronto-Ottawa-Montreal corridor, if only to meet international competition. This corridor looks to compete with New York, London, and Tokyo, not with other Canadian regions, and particularly not with the Maritime provinces. The observation of a Toronto-based advertising executive whose firm produced a prominent commercial for the Super Bowl is revealing. He said: 'The fact that we're from Toronto, a relatively small place, the international exposure will hopefully help us.'[103] If Toronto is considered a relatively small place to compete in the global economy, one can only imagine how residents of the Toronto-Ottawa-Montreal corridor must think of Halifax or Moncton.

In recent years, Ottawa has introduced new measures to isolate important national programs and its investment in economic development from political or regional considerations. In February 2002, the government of Canada launched a ten-year innovation strategy designed 'to move Canada to the front ranks of the world's most innovative countries'[104] by turning to arm's-length foundations to deliver the programs.

Lucienne Robillard, the industry minister between December 2003 and July 2004 in the Martin government, looked to the United States and to key sectors located in Ontario and Quebec to guide the work of her department. It is worth quoting her at some length: 'The department's analysis indicates that U.S. productivity growth has outpaced productivity growth in Canada for the following reasons. On average, U.S. firms invest more strongly in capital equipment, which translates directly into higher productivity. There is a large Canada-U.S. innovation gap, reflected in higher levels of R&D spending in the U.S. relative to the size of their economy.' However, she added, 'Canadians have every right to be confident in our economy. We have innovative leaders on the cutting-edge in areas like ICT, biotechnology and nanotechnology. Our automotive industry continues to demonstrate that it has what it takes to attract new investment. We possess an aerospace industry that is of global prominence.'[105]

Ottawa's 2002 'innovation strategy' set a target of developing at least ten internationally recognized technology clusters in Canada by 2010. Existing strengths and clusters already in various stages of maturity were noted, including 'wine in Niagara, aerospace in Montreal, new media in Vancouver, agricultural biotechnology in Saskatoon, information and communications technologies in Ottawa, Toronto and Kitchener-Waterloo ... and a well-established financial services cluster in Toronto.'[106]

Responding to pressure from MPs from Atlantic and western Canada, Industry Canada produced a report in January 2003 on regional perspectives on innovation. The report argued that 'industrial R & D worker per capita is highest in central Canada where opportunities have historically been the greatest' and that 'business investment in R & D is relatively weak in most regions with only Ontario and Quebec being above the national, per capita average.' In the case of the Maritime provinces, the report says that 'private sector R & D performance lags [behind] the rest of the country, industry receptor capacity is a critical challenge and cluster development is in early stages.' It added that 'the [Maritime] region's small and medium-sized universities have diffi- culty competing for R & D programming as currently designed and provincial governments have limited capacity to invest in university growth.' It concluded, however, that ACOA's Atlantic Innovation Fund (AIF) 'has had positive impact, encouraging key industry stakeholders to act in a coordinated fashion.'[107]

The innovation strategy has invested billions in research and devel- opment, the new economy, and in the creation of at least ten interna- tionally recognized technology clusters. The bulk of the investment is being delivered through arm's length agencies or foundations operat- ing free from political interference. As a senior federal official and a key architect of the strategy explained, 'The problem when you launch a new program is that ministers and MPs are always on the lookout to get their share of the spending. The innovation strategy is vitally important to Canada's economic future and we decided to isolate it from this problem. We created foundations where decisions are made strictly on the basis of merit.'[108]

In addition to the innovation strategy, the federal government has funded a number of foundations over the past several years and today they operate completely free of political direction. They include the Canada Foundation for Innovation (given over $3 billion to date), the Canada Research Chairs, the Canada Millennium Scholarship Founda- tion ($2.5 billion), Genome Canada ($435 million), Canadian Health Services Research Foundation ($126 million), Canada Health Infoway Inc. ($500 million), the Trudeau Foundation ($120 million), and the Canada Foundation for Sustainable Development Technology ($100 million). Much like the head offices and activities of the thirty-two Crown corporations established during the Second World War years, these foundations, their head offices, and their activities have little presence in or impact on the economy of the Maritimes. And, much like the Crown corporations, these foundations have had and will continue to have a significant impact on the economies of Ontario, Quebec, and to a lesser extent Alberta and British Columbia.

The foundations are part of neither the private nor public sector; they operate in a kind of no-man's-land. The former head of the Canada Foundation for Innovation (CFI), David Strangway, insists that the foundation is 'a non governmental organization.'[109] He is right, given that ministers, the government, and Parliament have no authority to direct, control, hold to account, or impose sanctions on them. Yet, they are also not part of the private sector because they are not subject to market forces. They are, in fact, self-governing entities that spend public funds but are accountable to no one other than themselves. They are free to operate away from political requirements and regional considerations and that is what they have done.

The innovation strategy and the spending programs of the foundations have concentrated their efforts in southern Ontario, Montreal, to some extent Vancouver, and in some instances in Alberta. The Maritime provinces have been virtually left out. The CFI, for example, has allocated less than 3 per cent of its resources to research activities in the three Maritime provinces, the Canadian Institutes of Health Research about 2.5 per cent, the Canadian Space Agency less than 3.0 per cent, and the Networks of Centres of Excellence less than 2.0 per cent.[110] Per capita spending by the CFI reveals that Quebec secured $63.41 per person and Ontario $51.07. Compare this to $35.37 per person for Prince Edward Island, $33.08 for Nova Scotia, and $15.34 for New Brunswick.[111] Much like the Crown corporations, the head offices of these foundations are located in the Toronto-Ottawa-Montreal corridor. Given this situation, it is difficult to imagine how the Maritime provinces will ever catch up or, for that matter, why Maritimers would favour a strong role for the federal government in economic development. Ottawa's purpose in creating the foundations was to strengthen the 'national' economy and productivity in relation to the United States.

Ontario did very well under foundation programs. The province was awarded over 40 per cent of the funding under the Canadian Institutes of Health Research, 34 per cent under Networks of Centres of Excellence, and 38 per cent under the CFI. It also secured 39 per cent of the funding of the investment in natural science and engineering research. This and other evidence suggest that those who argue that free trade and the north-south economic pull are such that Ontario's economic interests are now less tied to east-west economic relations may well have overstated their case. Interprovincial trade remains important to Ontario, accounting for about 30 per cent of its total trade. Ontario is the centre of Canada's financial services industry, it houses the bulk of head offices of Canadian companies, and the national government and its public service are in tune with Ontario's economic interests. Ontario firms draw more from Canada's network of embassies, and its strong diplomatic presence in the United States, than any other region.[112]

Responding to pressure from Atlantic MPs, the Prime Minister's

Office acknowledged that the government's innovation strategy was bypassing the Atlantic region. As we saw in chapter 8, the Department of Finance, ACOA, and the Prime Minister's Office were asked jointly to produce a $300 million, five-year program designed to strengthen the economy of the four provinces by accelerating the development of knowledge-based industries. The Atlantic Innovation Fund was political in the sense that it held considerable appeal to Atlantic MPs. But it also served to leave the national innovation agenda intact, free from having to deal with regional considerations. The AFI has been no less successful than CFI or other national efforts. Indeed, a mid-term evaluation audit of the AIF conducted in 2004 by an Ottawa-based consulting firm concluded that the program was successful, that it had supported some hundred projects with a total value of more than $625 million, and that it was 'meeting a need that is not met by any other federal program.'[113]

There are limited data on tax expenditures and their regional impact. However, this much we know. The Department of Finance produced an extensive report on tax expenditures and evaluations in 2002, which provided detailed data on personal and corporate income tax expenditures and GST tax expenditures. It had nothing to say, however, about their regional breakdown.[114] Still, the report reveals that the 'scientific research and experimental development investment tax credit' was worth $1.4 billion in 2003; 'partial inclusion of capital gains $2.0 billion, and non taxation of capital gains on principal residences $975 million.'[115] The department produced yet another report on tax expenditure in 2003 and again it was silent on the regional breakdown. It did, however, have a great deal to say about several other issues, including aging baby boomers and the consequent impact on retirement savings.[116] We know from earlier reports, however, that Ontario, Quebec, Alberta, and British Columbia traditionally earn the lion's share of tax expenditures – over 80 per cent of all corporate tax spending. The three Maritime provinces trail these provinces badly, and tax expenditures play only a negligible role in Ottawa's fostering of regional economic development. One federal finance official speculated that tax expenditures with a specific regional development purpose never amount to more than 2 per cent of the total federal tax expenditure budget.[117] But, unlike federal transfer payments, tax expenditures are hardly visible, so it is difficult, without Ottawa's cooperation, to produce a regional breakdown to establish winners and losers.

It is important to note once again that ACOA has met with precious little success in pursuing its advocacy mandate. We saw in chapter 6 that advocacy was one of four mandates given to ACOA when it was established in 1987. It will also be recalled that the 'principal focus of the advocacy function is to influence national decision-making processes, both proactively and relatively.'[118] The agency, even by its own admission, has virtually failed on both of these fronts.[119] Senior agency officials report that, given their limited resources, it is best to employ them where they have an opportunity to make an impact. The advocacy mandate offers no such opportunities.[120]

What about the Provinces?

To be sure, the Maritime provincial governments have long argued that many federal programs have had little impact in the region and that, as a result, they themselves have had to fill in the breach. A body of literature contrasting province building and nation building outlines some of the economic development efforts sponsored by provincial governments, particularly since the 1960s.[121] We know, for example, that both Richard Hatfield and Frank McKenna made economic development a top priority in New Brunswick during their respective tenures as premier (1970 to 1997).

But things have changed of late. The three provincial governments are no longer as active in the field as they once were. For one thing, most of their financial resources are now committed to maintain current levels of services in areas such as health care and education. The government of New Brunswick, for example, allocated $2.06 billion to health care and $1.15 billion to education out of a total expenditure of $5.7 billion in 2004–5.[122] These two sectors account for 56 per cent of the province's total expenditure budget and they represent the two fastest growing spending departments. In comparison, the province allocated only 45.3 per cent of its 1993–4 budget to health and education ($1.8 billion out of a total expenditure of $4 billion).[123] These two sectors have restricted the ability of provincial governments to intervene to promote economic development. Tom Courchene writes that the 1995 federal budget cuts 'compromised every provincial program except health care, since for provincial governments gutting medicare would spell certain electoral defeat ... After balancing the books in 1997 and presenting surpluses ever since, Ottawa has used the fiscal dividend to move into areas of exclusive provincial jurisdiction, such as cities and education, while the cash-starved provinces look on, helpless to spend any new money in their own constitutional domains. While none of this was part of a grand design, Machiavelli would be proud.'[124]

The federal government no longer partners cost-shared agreements with provincial governments in regional economic development. As we saw in earlier chapters, it signed a multitude of cost-shared agreements between 1972 and 2002, transferring funds to the three Maritime provinces to enable them to develop an economic planning capacity and to sponsor wide-ranging projects in every economic sector. These agreements provided 'new' money to the three provincial governments to enable them to become prominent actors in the field and to play an activist role in every economic sector. At least in the Maritime provinces, these were the golden years of province building. Tom Kent explained: 'The region appears to be infected with galloping provincialism. Industrial promotion was in the hands of small provincial units operating in competition with each other.'[125]

The federal government decided to discontinue these agreements in the Maritimes because they did not generate sufficient visibility for the spending of federal dollars. Yet, in 2003 it decided to enter into a new series of federal-provincial economic development agreements with the four western provinces.[126] Without federal dollars specifically allocated for the purpose, the three Maritime governments are much less present in every economic sector than they were twenty or thirty years ago. With few resources available to them, they have had no choice but to abdicate. Ottawa has picked up the slack through its spending power and has sponsored a series of 'national' initiatives, which have had only a modest impact on the region.

Looking Back

Politicians from all regions share one characteristic – they continually seek to influence the geographic distribution of federal employment and contracts. Canadian federal politicians, particularly these from the two most populous provinces, together with the federal policy advisers in Ottawa, are invariably preoccupied with national unity, the economic powerhouse to the south, and the health of Canada's economic heartland. The two central provinces decide which party will form the government and there are precious few checks and balances within the federal government to enable the smaller provinces and regions to have their views count in Ottawa. Big dogs not only eat first, they also have a

large appetite to satisfy when it comes to national economic development policies, federal investment, and the location of federal government activities.

The federal government has an Ontario-Quebec mindset. Its 'national' policies and 'national' programs to promote economic development are particularly well suited to the economic circumstances of
Ontario and, albeit to a lesser extent, Quebec. In any event, national
unity concerns and Canadian prime ministers ensure that Quebec interests will be accommodated by the federal government. At the same
time, national programs, notably foundations that operate away from
political direction, are underrepresented in the Maritime provinces.
National programs to promote economic development have terms and
conditions that inhibit the ability of the Maritime region to participate
(e.g., matching funds, cost-sharing ratios), and in some cases the design
of the program falls outside the region's capacity to participate (e.g.,
federal government investment and innovation).

Transfer payments to the have-less provinces have come in handy as
a form of compensation for the uneven application of these policies and
programs. These payments, however, have fallen out of favour. Some
believe that they hinder economic efficiency. Others insist that they
treat Canadians differently, depending on where they live, with income
being transferred from poorer Canadians in richer regions to richer
Canadians in poorer regions. Ottawa has been listening to these concerns.[127] It has sought to replace transfers to provinces with direct
transfers to individuals (e.g., the Millennium Scholarship Foundation,
the Child Tax Benefit, and the Atlantic Innovation Fund), rather than
through federal-provincial agreements.

Transfer payments are highly visible and lend themselves to comparing which regions gain and which contribute more than they receive.
The government of Ontario and some economists (e.g., Tom Courchene
et al.) led the charge for fair-share federalism, insisting that Ontario was
being short-changed in Ottawa's transfers to the provinces. However,
Ontario and the same economists have been completely silent about the
application of national programs, federal investment in research and
development and innovation, the concentration of the federal policy
capacity in Ottawa, assistance to the auto sector, and so on. Notwithstanding commitments by two former prime ministers (Trudeau and
Mulroney) and calls by such organizations as the Canada West Foundation, there has been no accounting of the regional application of na-

tional programs. Ottawa-based policy makers and their advisers have little interest in undertaking such a study. Big dogs prefer focusing on their own appetites and needs, and the less said about this the better.

There is some comfort for Maritimers in knowing that their relative underdevelopment is not entirely the result of their own failure. National political and administrative institutions designed for a relatively small unitary state (in geographical terms) have, when imported to Canada, defined things as national items that favour the most populous regions (coincidentally, those having the largest number of MPs). Such views reinforced the goal of building a national economy capable of competing with the United States. Thus, the combination of our parliamentary system with the need to forge a strong national economy from a relatively small population base have served to define a national perspective that speaks to the economic interests of central Canada and to concentrate Ottawa's economic development efforts in this region.

Economic development activities are thus to be concentrated to benefit the national economy or the Windsor–Quebec City economic corridor. Economic development activities elsewhere should be tied to local circumstances (e.g., oil and gas in western Canada and the fishery in the Maritime provinces), but they should not be seen to weaken the national economy or what belongs to it (see, for example, Ottawa's decision to abolish the Department of Regional Economic Expansion after it was able to entice Mitel to set up a plant in Bouctouche, New Brunswick, or the awarding of the CF18 contract to a Montreal firm rather than to the lowest bidder from Winnipeg). Ottawa will also not hesitate to overhaul its economic policies at the first hint that the Windsor–Quebec City economic corridor may be weakening. National political cohesion, meanwhile, would be maintained by instituting a system of transfer payments designed to underwrite the cost of uneven economic development but leaving intact the economic relationships that gave rise to uneven development. This in turn has led to embedded ideas among 'national' policy makers and their advisers that Maritimers are less entrepreneurial and less productive and, for these reasons, more dependent on transfer payments than are other Canadians.[128] Institutions and economic interests have over time embedded these ideas, and it is now extremely difficult to change this mindset.

Though Maritimers have learned important lessons, particularly in their dealings with the federal government, the situation will not be helped by moaning about how Confederation dealt the region a bad hand. Such complaints just create despair and ultimately serve to disempower the region. Nurturing a sense of betrayal suggests that the region can never succeed, can never compete with other regions at home or abroad, and that it should simply accept its place in the Canadian family as being 'below the salt.' In any event, establishing the fact that Canada's national political and administrative institutions have a geographical bias is important, but it answers, at best, only half of Paul Martin's question: 'What is the problem and what is the solution?' The next chapter explores the second half of the question.

11 The Solution: Where Can Little Dogs Eat?

In our review of theories of economic and regional development in chapter 3, we concluded that none were just plain wrong, none disobeyed the rules of logic or were flagrant in conflict with known facts. We also saw that, for the most part, they offer little in the way of policy prescriptions that might set the Maritimes on a successful trajectory. This study makes the case that all regional economies depend on some government activism and intervention if they are to grow. Indeed, Canada's economic development has been to some extent shaped by state development strategies, strategies that have had a profound impact on the location of economic activities. The study also shows that national political and administrative institutions and relatively self-contained historical accidents, together with events shaped by public policy decisions, have set in motion cumulative processes of self-reinforcing economic decline in the Maritime provinces.[1] In this chapter we pursue these observations and then look to them to identify prescriptions for economic development in the Maritime provinces.

Accidents of Geography and History

Henry Ford is reported to have said that 'history is just one damn thing after another.' Had Henry Ford been brought up in Calais, Maine, next door to New Brunswick, rather than Dearborn, Michigan, next door to Ontario, the economy of the Maritime provinces may well be vastly different from what it is today. His business acumen and his innovations led to one damn thing after another in the manufacturing sector in Michigan and later in Ontario. The fact that the Maritime provinces have some of the best natural harbours in the world (e.g., Halifax) and that an important part of Canada's oil and gas reserves is in Alberta are also accidents of history. Accidents of history have little connections to the work of national political and administrative institutions, but they will very often favour some economic regions over others. Communities and regions can hope to be visited by positive accidents of history but there is not a great deal that they can do to generate them.

Not all major economic development events or activities flow from accidents of history. Canada's public policy decisions have also given birth to historical events that have shaped economic development for years, influenced the location of economic ventures, and favoured one region over another. The government of Canada engages in a number of endeavours that influence the performance of the economy and the location of economic activities: its broad monetary and fiscal policies; programs that influence the economy whether the consequences are intended or not; programs to assist specific sectors, industries, firms, regions, and communities; trade promotion; investment in research, development, and innovation; government purchases and the location of its own personnel and activities. All of these give rise to historical events that can have a profound influence on the location of economic activities.

Canada, because of the nature and operation of its national political and administrative institutions, has given rise to an abundance of such historical events. Canada, as the Organization for Economic Cooperation and Development pointed out in 2002, has not one economy, but several regional ones with differing characteristics and circumstances.[2] Federal cabinet ministers, departments, and agencies have also spoken of the regional dimension of Canada's economies. However, Canada's political and administrative institutions have operated for the most part as if the country had one national economy. In consequence, some regions have benefited from this perspective while others, in particular the Maritime provinces, have paid a steep price. Canada's economic policies have been 'regionalized' only at the margins and involve the delivery of regional economic development programs and federal transfers both to provincial governments (equalization) and individuals (employment insurance program). But even here the 'national' pull has been and continues to be felt. We saw in earlier chapters how Canada's regional economic development programming was pushed and pulled to every region. Tom Kent, the first deputy minister of the Department of Regional Economic Expansion (DREE), put it succinctly when he wrote, 'if there were incentives for industry in Moncton, why not in

Montreal? ... If a policy applies to all regions, it's national, not regional. What the political doubletalk really meant was that federal measures for economic development gave less and less attention to eastern Canada. So it became easy to say that DREE was a failure and should be abandoned. But the main reason why it so much disappointed expectations was that most of the Ottawa establishment never liked it. The political will behind DREE very soon withered away.'[3] We also saw that even federal-provincial agreements for health care and postsecondary education were placed on a per capita basis shortly after Ontario's campaign for fair-share federalism. Even Ottawa's equalization formula has now been amended to introduce a per capita calculation.

Where Henry Ford grew up may well be an accident of geography, but the Canada-U.S. Auto Pact is not. It was an historical event. The Auto Pact allowed firms to bring parts and autos into Canada without any tariff, provided that the firms created jobs and investment in Canada. The Auto Pact was signed in January 1965 by Prime Minister Lester Pearson and President Lyndon Johnson after months of Washington–Ottawa negotiations.

The agreement benefited large American auto makers and southern Ontario. In exchange for tariff-free access to the Canadian market, the Big Three U.S. auto makers agreed that automobile production in Canada would not fall below 1964 levels and that for every five new cars sold in Canada, three new ones would be built here. The Auto Pact had an immediate effect. In 1964 only 7 per cent of the automobiles built in Canada were sold in the United States; the proportion jumped to 60 per cent by 1968. By 1999 Canada had become the fourth largest auto maker in the world.[4] This sector is the largest component of Canada-U.S. trade: it went from just $715 million in 1964 to $104.1 billion in 1999. There were 146,495 Canadians working in the auto, vehicle, and auto-parts manufacturing industry in 2002.[5] Ontario is home to 130,000 of these jobs – that is, about 90 per cent of all jobs in the industry in Canada.[6] As Jim Stanford explains, all of this development did not 'happen by accident': 'the main instrument [for their developments] was the 1965 Canada-US Auto Pact.'[7] The Auto Pact was a free-trade agreement in one sector in the interest of one region, a region whose economic interests, from an Ottawa point of view at least, flowed quite nicely into a national perspective. It explains why both politicians and senior career officials in Ottawa worked to ensure its signing and implementation. The industry has also been able to secure federal funding in recent years to modernize its operations.[8]

The Auto Pact is hardly the only historical event that has favoured just one region. We saw in chapter 2 that the decision to favour Ontario's iron and steel industry through a tariff was at the expense of Cape Breton's industry and that it had a profound impact on the Maritime region. The Maritime advantage in mining local coal gave way as the federal government pursued the national policy through its tariff structure to permit Ontario to develop its own steel industry using coal imported duty free from the United States. The decision to locate all Crown corporations in Ontario and Quebec during the Second World War and the construction of the St Lawrence Seaway, which served to undercut the superb Maritime ports, strengthened the economy of central Canada, often with serious implications for the Maritime region.

National institutions once again shaped historical events when the federal government put in place a postwar strategy to assist wartime production facilities to make the transition to peacetime production. This strategy greatly assisted central Canadian manufacturing firms to take root and prosper. Not so those in the Maritimes.

The same can be said about the development of the high-tech sector. In a *Saturday Night* magazine article, Charlotte Gray documents by just how much. She writes that the federal government 'is the reason that technology companies took root here [Ottawa and Kanata]. It all began over half a century ago, during the Second World War, when the federally-funded National Research Council attracted a generation of high-calibre scientists to Ottawa.'[9] Gray also explains that Northern Electronic Co. (now Nortel) in 1961 decided to locate its research laboratory just outside Ottawa 'because it wanted its engineers to be close to the government-sponsored scientific community.'[10] Gray could have added that the federal government also helped this Ottawa-based industry with strategic purchases and research and development grants throughout the 1970s, 1980s, and 1990s.

The concentration of Canada's aerospace industry in Montreal began when the federal government decided to locate Canadair in that city during the Second World War. The industry expanded when Saint-Hubert was selected for the Space Agency in the early 1990s. More recently, billions of federal dollars have gone to support the Quebec firm Bombardier in the form of research grants and loan guarantees, including about $1 billion in research and development funds since 1972. Bombardier has repaid only $275 million of the research and development money.[11] The Canadian government has played and continues to play a key role in the industry in other ways: it supports the National Research Council wind tunnels in which newly designed aircraft can be tested, it pays for costly projects like the Canadarm, and provides funds directly to the industry for a variety of purposes.[12] Quebec business and labour leaders recently urged the federal government to commit itself more fully with funds to the aerospace sector and also to recognize that Quebec is 'the logical place' to concentrate new activities 'since 62 percent of the country's aerospace sector is in the province.' The group urged Ottawa 'to hand over to the aerospace industry the remaining $500-million from a $1 billion R & D fund, after lavishing half of it on Ontario's auto sector.'[13] In fact, through the establishment of Crown corporations and its interventionist policies and programs, Ottawa sought to create clusters long before the term became fashionable in the literature. The clusters, however, were concentrated in southern and eastern Ontario, notably Ottawa, and in Montreal. Historical events shaped by public policy initiatives, which were in turn shaped by Canada's national political-administrative institutions, account for the development of these clusters. They were not just historical accidents.

The Maritime provinces have often looked to Ottawa to create regional economic development programs and for redistributive spending. Redistributive spending explains why Ottawa has traditionally been able to count on the three Maritime provinces to support a strong interventionist role for the federal government. However, the language of both redistributive spending and regional economic development is no longer as politically saleable as it once was. For one thing, it lacks the cachet of the language of national economic development. Though the facts may not square with the notion, national economic development implies no regional favourites, while regional economic development does. The regional language has always run the risk of being perceived in Ottawa as detracting from the national policy. But Ottawa's regional policies, as previous chapters show, have always been borderline, best described as add-ons, often politically motivated to meet the expectations of MPs from slow-growth regions. Described by Janine Brodie as 'patching the cracks of uneven development,' they have been tolerated in Ottawa but never accepted as an integrated part of national economic policies and programs.[14] Dalton Camp observed, after working as senior adviser in the Privy Council Office in the late 1980s, that the 'Ottawa system fights off regional economic development issues like antibodies.'[15] The rise of the global economy and the consequent desire to be competitive in the global economy has also served to put downward pressures on federal transfers or interregional transfers to slow-growth provinces.

As well, the national mindset is fuelled by the strength of the political power in the two central provinces, in particular Ontario. There is the financial pull of Toronto, the intellectual influence of the academic communities in the Windsor–Quebec City corridor, the national media, and the policy-advisory capacity of the national public service located in Ottawa virtually in its entirety. Then there are the think-tanks, research institutes, lobbyists, and policy consultants also operating, for the most part, out of Ottawa. The regional policy mindset, meanwhile, is left to some members of Parliament, the local media, provincial governments, and regional business communities. This mismatch is such that the government of Canada has not been able to think about the economy in both a national and regional context. The result is that the national mindset inevitably protects the economic interests of the Windsor–Quebec City corridor. In short, the national interest and the interest of the manufacturing heartland of central Canada flow quite nicely into one another and they have come together on many occasions to create positive historical events. Moreover, whenever threatened by the regional interests of either western or Atlantic Canada, the national mindset wins.

The Political-Administrative Framework Is No Accident

Margaret Conrad writes that 'the structure of Confederation created the framework for the [Maritime] region's marginalization ... Small political jurisdictions had little chance of shaping national policy to meet their needs.'[16] Sir John A. Macdonald wanted the British unitary model of legislative union and, if it were not possible to eliminate the provinces altogether, he wished to minimize their role so that all substantive issues would be the responsibility of the central government. He labelled this model 'the best, the cheapest, the most vigorous, and the strongest system of government we could adopt.'[17] However, legislative union was not acceptable: Quebec and a good number of political leaders from the Maritime provinces would have certainly opposed such a model. The solution was federalism, which Macdonald reluctantly accepted. Federalism was a new concept in 1867 and the only model available was the American one. As Jennifer Smith writes: 'It was not terribly popular [and], at the time the Canadians were embarking on the Confederation project, the Americans were fighting a civil war. The federal system, or at least the American version, was suspected to be a contributing factor.'[18] Macdonald and other Fathers of Confederation of like mind saw little merit in moving too far away from the British unitary model by embedding in the constitution or in national political institutions effective mechanisms for small provinces to protect their economic interests. The mother country had made no provision for this, and they saw little need for it in Canada. It explains why they looked to the British House of Lords rather than to the American Senate as a model for the upper house in Canada's Parliament.

Some Maritime leaders did express deep concern over the Confederation framework. Joseph Howe of Nova Scotia argued that political power would always be in central Canada because there would be no countervailing forces outside of that region to offset it.[19] A.J. Smith of New Brunswick urged the authors of Canada's constitution to 'give small provinces at least the guard which they have in the United States (i.e., an equal and effective Senate), although we ought to have more, because, here, the popular branch [i.e., the executive branch] is all-powerful.'[20]

Macdonald and others at the Confederation conference maintained that if the smaller provinces needed an advocate in Ottawa, then cabinet would be their voice. Christopher Dunkin, who would become minister of agriculture in the government of Sir John A. Macdonald, argued in 1865 that the 'cabinet here must discharge all that kind of function which in the United States is performed in the federal sense, by the Senate.'[21] Cabinet, however, has never been an effective vehicle for the regional perspective, leaving aside the odd 'breakaway' generated by the likes of Maritimers Allan J. MacEachen and Roméo LeBlanc. The role of regional ministers has been in decline for the past twenty years. Jim Meek, a Halifax-based journalist, writes: 'Atlantic Canada hasn't had a godfather in the federal cabinet since the Mulroney era when John Crosbie played that part so bombastically on the region's behalf. In the Trudeau years, the ministerial power broker for the region was Allan J. MacEachen. I spent twenty years criticizing the politics that MacEachen and Crosbie represented, but now that they and their like have disappeared from the landscape, I sort of miss the breed ... These guys actually got things done.'[22]

Effective political power has shifted from powerful regional ministers and even full cabinet to a small group of 'carefully selected courtiers,' mainly in the Prime Minister's Office, but also in the Privy Council Office and the Department of Finance. Hand-picked pollsters and some members of cabinet are also part of this select group.²³ In any event, the regional composition of the federal cabinet, which is not established in the constitution, has changed considerably over time. The notion that one-third of the cabinet would be from the Maritime provinces can now be found only in history books. One would be hard-pressed to imagine how, today, cabinet could be described as acting within the national government to protect the interests of small provinces.

Such facts are not to suggest that the regional perspective has entirely withered away. Provincial premiers have stepped up to the plate. They and their governments not only develop and manage provincial policies and programs, but they also represent the interests of their provinces in Ottawa and, increasingly in recent years, in international fora. The result is that the role of provincial premiers has expanded far beyond what the Fathers of Confederation anticipated.

Provincial premiers have become particularly adroit at pushing Ottawa for more federal money to deliver health-care services, education, and federal-provincial programs. Federal-provincial conferences have certainly served to make the premiers more visible on the national scene and contributed to the notion of an equitable regional distribution of the economic benefits of Canadian federalism. Premiers can take on the prime minister before television cameras and push the envelope as far as they wish in the interests of their province. They have all the incentives to do so and suffer no consequences if they go too far. Goading Ottawa to do more is always good politics back home; moreover, the premiers have no responsibility if the federal treasury goes into deficit or if a particular goal of federal spending miscarries.

That said, there are significant limits on the role of provincial premiers. It is the federal government that calls for federal-provincial conferences and that usually shapes the agenda. These conferences are necessary for holding constitutional talks, as was the case in the early 1980s, and for striking new fiscal arrangements. They do not, however, always have to be held before television cameras. Jean Chrétien, for example, avoided televised conferences whenever he could, knowing full well that they provided an opportunity for the premiers to play to the audience back home. In addition, though the premiers will try to influence many public policy issues, their political legitimacy centres around amending the constitution and fiscal federalism, not on federal government programs.

It is one thing to agree on the need for Ottawa to transfer more money to the provinces for health care, it is quite another to agree on the shape of national economic policies. When it comes to the latter, premiers, no matter their political affiliation, stand where they sit. The premiers of Ontario and New Brunswick will have perspectives vastly different from each other, whether they are Liberal, NDP, or Conservative. In addition, provincial premiers do not work in Ottawa, where national economic policies take shape, new public investments in research and development and Crown corporations are struck, and key program decisions are made.

In many instances, premiers learn of new initiatives through the media like the rest of us, when it is too late to influence their direction. This explains in part why the premiers agreed in December 2003 to create a Council of the Federation and locate its offices in Ottawa. The council has several purposes, including analysing 'actions or measures of the federal government that in the opinion of the members have a major impact on provinces and territories. This could include joint review and comment on bills and acts of the Parliament of Canada, as is currently done by provinces and territories individually. One of the purposes of this analysis is to support productive discussions with the federal government on issues of importance to Canadians.'[24] The council may be located in Ottawa but that doesn't make it part of the federal machinery or of its national political institutions. The council, like the premiers, will be on the outside, looking in, as national economic policies take shape. 'The bottom line,' as Jennifer Smith writes, 'is that no body within the federal government is designed to represent the provinces or to speak for them in federal councils.'[25] This, together with the majoritarian bias of Parliament, explains in no small measure why Ottawa has national economic policies driven by the economic interests of Canada's heartland, and redistributive policies that are geared to the slower-growth provinces. Redistributive policies have been the price Ottawa has decided to pay to pursue a regional policy for central Canada, disguised as national policy. However, the past fifty years have shown that redistributive policies do not produce positive historical events in economic development. The past twenty years have shown that Ontario is less and less willing to support redistributive policies, as the fair-share-federalism and closing-the-gap debates reveal.

What to do? It is hardly original to write that in a federation as large and as diverse as Canada, national political institutions need a capacity to speak for smaller provinces and regions. We can only stress that Senate reform, which would serve to give voice to the smaller provinces at the national level, is long overdue. We also stress that it would not weaken the national government. Roger Gibbins explains that, in the case of the United States, 'Effective territorial representation within national political institutions has promoted national integration, strengthened the national government, broadened its reach, and reduced the power of state governments to a degree unimagined in the founding years of the American republic.' He adds that 'strengthening regional representation at the centre would provide a mechanism for the further nationalization of Canadian policies.'[26] One could add that, coincidentally or not, American regional economic development policy has been quite different from the Canadian experience; in the United States, different regions have taken turns at high growth far more than they have in Canada.[27] There are powerful forces in Canada resisting Senate reform. Otherwise it would have been done a long time ago. Much as big dogs do not easily share their food, there are clear advantages for certain provinces and regions to leave well enough alone when they see no reason for change.

Creating Regional Perspectives in National Policy

A genuine regional perspective has had little currency in Ottawa over the years. Canada's political leaders claim to recognize that there is a problem – or at least say they do. Shortly after becoming leader of the Liberal Party, Paul Martin lamented the fact that 'when a regional issue arises in central Canada it very quickly becomes a national issue,' but that this is not the case for other regions. He added: 'We cannot allow national issues in British Columbia to be relegated to the sidelines as regional issues,'[28] and then explained: 'What I am talking about is the absolute necessity of reducing the distance between the nation's capital and the regions of the country, a distance which is not measured in kilometres, but a distance which is often measured in attitude.'[29] Stephen Harper, for his part, has continuously stressed the need for 'a greater voice for regions outside Quebec and Ontario.'[30] Even the Ottawa-based senior public service has started to recognize the problem in recent years. A task force consisting of senior career officials tabled a report in 2002 which concluded that what 'works in one part of the country may not work in another [, that] ... structures and processes for working together vary from region to region,' and that there was a 'weak federal ability to respond nationally to key regional issues.'[31]

Canada's political leaders – even those in Ottawa – can blame particular provinces for the country's inability to reform national political institutions, most notably, of course, the Senate. But the government of Canada is free to overhaul its own policy-making and administrative machinery, if it so wishes. There is no federal-provincial agreement, nor are there any constitutional requirements, that would stop it from substantially decentralizing its policy-advisory capacity, its operations, or its internal policy-making process. Indeed, the federal government could do away with sectoral departments (such as transport or fisheries and oceans) and replace them with spatial or regional departments to assume their functions and programs simply by submitting a bill to Parliament and securing its approval.

The challenge to the federal government, then, is to adjust its administrative practice to acknowledge the fact that Canada's economy is made up of several regional economies and that economic policies (with the exception of monetary policy) can be recast from a regional perspective. To do so would serve Canada and its regions well. How much more evidence do we need to prove that redistributive policies will not help the economies of the Maritime provinces to grow? Different historical events need to be generated in these regions, and federal policies could play a crucial part in doing so. Western Canada, too, has expressed deep concern over the years about its ability to be heard in Ottawa. Robert Roach of the Canada West Foundation writes: 'Westerners are not complaining about not getting their way – they are frustrated by the fact that their ideas, aspirations and concerns are often misunderstood or ignored in Ottawa.'[32]

At the risk of oversimplification, the federal government policy-making machinery works as follows. The prime minister and a handful of advisers run the policy process and shape the government's policy agenda to the extent they wish or their crowded agenda will allow. We know that the role of the national media is vitally important to the prime minister and his or her immediate advisers. They monitor it, and they are deeply influenced by it. Public opinion surveys and focus groups are also important in shaping the agenda. When policy issues matter a great deal to them or go to the heart of the government's political interests, all the policy levers at the centre of government will be employed to shape the government's response. The same applies when the prime minister wishes to pursue a specific policy initiative. We saw in the previous chapter the comparatively recent practice of policy by announcement. This practice also serves to strengthen the hand of the prime minister and his close advisers.[33]

For the most part, however, new policies and new programs emerge from an elaborate, porous consultative and policy-making process and are increasingly the product of many hands. The relevant line department may initiate the process, but it cannot get very far without engaging in elaborate interdepartmental meetings. From there, 'stakeholders' have to be consulted and a public consultation process put in place. A typical process can take up to two years and involve over twenty federal departments and agencies.[34]

In both instances, the process is lodged in Ottawa and is the product of Ottawa hands. Central agencies (the Prime Minister's Office, the Privy Council Office, the Department of Finance, and the Treasury Board Secretariat) oversee the process. Together they employ close to 4,000 mostly career officials, who, again, all work in Ottawa. They do not manage programs or deliver services to Canadians. Rather, they advise on policy, ensure some degree of interdepartmental policy coherence, prepare the fiscal framework and an annual budget, and oversee the expenditure budget and human management issues within government. When it comes to shaping policy, they deal with policy units in line departments and agencies headed by an assistant deputy minister, or the level just below the deputy minister, who is the administrative head of departments. Virtually all of these people and their staffs live and work in Ottawa. They brief ministers, attend interdepartmental policy meetings, and draft policy or program proposals. They spend an inordinate amount of time working out conflicts or potential conflicts with other departments. Yet, with all the talk about horizontal government, line departments still operate as silos and still pursue their sectoral interests and protect their departmental turf.[35]

The regional perspective is left to regional agencies – the Atlantic Canada Opportunities Agency and Western Economic Diversification Canada (WD). In addition, a good part of the federal program- and service-delivery capacity is located in regional offices. Ottawa-based officials will turn to regional agencies and offices for regional input. Yet the ability of either to influence Ottawa has been modest. For one thing, program managers are not policy specialists, and they do not have the skills or the time to participate in a more than cursory way in the policy process. Policy specialists in regional offices are few in numbers and have difficulty in being heard in policy units in line departments, let alone in central agencies. As we saw in chapter 5, Ottawa-based officials have borrowed from the British Empire the phrase 'going native' to describe federal regional officials who have come to identify with the region and its interests, while paying insufficient attention to the national interest.[36]

The Atlantic Canada Opportunities Agency (ACOA) has had little success in advocating the economic interest of Atlantic Canada because of limited resources. The fact that the federal government and Parliament would delegate the 'advocacy function' to a small government agency with its head office in Moncton speaks volumes. The ACOA act reads: 'The object of the Agency is to support and promote opportunity for economic development of Atlantic Canada ... through advocacy of the interests of Atlantic Canada in national economic policy, program and project development and implementation.'[37] It would be unthinkable for the federal government to delegate such responsibility for Ontario to a single agency. Again, one can only underline that the regional interests of Ontario are considered central to the national policy, while those of the Atlantic provinces might as well be delegated to a small agency on the periphery of the Ottawa machinery of government. At the same time, federal departments have virtually no policy specialists in the Maritime region.[38]

Regional ministers thus have little support from the bureaucracy to draw from in trying to influence the Ottawa policy- and decision-making process. They can ask the relevant provincial government for support, but this is hardly practical for obvious political, administrative, and accountability reasons. In brief, regional ministers, other ministers, and members of Parliament already have a community and a provincial and regional perspective to support, but they have no place to turn to for assistance in developing a case in Ottawa for their region. They also have no capacity to assess the application of federal programs in their communities and regions or to look at emerging policy issues and the likely impact on their regions. Examples abound: what does the emerging 'cities agenda' or the Kyoto protocol mean for the Maritime provinces, and how can federal research and development measures be tailored to correspond to the region's economic circumstances? Without a capacity to influence policy from a regional perspective, regional representatives will simply paw at the cabinet table and at the Ottawa system in the hope of bringing as many juicy morsels of government spending as they can to their community and region. Little dogs too have an appetite.

The problem is not limited to the lack of effective means of articulating a regional perspective in the policy process. There is also a lack of

program coordination on the ground, as attested to by public consultations held for Canada's Innovation Strategy and the Prime Minister's
Task Force on Urban Issues. Community leaders raised the point over
and over again that federal programs are 'un-coordinated' and 'poorly
integrated.'[39]

Moving a few organizational boxes around will achieve little. The
goal should be to transform government operations on the ground and
to strengthen the regional voice in shaping national policies. This would
also have a number of positive spin-offs: for businesses it would mean
easier access to government programs; for individuals, more programs
tailored to their personal needs; and for communities, government
programs with a community focus rather than a sectoral one. Government policies would be better able to blend social and economic perspectives, and, for national policy matters, there would be a greater
understanding of regional opportunities and socioeconomic realities.

The lack of program coordination is particularly visible on the ground
where programs and services are delivered. The entrepreneurs and the
business community in New Brunswick or Nova Scotia, as in all other
provinces, must navigate programs lodged in several federal departments, agencies, and Crown corporations – some with small offices in
their communities but in most cases not – to explore what services may
be available. In addition, while separating economic from social policy
may make sense in Ottawa, it does not on the ground.

National requirements in program implementation can play havoc
with economic development measures in the regions. An example will
make the point. ACOA has a program to assist its managers to provide
for 'easy and immediate access to consultant support' to deal with
problems or opportunities. Funding is modest, on average less than
$4,600 per case. ACOA decided to enter into an agreement with Con-
sulting and Audit Canada, a unit with the federal Department of Public
Works and Government Services (PWGS) to deliver the services. Given
the modest amount of funding, the selection process of consultants was
straightforward: a consultant (for example, a retired business person)
could be selected and out in the field working within only a few days.

In the aftermath of the sponsorship scandal, PWGS introduced more
demanding requirements in selecting consultants: a list of potential
consultants has to be produced and a process has to be in place to select
the winner of the contract. The process now takes on average more than
two weeks to produce a contract worth on average $4,600.[40] The condi-
tions were imposed because of developments in Quebec, not in Atlantic

Canada, but ACOA has to live with them. In addition, the conditions make little sense for a program that is designed to respond quickly to opportunities or problems and that involves only a modest sum of public money. A capacity to view program implementation from a regional perspective would have kept in place the simple decision-making process. ACOA officials insist that the program has, in the past, prevented a number of small businesses from shutting down and permitted others to pursue new opportunities, but that new administrative requirements are seriously inhibiting its continued success.[41]

Lack of policy and program capacity on the ground has also led to roadblocks that have inhibited economic development. One case will illustrate the point. As Frank McKenna reported in a March 2004 speech before the Atlantic Mayors' Congress: 'To obtain a permit to drill for oil or gas, it takes approximately 180 days in the United Kingdom, 200 days in Norway, 300 days in the Gulf of Mexico and 650 days in Atlantic Canada.'[42] Governments cannot guarantee the quantity of the resource that might be available, or the depth of the water and climate that the industry must deal with to access oil and gas under the area. But governments can control their regulatory regimes. One can speculate, however, that it would take much less than 650 days if Ontario or Quebec had substantive oil and gas reserves. As Brian Crowley writes: 'Only Ottawa, the owner of the resource, has the power to clean up the mess ... Where is Ottawa's so-called Smart Regulation initiative when you really need it?'[43]

Changes are needed at the very top to give voice to the regional perspective in Ottawa. A new senior-level cabinet committee, made up of the prime minister and all regional ministers, should be established to which all economic and social development proposals would be submitted. If the past forty years have taught us anything, it is that setting up a never-ending parade of regional development departments and agencies in the hope that someday the problem will go away – so that more serious matters like Ontario's competitiveness, new developments in the auto or the aerospace sectors, and national unity concerns can be properly addressed – does not work.

The regional perspective is in large part a matter of politics, and, to find its footing in Ottawa, it needs political commitment. The fact that the federal public service is still organized along functional or sectoral lines, with line departments pursuing specific sectoral objectives, not regional ones, is a political matter, not an administrative one. The fact that the great majority of senior public service positions are in Ottawa, not in the regions, is a political decision, not an administrative one. The fact that no sustained effort has ever been made to document and understand the effect of departmental policies and programs on specific regions – despite firm commitments made by Prime Ministers Trudeau and Mulroney that such investigations would be done – is a political failure, not an administrative one. And Ottawa's decision to abandon its policy of decentralizing federal government jobs from Ottawa to slow-growth regions was a political decision, not an administrative one.

Assuming that the required political will exists, central agencies should decentralize part of their operations to those regions where a new regional policy capacity needs to be created. The capacity should deal with all important economic sectors in the region and be concentrated in a single office. Regional ministers should be given support through dedicated staff from central agencies to represent the regional perspective in Ottawa.

A new regional agency patterned on ACOA, WD, and CED (Canada Economic Development for Quebec Regions) should be established for Ontario and smaller ones for the North and for Newfoundland and Labrador.[44] This would provide a symmetrical approach to economic development. The symmetrical approach would in turn bring *all* regional perspectives to the policy table in Ottawa on an equal footing. In fact, Joe Volpe, Ontario's regional minister in the Martin government, has already proposed a regional agency patterned on ACOA to his Ontario colleagues.[45] To be sure, the economic challenges confronting Ontario are vastly different from those facing the Maritime provinces, but they exist, just the same. Ontario continues to need skilled knowledge workers and the continued competitiveness of some sectors, including automobiles and steel, needs to be addressed. At the moment, Ontario (leaving aside FedNor) does not have a regional agency, but now, no less than other regions, it has its regional economic interests to promote. The global economy and the north-south economic pull resulting from NAFTA entail different challenges for Ontario than was the case some twenty years ago when east-west trade links were stronger. Canada's North is also very different from what it was when federal regional economic development efforts were first introduced. There are significant economic opportunities emerging in the North and a regional perspective, and a stronger voice from the North may well be necessary if they are to be successfully pursued.

Today's economic circumstances are a far cry from the days when

Ottawa's modern machinery of government was put in place by the Trudeau government in the late 1960s and early 1970s. The 'one size fits all' policy framework has never squared well with all regions. It will make even less sense in the coming years. Consider this: Canada's three largest cities face problems of fiscal capacity and physical infrastructure, as well as social issues. Such concerns are of little direct interest to the Maritime provinces, but they matter a great deal to Ontario, Quebec, and British Columbia, and will some day to Alberta. The next twenty-four largest cities will wish to focus on entrepreneurship, investment, trade, and promoting innovation networks with other communities, which will be of some interest to the Maritime region because of the Halifax–Moncton economic corridor. The next hundred cities and towns will look to the primary resource sectors for continued economic development, which will be of strong interest to the Maritime region. Finally rural, remote, and Native communities all have serious economic challenges, most notably a continuing loss of population, and such concerns will be of strong interest to the Maritimes.[46] All of these communities have to think in terms of the global economy and look to regions outside Canada as much as to other Canadian regions for future economic development. The federal government needs to have the machinery to respond to this changing reality, even if in some instances the solution is to do nothing or to propose measures that may be difficult to sell politically, such as encouraging out-migration from some communities.

It is worth quoting at length Tom Courchene on the changing nature of Canada's national economy. He writes:

'The bottom line is as profound as it is daunting – Canada is progressively less and less a single national economy and more and more a series of regional cross-border economies. One way to appreciate what is at stake here is to recognize that Canada's 1879 'National Policy' (which combined high tariffs, subsidized east-west rail links and the settlement of the West) was designed to forge an east-west country in the face of the north-south pull of population, trade and geography. The fact that Canada is perennially at or near the top of the United Nations Human Development Index serves as convincing testament to the success of this nation-building strategy. However, under FTA/NAFTA as both catalyst and driver, the upper half of North America is now in full evolutionary flight – the tariffs are gone, the west is settled, and the railways themselves are veering north-south, with the result that trade is reverting to patterns more consistent with continental geography and population centres.'[47]

If Canada's economy is to be recast in a series of regional economies to a greater extent than it is at the moment, then Ottawa's machinery of government also needs to be recast accordingly.

Ottawa must reform the machinery of government to give voice to all regions on an equal footing. This in itself would likely attenuate regional tensions in the country – with Ontario ministers often making the case that they do not have access to a regional agency, while ministers from other regions claiming that Ontario receives the bulk of federal funding and that federal policies and activities are invariably designed to promote Ontario's interest. But it would also strengthen the ability of the cabinet and ministers to play an active role in federal-provincial and community relations, promote a stronger program coordination on the ground, and contribute to a better country-wide ability to deal with competition and economic-adjustment issues.

A new regional policy capacity could undertake a number of initiatives. It could look at trade promotion from a regional rather than from a national perspective. If, with the Canada–U.S. and North American free trade agreements, trade patterns are reverting to those more consistent with continental geography, then Canada's machinery of government needs to respond. It could, for example, look at immigration policy and see how new Canadians could be encouraged to settle outside of Toronto, Vancouver, and Montreal.

As another initiative, the federal government could carry out a cost-benefit analysis of locating government units outside of Ottawa. One thing is clear – the number of public servants in the National Capital Region in general and central agencies in particular has grown since the program review of the mid-1990s. Between 1994 and 2004, as the regions' share of federal public servants dropped by nearly 25 per cent, the National Capital Region's share gained by several percentage points, and the Privy Council Office by 24 per cent.[48] Some studies have concluded that government units are more productive (less staff turnover) and cheaper to operate in the regions than in Ottawa. There is also reason to believe that federal public servants in the regions have not been plagued by the kinds of morale problems that have been evident for the past twenty years or so in Ottawa.[49] If the need to strengthen productivity in the private sector is being felt, the need applies equally to the public sector. Canada could benefit from Britain's example, where a 'review of public sector relocation from London and the South East' identified '20,000 jobs that could be relocated as a first tranche.'[50] If this makes sense in Britain, a country not nearly as regionalized as Canada, then it certainly warrants serious consideration in Ottawa. The prime minister and cabinet need a thorough and objective review of government decentralization, to assess its potential as an economic development tool and to determine the validity of claims that government units operating outside of Ottawa are more efficient and productive than those in Ottawa.[51]

Looking in the Mirror

The previous chapters make the case that regional problems are not simply a matter of Maritimers and Westerners nurturing a sense of betrayal or victimization. They are rooted in history and go to the heart of the inability of our national political and administrative institutions to accommodate Canada's regions, particularly the outer regions. Maritimers should understand that their region's relative underdevelopment is not entirely their own fault. Canada's national policies and its political administration have dealt the region a bad hand. A look at history will highlight the damage that has been done by over one hundred years of being relegated to the periphery of the national economy and, to some extent, by historical accidents and historical events shaped in large measure by national policies.

It may well provide a degree of comfort to Maritimers to recognize that their region's relative underdevelopment is not all their doing, but its value is essentially limited to this realization. For one thing, in the ahistorical world of politics and public policy, there is no market for this line of argument outside the region, as it speaks to the past, not the future. Kelly Toughill, of the *Toronto Star*, attended the fiftieth anniversary of the Atlantic Provinces Economic Council in October 2004 and reported: 'Many politicians here conjure up the Maritimes' pre-Confederation glory days as a starting point for a long diatribe about how the region has been hard-done by Canada.'[52] Yes, Confederation did deal the region a bad hand. But to dwell on the past is to give up, to accept that the region can never transform its economy, can never compete at home or abroad. However, given NAFTA and the fact that the Maritime region is now unfettered from the National Policy and its explicitly discriminatory tariff policies, perhaps it's time to bury the past and look to the future.

The Maritime provinces remain a 'region of the mind,' if only because Canada's constitution creates provincial communities, not regional ones.[53] Regions of the mind have little in the way of policy instruments to promote economic development. The constitutional framework empowers provincial governments to establish policies and programs, and, by ricochet, it inhibits a multi-province or regional perspective. There is a built-in inertia at the political, institutional, and bureaucratic levels that makes regional planning and integration extremely difficult. The individual Maritime provinces have shown little enthusiasm in the past to get together to promote regional economic development. The result is that regional issues will surface only when the premiers see a political advantage in raising them or when they wish to pressure Ottawa for additional transfer payments and the like to the three provinces.

Much has changed in the national and global economies over the past thirty years, but the structure of our institutions has not, and this is also true of our provincial governments – particularly so in the case of the three Maritime provincial governments, where a kind of institutional sclerosis has set in. Efforts to promote Maritime union or, failing that, closer interprovincial cooperation as attempted by former New Brunswick premier Louis J. Robichaud, amounted, in the end, to little. In 1979 the Atlantic Provinces Economic Council (APEC) claimed that the 'Atlantic region appears to be infected with galloping provincialism.' It went on to argue that economic development was in the hands of 'small provincial units operating in competition with each other.' Separately, the APEC maintained, the units were too 'unsophisticated' and lacked 'coordination among them.'[54]

Since 1979 the economy of the three Maritime provinces has become weaker and is poised to become weaker still. The old economy will continue to shrink, and the new economy involves research and development, scientific and technological sophistication, and an ability for governments and entrepreneurs to work together. With increasing regional integration spanning the U.S.-Canada border, size is becoming more significant. Roger Gibbins goes to the heart of the matter when he writes, 'If regions are in fact important motors for the new global economy, then the Canadian regions best equipped to compete in the global economy are the provincial regions, Ontario and Quebec. Only they possess a single government and thus the capacity to act quickly and strategically.'[55]

The federal government pays lip service to the importance of interprovincial cooperation but does not promote it with any degree of enthusiasm. Federal regional development efforts, as earlier chapters show, have been until recently a history of federal-provincial agreements, not federal-regional agreements. Tom Kent, DREE's first deputy minister, says that when the Council of Maritime Premiers was being established, he suggested that 'if the three provinces pooled their efforts at industrial promotion, creating one regional agency at least for a trial period of a few years, DREE would undertake to reimburse half of the agency's costs. The offer was received with polite inaction.'[56] The response speaks not only to Ottawa's reluctance to promote interprovincial cooperation aggressively through its spending powers, but equally to the unwillingness of the three provincial governments to cooperate, even when financial incentives are made available.

If the Maritime region wishes to become an actor on the world stage, the three provincial governments will have to cooperate closely and join forces to mount an economic development strategy. The economic literature tells us that 'population and employment will continue to concentrate in and around large urban areas; the effect of technological change has been to facilitate the geographic concentration of employment; distance is not dead, out-migration of the young and the educated makes job creation more difficult, knowledge-based institutions are sensitive to volume (i.e., quality and quantity of the knowledge infrastructure), peripheral regions can succeed but city size and location matter.'[57] Public-policy analysts and practitioners also agree that a Maritime perspective and joining of forces would be more effective than the three provincial units operating separately. Premier Binns of Prince Edward Island maintains that the prosperity of his province depends on 'people, energy, transportation and government policy,'[58] yet it is difficult to imagine that a jurisdiction with only 130,000 residents can mount an effective public policy strategy for these sectors on its own.

Former New Brunswick premier Frank McKenna has called for a regional securities regulator, more ambitious research and innovation, greater regional cooperation in energy, new emphasis in human-resources development, and greater efforts to attract new Canadians to the region. He concludes his wish list by saying that 'cooperation is easy to say, but hard to do. We have been afflicted by decades of parochialism, both amongst our provinces and within our provinces.'[59] He outlined several areas for closer cooperation, ranging from transportation to education. The former president of New Brunswick Power, Stewart MacPherson, argued that 'New Brunswick and the Maritimes are too small' and that what is needed at 'a minimum is one Maritime market.'[60] David Cameron recently took stock of regional cooperation in postsecondary education going back several decades and suggested that the region might 'increase its competitiveness as a region if it could somehow pool its resources so as to take on the big players in central and western Canada, not to mention the United States.' He writes: 'The story of post-secondary education in Atlantic Canada is the story of forces pulling in opposite directions, one toward integration and the other toward provincial independence. There is a price to be paid for this, but so far it is one the region seems willing to pay.'[61] It is interesting to note that, despite Cameron's analysis, postsecondary education is one sector that has made progress, in relative terms, in promoting a multiprovince perspective in the Maritime region.

All in all, the Maritime provinces, acting as a single entity rather than three separate ones, would stand a much better chance of attracting new Canadians, marketing their economic strengths and products abroad, rationalizing their physical infrastructure, promoting greater coherence and efficiency in human-resources development, and assisting small businesses to identify new markets in other regions and abroad. A specific case will clarify the point. As in other regions, urban areas are showing strong growth and solid job creation in the Maritimes. A new urban concept, the Halifax–Moncton corridor, has emerged in recent years because of its economic development potential. The corridor's population represents nearly 40 per cent of the population of New Brunswick and Nova Scotia, and its population in recent years has grown much faster than either the Nova Scotia and New Brunswick averages. Since 1988 over 35,000 people (net) have moved into the corridor; its age profile is younger than the provincial averages; new Canadians prefer moving here over other parts of the Maritime region; the number of employment insurance claimants has declined faster than elsewhere in the region; and taxpayers in the corridor pay more income taxes (from 7.9 to 17.4 per cent) than in other parts of the region. These positive developments, along with new investment, are taking place not only in Halifax and Moncton but in numerous communities between the two cities, hence the reference to a corridor.[62]

Community economic development associations in both Halifax and Moncton have sought to promote the corridor's development through new research and development and by attracting investment and marketing initiatives. The provincial governments, however, have not been enthusiastic about the initiative. Prince Edward Island, of course, sees no immediate benefit for itself from the corridor. In the case of New Brunswick and Nova Scotia, provincial political and bureaucratic actors play to their audiences, and their responses reflect past experience and province-centred political bureaucratic structures. But, much as political will is required in Ottawa to give voice to the regional perspective within the federal government, so political will is also needed in the three provincial capitals in the Maritimes if the region is to capture emerging economic opportunities and position itself in the continental and global economy.

It is hardly possible to point to a single policy field where the Maritime region would not benefit from a multiprovince perspective: regulatory policies; tax policy; trade and investment promotion; attracting new Canadians; research and development; securing more risk capital to move the region's industrial structure up the value chain; increasing value-added to its natural resources; Internet commerce; and using knowledge. Any hope of success for such an ambitious agenda hinges on the collaboration of both senior orders of government, but it also requires that the three provinces put aside parochialism. In brief, the region faces a number of important challenges if it is to improve its competitive position in the global marketplace. Partnering, collaboration, networking, and strategic alliances are all important themes in today's economic development literature. If such alliances are vital to large urban centres and regions, they are even more so in the case of three small provinces that are poised to be left even further behind than they are now.

The region may get its share of historical accidents in future, such as the discoveries of new oil and gas reserves. It is highly unlikely, however, that it can generate positive historical events in economic development if it operates as three small jurisdictions competing against one another on the periphery of the North American economy. Maritimers and their provincial governments can blame only themselves, not the government of Canada, for this state of affairs. Both senior orders of government will have to adjust along the lines suggested above. But the private sector and a market economy will need to show the way if the region is to prosper.

Looking to the Market

Forty years of federal efforts at promoting regional economic development have taught us many important lessons, including the realization that market-based economic development holds more promise for the Maritime provinces than any other approach. Moreover, it is increasingly confirmed that the private sector and market forces create thriving regional economies. The Maritime region should be no exception. In any event, economic theory is not always wrong: higher productivity translates into economic growth and lower costs translate into more employment.[63]

There are profound changes underway that hold potentially long-term consequences for all Canadian regions. Global capital markets, international outsourcing (Moncton recently lost some 150 high-paying software-programming jobs to India), and instantaneous electronic commerce are redefining the relationship between government and private firms and between private firms and their clients. Governments will be able to influence private firms through taxation and regulations, but the days of directing a firm to set up shop in a particular region are over. Any attempt to do so would result in firms simply picking up and moving to a more congenial environment. Moncton lost those jobs to India because it made economic sense to relocate them to a country where people have the necessary knowledge and skills and were readily available at lower wages. This is a hard lesson, but it is reality.

We may pine for the days when governments could embark on a strategy with programs that provided both 'carrots and sticks' to direct the pace and location of economic activities behind a protected economy. Those days, for the most part, are gone. The rapid liberalization of the international economic system is substantially changing regional economies. Large firms, like Ford or Bombardier, with plans to create or 'save' thousands of jobs, may force the hand of governments, including the Canadian government, to come up with cash to revitalize industries in southern Ontario or Quebec. It is difficult to imagine, however, many such opportunities for the Maritime region.

Yet no government, in the Maritimes or elsewhere, should avoid trying to prevent or slow down needed adjustments. The success of all regional economies in Canada will depend on a number of things, including the reallocation of resources to more productive, competitive, and higher-value activities. This suggests that the federal government needs to take a fresh look at its transfers to individuals in the Maritime provinces (i.e., the employment insurance program) in order to help the region become more competitive. Ottawa would be wise to take into account the growing body of work that offers specific recommendations on how to reform the program so as to remove incentives to economic dependence.[64]

A regional perspective to policy making requires the federal government to adjust its own operations, not just its policy-making process, to enable the private sector to expand. There are two sides to the regional perspective: the federal government should tailor its policies and programs to accommodate the region's circumstances, and the region itself must recognize that it needs to adjust its expectations with regard to federal salaries and wages. They should not be determined by national pay scales applicable equally across Canada.[65] In the Maritimes these are higher because of pressures for national parity in the public sector. A national salary scale is also incompatible with the fact that the Maritime economy is different from that of, say, Ontario and that regionally tailored policies are required. Moreover, it is not compatible with private-sector practices in the regional economy: 40 per cent of Canadian manufacturers plan their pay based on regional differentials, an approach that is widely employed in the United States. The pay for manufacturing employees is far higher, for example, in Fort McMurray, Alberta, than in the Maritimes, with the gap as wide as 25 per cent.[66]

To be sure, it is understandable that federal public servants in the Maritimes would prefer having their salaries tied to national standards. But this preference must be weighed against the fact that no salaries are going to the unemployed. Paying national salary levels makes sense if it is required to attract highly qualified people, but, if not, it can create unemployment. The central point here is that the federal government should follow the private sector, not lead it. That is, if the private sector decides that it needs to pay national salary levels to attract certain skills, then the federal government should do the same. But the obverse also applies. Currently, the federal government inhibits economic development and job creation in the Maritimes by paying higher salaries and wages than does the private sector. If these were lower than the national standards, the region would be more competitive in the public sector itself, and the case to locate more federal government units in the region would be strengthened. High salary levels can create an upward trend in salaries and wages and, by ricochet, reduce demand for labour and make a region less competitive.

Salaries of federal public servants are also relatively high by national standards. Data from Statistics Canada reveal that the average salary in the federal public service was 21 per cent higher in 2004 than the average salary in the goods-producing sector. Further, the average salary of federal public servants was in the ninety-fifth percentile of the published service-sector salaries in the same year.[67] In 2005 the federal government advertised an opening for a policy analyst position in Moncton. The position does not require management experience and calls for a university degree in social sciences and some experience in preparing reports, research papers, and the like. It pays between $71,500 and $82,706, plus very generous fringe benefits.[68] I know of no private-sector position in the Maritime provinces that would pay anywhere near this salary for similar responsibilities and comparable knowledge and skills.

The same principle should apply to other public-sector jobs in the region, including those in health and education. Equalization payments are responsible for 20 per cent of the salaries of all provincial public servants. If the goal is for the regional economy to generate sufficient resources to pay for public services consumed in the region, then adjustments have to be made to enable the private sector to generate economic activities. Equalization payments can serve to prop up the salaries of provincial public servants in the Maritime provinces, and great care must be taken not to distort private-sector salaries. Potential employees, for their part, will have to weigh lower salaries against the superior lifestyle and other advantages, including much lower housing costs, described in earlier chapters.

Costs, including salaries, wages, and qualified workers, matter to existing businesses and aspiring entrepreneurs. Why else would an American firm transfer 150 computer-programming jobs from Moncton to India? Employers will move activities from large urban centres to the Maritime provinces only if it makes business sense to do so, and the cost of doing business is often the determining factor.

As the Maritime provinces shift more and more to a market economy, whether enthusiastically or not, they will require outside investment and entrepreneurs. Risk taking is more socially acceptable in competitive open economies, hence the need to introduce greater wage flexibility.[69] Successful entrepreneurs will have to assume risk and innovate. Their training might be in anything – successful entrepreneurs may have been trained in engineering economics, computer science, physics, law, almost anything.

Yet in today's economic and sociological environment, 'entrepreneurship' is more often a matter of teamwork, in which a variety of people with different sorts of training participate. In any enterprise, anyone who participates in decisions regarding start-up, choice of product(s), location(s) of the firm, markets, technology to be used, skills of the labour force, type of equipment to be created or bought, scale of operation, organization of the enterprise, or changes in any or all of these, is an 'entrepreneur.' It follows that it is not possible to recognize a 'good entrepreneur' or a 'bad entrepreneur' by a person's characteristics, in advance.

The Maritime region is quite prolific at creating new small businesses, but Maritimers, including business leaders, do not appear to value home-grown, local medium and large firms. A survey of the most admired and respected Canadian corporations, as ranked by regional chief executive officers, revealed that the five most admired corporations in the region were all from away (Royal Bank, Bank of Nova Scotia, Enbridge, Tim Horton's, and Wendy's). The Irving group, McCain Foods, and Sobey's did not make it into the top five. Compare that to Quebec, where Bombardier, Jean Coutu, Power Corp, and BCE, all Quebec-based firms, were in the top five, and Ontario, where four of the five were from Ontario, the one exception being Bombardier.[70] Maritimers appear to be reluctant to recognize that medium and large firms are vitally important: they tend to be more innovative, sponsor more research and development, purchase more new technology and equipment to strengthen their competitiveness, and account for more venture capital than small businesses. They are also more likely to pursue export markets.

How then can the region encourage not only small business start-ups but also medium-sized firms? Risk capital is particularly important if small firms are to grow to medium-sized enterprises and if medium-sized firms are to prosper. We saw in chapter 10 that the region lags in generating venture capital and in chapter 8 that federal government reports indicate the region has insufficient access to capital. We do not think that this situation should be remedied by the government's stepping in with cash grants. The region has already paid a heavy price for the stereotype of always being on the receiving end of handouts. The fact that governments actually spend less on businesses in the Maritime provinces than elsewhere does not seem to have changed the public perception. Quite apart from this, forty years of regional economic development efforts offer fairly convincing evidence that government cash grants to businesses are not effective instruments in promoting economic development.[71] Nor do cash grants hold much appeal for entrepreneurs and aspiring entrepreneurs. A survey was conducted in the four Atlantic provinces to explore the issue of start-up assistance with entrepreneurs. When asked to indicate the kinds of assistance considered most important to people starting up a new business, 60 per cent checked 'information' first, followed by loans (39 per cent), planning/marketing assistance (36 per cent), and management training

(36 per cent). Other financial-assistance programs were considered less important (grants, 27 per cent; interest-rate subsidies, 26 per cent; loan guarantees, 17 per cent; equity investment, 11 per cent).[72]

Rather than turning to cash grants yet again or attempting to enter the venture capital business, governments could encourage pension funds to become more active players in the venture capital market, turn to its taxation policy, and review its securities regulations. Jack Mintz and Yvan Guillemette quote an OECD study to make the case that Canada 'on the regulatory front has one of the most restrictive regimes on foreign investment.'[73] It is very difficult to understand, from a Maritimer's perspective at least, why governments would wish to restrict or inhibit foreign investment. The C.D. Howe Institute, for one, argues that what is required in the region is an investment tax credit that would apply only to the region. The credit would only be triggered by an investment in the region, not by simply shifting income from another region.[74]

We do not know if the reason the region has not had much success in generating venture capital is because of a lack of supply or a lack of demand. The Atlantic Canada Equity Fund was set up by the federal government, the four Atlantic provinces, and some private-sector money from chartered banks in 1996 and given $30 million to invest. By November 2004, it had invested $17 million and announced that it was close to the end of its investment cycle in new companies and that it would retain the balance of its capital to support its existing portfolio. It also announced that it was planning to establish a new fund to invest in early-stage technology-based companies.[75] Though the fund has been able to resist political considerations and provincial lobbying in its operations and decisions, its presence in the region has hardly been felt. It has invested in ten companies, two of which are no longer in business. Some argue that the fund has had little success simply because it is too small, while others believe that the problem is not one of supply but rather demand.[76] It is impossible to determine which interpretation is more valid. But the business community itself, from the survey of Atlantic entrepreneurs described above, as well as the region's best-known business leaders, such as Harrison McCain, point to tax credits or lower taxes as the most promising instrument to promote economic development in the region.[77]

It is important to recognize that direct corporate taxes account for a relatively small amount of revenue for both senior orders of government. Direct taxes from both corporations and government enterprises represented only about 9.1 per cent of all direct and indirect taxes paid in the Maritimes federally and provincially in 2001, or 8.5 percent over the ten-year period between 1991 and 2001.[78] The point is that it would be relatively inexpensive to create an extremely attractive tax environment, one that would entail no administrative overhead cost. Frank McKenna, however, has a warning about a tax incentive for the region. He argues:

> If you piddle around with taxes one or two points, just keep your money because it won't make a difference. If you are going to be a bear on this, be a grizzly. You have to go after the people around the world who will pay attention to this kind of incentive. The logic is simple; if you lower input cost for business, it results in accelerated business. This creates more growth, more jobs, more prosperity, ultimately it leads to better services for our citizens and it means we receive less from the rest of Canada and pay more back to the rest of Canada, making this a win situation for us and a win situation for the rest of Canada ... I don't think the Government of Canada would lose a nickel on this deal. In Ireland, tax rates were reduced 12–12.5 percent and corporate tax revenues actually increased.[79]

Businesses now are less loyal to their region of birth, and both business and capital are more mobile than was the case as recently as twenty years ago. The large Canadian brewery Molson initiated merger talks with Coors because it 'got trapped ... It became too big for the Canadian market yet too small and inexperienced to play the global, or even the continental game.'[80] Thirty years ago Reuben Cohen, a well-known Maritime investment banker, sold Maritime Life to John Hancock of Boston and extracted from Hancock the promise that the head office would remain in Halifax.[81] Businesses in the Maritimes are bought and sold these days and no thought is given to 'extracting' such commitments.[82]

It takes skilled people to grow small businesses into medium-sized firms, to innovate and to network in the new economy. This, and strengthening the region's physical and research and development infrastructure, is where the role of government comes in. It is hardly original to write that economic development in future will be driven by productive and creative workers. What is important for the Maritime region is that, as things presently stand, it will be extremely difficult to attract and retain a high-quality labour force. Richard Florida, in a recent *Harvard Business Review* article, expressed concern that even the United

States, with its sophisticated research and development infrastructure, may be losing its competitive edge in this area. He writes that 'the United States may well have been the Goliath of the twentieth-century global economy, but it will take just half a dozen twenty-first-century Davids to begin to wear it down.'[83] He writes about a looming crisis, a shortage of creative talent caused by boomers retiring in massive numbers at a time when there are simply not enough young workers to take over. He adds, 'You don't have to be a rocket scientist to figure out that there is only one way for the United States to fill the gap: foreign talent.'[84]

Competition for foreign talent will be intense in the coming years, and, given the Maritime region's unimpressive record in attracting new Canadians, this is cause for grave concern. To be sure, there has been no shortage of people calling attention to the need to attract more new Canadians to the Maritimes. It is one issue on which everyone agrees, from politicians representing all parties, to business leaders, to virtually every think-tank and researcher in the region.[85] The more important question is how to go about it. Frank McKenna suggests that the federal government should simply take the lead and direct new Canadians to the region. He explains: 'A century ago, Western Canada was settled through waves of immigration resulting from generous and carefully planned inducements from the Government of Canada. It's now our turn. We must demand a regionally differentiated immigration policy.'[86]

The Maritime region, however, also needs to do its part. The talented people needed by the new economy often get their start at universities. Many foreign students who like their new communities decide to stay after completing their studies. There is no shortage of universities (one in Prince Edward Island, four in New Brunswick, and six in Nova Scotia) or community colleges in the Maritime provinces. The region has more postsecondary institutions per capita than anywhere else in Canada. The universities, together with the three orders of government, could collaborate on an aggressive strategy to attract new Canadians to study or undertake research in the region.

The region also needs to focus on new entrants to the labour market and the existing workforce. The region is in an ideal position, given its size and its economic challenge, to act as a test case, a pilot project, to try new human-resources development policies. The three Maritime provincial governments should put aside jurisdictional concerns and collaborate with one another and with Ottawa to develop a made-in-the-Maritimes human-resources policy. All relevant government pro-

grams should be on the table – including minimum wages, employment insurance, and social assistance. The purpose would be to up-
grade worker skills and encourage labour mobility. Incentives to
encourage potential entrants to the labour force to stay in school, college, or university as long as possible before joining the workforce
should be looked at. This may prove difficult if predictions hold true
that North America, including the three Maritime provinces, may be
facing a serious labour shortage in several years.

The region also needs to develop its networking abilities and to
continue to look south to New England to strengthen its economy.
Many public-policy analysts and economists make the case that FTA
and NAFTA are transforming the Canadian economic space from the
traditional east-west to a north-south trading axis.[87] The Maritime region is now in a position to return to trade patterns that flourished
before Ottawa's National Policy was implemented. Trade between the
Maritime region and the United States has increased substantially since
the FTA and NAFTA were signed. If, as Maritimers often claim, Confederation and the National Policy pushed the Maritimes a thousand miles
further out to sea and away from its natural markets, then NAFTA has
brought the region back in, close to its natural trade partners. Recent
economic data suggest that the region is successfully rediscovering its
old north-south trade patterns.

Other reasons make it natural for the region to look south. Economic
and family links between New England and the Maritime provinces go
back in history. There is likely not an Acadian family without relatives
in the Waltham-Leominster area around Boston and not a single Cape
Bretoner without relatives, to employ a local expression, in the Boston
states. Thus the basis for business networking exists. The need for a
genuine regional perspective in national economic policy remains, of
course, but the fact that economic development in the future will be a
much more collaborative process involving government, the private
sector, research institutions, the global economy, the Internet, and regional trade agreements all point to stronger exchanges between New
England and the Maritimes.

Several ongoing collaborative mechanisms already are strengthening
economic ties between the two trading regions. Norm Mineta, the U.S.
Secretary of Transportation, has pledged to launch a multi-modal study
of the transportation corridor that stretches from Halifax through New
Brunswick, Maine, Vermont, and northern New York to the Ontario
border. State and provincial governments in the two regions have agreed

to support a Northeast Business Network. Business groups and think-tanks from both countries have come together to promote an 'Atlantica' concept. Sponsors of the concept insist that the private sector has to lead the way, as governments have been too slow in promoting its potential.[88] The goal is to create a natural economic zone and trade corridor, facilitate business exchanges between the two regions, and look to the two economic regions, in particular on the Canadian side, to build stronger trade ties with Europe.

This book ends where it began, with the Maritime region exploring new markets and looking south for economic opportunities. The difference is that the region has lost both economic and political clout along the way, and its presence in the Canadian family is considerably less significant than it was 140 years ago. However, we have learned a great deal along the way. We have learned that Canada's national economic policies have benefited certain regions at the expense of others, that spending in the name of economic development is not necessarily a sound investment, that the best regional economic development policy is one where the national government can simultaneously accommodate both national and regional perspectives and where national economic policies are adjusted to reflect regional circumstances, rather than falling back on 'add-ons,' transfer payments, or 'guilt money.'

The challenge for the Maritime region is not to hope for historical accidents but to generate positive historical events. Certainly, historical events were created on the days that the FTA and NAFTA were signed, and they will continue to benefit the region. Other such positive historical events will require the federal government to think in both a national and a regional context and to adjust its machinery of government accordingly. As well, the three Maritime provinces must establish mechanisms with teeth to ensure close cooperation in every economic sector. They must recognize that political boundaries have lost a great deal of their previous economic significance and that a market economy and a strong business climate are the best bet for the region to thrive in a competitive global economy. None of this is likely to transform the Maritime economy overnight, but it does offer the hope that some day people who left the region in search of better opportunities can return home to visit, happy in the knowledge that their grandchildren had no need to follow them down the road.

Notes

Preface

1 'Maritime Mafia Seeking New Guard,' *Globe and Mail*, 27 March 2004, B1. and B4.
2 'Harper Holds to View of East Coast,' *Globe and Mail*, 26 May 2004, A7.

1. Introduction

1 See, for example, Mildred A. Schwartz, *Politics and Territory: The Sociology of Regional Persistence in Canada* (Montreal: McGill-Queen's University Press, 1974), 5–6.
2 See, e.g., Canada, Royal Commission on Maritime Claims, *Report of the Royal Commission on Maritime Claims* (Ottawa, 1926).
3 See, among others, Donald J. Savoie and Irving Brecher (eds), *Equity and Efficiency in Economic Development: Essays in Honour of Benjamin Higgins* (Montreal and Kingston: McGill-Queen's University Press, 1992).
4 Canada, *Proceedings of the Standing Senate Committee on National Finance*, no. 12, 22 March 1973, 14:24.
5 D.D. Husband, 'National versus Regional Growth,' *Canadian Public Administration* 14, no. 2 (1971): 548.
6 'Copps' Battle a Symptom of Liberal Infighting,' *Globe and Mail*, 17 January 2004, A6.
7 'MP Suffers Humiliating End to 16-Year Career,' *Ottawa Citizen*, 30 March 2004, B1.
8 Benjamin Higgins and Donald J. Savoie, *Regional Development Theories and Their Application* (New Brunswick, NJ: Transaction Publishers, 1995).
9 Ben Higgins made this point in many of his publications. See, for example,

Benjamin Higgins, 'Equity and Efficiency in Development: Basic Concepts,' in *Equity and Efficiency in Economic Development*, 21–50.

10 Consultations with a senior public servant, Ottawa, 1 June 2004.

11 'Ministers and Deputy Ministers Holding Office in Selected Federal Departments between September 1984 and May 2004,' *Parliamentary Research Branch*, Ottawa, 28 May 2004, 1.

12 Consultations with a senior public servant, Ottawa, 1 June 2004.

13 Thomas J. Courchene, *A State of Minds: Toward a Human Capital Future for Canadians* (Montreal: IRPP, 2001), and by the same author, 'A Human Capital Future for an Information Era' (keynote address to the CERF/IRP Conference, Ottawa, 4–6 May 2000), 16.

14 Robert Campbell, 'The Character of Canada Post Corporation: A Conceptual and Comparative Perspective' (Wilfrid Laurier University, May 2004, mimeo), 23.

15 J.R. Mallory, *The Structure of Canadian Government* (Toronto: Macmillan, 1971), 28.

16 Donald Creighton, *Towards the Discovery of Canada* (Toronto: Macmillan, 1972), 283.

17 Lawrence Martin, 'Stephen Harper Can't Win the Election Being Stephen Harper,' *Globe and Mail*, 1 April 2004, A13.

18 See, among others, Peter C. Newman, *Renegade in Power: The Diefenbaker Years* (Toronto: McClelland and Stewart, 1963).

19 'Eastern Canada's New Boss of Bosses,' *Globe and Mail*, 17 October 2000, A19.

20 Quoted in Campbell Morrison, 'Manley No Friend of Atlantic Canada,' *Moncton Times and Transcript*, 18 October 2000, A2.

21 Consultations with Brian Crowley, president of Atlantic Institute for Market Studies (AIMS), Halifax, 10 November 2003.

22 See, among others, Donald J. Savoie, *Regional Economic Development: Canada's Search for Solutions* (Toronto: University of Toronto Press, 1992), 248.

23 In particular, see ibid., and Higgins and Savoie, *Regional Development Theories and Their Application*.

2. History Matters

1 Dan Usher made a similar point in his 'Some Questions about the Regional Development Incentives Act,' *Canadian Public Policy* (Fall 1975): 557–75.

2 D.A. Muise, 'Prologue: The Atlantic Colonies before Confederation' in

E.R. Forbes and D.A. Muise (eds), *The Atlantic Provinces in Confederation* (Toronto: University of Toronto Press, 1993), 4.

3 T.W. Acheson, 'The Maritimes and Empire Canada,' in D. Bercuson (ed.), *Canada and the Burden of Unity* (Toronto: Macmillan, 1977), 90.

4 J.M.S. Careless, 'Aspects of Metropolitanism in Atlantic Canada,' in M. Wade (ed.), *Regionalism in the Canadian Community, 1867–1967* (Toronto: University of Toronto Press, 1969), 124.

5 W.T. Easterbrook and Hugh Aitken, *Canadian Economic History* (Toronto: Macmillan, 1967), 247.

6 Ibid., 248.

7 Ibid.

8 Muise, 'Prologue,' 9.

9 G.A. Rawlyk and Doug Brown, 'The Historical Framework of the Maritimes and Confederation,' in G.A. Rawlyk (ed.), *The Atlantic Provinces and the Problems of Confederation* (St John's: Breakwater, 1979), 1.

10 See, among many others, Forbes and Muise (eds), *The Atlantic Provinces in Confederation.*

11 Rawlyk and Brown, 'Historical Framework,' 4.

12 Claude Bélanger, 'The Maritime Provinces: The Maritime Rights Movements and Canadian Federalism' (mimeo, Marianopolis College, 2001), 8.

13 Rawlyk and Brown, 'Historical Framework,' 7.

14 Easterbrook and Aitken, *Canadian Economic History*, 244.

15 Donald Creighton, *The Road to Confederation: The Emergence of Canada, 1863–67* (Toronto: Macmillan, 1964), 26.

16 W.M. Whitelow, *The Maritimes and Canada before Confederation* (Toronto: Oxford University Press, 1934), 201.

17 S.A. Saunders, *The Economic History of the Maritime Provinces* (Fredericton: Acadiensis, 1984), 23.

18 See, among others, Rawlyk (ed.), *The Atlantic Provinces*, 9.

19 Ibid., 10.

20 See, for example, W.S. MacNutt, *New Brunswick: A History, 1784–1867* (Toronto: Macmillan, 1963), 414–86.

21 Ibid., 454–5.

22 Ibid., 455.

23 John Ibbitson, *Loyal No More: Ontario's Struggle for a Separate Destiny* (Toronto: HarperCollins, 2001), 28.

24 Roger Gibbins, *Regionalism: Territorial Politics in Canada and the United States* (Toronto: Butterworths, 1982), 29.

25 Easterbrook and Aitken, *Canadian Economic History*, 388.

26 Nova Scotia, *Debates and Proceedings of the Nova Scotia House of Assembly* (1885), 10.
27 W.L. Morton, *The Kingdom of Canada* (Toronto: McClelland and Stewart, 1963), 465.
28 Ibid., 479.
29 See, among others, Janine Brodie, *Political Economy of Canadian Regionalism* (Toronto: Harcourt Bruce Jovanovich, 1990), 145.
30 Ernest Forbes, quoted in 'Shafted,' *Atlantic Progress* (Halifax), June 1999, 36.
31 Hugh G. Thorburn, *Politics in New Brunswick* (Toronto: University of Toronto Press, 1961), 16.
32 Ibid.
33 Philip A. Buckner, 'The 1870s: Political Integration,' in Forbes and Muise, *The Atlantic Provinces in Confederation*, 49.
34 D.A. Muise, 'The 1860s: Forging the Bonds of Union,' in ibid., 39.
35 Ibid., 24.
36 David G. Alexander, *Atlantic Canada and Confederation: Essays in Canadian Political Economy* (Toronto: University of Toronto Press, 1983), 4.
37 Thorburn, *Politics in New Brunswick*, 16.
38 Nova Scotia, *Journal of the Nova Scotia Assembly* (1886), 147–8.
39 David Frank, 'The 1920s: Class and Region, Resistance and Accommodation,' in Forbes and Muise, *The Atlantic Provinces in Confederation*, chap. 7.
40 J.R. Mallory, *The Structure of Canadian Government* (Toronto: Macmillan, 1971), 124.
41 Donald J. Savoie, *The Politics of Public Spending in Canada* (Toronto: University of Toronto Press, 1990), chap. 10.
42 Ibid., 13.
43 Carman Miller, 'The 1940s: War and Rehabilitation,' in Forbes and Muise, *The Atlantic Provinces in Confederation*, 325.
44 Alexander, *Atlantic Canada and Confederation*, 68.
45 See, among others, Paul Bairoch, *Cities and Economic Development: From the Dawn of History to the Present* (Chicago: University of Chicago Press, 1988).
46 L.D. McCann, 'Shock Waves in the Old Economy: The Maritime Urban System during the Great Transformation 1867–1939,' in George J. DeBenedetti and Rodolphe H. Lamarche (eds), *Shock Waves: The Maritime Urban System in the New Economy* (Moncton: Canadian Institute for Research on Regional Development, 1994), 9–42.
47 Ibid., 12.
48 Ibid., 14.

49 Canada, Department of Reconstruction and Supply, *Employment and Income with Special Reference to the Initial Period of Reconstruction* (Ottawa: King's Printer, 1945), 21.

50 A.W. Johnson, *Social Policy in Canada: The Past as It Conditions the Present* (Ottawa: Institute for Research on Public Policy, 1987), 1.

51 Harold Innis, 'Decentralization and Democracy,' in H. Innis (ed.), *Essays in Canadian Economic History* (Toronto: University of Toronto Press, 1956), 371.

52 Canada, *The Atlantic Region of Canada: Economic Development Strategy for the Eighties* (St John's: Atlantic Development Council, 1978), 39.

53 Rawlyk and Brown, 'Historical Framework,' 26.

54 Frank, 'The 1920s,' 253.

55 For an excellent history of the movement, see Ernest R. Forbes, *The Maritime Rights Movement, 1919–1927: A Study in Canadian Regionalism* (Montreal: McGill-Queen's University Press, 1979).

56 Ibid., 29.

57 Ibid., 158.

58 Canada, *Report of the Royal Commission on Maritime Claims* (Ottawa: King's Printer, 1927), 44.

59 Frank, 'The 1920s,' 258.

60 Quoted in Alexander, *Atlantic Canada and Confederation*, 36.

61 D.A. Muise, 'The 1860s,' 36.

62 See ibid., 21.

63 Ibid., 37.

64 Donald J. Savoie, *Regional Economic Development: Canada's Search for Solutions* (Toronto: University of Toronto Press, 1992), 167.

65 Frank, 'The 1920s,' 261.

66 See ibid., 229.

67 Donald Smiley (ed.), *The Rowell-Sirois Report*, Book 1 (Toronto: McClelland and Stewart, 1963), 2.

68 Janine Brodie adds, 'measures to reconstruct a peacetime economy.' See *Political Economy of Canadian Regionalism*, 149.

69 Morton, *The Kingdom of Canada*, 465.

70 Ibbitson, *Loyal No More*, 5.

71 Carman Miller, 'The 1940s: War and Rehabilitation,' in Forbes and Muise, *The Atlantic Provinces in Confederation*, 326.

72 Ibid., 479.

73 See, among others, Brodie, *Political Economy of Canadian Regionalism*, 145.

74 Miller, 'The 1940s,' 328.

75 Ibid.

76 Margaret Conrad, 'The 1950s: The Decade of Development,' in Forbes and Muise, *The Atlantic Provinces in Confederation*, 407.
77 See, among others, H. Lithwick, 'Federal Government Regional Economic Development Policies: An Evaluative Survey,' in K. Norrie (ed.), *Disparities and Interregional Adjustment* (Toronto: University of Toronto Press, 1986), 116.
78 See, among others, 'The Fredericton Conference of Atlantic Premiers,' *Atlantic Advocate* (September 1956), 28. See also Conrad, 'The 1950s,' 408.
79 W.S. MacNutt, 'The Fredericton Conference: A Look Backward and a Look Forward,' *Atlantic Advocate*, Fredericton (September 1956), 13.
80 Canada, *Report of the Royal Commission on Canada's Economic Prospects* (Ottawa: Queen's Printer, 1957), 494.
81 See Peter C. Newman, *Renegade in Power* (Toronto: McClelland and Stewart, 1963).
82 See the *Atlantic Advocate* (July 1957), 11.
83 See Conrad, 'The 1950s,' 413.
84 Ian M. Drummond with Peter George, Kris Inwood, Peter Sinclair, and Tom Traves, *Progress without Planning: The Economic History of Ontario from Confederation to the Second World War* (Toronto: University of Toronto Press, 1987), 104.
85 Ibid., 114.
86 See, among others, D.M. Ray, 'Regional Economic Development and the Location of U.S. Subsidiaries,' in Paul Phillips (ed.), *Incentives, Location and Regional Development* (Winnipeg: Economic Development Advisory Board, 1975), 20–5.
87 Ibbitson, *Loyal No More*, 4–5.

3. Theories Matter Less

1 The reader should consult Benjamin Higgins and Donald J. Savoie, *Regional Development Theories and Their Application* (New Brunswick, NJ: Transaction Publishers, 1995), chaps 5, 8, and 10. I borrow from our book particularly from chapters 3, 4, 6, 9, 11, 20, and 21.
2 Quoted in André Raynauld (ed.), *Seminar on Regional Development in Canada: Transcript of the Proceedings* (Montreal: Centre de recherche en développement économique de l'Université de Montréal, 1980), 105.
3 *Living Together* (Ottawa: Economic Council of Canada, 1977).
4 Harold A. Innis, *Fur Trade in Canada: An Introduction to Canadian Economic History* (Toronto: University of Toronto Press, 1956), 358.
5 Ibid.

6 James P. Bickerton, *Nova Scotia, Ottawa and the Politics of Regional Development* (Toronto: University of Toronto Press, 1990), 12–13. See also John H. Dales, *The Protective Tariff in Canada's Development* (Toronto: University of Toronto Press, 1966).

7 See, among others, W.T. Easterbrook, 'Recent Contributions to Economic History: Canada,' *Journal of Economic History* 19 (1959): 76–102; and John H. Dales, *Hydro Electricity and Industrial Development in Quebec, 1898–1940* (Cambridge: Harvard University Press, 1957).

8 *Living Together*, 24–5.

9 See, for example, David Easton, *A Systems Analysis of Political Life* (New York: Wiley, 1965).

10 Ernest R. Forbes, 'In Search of a Post-Confederation Maritime Historiography 1900–1967,' in D.J. Bercuson, and P.A. Buckner (eds), *Eastern and Western Perspectives* (Toronto: University of Toronto Press, 1981), 48–9.

11 *Living Together*, chap. 4.

12 Ibid., 103.

13 Ibid., 27.

14 Thomas J. Courchene, 'A Market Perspective on Regional Disparities,' *Canadian Public Policy* 7, no. 4 (1981): 515.

15 Ralph Matthews, *The Creation of Regional Dependency* (Toronto: University of Toronto Press, 1983), 75.

16 Ibid.

17 Ibid. Matthews also suggests that 'dependency theory sees migrants as the victims of an exploitative economic system' (76).

18 Andrew Stark, 'Preface,' in Thomas J. Courchene with Colin R. Telmer, *From Heartland to North American Region State* (Toronto: Monograph Series on Public Policy, Centre for Public Management, 1998), iv and 86.

19 Thomas Walkom, 'The Year Ottawa Elected Its Own PM,' *Toronto Star*, 29 December 1990, D4.

20 *Competing in the New Global Economy*, 3 vols. (Toronto: Government of Ontario, 1988–9).

21 Richard Simeon, 'Thinking about Constitutional Futures: A Framework' (paper prepared for the C.D. Howe Institute, December 1990), 12.

22 See, among others, Michel Cormier, *Louis J. Robichaud: Une Révolution si peu tranquille* (Moncton: Éditions de la Francophonie, 2004), and Hugh Thorburn, *Politics in New Brunswick* (Toronto: University of Toronto Press, 1961).

23 Discussions with Michael MacDonald, a senior ACOA official in the agency's early years and later head of the Greater Halifax Partnership, various dates.

24 Joseph Schumpeter, *The Theory of Economic Development* (Cambridge: Harvard University Press, 1934).
25 David C. McClelland and David C. Winter, *Motivating Economic Achievement* (New York: Free Press, 1973), 30.
26 David Hume, 'On the Balance of Trade,' *Political Discourses* (1752), reprinted in A.E. Monroe (ed.), *Early Economic Thought: Selections from Economic Literature Prior to Adam Smith* (Cambridge: Harvard University Press, 1948), 327.
27 Adam Smith, *The Wealth of Nations* (New York: P.F. Collier, 1902).
28 John Stuart Mill, *Principles of Political Economy: With Some of Their Applications to Social Philosophy* (London: Longmans, Green, 1865).
29 J.E. Cairnes, *The Character and Logical Method of Political Economy* (New York: Kelley, 1888).
30 J.S. Nicholson, *Principles of Political Economy*, 2nd ed. (London: A and C Black, 1901–3), 2:294; Bertil Ohlin, *Interregional and International Trade* (Cambridge: Harvard University Press, 1933), 52.
31 P.T. Ellsworth, *The International Economy* (New York: Macmillan, 1958).
32 Frank Taussig, *International Trade* (New York: Macmillan, 1928), 67–8 and chap. 6.
33 Ellsworth, *The International Economy*, 123.
34 Benjamin Higgins and Donald J. Savoie (eds), *Regional Economic Development: Essays in Honour of François Perroux* (London and Boston: Allen & Unwin, 1988).
35 François Perroux, 'Economic Space: Theory and Applications,' *Quarterly Journal of Economics* 64 (1950): 89–104.
36 Ibid., 96.
37 François Perroux, 'A Note on the Notion of Growth Pole,' *Économie appliquée*, nos. 1/2 (1955): 6.
38 Karen Polenske, 'Growth Pole Theory and Strategy Reconsidered: Domination Linkages, and Distribution,' in Higgins and Savoie, *Regional Economic Development*, 93.
39 François Perroux, 'The Pole of Development and the General Theory of the Economy,' in Higgins and Savoie, *Regional Economic Development*, 49.
40 For those unacquainted with Boudeville's work, the best introductions might be *French Regional Polarization and Planning* (Paris: Plon, 1976), and 'Functional Regional Analysis: An Elementary Exposition on Some Selected Topics,' in J.H.P. Paelinck and A. Sailez (eds), *University of Toronto Lectures* (Paris: Association de science régionale de langue française, 1977). See also Anthony Kuklinski, *Polarized Development and Regional Policies: Tribute to Jacques Boudeville* (The Hague: Mouton, 1981).
41 Higgins and Savoie, *Regional Economic Development*, 54, 56.

42 Ibid., chap. 4.
43 Allen J. Scott and Michael Storper, 'High Technology Industry and Regional Development: A Theoretical Critique and Reconstruction,' *International Social Science Journal*, no. 112 (May 1987): 220.
44 Robin Marris, 'Equity, Efficiency and the Managerial Paradigm,' in Donald J. Savoie and Irving Brecher (eds), *Equity and Efficiency in Economic Development: Essays in Honour of Benjamin Higgins* (Montreal: McGill-Queen's University Press, 1992).
45 Scott and Storper, 'High Technology Industry,' 220.
46 Ibid.
47 Fu Chen Lo and Kamal Salih, 'Growth Poles and Regional Policy in Open Dualistic Economies: Western Theory and Asian Reality,' in Lo and Salih (eds), *Growth Pole Strategy and Regional Development: Alternative Approaches* (Oxford: Pergamon Press, 1978), 243–70.
48 Philippe Aydalot, 'La Division spatiale du travail,' in Jean H.P. Paelink and Alain Sallez (eds), *Espace et localisation* (Paris: Economica, 1983), 175.
49 Ibid., 176–9.
50 Michael E. Porter, *The Competitive Advantage of Nations* (New York: Free Press, 1998).
51 Porter, quoted in Clifford Bekar and Richard G. Lipsey, 'Clusters and Economic Policy' (paper prepared for Finance Canada, Human Resources Development Canada, Industry Canada and Policy Research Initiative, Ottawa, 16 July 2001), 5.
52 Richard Florida, *The Rise of the Creative Class: And How It's Transforming Work, Leisure, Community, and Everyday Life* (New York: Basic Books, 2003).
53 Richard Florida, in www.washingtonmonthly.com, May 2002, p. 4.
54 Florida, *Rise of the Creative Class*, 7–8.
55 Lester C. Thurow, *The Future of Capitalism* (New York: William Morrow, 1996), 8, 68.
56 Thomas J. Courchene, *A State of Minds: Toward a Human Capital Future for Canadians* (Montreal: IRPP, 2001), and, by the same author, 'A Human Capital Future for an Information Era' (keynote address to the CERF/IRPP Conference, Ottawa, 4–6 May 2000), 16.
57 Ibid.
58 Joan Robinson, *Economic Philosophy* (New York: Doubleday, 1964), 63, 73–4.
59 Richard Lipsey quoted in Raynauld, *Seminar on Regional Development in Canada*, 105.
60 Albert Breton, 'The Status and Efficiency of Regional Development Policies,' in Savoie and Brecher, *Equity and Efficiency in Economic Development*, 161.
61 See, for example, Thomas J. Courchene, 'A Market Perspective on Regional Disparities,' *Canadian Public Policy* 7, no. 4 (1981): 513.

62 Hon. Pierre DeBané, quoted in Donald J. Savoie, *Regional Economic Development: Canada's Search for Solutions*, 2nd ed. (Toronto: University of Toronto Press, 1992), 157.

4. Trying This

1 John Ibbitson, *Loyal No More: Ontario's Struggle for a Separate Destiny* (Toronto: HarperCollins, 2001), 87–8.
2 See, among many others, Canada, *Fiscal Federalism in Canada* (Ottawa: Supply and Services, 1981), chaps 3–6.
3 Canada, *Report of the Royal Commission on Bilingualism, and Biculturalism*, Book II (Ottawa: 1967), xliv.
4 Frank Walton, 'Canada's Atlantic Region: Recent Policy for Economic Development,' *Canadian Journal of Regional Science* 1, no. 2 (1978): 44.
5 See, among others, Anthony Careless, *Initiative and Response: The Adaptation of Canadian Federalism to Regional Economic Development* (Montreal: McGill-Queen's University Press, 1977), 39–88.
6 See, among others, Thomas N. Brewis, 'Regional Development in Canada in Historical Perspective,' in N.H. Lithwick (ed.), *Regional Economic Policy: The Canadian Experience* (Toronto: McGraw-Hill Ryerson, 1978), 220.
7 Walton, 'Canada's Atlantic Region,' 44.
8 Re Pickersgill, see Careless, *Initiative and Response*, 113–16; discussion of reasons for failure based on interview with a former DREE official.
9 See Careless, *Initiative and Response*, 91–108.
10 Ibid., chaps 2 and 3.
11 Quoted in Richard W. Phidd and G. Bruce Doern, *The Politics and Management of Canadian Economic Policy* (Toronto: Macmillan, 1978), 324.
12 Marchand declared, 'Because things are boiling over in central Canada, monetary conditions have to be tightened in order to head off inflation; the restraint may be felt here [Atlantic Canada] even though, far from the economy boiling over, there is persistent and severe unemployment.' See DREE, Atlantic Conference '68, 'Address by the Honourable Jean Marchand: A New Policy for Regional Development,' 29 October 1968, 7.
13 See the policy discussion document DREE, *Regional Policy in the Canadian Context* (Ottawa: DREE, 1978), 6. See also J.P. Francis and N.G. Pillai, 'Regional Economic Disparities and Federal Regional Development Policies in Canada,' in *Regional Poverty and Change* (Ottawa: Canadian Council on Rural Development, 1973), 123–60.

14 Canada, *House of Commons Debates* (20 March 1969), 6893–5.
15 Interview with former DREE officials.
16 Interview with Jean Marchand and a former official of the Privy Council Office. These interviews were conducted in Ottawa for my earlier book on regional development, *Regional Economic Development: Canada's Search for Solutions* (Toronto: University of Toronto Press, 1992).
17 The account that comprises the rest of this chapter is based on the interview with Jean Marchand.
18 See Geoffrey Stevens, *Stanfield* (Toronto: McClelland and Stewart, 1973), 3–11, Canada, *House of Commons Debates* (27 February 1969): Stanfield, p. 6020; Douglas, p. 6024.
19 Canada, *House of Commons Debates* (27 February 1969): Trudeau, p. 6016; Marchand, p. 6894.
20 Interview with a member of Parliament.
21 Canada, Government Organization Act, *Statutes of Canada*, 1969, part IV, subsequently consolidated in the Department of Regional Economic Expansion Act, *Revised Statutes of Canada*, 1970, chap. R-4.
22 Richard Higgins suggests that perhaps 'the failure to achieve objectives in public life often results in severe criticism from the press, opposition parties and others. The rewards are usually meagre, to say the least, for a well-prepared and hard-fought initiative which falls short of expectations.' See Canada, *Proceedings of the Standing Senate Committee on Finance*, no. 3 (21 November 1978): 6.
23 See, among many others, Francis and Pillai, 'Regional Economic Disparities and Federal Regional Development Policies in Canada,' 136–7.
24 Robert S. Woodward, 'The Effectiveness of DREE's New Location Subsidies,' in N.H. Lithwick (ed.), *Regional Economic Policy: The Canadian Experience* (Toronto: McGraw-Hill Ryerson, 1978), 243–56.
25 DREE, *Annual Report, 1969–1970*, 10–12.
26 Commenting on planning in his new department, Marchand spoke of 'planning to attract new industries, to stimulate and aid the modernization and expansion of existing industries, to find customers outside the region, the kind of growth that is reproductive in the sense that one thing leads to another'; DREE, Atlantic Conference '68, 'Address by the Honourable Jean Marchand,' 14.
27 Interview with former DREE officials. See also DREE, *Annual Report, 1971–1972*, 21.
28 DREE, *Annual Report, 1971–1972*, 14, 22.
29 Tom Kent made this point in numerous speeches and presentations.

5. Trying That

1 Pierre Normandin (ed.), *The Canadian Parliamentary Guide* (Ottawa: n.p., 1973), 512.
2 Donald J. Savoie, *Federal-Provincial Collaboration: The Canada–New Brunswick General Development Agreement* (Montreal: McGill-Queen's University Press, 1981), 26.
3 Canada, Department of Regional Economic Expansion, *The New Approach* (Ottawa, 1976).
4 See, for example, DREE, *Canada-Saskatchewan General Development Agreement* (Ottawa: Information Canada, 11 February 1974).
5 See, for example, DREE, *Canada–Nova Scotia Industrial Development* (Ottawa and Halifax, 22 June 1976), 5.
6 Savoie, *Federal-Provincial Collaboration*, chaps 4 and 5.
7 Ibid.
8 See DREE, *Les Ententes de développement du MEER*, various dates. The last such report was issued in 1981 by the Department of Supply and Services.
9 Donald J. Savoie, *Regional Economic Development: Canada's Search for Solutions* (Toronto: University of Toronto Press, 1992), 275.
10 Ibid., 207.
11 Canada, *Atlantic Region Industrial Parks: An Assessment of Economic Impact* (Ottawa: Department of Regional Economic Expansion, n.d.), 18–72.
12 See N.H. Lithwick, 'Regional Policy: The Embodiment of Contradictions,' in G. Bruce Doern (ed.), *How Ottawa Spends Your Tax Dollars, 1982* (Toronto: Lorimer, 1982), 131–46.
13 Interview with a former MSERD official. This view was fairly widespread in Ottawa, notably in central agencies, but also to some extent even in the DREE head office.
14 Interview with a former DREE Atlantic regional official.
15 Canada, Proceedings of the Senate Standing Committee on Agriculture, *Minutes of Proceedings* (Ottawa, 1977), 11–19.
16 Savoie, *Federal-Provincial Collaboration*, chap. 7.
17 'No Fisheries Accord – LeBlanc,' *Moncton Times*, 11 February 1977, 1.
18 See Donald J. Savoie, 'The GDA Approach and the Bureaucratization of Provincial Governments in the Atlantic Provinces,' *Canadian Public Administration* 24, no. 1 (1981): 116–31.
19 Canada, Department of Regional Economic Expansion, *The New Approach*, 25.
20 DREE, *Montreal Special Area* (Ottawa, n.d.).
21 This commitment led to the signing of a subsidiary agreement for eastern

Ontario. See DREE, *Canada-Ontario Subsidiary Agreement – Eastern Ontario* (Toronto and Ottawa, 20 December 1979).

22 See Savoie, 'The GDA Approach,' 116–31.

23 See Richard Simeon (ed.), *Must Canada Fail?* (Montreal: McGill-Queen's University Press, 1977), chaps 2, 13, 16, and 17.

24 Canada, Conseil économique, *Treizième exposé annuel* (Ottawa: Supply and Services, 1976). This annual report dealt at length with the problem of inflation.

25 Thomas J. Courchene, 'Avenues of Adjustments: The Transfer System and Regional Disparities,' in *Canadian Confederation at the Crossroads: The Search for a Federal-Provincial Balance* (Vancouver: Fraser Institute, 1978), 145–77.

26 DREE, *Annual Report, 1978–1979*, 3, 2.

27 Ibid., 3.

28 Canada, *Proceedings of the Standing Senate Committee on National Finance*, no. 3 (21 February 1978): A7 and A8.

29 DREE, *Economic Development Prospects in Ontario* (December 1979), 2.

30 Ibid., 1–14, 58–9.

31 Ibid., 2.

32 DREE, *Economic Development Prospecst in the Western Region* (December 1979).

33 DREE minister Marcel Lessard declared: 'Clearly, one of the principal advantages of the GDA mechanism is its flexibility, a characteristic which ... is absolutely essential in a country with such diverse economic regions'; Canada, *Proceedings of the Standing Senate Committee on National Finance*, no. 3 (21 February 1978): A17.

34 See, among others, Savoie, *Federal-Provincial Collaboration*, chap. 7.

35 Quoted in *Atlantic Insight*, 17 April 1979, 12, 19.

36 Ibid., 12. See also Mike Forestall, MP for Dartmouth–Halifax East, 'Regional Development: A Failed and Forgotten Commitment' (mimeo, n.d.). Interview with former DREE officials and with Elmer MacKay.

37 'A Maverick in the Liberal Ranks,' *Ottawa Journal*, 23 July 1980, 4; Pierre De Bané, 'A New Regional Development Policy' (mimeo, n.d.).

38 Interview with Pierre De Bané. See also 'Pierre De Bané a eu le seul ministère qui l'intéressait – Des chances égales pour tous,' *Le Droit* (Ottawa), 20 August 1980, 1.

39 Interview with Pierre De Bané.

40 DREE, *Senior Staff Conference*, 17 and 18 June 1980, 22.

41 Ibid., 23–4.

42 'A Maverick in the Liberal Ranks,' 4.

43 'De Bané's Future Appears Bright Despite New Post,' *Montreal Gazette*, 13 January 1982, 13.

44 DREE, 'Notes for a Speech by Russell MacLellan, MP, Parliamentary Secretary to the Honourable Pierre De Bané, Federal Minister of Regional Economic Expansion, to the 13th Annual Conference of the Industrial Developers Association of Canada, Quebec' (21 September 1981), 5.

45 'La Venue de 2 usines à Bouctouche créera 1,000 emplois dans Kent,' L'Évangéline (Moncton), 17 July 1981, 3.

46 See 'Bickering Over Car Plant Led to Cabinet Shake-up,' Toronto Sunday Star, 17 January 1982, 1.

47 The controversy led to a series of charges and counter-charges between Ottawa and Quebec City. See DREE, 'Statement by the Honourable Pierre De Bané on the Decision by Volkswagen' (13 October 1981), 5.

48 Statement by Bruno Rubess, president of Volkswagen Canada (13 October 1981), 1.

49 Canada, Office of the Prime Minister, 'Reorganization for Economic Development' (news release, 12 January 1982).

50 Canada, Department of Finance, Economic Development for Canada in the 1980s (Ottawa, November 1981), 11.

51 Canada, Department of Energy, Mines and Resources, 'Notes for an Address by the Honourable Marc Lalonde, Minister of Energy, Mines and Resources, to the Second Atlantic Outlook Conference' (Halifax, 18 February 1982), 2.

52 Finance, Economic Development for Canada in the 1980s, 17; Ministry of State for Economic and Regional Development (MSERD), 'Notes for an Address by the Honourable Bud Olson, Minister of State for Economic Development – Mega Projects' (mimeo, n.d.), 2–3.

53 See, among others, Ronald W. Crowley, 'A New Power Focus in Ottawa: The Ministry of State for Economic and Regional Development,' Optimum 13, no. 2 (1977): 5–16.

54 MSERD, 'Contacts in Federal Economic and Regional Development Departments' (January 1984), 2.

55 Canada, Ministry of State for Economic Development, 'Notes for an Address by the Honourable Bud Olson, Minister of State for Economic Development – A FEDC for PEI' (n.d.).

56 CBC, As It Happens, 24 February 1982, transcript, 5–6.

57 Canada, House of Commons, Bill C-152, An Act Respecting the Organization of the Government of Canada and Matters Related to or Incidental Thereto – As Passed by the House of Commons, 25 October 1983, schedule 11, sec. 35, p. 22.

58 Canada, 'Reorganization for Economic Development'; Finance, Economic Development for Canada in the 1980s, 10.

59 See, for example, MSERD, 'Canada-Saskatchewan Economic and Regional Development Agreement' (Ottawa and Regina, 30 January 1984).

60 Canada 'Reorganization for Economic Development' (news release), Office of the Prime Minister, 12 January 1982).

61 Over a five-year period from the late 1970s to the early 1980s, the GDA spending pattern saw 45 per cent of the funds going to the four Atlantic provinces, 30 per cent to Quebec, 6 per cent to Ontario, and 20 per cent to the western provinces. Consultations with federal government officials, various dates.

62 'Reorganization for Economic Development.'

63 Peter Aucoin and Herman Bakvis, 'Organizational Differentiation and Integration: The Case of Regional Economic Development Policy in Canada,' *Canadian Public Administration* 27, no. 3 (1984): 366.

64 'Bickering over Car Plant Led to Cabinet Shake-up,' *Toronto Sunday Star*, 17 January 1982, 1.

65 DRIE, 'Speaking Notes – The Honourable Ed Lumley to the House of Commons on the Industrial and Regional Development Program' (27 June 1983), 1, 2.

66 See appendices B and C of Donald J. Savoie, *Regional Economic Development: Canada's Search for Solutions* (Toronto: University of Toronto Press, 1986) for a detailed outline of how the IRDP program operated and how the tier system actually worked.

67 APEC, *An Analysis of the Reorganization for Economic Development* (Halifax: Atlantic Provinces Economic Council, August 1982); Canada, *Government Policy and Regional Development* (Report of the Standing Senate Committee, September 1982).

68 'Trudeau–Pitfield Bureaucracy First Item on Turner's Overhaul,' *Globe and Mail*, 2 July 1984, p. 5; Canada, Office of the Prime Minister, 'Government Organization Measures' (release, 30 June 1984).

6. Mulroney: Inflicting Prosperity

1 See Michael J. Prince, 'The Mulroney Agenda: A Right Turn for Ottawa,' in Michael J. Prince (ed.), *How Ottawa Spends, 1987–88: Tracking the Tories* (Toronto: Methuen, 1987), 9.

2 Quoted in Claire Hoy, *Friends in High Places* (Toronto: McClelland-Bantam, 1988), 84.

3 Ibid.

4 'Background Notes for an Address by Brian Mulroney P.C., M.P.,' Toronto, Progressive Conservative Party, 28 August 1984.

5 Canada, Department of Finance, 'Economic and Fiscal Statement' (8 November 1984), 3–4.
6 Ibid., 55.
7 See Statement by Honourable Brian Mulroney at Halifax, 2 August 1984, Progressive Conservative Party of Canada, Annexe A, 1.
8 See Donald J. Savoie, 'ACOA: Something Old, Something New, Something Borrowed, Something Blue,' in Katherine A. Graham (ed.), *How Ottawa Spends, 1989* (Ottawa: Carleton University Press, 1989), 107–30.
9 DRIE, 'Adjustments to Industrial and Regional Development Program' (news release, 9 November 1984); 'Provinces May Get More Clout on Grants,' *Toronto Star*, 22 January 1985, 7. See also 'Développement régional: Stevens est prêt à laisser la maîtrise d'œuvre aux provinces,' *Le Devoir* (Montreal), 22 January 1985, 1.
10 MSERD, 'Canada-Ontario Economic Development Ministers Meet' (news release, 2 November 1984).
11 DRIE, 'Canada and British Columbia Sign New Economic and Regional Development Agreement' (news release, 23 November 1984).
12 'Quebec Signs New Economic Development Agreement,' *Montreal Gazette*, 15 December 1984, 2.
13 DRIE, *Canada-Quebec Economic and Regional Development Agreement*, 14 December 1984. See also DRIE, 'Canada-Quebec Economic and Regional Development Agreement' (news release, 14 December 1984).
14 Canada, Department of Finance, *The Budget Speech*, 23 May 1985, 11.
15 See Donald J. Savoie, *An Economic Development Plan for Cape Breton and Cape Bretoners* (Moncton: Canadian Institute for Research on Regional Development, June 1990), 18.
16 Ibid., 22.
17 Ibid., 30.
18 DRIE, 'Intergovernmental Position Paper on the Principles and Framework for Regional Economic Development' (June 1985), 5–6.
19 Ibid., 6–14.
20 Ibid., 15.
21 Donald J. Savoie, *Establishing the Atlantic Canada Opportunities Agency* (Ottawa: Office of the Prime Minister, May 1987), 14.
22 Ibid., 27.
23 Ibid., 30.
24 Ibid., 34.
25 See Canada, *The Atlantic Enterprise Program* (Ottawa: Department of Regional Industrial Expansion, 1987).
26 DRIE, Economic and Regional Development Agreements – Mid-term assessment, January 1987, 1.

27 Ibid., 14.
28 Ibid.
29 Ibid., 16.
30 Ibid.
31 Ibid., 17.
32 DRIE, *Report of the Federal-Provincial Task Force on Regional Development Assessment* (n.d.), 47. The report was submitted to the Annual Conference of First Ministers, Toronto, 26–7 November 1987.
33 Ibid.
34 Ibid., 2–3.
35 Ibid., 13–18.
36 Canada, Royal Commission on the Economic Union and Development Prospects for Canada, *Report*, vol. 3 (Ottawa: Minister of Supply and Services, 1985), 213.
37 Ibid., 214.
38 Ibid., 215.
39 Ibid., 220.
40 'Mr. Stevens Departs,' *Globe and Mail*, 13 May 1986, A6.
41 Canada, Commission of Inquiry on Unemployment Insurance, *Report* (Ottawa: Ministry of Supply and Services, 1986).
42 See Savoie, *Establishing the Atlantic Canada Opportunities Agency*, 20–36.
43 Canada, *Hansard*, 1 October 1986, 12.
44 I was asked in October 1986 to consult with a cross-section of Atlantic Canadians and to prepare a report for the prime minister on the establishment of ACOA. At the time, I was executive director of the Canadian Institute for Research on Regional Development at the Université de Moncton.
45 Consultations with officials from the Prime Minister's Office when I was working on the report to establish ACOA.
46 DRIE, 'Minister Tables DRIE Financial Studies' (news release, 13 October 1987).
47 'Party Comes First, Unhappy Côté Says in Deciding to Quit,' *Globe and Mail*, 23 August 1988, A1.
48 Savoie, *Establishing the Atlantic Canada Opportunities Agency*, 33.
49 I was asked by Premier Hatfield on 30 August 1986 to prepare the paper.
50 See, among others, Audrey D. Doerr, *The Machinery of Government in Canada* (Toronto: Methuen, 1981), 12–41.
51 See Savoie, *Establishing the Atlantic Canada Opportunities Agency*, chap. 2.
52 Ibid, 22.
53 Ibid.
54 Ibid., 24.

55 Ibid., 33.
56 Ibid., 18. This in turn was borrowed from William Alonso, 'Population and Regional Development,' in Benjamin Higgins and Donald J. Savoie (eds), *Regional Economic Development: Essays in Honour of François Perroux* (Boston: Unwin Hyman, 1988), 131.
57 Ibid.
58 Ibid, 68–71.
59 Ibid.
60 Ibid.
61 Ibid., chap. 3.
62 See, among many others, 'PM Launches New Agency for Atlantic Canada,' *Halifax Sunday Herald*, 7 June 1987, 1.
63 'Atlantic Canada Gets Big Boost,' *Fredericton Daily Gleaner*, 8 June 1987, 1.
64 *'Newshour'* CKO-FM (Halifax), 8 June 1987, MIT Media Tapes and Transcripts.
65 'Hatfield, McKenna Voice Support,' *Fredericton Daily Gleaner*, 9 June 1987, p. 1. See also 'Regions Leaders' Reaction Positive,' ibid., 8 June 1987, 2.
66 CBC Radio News (Halifax), 8 June 1987, MIT Media Tapes and Transcripts.
67 'Atlantic Canada Gets Big Boost,' 1, 3.
68 Ibid.
69 'Two Maritimers Will Be in Control,' *Fredericton Daily Gleaner*, 8 June 1987, 3.
70 Canada, An Act to increase opportunity for economic development in Atlantic Canada, to establish the Atlantic Canada Opportunities Agency and to make consequential and related amendments to other acts, assented to 18 August 1988, chapter 50, p. 7.
71 Ibid.
72 Ibid., 4.
73 Ibid., 3.
74 Ibid., 13.
75 See, 'Tories Threaten Commons Delay of Liberals' Split ACOA Bill,' *Halifax Chronicle-Herald*, 16 June 1988, 4.
76 Canada, Report of the Minister for the fiscal year 1988–9 (Moncton: Atlantic Canada Opportunities Agency, 31 August 1989), 31.
77 Ibid., 32.
78 Ibid.
79 Ibid.
80 Ibid.
81 Consultations with senior ACOA officials, various dates.

82 Ibid.

83 Ibid.

84 Canada, Report of the Minister for the fiscal year 1988–9, 33.

85 Ibid.

86 See, among others, Donald J. Savoie, *The Politics of Public Spending in Canada* (Toronto: University of Toronto Press, 1990), chap. 7.

87 Canada, Privy Council Office, 'Background Paper on New Cabinet Decision-Making System' (n.d.).

88 'Ottawa Cuts Atlantic Canada Development Aid,' *Globe and Mail*, 16 May 1989, A1.

89 See *An Information Package for the Participants to the Ministerial Consultation on Regional Economic Development in Atlantic Canada* (Moncton: Atlantic Canada Opportunities Agency, September 1989).

90 Canada, *The Budget Speech*, Department of Finance, 27 April 1989, 7.

91 See 'PM Was Warned ACOA Could Be Slush Fund,' *Saint John Telegraph Journal*, 27 January 1988, 1.

92 Quoted in 'Suspicions Linger about ACOA Intent,' *Saint John Telegraph Journal*, 14 March 1988, 3.

93 See Speaking Notes for Peter O'Brian, Director, Federation of Independent Business, for a presentation to the Consultation Session on ACOA, Halifax, 11 and 12 September 1989).

94 'Petty Bureaucrats Pull Shabby Coup,' *Toronto Sunday Star*, 20 July 1989, B3.

95 Frederick W. Mayer, *Interpreting NAFTA* (New York: Columbia University Press, 1998).

96 The *Canadian Journal of Regional Science* produced a special issue on the Canada-U.S. Free Trade Agreement for vol. 13, nos 2 and 3 (1990).

97 Jean Chrétien, 'A Modern Foreign Policy' (speech to the Empire Club of Canada, Toronto, 8 March 1990), 6–7.

98 Fredericton, New Brunswick Information Service, statement by Premier Frank McKenna, *Canada-US Free Trade Agreement* (16 December 1987), 1–2.

99 Notes for remarks by the Hon. David Peterson to the Canadian Club and Empire Club (Toronto, 4 November 1987), 13–14.

100 See 'Tories Seek to Regain Support with Western Diversification Plan,' *Ottawa Citizen*, 9 August 1987, 3.

101 Canada, Western Diversification Initiative (news release, Office of the Prime Minister, 4 August 1987).

102 Canada, 'Notes pour une allocution du Premier Ministre Brian Mulroney sur le développement régional devant les Chambres de Commerce

d'Edmonton et de l'Alberta' (Office of the Prime Minister, 4 August 1987), 3 (my translation).
103 'Aid Package Focus of PM's Trip,' *Globe and Mail*, 1 August 1987, A6.
104 'Tory Activists, Friends Fill New Board,' *Globe and Mail*, 21 November 1987, B3.
105 See Canada, *Canada-Quebec Subsidiary Agreement on the Economic Development of the Regions of Quebec* (Ottawa: Department of Industry, Science and Technology, 9 June 1988), schedules B, C, and D.

7. Chrétien

1 Jean Chrétien, *Straight from the Heart* (Toronto: Key Porter Books, 1985), 18.
2 I was present at the meeting when this point was made to Mr Chrétien. Others present at the November 1989 Ottawa meeting were Rod Bryden, Mike Kirby, Roméo LeBlanc, and David Dingwall.
3 Ibid.
4 See, for example, Carol Goar, 'Liberal Leadership Race Lacks Fresh Ideas,' *Toronto Star*, 16 June 1990, D1.
5 *Creating Opportunity: The Liberal Plan for Canada* (Ottawa: Liberal Party of Canada, September 1993), 59.
6 Canada, 'Priorities for the 1980s, Text of Remarks by the Honourable Jean Chrétien, president of the Treasury Board, to the Annual Conference of the Institute of Public Administration of Canada' (3 September 1975), 5.
7 Canada, 'Statement by the Honourable Jean Chrétien, minister responsible for the federal government decentralization paper' (3 October 1977).
8 Interview with a federal official and member of the Task Force on Decentralization.
9 Canada, 'Statement by the Honourable Sinclair Stevens, President of the Treasury Board' (15 August 1979).
10 Canada, 'Statement by the Honourable Donald Johnston, President of the Treasury Board on the Federal Government Decentralization Program' (n.d.).
11 'GST Centre to Be Built in Summerside,' *Globe and Mail*, 4 May 1990, A1.
12 See Donald J. Savoie, *The Politics of Public Spending in Canada* (Toronto: University of Toronto Press, 1990), chap. 8. See also 'Ottawa Loses to Winnipeg as Site for World-class Lab,' *Ottawa Citizen*, 8 October 1987, 1.
13 'Where Did Gun-Registry Money Go?' *Halifax Chronicle-Herald*, 11 December 2002, 1.
14 See, among many others, John Geddes, 'The Ontario Factor,' *Maclean's*, 22 March 2004, 21.

15 Consultation with a former cabinet minister in the Chrétien government (1993–7), Ottawa, November 2003.

16 The consultation session was held at the Beauséjour Hotel, Moncton, 22 November 2002.

17 'Mais seuls cinq fonctionnaires ont suivi,' *Le Soleil* (Quebec), 5 August 1978, 1.

18 Ottawa, 'Statement by the Honourable Sinclair Stevens, President of the Treasury Board' (27 July 1979).

19 Interview with a former member of the task force.

20 'Productivité accrue,' *Le Soleil* (Quebec), 5 August 1978, 1. The director at Shediac made his observation at a meeting of federal officials to which I was invited. The meeting was chaired by the FEDC for New Brunswick.

21 See Peter Aucoin and Donald J. Savoie, 'Launching and Organizing a Program Review Exercise' (paper prepared for the Canadian Centre for Management Development, Ottawa, 1988), 2.

22 Ibid.

23 See, for example, Amelita Armit and Jacques Bourgault (eds)., *Hard Choices or No Choices: Assessing Program Review* (Toronto: Institute of Public Administration, 1996).

24 See, for example, Donald J. Savoie, *Governing from the Centre: The Concentration of Power in Canadian Politics* (Toronto: University of Toronto Press, 1999), 78.

25 Arthur Kroeger, 'The Central Agencies and Program Review' (paper prepared for the Canadian Centre for Management Development, Ottawa, n.d.), 2.

26 Savoie, *Governing from the Centre*, 179.

27 Ibid.

28 Edward Greenspon and Anthony Wilson-Smith, *Double Vision: The Inside Story of the Liberals in Power* (Toronto: Doubleday, 1996), 225.

29 Ibid., 211.

30 *Action Plan – Program Review* (Moncton: Atlantic Canada Opportunities Agency, 22 September 1994). This document was made available to me by senior ACOA officials.

31 Canada, Commission of Inquiry into the Sponsorship Program and Advertising Activities, Hon. David Dingwall, 21 January 2005, vol. 60, p. 10549.

32 This view is based on various discussions I had with Jean Chrétien while he was MP for Beauséjour and leader of the Opposition (*ca* 1990–3).

33 See, among others, Savoie, *Governing from the Centre*, chap. 10.

34 Atlantic Canada Opportunities Agency, *Report to Parliament, 1993–1998* (Moncton: ACOA, 1998), 40.

35 Consultations with senior ACOA officials, Moncton, various dates, 1995–2004.
36 Atlantic Canada Opportunities Agency, *Report to Parliament*, 14.
37 See, among others, 'Canada Voters Create Political Patchwork,' *Washington Post*, 4 June 1997, A26.
38 The industry portfolio consisted of ACOA, the Business Development Bank of Canada, Canada Economic Development for Quebec Regions, the Canadian Space Agency, the Canadian Tourism Commission, Competition Tribunal, the Copyright Board of Canada, Enterprise Cape Breton Corporation, Industry Canada, Infrastructure Canada, the National Research Council of Canada, the Natural Sciences and Engineering Research Council of Canada, the Social Sciences and Humanities Research Council of Canada, the Standards Council of Canada, Statistics Canada, and Western Economic Diversification Canada.
39 See Canada, Atlantic Canada Opportunities Agency, *Five-Year Report to Parliament, 1998–2003* (Moncton: ACOA, 2003).
40 Canada, Budget Document, Budget Speech, Department of Finance, 16 February 1999.
41 Canada, *Budget Documents: Making Canada's Economy More Innovative* (Department of Finance, 28 February 2000).
42 Consultation with a member of Parliament from the Maritime provinces, Ottawa, December 2003.
43 *Atlantic Canada: Catching Tomorrow's Wave* (Ottawa: Liberal Party, Atlantic Caucus, 31 May 1999), 91.
44 Premier Frank McKenna's speech at the Atlantic Vision Conference, Moncton, New Brunswick (9 October 1997), 5.
45 The government of Canada made $150 million available over five years to provide financing assistance to buyers and lessees of Canadian-built ships. The initiative was updated on 3 March 2003. See Canada, 'News Release – Minister Rock Announces Improvements to the Structured Financing Facility for Shipbuilding' (Industry Canada, 3 March 2003).
46 *Catching Tomorrow's Wave*, p. 120.
47 Consultations with senior ACOA officials, various dates, and with a former senior PMO official, Ottawa, December 2003.
48 'Prime Minister Announces New Atlantic Investment Partnership' (Office of the Prime Minister, News Release, 29 June 2000).
49 Canada, 'Invest in the West: Federal and Provincial Government Sign New $50 Million Agreement for Alberta,' Western Economic Diversification, *News Release*, 5 December 2003.
50 See 'Atlantic Innovation Fund' at www.acoa-apeca.gc.ca.

51 Consultations with senior ACOA officials, Moncton, April 2004.

52 Canada, Atlantic Canada Opportunities Agency, *Five-Year Report to Parliament 1998–2003* (Moncton: ACOA, 2003), 9–10. The statutory payments include liabilities under the Small Business Loans Act, and the Canada Small Business Financing Act and liabilities for loans or credit pursuant to the Government Organization Act, Atlantic Canada, 1987.

53 Ibid., 11.

54 See various ACOA publications on its Web site www.acoa-apeca.gc.ca, in particular the *Five-Year Report to Parliament, 1998–2003* and *Outlook on Program Priorities and Expenditures,* various dates.

55 Consultations with senior ACOA officials, Moncton, various dates.

56 ACOA, *Five-Year Report to Parliament, 1998–2003,* 48–55.

57 Ibid., 16–19.

58 'Chrétien Declared Winner of Canadian Election,' www.cnn.com (accessed 27 November 2000).

59 'The Rising Tide: Continuing Commitment to Atlantic Canada' (discussion paper, Atlantic Liberal caucus, November 2002 and 23 July 2003).

60 Ibid., 8.

61 Canada, Speech from the Throne (Office of the Prime Minister, 2 February 2004).

62 This observation was made to me by a senior ACOA official who had attended a meeting in Ottawa on the 'Rising Tide' document in March 2004.

63 Can-West News Service, 'Regional Development Reviewed,' reprinted in *St John's Telegraph,* 28 February 2003, A7.

64 Consultation with a minister in the Paul Martin government, Ottawa, April 2005.

65 Canada, *Budget 2005* (Ottawa: Department of Finance), chap. 4, 'Investing in Regions and Sectors,' 1–9.

66 Ibid.

67 Canada, *Expenditure Review for Sound Financial Management* (Ottawa: Department of Finance, 2005), 15–16.

68 Canada, *Offshore Resources Accords: Status and Backgrounds* (Ottawa: Department of Finance, 14 February 2005). See also, 'Provinces Rebel over Offshore Agreement,' *Globe and Mail,* 12 February 2005, A1 and A7.

69 Consultations with senior ACOA officials, Moncton and Ottawa, various dates between March and April 2005.

70 Stephen Harper, 'Harnessing the Potential: An Economic Revitalization Plan for Atlantic Canada' (n.d.), 1–7.

71 'Harper Questions ACOA,' *PEI-CBC,* www.pei-cbc.ca (accessed 6 April 2004).

72 'Harper Pledges Strategy to Boost Region,' *Saint John Telegraph Journal,* 21 March 2005, 1.

73 'Jobs! Jobs! Jobs!' *ACOA Watch* 1, no. 1 (March 2003): 1–3.

74 'Newsletter Attacks ACOA Members,' *Moncton Times and Transcript,* 27 March 2003, 4.

75 'It's Time to Re-think ACOA,' *AIMS* at www.aims.ca and reproduced in several newspapers in the Maritime provinces, 1996.

76 'Patron Saints of Port,' *Globe and Mail,* 16 October 1996, A20.

77 'Spector Takes Leave of Atlantic Provinces,' *Globe and Mail,* 29 June 1996, A1.

78 Report of the Auditor General of Canada to the House of Commons, *Atlantic Canada Opportunities Agency – Economic Development* (Ottawa: Minister of Public Works, 2001), 29.

79 Ibid., 28–9.

80 See Canada, *Estimates: Part I, II and III* (Ottawa: Treasury Board Secretariat, various years, 2000–1 to 2003–4).

81 For a more detailed review of the APEC study based on data from Statistics Canada, see Savoie, *Regional Economic Development: Canada's Search for Solutions* (Toronto: University of Toronto Press, 1986), 245.

82 Jack M. Mintz and Michael Smart, *Brooking No Favourites: A New Approach to Regional Development in Atlantic Canada* (Toronto: C.D. Howe Institute, December 2003), 2.

83 Ibid., 17.

84 Ibid., 18–19.

85 Ibid., 17.

86 Canada, *Annual Report, 2003* (Montreal: Business Development Bank of Canada, n.d.), 29.

87 Based on information provided by senior ACOA officials, April 2004.

88 Consultation with a senior Industry Canada official, April 2004.

89 Canada, 'Audit of Technology Partnerships Canada,' Audit and Evaluation Branch, October 2003, 6.

90 Consultations with a senior Industry Canada official, Ottawa, 21 April 2004.

91 Jeff Sallot, 'Ottawa Puts Firms' Funding on Hold,' *Globe and Mail,* 15 April 2004, A4.

92 William Watson, 'How to Cut Taxes,' *Financial Post,* 28 February 2004, FP11.

93 Consultation with a former adviser to Prime Minister Chrétien, Ottawa, December 2003.

8. Heal Thyself

1 See, among others, Donald J. Savoie, *Pulling against Gravity: Economic Development in New Brunswick during the McKenna Years* (Montreal: IRPP, 2001), 177.

2 'Harper Confronts Comments about Atlantic Canada's Culture of Defeat,' *Halifax Chronicle-Herald*, 20 September 2002.

3 Donald J. Savoie, *Establishing the Atlantic Canada Opportunities Agency* (Moncton: Canadian Institute for Research on Regional Development, 1987), 33.

4 John Lownsbrough, 'The Energizer Premier,' *Report on Business*, March 1993, 31.

5 Josh Beutel, 'What Makes Frankie Run,' in Josh Beutel (ed.), *The Blue Grit: A Frank McKenna Review* (Saint John: Lanceman Production, 1996), 9.

6 *Toronto Globe*, August 1906, 4.

7 J. Murray Beck, *The History of Maritime Union: A Study in Frustration* (Fredericton: Maritime Union Study, 1969).

8 See Ernest R. Forbes, *The Maritime Rights Movement: A Study in Canadian Regionalism* (Montreal: McGill-Queen's University Press, 1975).

9 Beck, *History of Maritime Union*, 44.

10 Richard H. Leach, *Interprovincial Cooperation in the Maritime Provinces* (Fredericton: Maritime Union Study, 1970), 30.

11 Ibid., 31.

12 Ibid.

13 Notes for an Opening Address by Honorable Hugh John Flemming, Premier of New Brunswick, at the Atlantic Premiers' Conference held in Fredericton, 9 July 1956, 4.

14 Leach, *Interprovincial Cooperation*, 32.

15 Ibid., 28–102.

16 Paul H. Evans, *Report on Atlantic/Maritime Interprovincial Cooperation between 1950 and 1971* (Halifax: Council of Maritime Premiers, 1985), 3.

17 Ibid., 55.

18 Ibid., 100. It should also be noted that the four provinces agreed to open an Atlantic Pavilion at Expo '67 and to send joint trade missions to New England in the late 1960s.

19 Quoted in 'Atlantic Union Suggested,' *Halifax Chronicle-Herald*, 2 September 1964, 1.

20 New Brunswick, 'Proposal Regarding the Political Union of the Atlantic Provinces submitted to the Atlantic Premiers Conference' (September 1964), 1.

21 Ibid., 3.
22 Quoted in Flemming, Notes, 95.
23 Ibid.
24 Evans, *Report on Atlantic/Maritime Interprovincial Cooperation*, 2.
25 *The Report of the Maritime Union Study* (Fredericton: Queen's Printer, 1970), 1.
26 Quoted in Evans, *Report on Atlantic/Maritime Interprovincial Cooperation*, 94.
27 Ibid., chap. 3.
28 *Report of the Maritime Union Study*, 2–3.
29 Ibid., see appendix A.
30 Ibid., 108–9.
31 Ibid., 9.
32 Ibid., 66–7.
33 Ibid., 75.
34 Ibid., 76.
35 Ibid., 77.
36 Ibid.
37 Ibid., 79.
38 Notes for an address by Fred Drummie to the annual meeting of the Institute of Public Administration of Canada, Halifax, 13 September 1976, p. 2.
39 See 'Premiers Accept Three Union Study Proposals,' *Halifax Chronicle-Herald*, 27 January 1971, 1.
40 See, for example, Council of Maritime Premiers, 'The Future of Maritime Cooperation' (news release, 2 June 1981).
41 See 'The Record of Cooperation in the Maritimes,' notes for remarks by Emery M. Fanjoy to the conference 'Regional Cooperation in the Maritimes: The Recent Issues and Prospects,' Halifax, 21 April 1981. It is also important to note that there are now over 200 regionally funded post-secondary programs, including a common medical school, dental school, and forest-ranger school, among others.
42 See L.F. Kirkpatrick, 'Regional Co-operation in the Electrical Generation – A Review,' remarks to the conference 'Regional Cooperation in the Maritimes: The Recent Issues and Prospects,' Halifax, 21 April 1981.
43 Charles J. McMillan, *Standing Up to the Future: The Maritimes in the 1990s* (Halifax: Council of Maritime Premiers, 1989), 1.
44 Ibid., 10–11.
45 Ibid., 11.
46 Ibid., 3.
47 Ibid., 46.

48 Ibid.
49 Ibid.
50 Ibid., 44.
51 Ibid., 46.
52 Ibid., 45.
53 'Premiers Committed to Regional Cooperation?' (Council of Maritime Premiers, news release, 27 October, 1999).
54 Council of Atlantic Premiers, 'Establishment of Council of Atlantic Premiers' (Halifax, 15 May 2000).
55 Consultation with a former official with the Council of Maritime Premiers, Moncton, 18 May 2004.
56 Consultations with an official with the Council of Atlantic Premiers, Moncton and Halifax, 17 May 2004.
57 'Establishment of Council of Atlantic Premiers.'
58 Ibid., 2.
59 See Backgrounder, in ibid., 3, 4.
60 'Premiers Agree on Several National and Regional Issues' (Council of Atlantic Premiers, news release, 10 June 2002).
61 Council of Atlantic Premiers, 'CAP Initiatives' (Halifax, n.d.), 1.
62 'Atlantic Premiers Discuss Equalization' (Council of Atlantic Premiers, news release, 4 December 2000).
63 Quoted in 'Is Newfoundland Part of the Maritime Family?' *Halifax Chronicle-Herald*, 23 May 1991, A2.
64 Quoted in 'Newfoundland's Role in Maritime Union Key Item for Talks,' *St John's Evening Telegram*, 22 May 1991, 1.
65 'A Boat to Miss?' *St John's Evening Telegram*, 26 May 1991, 4.
66 Wade Locke and Stephen G. Tomblin, 'Good Governance, a Necessary but Not Sufficient Condition for Soliciting Economic Viability in a Peripheral Region: Cape Breton as a Case Study' (discussion paper prepared for the Cape Breton Regional Municipality, Sydney, Nova Scotia, October 2003), 11 and 48.
67 Donald J. Savoie, *Federal-Provincial Collaborations: The Canada–New Brunswick General Development Agreement* (Montreal: McGill-Queen's University Press, 1981), chap. 9.
68 Benjamin Higgins and Donald J. Savoie, *Regional Development Theories and Their Application* (New Brunswick, NJ: Transaction Publishers, 1995), chap. 3.
69 Joseph Schumpeter, *The Theory of Economic Development* (Cambridge: Harvard University Press, 1934).
70 Canada, *The Implementation of an Entrepreneurship Development Strategy in Canada* (Moncton: Atlantic Canada Opportunities Agency, 1996), 32.

71 *Small Is Big: National Poll Results on Canadians' Attitudes about Small Business,* report by Goldfarb Consultants for Canadian Federation of Independent Business and Scotiabank, October 1999, p. 5.
72 As told to me by Harrison McCain, Florenceville, New Brunswick, various dates between 1998 and 2003.
73 *Atlantic Progress,* September 1996, 23.
74 Ibid., 32.
75 Canada, *The State of Small Business and Entrepreneurship in Atlantic Canada* (Moncton: ACOA, 1991), v.
76 Ibid., xvi.
77 Ibid.
78 Ibid., xxiv.
79 Canada, *The State of Small Business and Entrepreneurship* (Moncton: ACOA, 1994), 10.
80 Ibid., 6.
81 Ibid., 11.
82 Ibid., 21.
83 Ibid., 30.
84 Ibid., 43.
85 Ibid., 44.
86 Ibid., 46.
87 Ibid., 48.
88 Ibid., 54.
89 Ibid., 59.
90 Ibid., 60–1.
91 Canada, *The State of Small Business and Entrepreneurship in Atlantic Canada* (Moncton: ACOA, 1998), v.
92 Ibid.
93 Consultations with a senior ACOA official, Moncton, 31 March 2005.
94 As told to me by Professor Benjamin Higgins.
95 Canada, *The State of Small Business and Entrepreneurship* (Moncton: ACOA, 2004), 24.
96 Ibid., viii.
97 Ibid., 52.
98 Wayne T. Vincent, *Reasons for Failure of Small Retail Business in Atlantic Canada,* p. 4. A copy of the report is available in the ACOA library, Moncton, New Brunswick.
99 Ibid., 1.
100 Ibid., 4.
101 Ibid., 5.

102 Ibid., 12.
103 Ibid.
104 Ibid., 111.
105 Ibid., 115.
106 Ibid., 126.
107 Ibid., 129.
108 Ibid., 128.
109 Ibid., 131.
110 Ibid.
111 Ibid., 132.
112 See, for example, David G. Alexander, *Atlantic Canada and Confederation: Essays in Canadian Political Economy* (Toronto: University of Toronto Press, 1983), 89.
113 Quoted in Savoie, *Pulling against Gravity*, 1.
114 *Small Is Big*, 5–7.

9. The Region Then and Now

1 Galbraith made this observation with the local media after his Josiah Wood Lecture at Mount Allison University, Fall 1986.
2 Quoted in 'Economics Focus: Cycle and Commitment,' *Economist*, 16 October 2004, 74.
3 Donald J. Savoie, *Aboriginal Economic Development in New Brunswick* (Moncton: Canadian Institute for Research on Regional Development, 2000), 77–9.
4 Michel Cormier, *Louis J. Robichaud: A Not So Quiet Revolution* (Moncton: Faye Editions, 2004).
5 David Alexander, 'New Notions of Happiness: Nationalism, Regionalism and Atlantic Canada,' *Journal of Canadian Studies* 15, no. 2 (1990).
6 See, among others, Donald J. Savoie, *Regional Economic Development: Canada's Search for Solutions* (Toronto: University of Toronto Press, 1992), chap. 9.
7 Linda Duxbury and Chris Higgins, *Where to Work in Canada: An Examination of Regional Differences in Work-Life Practices* (Ottawa: Health Canada, September 2003), 7.
8 Quoted in 'Ontarians Earn More, East Coast Folks Happy,' *National Post*, 20 November 2003, 1.
9 Duxbury and Higgins, *Where to Work in Canada*.
10 See Economic Council of Canada, *Living Together*, chap. 4.
11 Consultation with a senior government of Canada official, Ottawa, 20 August, 2004.

12 See, among many others, Savoie, *Regional Economic Development*, and *Pulling against Gravity: Economic Development in New Brunswick during the McKenna Years* (Montreal: Institute for Research on Public Policy, 2001).

13 Based on material that Industry Canada provided to the author in September 2003.

14 See, among others, 'New Brunswickers, Come Home,' *Ottawa Citizen*, 10 March 2004, C1.

15 See various papers presented to the APEC's fiftieth anniversary held in Moncton, September 2004. The papers are available on the APEC Web site: www.apec-econ.ca

16 Harry Bruce, 'Let's Find a Way to Attract Immigrants,' *Halifax Chronicle-Herald*, 24 October 2004, 7.

17 Ibid.

18 Quoted in ibid. See also *A Framework for Immigration: A Discussion Paper* (Halifax: Government of Nova Scotia, Department of Education, August 2004).

19 Bruce, 'Let's Find a Way to Attract Immigrants.'

20 Based on data provided by Statistics Canada to the author.

21 Joe Ruggeri and Yang Zou, *From Labour Surpluses to Labour Constraints in Atlantic Canada* (Fredericton: Policy Studies Centre, UNB, 2005), 64–5.

22 Calculations in this paragraph are based on Statistics Canada data provided to the author.

23 See Savoie, *Pulling Against Gravity*, 18.

24 Ibid., 93, 96.

25 Statistics Canada, *Labour Force Survey*, CANSIM II, V2461119 and tables 101–10K.

26 This information was made available to me by Industry Canada in August 2003. It is based on data provided by Human Resources Development Canada.

27 See Richard Florida, 'The Economic Geography of Talent,' *Annals of the Association of American Geographers* 92, no. 2 (2002): 743–55 and Meric S. Gertler, Richard Florida, et al., *Competing on Creativity: Placing Ontario's Cities in North American Context* (Toronto: Ontario Ministry of Enterprise, Opportunities and Innovation and the Institute for Competitiveness and Prosperity, 2002).

28 The table shows the percentage of jobs that ranked in the top decile in terms of service-sector pay. Statistics Canada's annual estimates of employment, earnings, and hours (AEEEH) do not list every service-sector job because of confidentiality purposes; therefore, when talking about deciles we are referring only to publishable employment data. AEEEH

ranked, according to weekly wages, the service-sector jobs, then matched the rankings to 2001 census data to show how many of the top-decile jobs were located in a particular city. (It should be noted that AEEEH used NAICS 2002 definition and the census was done using NAICS 1997 definition; however, they are similar enough that you can still use the coordance tables to match categories.)

29 Frank McKenna, 'The Path to Self-Sufficiency,' speech to the Greater Moncton Chamber of Commerce, 101st annual banquet, 6 May 1992, 4.

30 Brian Crowley, quoted in 'Three Views of Atlantic Canada's Future,' *Policy Options*, December 2000, 14.

31 William Watson, *The Study in Brief* (Toronto: C.D. Howe Institute, 1995), 2.

32 Ibid., 3.

33 Doug May and Alton Hollett, *The Rock in a Hard Place: Atlantic Canada and the UI Trap* (Toronto: C.D. Howe Institute, 1995), 45.

34 Ibid., 51.

35 Ibid., 92.

36 Ibid., 98.

37 Canada, *Employment Insurance 2002 Monitoring and Assessment Report* (Ottawa: Canada Employment Insurance Commission, 31 March 2003). The business community was critical of the 2004 changes. See, among others, 'EI Change Is Cherry-Picking,' *Ottawa Citizen*, 12 May 2004, A3.

38 Jeffrey Simpson, 'Liberals Fall Back on That Old-style Sleight of Hand,' *Globe and Mail*, 12 May 2004, A7.

39 Consultation with a senior government official, Ottawa, 10 June 2004.

40 Quoted in 'Rich and Poor Provinces Split,' *Globe and Mail*, 26 October 2004, A1.

41 Premier McGuinty said, 'We are pleased with the new arrangement.' Quoted in 'PM, Premiers Reach $28 Billion Deal,' in Canada.comNews, 26 October 2004.

42 'The More Things Stay the Same,' *Globe and Mail*, 27 October 2004.

43 *The National*, CBC News, 27 October 2004.

44 'Deal Worth $28 Billion,' *Halifax Chronicle-Herald*, 27 October 2004, 1.

45 Quoted in 'Atlantic Premiers Protest,' *Toronto Star*, 29 September 2004, A7.

46 Jim Travers, 'King and Barons Divvy up Pie,' *Toronto Star*, 26 October 2004, A7.

47 Andrew Coyne, 'Equalization, without the Equalization,' *National Post*, 30 October 2004, A16.

48 'The Equalization Program and Atlantic Canada,' in Atlantic Provinces Economic Council Report, Winter 2001, 1–6.

49 Canada, *Health Care Renewal* (Ottawa: Health Canada, 25 September 2004), 5–7.

50 Canada, 'Address by Prime Minister Paul Martin at First Ministers Meeting' (Office of the Prime Minister, 13 September 2004), 5–7.

51 'New Federal Investments on Health Commitments on 10-year Action Plan on Health' (Health Canada news release, 16 September 2004). It should be noted that, combined with CHST tax points, the total transfer stands at $30.6 billion in 2005–6.

52 For a brief history of Canada's transfers to provinces, see Paul Boothe, 'Finding a Balance: Renewing Canadian Federalism' (Benefactors Lecture, C.D. Howe Institute, 30 October 1988).

53 Information provided by the Department of Finance to the author, 26 October 2004.

54 Andrew Sharpe, *The Canada–Atlantic Canada Manufacturing Productivity Gap: A Detailed Analysis* (Ottawa: Centre for the Study of Living Standards, December 2003), 1–12.

55 See *Trends in Economic Performance* (Halifax: Atlantic Provinces Economic Council, 2003).

56 *Subsidized to the Hill?* (Halifax: Atlantic Provinces Economic Council, September 2004), 1–15.

57 See, among others, Morley Gunderson, 'North American Economic Integration and Globalization,' in Patrick Grady and Andrew Sharpe (eds), *The State of Economics in Canada: Festschrift in Honour of David Slater* (Montreal and Kingston: McGill-Queen's University Press, 2001), 355–75.

58 See various papers in Thomas J. Courchene, Donald J. Savoie, and Daniel Schwanen (eds), *The Art of the State: Thinking North America* (Montreal: IRPP, 2004).

59 See Pierre-Marcel Desjardins, *Atlantic Canada's Exports, with a Focus on SMEs and Rural Regions* (Moncton: Canadian Institute for Research on Regional Development, 2003), 106.

60 Canada, *Canada's Growing Economic Relations with the United States*, Parts 1 and 2, a report prepared by the Micro-Economic Policy analysis (Ottawa: Department of Industry, n.d.).

61 See various studies prepared or sponsored by Industry Canada since the late 1990s. These studies are accessible by going to publications at www.ic.gc.ca.

62 See, for example, Savoie, *Regional Economic Development*, 65.

63 Canada, Speech from the Throne to Open the First Session of the 38th Parliament of Canada, 5 October 2004, 4.

64 Gordon Osbaldeston made this observation at a meeting attended by the author in Ottawa in March 1982.

10. The Problem

1 Quoted in *Halifax Chronicle Herald*, 29 May 2002, 1.
2 Editorial, *National Post*, 3 August, 2002.
3 John Ibbitson, 'McGuinty, Martin Need Each Other,' *Globe and Mail*, 19 July 2004, A6.
4 See, for example, Thomas J. Courchene, 'Fair-Share Federalism and the 1999 Federal Budget,' *Policy Options*, April 1999, 39–46.
5 Stéphane Dion, 'Speaking out for the Atlantic Provinces' (address to the Diplomatic Forum, Halifax, 19 October 2002), 6.
6 Ernest Forbes, *The Maritime Rights Movement, 1919–1927* (Montreal and Kingston: McGill-Queen's University Press, 1979), 22.
7 See, among others, Eric Sager and Louis R. Fisher, 'Atlantic Canada and the Age of Sail Revisited,' in Douglas McCalla (ed.), *Perspectives on Canadian Economic History* (Toronto: Copp Clark Pitman, 1987), 97–117.
8 See, among many others, 'Paul Martin Campaign: Policy Table on Economic Development,' Ottawa, 2 May 2003, p. 1.
9 See, for example, Donald J. Savoie, *Governing from the Centre: The Concentration of Power in Canadian Politics* (Toronto: University of Toronto Press, 1999).
10 Roger Gibbins, *Regionalism: Territorial Politics in Canada and the United States* (Toronto: Butterworth, 1982), 194.
11 Savoie, *Governing from the Centre*.
12 'Ontario Rescues Martin,' *Globe and Mail*, 29 June 2004, A1; CBC, *The National*, 26 May 2004.
13 'Harper Picks up the Pieces for Now,' *Globe and Mail*, 30 June 2004, A4.
14 In the early 1980s the Nova Scotia office of the federal Department of Regional Economic Expansion targeted Deutz engines, a German firm, to locate a plant in the province. When the DREE minister was briefed on the project, he alerted the Montreal DREE office of the potential project, and the Quebec region sought to locate the proposed project in that province.
15 John Ibbitson, 'Winners: The West and the PM's Pals,' *Globe and Mail*, 20 July 2004, A1, A4.
16 'A Capital without Clout: Just One MP in a Junior Post,' *Ottawa Citizen*, 21 July 2004, A1 and A4.
17 '$600 M for Light-Rail,' *Ottawa Citizen*, 14 May 2004, F1.
18 See, for example, Rand Dyck, *Canadian Politics: Critical Approaches* (Toronto: Nelson Thomson, 2000), 491.
19 Savoie, *Governing from the Centre*.
20 Christopher Dunn, 'Federal Representatives of the People and Government of Newfoundland and Labrador,' in *Research Volume 2: Royal Commis-*

sion on *Renewing and Strengthening Our Place in Canada* (St John's: Office of the Queen's Printer, April 2003), 42.

21 Donald V. Smiley and Ronald L. Watts, *Intrastate Federalism in Canada* (Toronto: University of Toronto Press, 1985), 78–81.

22 Geoffrey Stevens, *The Player: The Life and Times of Dalton Camp* (Toronto: Key Porter, 2003), 296.

23 J.E. Hodgetts, *Pioneer Public Service: An Administrative History of the United Canadas, 1841–67* (Toronto: University of Toronto Press, 1955), v.

24 Donald J. Savoie, *Breaking the Bargain: Public Servants, Ministers, and Parliament* (Toronto: University of Toronto Press, 2003), 25.

25 Hodgetts, *Pioneer Public Service*, 278.

26 Robert B. Bryce, *Maturing in Hard Times* (Montreal and Kingston: McGill-Queen's University Press, 1986), 1.

27 Philip A. Buckner, 'The 1870s: Political Integration,' in E.R. Forbes and D.A. Muise (eds), *The Atlantic Provinces in Confederation* (Toronto: University of Toronto Press, 1993), 49.

28 Ibid.

29 Richard Crossman, *The Diaries of a Cabinet Minister*, vol. 1 (London: Hamilton and Cape, 1975), 88–105.

30 Weber quoted in H.H. Gerth and C. Wright Mills, *From Max Weber: Essays in Sociology* (New York: Oxford University Press, 1946), 228.

31 V. Seymour Wilson, *Canadian Public Policy and Administration: Theory and Environment* (Toronto: McGraw-Hill, 1981), 49.

32 Savoie, *Breaking the Bargain*, 221–2.

33 See, among others, 'Ottawa Eyes Additional Office Space in Gatineau,' *National Post*, 26 November 2004, FP8.

34 Roger Gibbins and Robert Roach, *The West in Canada: An Action Plan to Address Western Discontent* (Calgary: Canada West Foundation, September 2003).

35 Donald Gow, 'Canadian Federal Administrative and Political Institutions' (PhD diss., Queen's University, 1967).

36 See Canada, Privy Council Office, *Former Clerks of the Privy Council* (Ottawa, n.d.)

37 The exception is Kevin Lynch, born in Cape Breton, who was deputy minister of Finance 2000–4 and deputy minister of Industry Canada, 1995–2000.

38 Canada, Commission of Inquiry into the Sponsorship Program and Advertising Activities, Jean Pelletier, 7 February 2005, vol. 71, p. 12432.

39 See Statistics Canada, 'Federal Government Employment, Wages and Salaries for Census Metropolitan Areas for the Month of September,' Cansim II, table 183003, compiled by the author.

40 Consultation with a senior Treasury Board Secretariat official, Ottawa, 30 January 2004.

41 Consultation with a senior Treasury Board Secretariat official, Ottawa, May 2004.

42 Savoie, *Breaking the Bargain*, chap. 9.

43 Consultation with B. Guy Peters, University of Pittsburgh, October 2003.

44 Australian Public Service, Statistical Bulletin, Canberra, Public Service and Merit Protection Commission, 2002–3, 7.

45 Consultation with a senior Treasury Board Secretariat official, Ottawa, 30 January 2004.

46 Stephen G. Tomblin, *Ottawa and the Outer Provinces* (Toronto: Lorimer, 1995), 16.

47 Harry Bruce, *Down Home* (Toronto: Key Porter Books, 2002).

48 Jeffrey Simpson, 'The Truth about Atlantic Canada's Economy,' *Globe and Mail*, 20 June 2001, A7.

49 R.A. Young, 'Teaching and Research on Maritime Politics: Old Stereotypes and New Directions,' in P.A. Buckner (ed.), *Teaching Maritime Studies* (Frederiction: Acadiensis Press, 1986), 153.

50 Edith Robb, 'It's Now Time to Change Our Image,' *Moncton Times and Transcript*, 10 July 2004, A3.

51 Ibid.

52 See, among others, Claire Morris, 'The New Brunswick Experience' (remarks before the Ontario Management Forum, June 1995), 11–12.

53 Ibid., 12.

54 Ibid., 13.

55 Quoted in 'Looking Back and Looking Ahead,' *New Brunswick Business Journal* 8, no. 1 (1991): 1.

56 Examples include Hawk Communications and Communications Plus, both in Moncton, and together employing about forty people.

57 Donald J. Savoie, 'Searching for Accountability in a Government without Boundaries,' *Canadian Public Administration* 47, no. 1 (2004): 15–20.

58 Consultation with Roméo LeBlanc, Grande-Digue, New Brunswick, September 2003.

59 Jacques Bourgault, *Le Rôle et les défis contemporains des sous-ministres du gouvernement fédéral du Canada* (Ottawa: Centre canadien de gestion, 2002).

60 Consultation with a senior Treasury Board Secretariat official, Ottawa, June 2004.

61 Canada, 'Ministers and Deputy Ministers Holding Office in Selected Federal Departments between September 1984 and May 2004' (Parliamentary Research Branch, 28 May 2004), 1.

62 Michael Prince, 'Soft Craft, Hard Choices, Altered Context: Reflections on 25 Years of Policy Advice in Canada' (University of Victoria, July 2004), 8.

63 Savoie, *Breaking the Bargain*, 254.

64 Jeffrey Simpson, *The Friendly Dictatorship* (Toronto: McClelland and Stewart, 2001), 174.

65 Based on information provided by the Atlantic Canada Opportunities Agency, Moncton, January 2004.

66 Consultation with Nick Mulder, November 1997, Ottawa.

67 Andrew F. Cooper, *In Between Countries: Australia, Canada and the Search for Order in Agricultural Trade* (Montreal and Kingston: McGill-Queen's University Press, 1997), 217.

68 'Canada Slips Again in Global Ranking,' *Globe and Mail*, 14 November 2004, B1.

69 Peter Leslie, *Federal State, National Economy* (Toronto: University of Toronto Press, 1987), 10.

70 Hon. Jean Chrétien, 'The Challenges of Canadian Federalism in the 1980s' (an address to the Empire Club of Canada, Toronto, 17 January 1980), 7.

71 See, for example, 'Ottawa Has Role Saving Auto Jobs,' *Toronto Star*, 15 June 2004, A26.

72 'Liberals Shower Auto Industry with Aid,' *Globe and Mail*, 12 June 2004, B1; 'Ontario to Lure Leading-edge Auto Plans,' *Globe and Mail*, 14 June 2004, B1.

73 See, among others, 'EDC Exposure to Aerospace Tops $9.3 Billion,' *Ottawa Citizen*, 10 April 2003, D1.

74 'Ex-EDC Head Blasts Nortel Aid,' *Globe and Mail*, 13 March 2004, B5.

75 *Creating Opportunity: The Liberal Plan for Canada* (Ottawa: Liberal Party of Canada, September 1993), 59.

76 Janet Atkinson-Grosjean, *Public Service, Private Interests* (Vancouver: W. Maurice Young Centre for Applied Ethics (UBC) and Centre for Policy Research on Science and Technology (Simon Fraser), 2003), 35.

77 Woodrow Wilson, 'The Study of Administration,' *Political Science Quarterly* 2, no. 2 (1887): 198.

78 'Federal Hiring Keeps Region's Economy Growing,' *Ottawa Citizen*, 29 September 2004, D1.

79 'Region to Land Federal Jobs as Part of Liberal Plan, Says MP,' *Saint John Telegraph Journal*, 28 October 2004, 1.

80 'Relocating Federal Jobs Won't Save Cash,' Canada.com News, at http://www.canada.com (accessed 23 October 2004).

81 'Federal Tourism Commission Heads West,' www.canada.com/news (accessed 29 March 2005).

82 'Illogical Tourist Body Move Angers Ontario,' *Toronto Star*, 31 March 2005, A7.

83 Donald J. Savoie, 'Le Programme fédéral de décentralisation: un réexamen,' *Canadian Public Policy* 12, no. 3 (1986).

84 Consultation with a deputy minister, Ottawa, 13 August, 2004.

85 See the AECL annual report for 2003–4, *Power through Partnership* (Ottawa: Atomic Energy of Canada Limited, 2004). The report, for example, reveals that the AECL has drawn over $100 million a year from 'Parliamentary appropriations for research operations' since 2000 including $136 million in 2002 (43).

86 'Seeking a Fair Deal for Ontario,' *National Post*, 6 April 2005, A18.

87 Quoted in 'McGuinty Bets Political Future on Assumption Ontarians Fed Up,' *Ottawa Hill Times*, 4 April 2005, 1.

88 Mary Tonigan, 'Yes, Ontario Is a Victim,' www.macleans.ca (accessed 18 March 2005).

89 Eric Reguly, 'It's Time Ontario Fought the Feds,' *Globe and Mail*, 15 February 2005, B2.

90 'Ontario's Burden Growing: CIBC Report,' www.thestar.com (accessed 19 April 2005).

91 Warren Lovely, *Killing the Golden Goose?* (Toronto: CIBC, 15 April 2005), 3.

92 'PM Rejects Ontario's Gripes,' *Globe and Mail*, 15 February 2005, A1.

93 'Martin Promises Ontario $5.75 Billion Package,' www.globeandmail.com (accessed 8 May 2005).

94 Donald J. Savoie, *Pulling against Gravity: Economic Development in New Brunswick during the McKenna Years* (Montreal: IRPP, 2001), 187.

95 Gibbins and Roach, *The West in Canada*, 9.

96 Ibid., 8.

97 Information obtained from the Atlantic Canada Opportunities Agency. The data were produced in July 2002, and the agency acknowledges that 'it is difficult to assess the exact value of CIDA contracts executed principally or sub-contracted by Atlantic firms, universities and not-for-profit organizations.'

98 Based on data obtained from ACOA, Moncton, June 2002.

99 Ibid., December 2003.

100 Mary Janigan, 'A Patronage Epidemic,' *Maclean's*, 14 June 2004, 22.

101 Margaret Conrad, 'To Have and Have Not,' *Globe and Mail*, 7 March 2001, A8.

102 'Museum Caught in Backlash: Some Disdainful Media Writers Toss Poison Darts at Asper's Stunning Project in Winnipeg,' www.thestar.com (accessed 25 April 2005).

103 'Super Bowl Viewers Love Canadian Ad,' *Globe and Mail*, 3 February 2004, B1.

104 Canada, *The Innovation Agenda* (Ottawa: Department of Industry, February 2002).

105 'Robillard Says Industry Is a Top Priority under PM Martin,' *Ottawa Hill Times*, 12–18 January 2004, 16.

106 Canada, *Innovation Target 13* (Ottawa: Industry Canada, n.d.), 1.

107 Canada, *Achieving Excellence: Regional Perspectives on Innovation* (Ottawa: Industry Canada, January 2003), 10–12.

108 Consultation with a senior federal government official, Ottawa, April 2004.

109 Canada, Parliament, House of Commons, Standing Committee on Industry, Science and Technology, *Evidence*, 3 April 2001 (Ottawa: Public Works and Government Services Canada, 2001), 8.

110 See, among others, Savoie, *Pulling against Gravity*, 181. The section is also based on data obtained from the Treasury Board Secretariat and the Atlantic Canada Opportunities Agency.

111 Data received from the head of the Canada Foundation for Innovation, Moncton, New Brunswick, 20 September 2004.

112 See 'Notes for an address by the Hon. Stéphane Dion, President of the Privy Council Office and Minister of Intergovernmental Affairs,' Distinguished Speaker Series, Faculty of Law, University of Western Ontario, 21 September 2001, 2. It is also worth noting that Prime Minister Chrétien broke with tradition when he appointed one of his former ministers from Ontario, Ron Irwin, as consul general in Boston, a position usually reserved for someone from the Maritime provinces.

113 See 'Audit Recommends Boost in Funding for Innovation Fund,' *Moncton Times and Transcript*, 11 August 2004, A1.

114 Canada, *Tax Expenditures and Evaluations, 2002* (Ottawa: Department of Finance, 2002).

115 Ibid. Note that these figures are presented in the document as 'projections.'

116 Canada, *Tax Expenditures and Evaluations, 2003* (Ottawa: Department of Finance, 2003), 59–68.

117 Savoie, *Regional Economic Development: Canada's Search for Solutions* (Toronto: University of Toronto Press, 1986), 184.

118 Consultations with senior ACOA officials, June 2004. See also Donald J. Savoie, *Rethinking Canada's Regional Development Policy* (Moncton: Canadian Institute for Research on Regional Development, 1997), 15–26 and Canada, *ACOA Five-Year Report to Parliament, 1998–2003* (Moncton: ACOA, October 2003), chap. 4.

119 Quoted in Savoie, *Regional Economic Development*, 202.

120 Consultations with senior ACOA officials, Moncton, various dates.

121 See Savoie, *Pulling against Gravity*.

122 New Brunswick, *Budget 2004–2005* (Fredericton: Department of Finance, 30 March 2004).

123 *Budget 1993–94* (Fredericton: Department of Finance, 21 March 1994).

124 Thomas J. Courchene, 'Hourglass Federalism: How the Feds Got the Provinces to Run Out of Money in a Decade of Liberal Budgets,' *Policy Options* 25, no. 4 (April 2004): 12.

125 Tom Kent turned to an APEC conference (1979) to support his view. See Tom Kent, 'A Future for Regional Policy' (paper presented to the APEC conference, Halifax, 30 July 2004), 1.

126 Western Economic Diversification Canada signed a series of new 'Western Economic Partnership Agreements' starting in late 2003. The agreements have a total cash value of $200 million over four years to be shared 50/50 with Ottawa. See Canada, Western Economic Diversification Canada at http://www.wd.gc.ca.

127 See, among others, Paul Boothe, 'Restore Balance to Canada's Intergovernmental Transfer System' (C.D. Howe Institute, press release, 30 October 1998).

128 This exception, of course, being Newfoundlanders and Labradorians.

11. The Solution

1 Paul Krugman makes a similar point with respect to historical accidents in his 'Increasing Returns and Economy Geography,' *Journal of Political Economy* 99 (1991): 483–99 and in 'Some Chaotic Thoughts on Regional Dynamics,' http://www.wws.princeton.edu/pkrugman/temin. html

2 *OECD – Territorial Reviews – Canada* (Paris: OECD, 2002).

3 Tom Kent, 'A Future for Regional Policy' (paper presented to the APEC conference, Halifax, 30 July 2004), 8.

4 See, among others, Maureen Appel Molot, Breakfast Talk on Canadian Auto Tariff Policy (Norman Paterson School of International Affairs, Carleton University, 28 October 1999).

5 See Canada, Economy of Canada, http://www.cia.gov/cia/publications/factbook

6 See Canada, Statistics Canada, Total Manufacturing Jobs – Motor Vehicle and Motor Vehicle Parts, table 2180024.

7 Jim Stanford, 'Canada's Auto Industry: Smokestack Sector or High-Tech Winner' (presentation to the Canadian Association of Business Economics, Kingston, August 2004).

8 See, among many others, 'Project Would Secure about 4,000 Jobs at Plant,' *Globe and Mail*, 8 September 2004, B18.

9 Charlotte Gray, 'Ottawa Dot Com,' *Saturday Night*, March 2000, 46.

10 Ibid.

11 'Ottawa Offers $1.5 Billion in Loan Guarantees to Bombardier for Jet Order,' www.canada.com.news, 29 October 2004, and 'New Brunswick Jet Wouldn't Come Cheap,' *Financial Post*, 23 February 2004, FP1. See also '$750 M Aid for Bombardier,' *National Post*, 13 May 2005, F1.

12 Canada, 'Government of Canada Supports Development of Advanced Aerospace Technology' (Industry Canada, press release, August 2003), 1.

13 'Ottawa Urged to Institute Aerospace Policy,' *Globe and Mail*, 19 November 2004, B5.

14 Janine Brodie, *The Political Economy of Canadian Regionalism* (Toronto: Harcourt Brace Jovanovich, 1990), 171.

15 Dalton Camp made this observation to the author over lunch in Ottawa in the early 1990s.

16 Margaret Conrad, 'When Ottawa Sends Money to Atlantic Canada, It's Called a Handout' (n.d.), available at www.uni.ca/lb_conrad_e.html

17 Quoted in Peter Waite, *The Life and Times of Confederation, 1864–1867* (Toronto: University of Toronto Press, 1963), 40.

18 Jennifer Smith, *Federalism* (Vancouver: UBC Press, 2004), 43.

19 Ibid., 46.

20 Quoted in ibid, 49.

21 Province of Canada, *Parliamentary Debates on the Subject of the Confederation of the British North American Provinces* (Quebec: Parliamentary Printers, 1865), 495.

22 Jim Meek, 'Wanted: One Political Godfather,' *Progress*, June 2004, 60.

23 Donald J. Savoie, 'The Rise of Court Government in Canada,' *Canadian Journal of Political Science* 32, no. 4 (1999): 635.

24 *Council of the Federation Founding Agreement* (Ottawa: Council of the Federation, 5 December 2003), p. 3.

25 Smith, *Federalism*, 102.

26 Roger Gibbins, *Regionalism: Territorial Politics in Canada and the United States* (Toronto: Butterworths, 1982), 195.

27 See Benjamin Higgins, Niles Hansen, and Donald J. Savoie, *Regional Policy in a Changing World* (New York: Plenum Press, 1990), 195.

28 Quoted in Dirk Meissner, untitled article, Canadian Press, reporting on Hon. Paul Martin's trip to Vancouver, http://www.canada.com, 9 July 2003.

29 'Martin to Emphasize Regions,' *National Post*, 23 September 2003, p. A1.

30 'Stephen Harper's Next Move,' *National Post*, 12 July 2004, A11.
31 Canada, *Delivering Federal Policies in the Regions: Final Report of the Task Force on the Coordination of Federal Activities in the Regions* (Ottawa: Privy Council Office, July 2002), 8–20.
32 Robert Roach, 'All for One and One for All,' *Ottawa Citizen*, 17 August 2004, A15.
33 See Donald J. Savoie, *Breaking the Bargain: Public Servants, Ministers, and Parliament* (Toronto: University of Toronto Press, 2003), 278.
34 Donald J. Savoie, 'Searching for Accountability in a Government without Boundaries,' *Canadian Public Administration* 47, no. 1 (2004).
35 See, among others, Donald J. Savoie, *Governing from the Centre: The Concentration of Power in Canadian Politics* (Toronto: University of Toronto Press, 1999).
36 See, among others, Donald J. Savoie, *Federal-Provincial Collaboration: The Canada–New Brunswick General Development Agreement* (Montreal and Kingston: McGill-Queen's University Press, 1981).
37 Canada, Atlantic Canada Opportunities Agency – Act, Department of Justice, R.S. 1985, chap. 41 (4th supp.).
38 Statistics on policy specialists in the Maritimes was provided to the author by senior ACOA officials.
39 As reported to the author by senior Industry Canada officials, Ottawa, 18 September 2003.
40 Consultations with ACOA officials, Fredericton, March 2005.
41 Ibid.
42 Frank McKenna, 'Address to the Atlantic Mayors' Congress and the Greater Moncton Chamber of Commerce' (Moncton, 26 March 2004), 17.
43 Brian Lee Crowley, 'East Coast Oil Is Not a Pipe Dream,' *National Post*, 1 September 2004, A11.
44 The focus of this study is on the Maritime provinces. It may be that British Columbia would wish to lay claim to its own regional agency.
45 'Volpe Ponders Aid Agency to Help Ontario,' *Globe and Mail*, 20 October 2004, A3.
46 See, among many others, T. Friedman, *The Lexus and the Olive Tree: Understanding Globalization* (New York: Strauss and Giroux, 1999).
47 Thomas J. Courchene, 'FTA at 15, NAFTA at 10: A Canadian Perspective on North American Integration' (Presidential Address to the North American Economics and Finance Association, January 2003), 12.
48 Based on information provided to the author by Treasury Board Secretariat officials, Ottawa, September 2004.
49 Savoie, *Breaking the Bargain*.

50 See the 'Lyons Review' at http://www.hon.treasury.gov.uk, consultations and legislation.

51 See, among others, 'Productivité accrue,' *Le Soleil* (Quebec), 5 August 1978, 1, and Donald J. Savoie, 'Le Programme fédéral de décentralisation: un réexamen,' *Canadian Public Policy* 12, no. 3 (1986).

52 Kelly Toughill, 'A Plan to Kick-Start Atlantic Canada's Economy,' *Toronto Star*, 2 October 2004, A8.

53 See D.E. Smith, 'The Prairie Provinces,' in D.J. Bellamy, J.H. Pammett, and D.C. Rowat (eds.), *The Provincial Political Systems: Comparative Essays* (Toronto: Methuen, 1976), 274.

54 Quoted in Kent, 'A Future for Regional Policy,' 2.

55 Roger Gibbins, 'Regional Integration and National Contexts: Constraints and Opportunities,' in Stephen G. Tomblin and Charles S. Colgan (eds), *Regionalism in a Global Society: Persistence and Change in Atlantic Canada and New England* (Peterborough, ON: Broadview, 2003), 54.

56 Kent, 'A Future for Regional Policy,' 1–2.

57 Mario Polèse and Richard Shearmur, *The Periphery in the Knowledge Economy* (Montreal: INRS, 2002), i–xxiv.

58 'A Plan to Kick-Start Atlantic Canada's Economy,' *Toronto Star*, 7 October 2004, A8.

59 Frank McKenna, 'Address to the Atlantic Mayors' Congress,' 57.

60 Stewart MacPherson, 'Competition, Restructuring and Markets in Eastern Canada' (paper for the AIMS Conference, 'Plugging in the International Northeast,' Moncton, 12 November 2003), 11.

61 David M. Cameron, 'Once Upon a Dream: Post-Secondary Education and Regionalism in Atlantic Canada,' in Tomblin and Colgan, *Regionalism in a Global Society*, 210.

62 Halifax–Moncton Growth Corridor: Asset Mapping, a working document prepared by Shiftcentral for the Greater Halifax Partnership. See www.greaterhalifax.com.

63 See, among others, Polèse and Shearmur, *The Periphery in the Knowledge Economy*, xxvi.

64 See, among others, Jack M. Mintz and Finn Poschmann, *Follow the Cash: Changing Equalization to Promote Sound Budgeting and Prosperity* (Toronto: C.D. Howe Institute, October 2004).

65 It should be noted that wages for some blue-collar workers are regionally differentiated.

66 'Regional Pay Differences Become Common Study,' *Globe and Mail*, 16 November 2004, B15.

67 Canada, Statistics Canada, *Annual Estimate of Employment, Earnings and*

Hours 1991–2004, based on the North American Industrial Classification System (NAICS – 2002).

68 Canada, Commission de la fonction publique du Canada, 'Analyste de politiques,' 20 April 2005, AC083866DL13GEN.

69 Marcus Olson, *The Rise and Decline of Nations* (New Haven, CT: Yale University Press, 1984).

70 'RIM Top Tech Firm in Respect Poll,' *Globe and Mail*, 20 January 2003, B5.

71 See Savoie, *Regional Economic Development*.

72 Lois Stevenson, *The State of Entrepreneurship in Atlantic Canada* (Moncton: ACOA, 1990).

73 Jack Mintz and Yvan Guillemette, 'Stop Scaring Away Foreign Investment,' *National Post*, 17 August 2004, A7.

74 Frank McKenna made this point in his speech to the Atlantic Economic Summit, Atlantic Provinces Economic Council, 29 September 2004, 8.

75 Information on the fund is available at http://www.acf.ca.

76 See, for example, Brian Lee Crowley, 'Here We Go Again,' *Halifax Chronicle-Herald*, 5 December 2001, 7, and consultations with Tom Hayes, a Halifax-based entrepreneur, 2 October 2004. Vancouver-based Growth Works launched in 2005 a new labour-sponsored venture capital fund for the East Coast. See, 'Atlantic Venture Fund Aids Small Businesses,' *Moncton Times and Transcript*, 14 February 2005, B3.

77 Harrison McCain made this point to me on several occasions.

78 Canada, Statistics Canada, Government Sector Revenue and Expenditure, Provincial Economic Accounts.

79 Frank McKenna made this point in his speech to the Atlantic Economic Summit, 11.

80 'Why Molson Needed to Merge,' *Time* (Canada), 2 August, 2004, 25.

81 Consultation with Reuben Cohen, Moncton, New Brunswick, 10 April 2004.

82 See, for example, Spielo, a Moncton firm employing about 300 people in producing video lottery terminals sold to a large U.S. firm, GTECH, on 30 April 2004.

83 Richard Florida, 'America's Looming Creative Class,' *Harvard Business Review* 82, no. 10 (2004): 124.

84 Ibid., 128.

85 Speaker after speaker at the Atlantic Economic Summit stressed its importance. But so has the Atlantic Provinces Economic Council. See http://www.apec-econ.ca and Atlantic Institute for Market Studies at http://www.aims.ca.

86 Frank McKenna made this point in his speech to the Atlantic Economic Summit, Atlantic Provinces Economic Council, 29 September 2004, 6.
87 See, among many others, Courchene, 'FTA at 15, NAFTA at 10,' 10.
88 For a full briefing of the Atlantica concept, visit http://www.aims.ca.

Index

144, 158; president, 88; and public service cuts, 158; Secretariat, 159, 168; secretaries, 9, 278, 286; as stand-alone agency, 177
Trois-Rivières, 91
Trudeau, Pierre Elliott, 8, 15, 16, 106, 114, 116, 118–19, 121, 123, 124–5, 132, 146; 1972 cabinet changes, 97; and constitutional renewal, 115; and DREE, 95; economic development reorganization, 118–19; and energy policy, 115; federal government machinery under, 324; as national politician, 10, 282; on national unity, 85; and Quebec's place in Confederation, 89; and regional development, 87, 95
Trudeau Foundation, 300
Tupper, Charles, 21–2, 24
Turner, John, 126, 128–9, 132, 161

unemployment, 34, 108; ADA and, 84; in Atlantic provinces, 137; in British Columbia, 52; in Cape Breton, 244; in Halifax, 244; in Maritime provinces, 132, 224; in Moncton, 244; in Montreal, 94, 107; and national unity, 85–6; in Quebec, 107; in rural areas, 244; salaries and, 332; in Toronto, 94
unemployment-employment insurance (UI-EI), 178, 184–5, 197, 250–3, 251; cuts to, 172, 178, 252, 253; in Halifax–Moncton corridor, 329; and incentives to find employment, 252, 253
Unemployment Insurance Fund, 41
United Nations Human Development Index, 324
United Province of Canada. See

Canada, United Province of
United States: banks and SMEs in, 228; and Canadia's national economy, 48–9; civil service in, 281; competitiveness of, 336–7; economic competition with, 9, 10, 12, 301, 306; exports to, 23table, 264–5; federalism in, 313–14; free trade with, 143, 160–2; influence on policy making, 288; location of subsidiaries in Canada, 47; Maritime competitiveness with, 224; natural resource exports to, 160–1; out-migration to, 198; productivity in, 299; R&D spending in, 299; reciprocity with, 19–20, 22–3, 48; regional comparisons with Canada, 109; regional economic development in, 317; regional pay differentials in, 332; Senate, 30, 281, 314, 317; trade with, 28, 264
universal applicability, 51
universities, 300, 337. See also postsecondary education
Upper Ottawa Valley, 102
urban centres, growth poles as, 65, 68, 69, 90
urbanization, 32–5, 236–7
Uruguay Round, 288
usury, 58

Vancouver: Canadian Tourism Commission in, 293–4; innovation strategy in, 301
venture capital (VC), 261, 262table, 334, 335
VIA Rail, 297
Vincent, Wayne T.: *Reasons for Failure of Small Retail Businesses in Atlantic Canada*, 227–9